HEMINGWAY'S QUARREL WITH ANDROGYNY

Hemingway's
Quarrel with
Androgyny

MARK SPILKA

University of Nebraska Press

Lincoln & London

Acknowledgments for the use of copyrighted material
appear on pages xi–xiii.

Copyright © 1990 by the University of Nebraska Press
Manufactured in the United States of America

The paper in this book

meets the minimum requirements of American National

Standard for Information Sciences –

Permanence of Paper for Printed Library Materials

ANSI Z.39.48-1984.

Library of Congress Cataloging in Publication Data

Spilka, Mark

Hemingway's quarrel with androgyny

Bibliography: p.

Includes index. 1. Hemingway, Ernest, 1899-1961 –

Knowledge – Psychology.

2. Androgyny (Psychology) in literature.

3. Sex role in literature. I. Title.

PS3515.E37 Z873   1989   813'.52   89-14701

ISBN 0-8032-4127-5

To my indispensable parents
Zella Fenberg Spilka Goda
and
Harvey Joseph Spilka
who set me going before they stopped
and to my inimitable aunt
Bertha Fenberg Stone
who was there long before me

Contents

ILLUSTRATIONS

Key to sources of photographs:
Ernest Hemingway Foundation, EHF
The Victoria and Albert Museum, VAM
Phaidon Press, PP

Acknowledgments

Since this book has been ten years in the making, a great many of my debts are now beyond recall. Let me begin then by apologizing to that small army of friends and abettors who will remain not simply unmentioned here but also unretrieved. Of those retrieved let me thank first the editors of several journals who accepted and printed early versions of chapters 1, 2, 3, and 11 and Appendix A and have granted permission to reprint modified versions of these essays: the late (and much lamented) Maurice Beebe, for "Victorian Keys to the Early Hemingway, Part I: *John Halifax, Gentleman," Journal of Modern Literature* 10 (March 1983): 125–50, and "Victorian Keys to the Early Hemingway, Part II: *Fauntleroy* and *Finn," Journal of Modern Literature* 10 (July 1983): 289–310; my astute colleagues at *Novel,* for taking "Victorian Keys to the Early Hemingway: Captain Marryat," *Novel: A Forum on Fiction* 17 (Winter 1984): 116–40, and "Hemingway's Barbershop Quintet: *The Garden of Eden* Manuscript," *Novel: A Forum on Fiction* 21 (Fall 1987): 29–55; and Charles "Tod" Oliver, for taking "A Source for the Macomber 'Accident': Marryat's *Percival Keene," Hemingway Review* 3 (Spring 1984): 29–37. I want to thank also Fritz Fleischmann, editor of *American Novelists Revisited: Essays in Feminist Criticism* (Boston: G. K. Hall, 1982), for soliciting and printing "Hemingway and Fauntleroy: An Androgynous Pursuit," which appears under my copyright in that anthology on pp.339–70; and editors Ian MacNiven and Lawrence Gamache, for similarly accepting "Original Sin in 'The Last Good Country'; or, The Return of Catherine Barkley," for inclusion in their *Festschrift* for the late Harry T. Moore, *The Modernists* (Rutherford, N.J.: Fairleigh Dickinson

University Press; London and Toronto: Associated University Presses, 1987), pp.210–33. The latter essay figures strongly in Chapters 5 and 10. In line with such encouraging support, let me thank also Wyman Herendeen, James Nagel, Susan Gubar, Al Cook, Suzanne Woods, Jackson Bryer, Gerry Brenner, and Edward Engelberg for the chance to test my views on Hemingway against live audiences at Toronto, Northeastern, the New York MLA, Brown, Madrid, Schruns, and Brandeis.

My debts to the National Endowment for the Humanities are also considerable. In 1977–78 the Endowment awarded me a research grant to pursue my larger project, then called "New Literary Quarrels with Tenderness," out of which came my previous book, *Virginia Woolf's Quarrel with Grieving* (Lincoln: University of Nebraska Press, 1980). Under the auspices of that grant I was also able to begin preliminary readings for the present study, which I ultimately completed some ten years later with the help of yet another grant from the NEH for spring and summer 1987. Let me again express thanks to my various referees for these projects: George Ford, Julian Moynahan, Patricia Spacks, Elaine Showalter, and Michael Reynolds. Readers of this book will quickly see that my debts to Spacks, Showalter, and Reynolds are intellectual as well as professional. To Reynolds especially, who not only read and liked this manuscript but who shared with me also his ongoing work on *The Young Hemingway* (1986), let me add my thanks for renewed faith in the collaborative nature of like-minded scholarship in these all too rivalrous times. But there are other Hemingway scholars who have generously shared findings with me, even when our views have been opposed: Scott Donaldson, notably, and Peter Griffin, especially during his spadework for *Along with Youth* (1985), when he was also willing to let me read (with much profit) his groundbreaking dissertation, "Ernest Hemingway: In My Beginning Is My End" (Brown University, 1979). Perhaps the late Carlos Baker should be included here, since he too was skeptical of my aims yet always willing to help me pursue them. Only a month before he died, for instance, he sent me a xerox of the letter from Allen Tate that figures so importantly in chapters 7 and 8.

More sanguinely, I am indebted to James Brasch for helpful Cuban findings, to Paul Smith, for useful corroborations of early hunches; to Robert W. Lewis, for permission from the Hemingway Foundation to quote from unpublished manuscripts in the Hemingway Collection at the Kennedy Library; and to correspondent William Adair for helpful derivations. I owe much thanks also to curators of that collection over the past ten years: notably Jo August Hills and Joan O'Connor; and to librarians elsewhere for their personal assistance—William Jerousek of the Oak Park

Public Library, and John Delaney at the Scribner Archives in Princeton University Library. And to my colleague Elmer Blistein at Brown for Shakespearean lore and grammatical severities. And to the office staff under the inimitable Ruth Oppenheim—notably Lorraine Mazza, Dorene Soscia, and Christine Stochowiak—for innumerable typings, wrappings, and mailings; and to Ruth Oppenheim herself, for keeping tabs on all my deliberations, and for much counsel and comfort. And to Barbara DeMaio and Verbatim, Inc., for heroic computerizations. And to the Brown University Faculty Development Fund for helping to defray publication and other costs.

Photos 1–17 and 21–23 are copyright © 1988 by The Ernest Hemingway Foundation and used by permission. Photo 18 is from Rodin, *Sculptures,* reproduced by permission of the Phaidon Press and the Musée Rodin. Photos 19 and 20 are courtesy of the Board of Trustees of the Victoria and Albert Museum.

What I owe to Ruth Dane, to whom I dedicated my last book, shall go unmentioned here if not unremembered or privately unsung. It should be noted, however, that she is in no way responsible for what I have made, or failed to make, of all I have learned from her. What I owe to my aunt, Bertha Fenberg Stone, to whom among others the present book is dedicated, is more readily mentionable. Her interview with Grace Hall Hemingway in 1927 has yielded the Fauntleroy clue which confirms my early arguments, and has served in this respect rather like a family heritage. The same might be said of her memories of Paris and Chicago in the late 1920s and early 1930s, and of the Marie Laurencin prints she bought then for her sisters, one of which now hangs in my bedroom, of embracing mermaids (whether mother and daughter, or perhaps simply older and younger sisters, or lovers, is unclear). At any rate, the example of her ongoing life as a reporter, writer, and teacher has much bearing on my own life, for which stirring influence much thanks and much love.

Finally, to a group of men with whom I work called Brother to Brother, let me add thanks for the lesson, however imperfectly learned, that none of us can afford to be holier than Hemingway. He too is our brother.

Introduction

✿

Hemingway's Secret Muses

> Male writers have needed the loving support of their muses, mistresses, or mothers in order then to put them aside, deny them, reject them, idealize them or kill them in their writing, but, in any case, to ingest them so as better to evacuate them, purify themselves, and identify with the Father—if only then to kill him like the good sons they are.
>
> ALICE JARDINE,
> in Susan Suleiman's *The Female Body in Western Culture*

In the summer and fall of 1958, Ernest Hemingway brought to rough completion a revised draft of a long novel called *The Garden of Eden* which he had begun in 1946 and then put aside to pursue other projects. It was the last full-length novel he would ever finish, and its subject—the sex-reversal experiments of two androgynous couples living in France in the 1920s—was itself something of a reversal for him. His lifelong interest in forms of masculine heroism—bullfighting, deep-sea fishing, soldiering, boxing, lion-hunting—had apparently given way to a study of role reversals in marriage. Actually his interest in the androgynous makeup of men and women had begun much earlier and had almost ended where it began. In *The Sun Also Rises* (1926), mannish Lady Brett Ashley and unmanned Jake Barnes are unable to consummate their love, ostensibly because of the sexual wound Barnes has sustained in the war, but more importantly because Brett herself—wearing a man's felt hat over her boyish bob as she stands at the bar

I

with other "chaps"—represents the arrival of the liberated woman of the 1920s, a type whose assumption of equality with men makes her much too difficult for Hemingway's heroes to handle even while it makes her more attractive. The question of equal strength between men and women was one Hemingway never could answer for himself, and when Brett puts the question of the love that might have been at the end of the novel—"Oh Jake . . . we could have had such a damned good time together"—Barnes replies with a dissenting "Yes . . . Isn't it pretty to think so?"

In his next novel, *A Farewell to Arms* (1929), Hemingway would establish the terms for that dissent. He would go back in time to the war that produced such desolate postwar lovers and would explore the "damned good time"—the romantic love—that was no longer available to them. And the androgynous nature of that love which in open and implicit ways this novel establishes would be the secret key to its dissolution. In *A Farewell to Arms* Hemingway would say farewell also to those feminine aspects of his own makeup, which he had tried honestly enough to confront, and would evade the question of equal strength by passing off the failure of love onto external and extraneous causes. The hair-matching motif which begins in this novel—where Catherine Barkley offers to cut her hair short if Frederic Henry will let his grow long—would recur in later fictions: in *For Whom the Bell Tolls* (1940), where Maria's close-cropped hair matches Robert Jordan's; in the posthumously published "The Last Good Country," where Nick Adams's kid sister Littless cuts her hair to resemble his; and in *The Garden of Eden* itself, where one couple has short hair in common and the other long. But the essential terms of the androgynous dilemma and the essential failure to resolve it would remain unchanged.

The great change, the important and startling change, was in Hemingway himself, in his late attempt to come to terms once more with his own androgynous nature. His masculinist pose had hardened through the 1930s, the period of public displays of virility and of fictional provings of masculine integrity. At the same time his awareness of female strength and stoic suffering became evident through types like Marie Morgan, Helen Gordan, and Pilar—women tough enough to confront or deflect the increasing brutality of male figures in his fictions yet resilient enough to avoid brutality themselves: female personas, then, with whom even a hardened author might identify, as opposed to bitch heroines like Margot Macomber who threatened his hegemony.

This polarization of internalized male and female toughness would in several ways relax by the 1950s. In "The Last Good Country" Hemingway would actively seek to recover those childhood affections which had sustained him through troubled adult relations with wives and mistresses; he would externalize and test the limits of those innocent loves with adoring sisters who endorsed his protective strength, and with whose brave supporting love he secretly identified. Thus twinned and fortified, he would revise *The Garden of Eden* manuscript he had begun in 1946, moving away from his originally lugubrious theme—"the happiness of the Garden that a man must lose"—toward recuperation of manly powers through artistic resistance to the hazards of androgynous adulthood. And with this late version of "the wound and the bow" approach to his own fiction, he would create for us, as for himself, a retrospective key to his own lifelong quarrel with androgyny.

In accordance with that key, androgyny seems to have been a childhood condition that initially promised great happiness to Hemingway but was soon resisted and repressed; a wounding condition, then, that could be overcome only through strenuous male activities, athletic and creative, as with his active or vicarious devotion to a variety of manly sports and his serious dedication to writing as to an athletic discipline. Judging from his own descriptions, in *The Garden of Eden* manuscript, it was also a bedevilling condition, an imagining of the secret muse within himself first as a devilish woman, inclined toward role reversals, lesbianism, and *ménages à trois,* whose degrading hold upon his passions and affections stirred him to manly resistance, then as a supportive woman who encouraged his recovery. Such an imagining helps to explain the curiously *sui generis* view of his own creativity that marks his previous writings about writing, as if he alone among the world's great male writers had no female muse to rely on while warring with his many literary fathers. Meanwhile, as he would ultimately reveal, he was wrestling furiously and secretly with devilish and adoring female versions of himself! That revelation in *The Garden of Eden* manuscript—as externalized by the devilish wife and her lesbian friend by whom the writer David Bourne is alternately provoked and soothed, castigated and encouraged, unmanned and remanned—seems to me of central importance to all future Hemingway studies and justifies my own long concern with the dynamics of androgyny in his life and art.

PARENTAL DEFINITIONS

Since 1978, when I began this study, evidence of Hemingway's androgynous predilections has mounted rapidly, abetted by sudden access to new collections of letters and manuscripts and by a spate of recent biographies and research aids. The exposure thereby of the peculiarities of his childhood, of the surprising range and voracity of his readings, and of the difficulties of

3

his sequential marriages and sporadic affairs, has made a new assessment of his life and work inevitable. Not until May 1986, however, when Scribner's released its narrowly selective version of *The Garden of Eden* manuscript, was the longer and more revealing version of that crucial document made available to scholars. Until then it had been placed "off limits" by Hemingway's widow, Mary Welsh Hemingway. But one scholar, Carlos Baker, had been allowed to read it in preparation for his biography of 1969, *Ernest Hemingway: A Life Story;* and another, Aaron Lapham, was able to read the opening and closing chapters and to scan the rest when the manuscript arrived for storage in the Hemingway Collection at the Kennedy Library, then in Waltham, Massachusetts.[1] From their reports of its contents it did not seem to advance appreciably the treatment of androgyny in previous works. Indeed, it seemed to confine itself to the excitement of matching hairstyles and experimental ways of making love, without giving any serious attention to motivations and emotions or to the basis for androgynous harmony; and its explicit theme—"the happiness of the Garden that a man must lose"— was a familiar one in earlier fiction. That theme would serve as well, for instance, for *A Farewell to Arms,* where the loss of androgynous happiness initially occurs.

It seemed significant, nonetheless, that Hemingway had conceived of androgynous love as an edenic garden that a man must lose or leave, that he had returned repeatedly in his fiction to the problem of its transience, and that he had tried to explore its childhood sources and its Parisian flowering in his closing years. With that much to go on, one could at least define androgyny in his life and work as a mixture or exchange of traditionally male and female traits, roles, activities, and sexual positions. Further, given his androgynous upbringing, one could connect such predilections historically with the way women began to define maleness in mid-nineteenth century as an expression or projection of their own wishes and desires, whether for power or recognition, as in the "feminine" stage of Elaine Showalter's feminine-feminist-female progression in *A Literature of Their Own.*[2] As I will argue in the pages ahead, Grace Hall Hemingway's "feminine" concept of her firstborn son's maleness was one such androgynous projection that would affect his life and work profoundly, as were her own late-nineteenth-century "feminist" propensities in the androgynous household she had established with her cheerfully cooperative husband Clarence. Their child-rearing experiments may be seen in this light as a peculiar blend of "feminine" and "feminist" propensities with an emerging postpioneer emphasis on outdoor skills for both sexes—which Clarence especially advocated. And with these interweaving yet opposing forms of androgyny in mind, one

4

could also, finally, look to Hemingway's boyhood reading for clues as to how these forms might affect his future life and work, and proceed then to an examination of the curve of his writing career.

That is what I have tried to do in the present study. My selective look at Hemingway's boyhood reading, largely in British literature, helps to show how he was raised by a blend of feminine and masculine versions of manhood which later became submerged and dominant strains, respectively, in his published fiction, and which began to reverse positions toward the end of his life, as his posthumously published fictions (e.g., "The Last Good Country" and *The Garden of Eden*) now reveal. My purpose, then, in Part One, is to examine these strands in his reading, especially as they offer "Victorian keys" to his formative years, and to analyze in Part Two "the return of the repressed"—the persistence of the submerged feminine strain and of the early Victorian impress, and the reascendance of the feminine in his closing years. Finally, as a fitting climax to this progress, my concluding chapter is devoted to the retrospective vision of androgyny that *The Garden of Eden* manuscript now affords: as a wounding condition, that is to say, against which Hemingway's artistic bow has always been manfully strung.

EARLY READINGS

It may help to know that my work on Hemingway is part of a larger study of the taboo on tenderness in modern fiction, whereby the old Victorian quarrel with sexuality has been replaced by our modern quarrel with the softer sentiments. That historical shift in taboos can be further understood as part of a cycle of reactions since the eighteenth century in British and American culture—reactions, that is, to the penumbra of sentiments surrounding Benevolent Man, in the eighteenth century; his Romantic and Victorian successor, the Benevolent Child, in the nineteenth; and the Benevolent or Love Generation of more recent times. Such early moderns as Joyce, Woolf, Lawrence, and Hemingway fall obviously in the trough between the second and third upswing of benevolent sentiments: witness, Hemingway's *A Farewell to Arms* and Lawrence's *Lady Chatterley's Lover,* which not only deflate Victorian sentiments as to love and war, in their embittered toughness, but also anticipate and minister to the sentiments of the "make love not war" generation of the 1960s and after.

My study of Hemingway's quarrel with androgyny proceeds, at any rate, from within that cyclical context, from which my own use of his boyhood reading as an index to his later development as a writer derives its sanction. Just as Joyce continues to deal with compassionate ineffectualities which go

5

back through Dickens to the eighteenth century, or Woolf with intensely personal reactions to the excesses of Victorian mourning, or Lawrence with those "tender passions" which many Victorians repressed but which (according to Peter Gay) some Victorians seem to have cultivated within and without the bonds or bounds of matrimony,[3] so Hemingway derives opposing yet overlapping strands of feeling about manhood from Victorian protofeminist and imperial fictions. Of course, he also derives them from his upbringing in a peculiarly British and androgynous home, where such fictions were amply shelved, and from the thirty or forty books his family brought with them from the Oak Park Library each summer to their cottage in northern Michigan, as well as from Oak Park schools where British rather than American literature was chiefly taught.

What is striking about the acculturation process, in this domestic and communal context of affluent Christian gentility, is how muscular the gentility as well as the Christianity proved to be in practice, how devoted to strenuous outdoor life as the most wholesome environment for childrearing and to ideals of stoic endurance and manly courage in the face of death—especially where consideration for and protection of women and children were concerned. As Michael Reynolds recently noted in *The Young Hemingway,* the spectacle of "women and children first" during the sinking of the *Titanic* had roused the manly hearts of Oak Parkers (the future author of *For Whom the Bell Tolls* among them), even though women and children were in other respects quite secondary in that restricted and restrictive community.[4]

For Hemingway's embarrassingly feminist mother, however, those restrictions did not always obtain. As the daughter of former British citizens who had emigrated to this country in mid-century and who had jointly raised her to avoid the kitchen and pursue a career in grand opera, she continued to insist on her primary status as a human being long after she abandoned opera for marriage—continued in fact to give music lessons and concert performances that helped to pay for cooks and maids whom her husband—who loved to cook and shop himself—was left to supervise; and, more vicariously, she continued also to admire adventurous Christian gentlemen and successful businessmen like her father and uncle, Ernest and Miller Hall, after whom she named and tried to model her first son, Ernest Miller Hemingway, as Peter Griffin has recently reminded us.[5] But if Grace prized muscular Christian gentility in her firstborn son, she also prized it through him for herself. She was in this respect like the first stage of women writers whom Elaine Showalter records in *A Literature of Their Own*—novelists like Dinah Mulock Craik, author of the bestseller of 1856, *John Halifax, Gentleman;* Frances Hodgson Burnett, author of the bestseller of

1886, *Little Lord Fauntleroy;* and Emily Brontë, author of the classic of 1847, *Wuthering Heights,* all of whom fashion model (or in Brontë's case, devilish) heroes who act and feel as these women writers would act and feel if they were men.[6] It seems significant, in this light, that *John Halifax, Gentleman,* the saga of an adventurous Christian businessman with a pastoral family retreat, was something of a family bible for Hemingway's parents at his birth; and that the manly little Fauntleroy and the ragamuffin Huck Finn were at first compatible parental models for his boyhood years, even as Catherine's Heathcliff and Cathy's Hareton served him as secret adolescent models for star-crossed uncrossed love, in keeping with Patricia Meyer Spacks's view of the adolescent standard that Brontë's novel sets against the world.[7]

But Emily Brontë's rough-hewn, bad-mouthed, antireligious heroes, wuthering imaginatively on the Michigan moors, were also more in keeping with Finn than Fauntleroy, who by this time seemed to Ernest a sissified hero like Edgar Linton of Thrushcross Grange, the Oak Park of its day. Ernest had in fact early opted for the likes of Huck, Hareton, and Heathcliff, conveniently suppressing the manlier aspects of Halifax and Fauntleroy and converting even his mother's lesson of protective concern for his sisters into the basis for adolescent rebellion against her. Thus Emily Brontë's novel provided a useful bridge—one still visible in *A Farewell to Arms,* "The Last Good Country," and *The Garden of Eden*—to the British imperial view of manhood he had already found in Captain Marryat, Rudyard Kipling, and John Masefield. These early male favorites had captured his imagination with images of runaway boys, naval and infantry combat, manly trades plied by future writers, types of cowardice and courage, heroic hankerings after death, antimarital and antifeminist stances, all in keeping with the postpioneer world of Mark Twain and his compatriots (Buffalo Bill et al.), from whom his machismo sentiments are usually said to derive. Actually, as Michael Reynolds has shown, Teddy Roosevelt was at this point a much greater American influence than Twain, and Teddy was our own imperial hero and international sportsman.[8]

Craik, Burnett, Brontë, Marryat, Kipling, Masefield—these are my six Victorian (in Masefield's case Edwardian) keys to those overlapping feelings about manhood from Hemingway's childhood, as shaped and reconfirmed by female and male writers whose views corresponded roughly to those of Hemingway's parents. His father, a physician and naturalist who collected Indian relics and taught all his children to shoot, fish, swim, boat, and cook, considered himself a frontier scout and Ernest his foremost disciple. His talented mother shared that view while raising Ernest and his older sister

7

Marcelline as her twin Dutch dollies, exposing all her children to music, painting, and literature, and preparing Ernest especially for genteel Christian manliness. Ernest meanwhile gradually withdrew in imagination and feeling to a world of "men without women" where "the softening feminine influence" is supposedly absent;[9] but in youth or adulthood it was always a world more imaginary than real. The absence of women would be belied, for example, by his serial marriages, by the recurring Brontë impress in his own romantic fictions, by the admiration for strong women he shared with Kipling, Marryat, and Masefield, and by the recurrence also of aspects of those early "gardens of Eden"—his twinship years with sister Marcelline in infancy and his adolescent romances with adoring younger sisters before and after World War I. Indeed, the "Papa-daughter" locutions which he adopted by his late twenties are best understood as imaginative co-options of the presiding role, in his infancy, of his maternal grandfather "Abba" Ernest Hall, whom his mother wanted him to emulate, and of the "softening feminine influence" on himself that his mother and older sister then provided and that his adoring younger sisters later reinforced.

These biographical peculiarities will be very much a part of my argument in the pages ahead; but one obvious advantage of placing them in the context of Hemingway's boyhood reading is to insist on their cultural as well as psychological importance and on their ultimate literary significance. If, as I believe, a writer's life may be seen as a struggle to express through his or her creations an engagement with cultural problems that beset us all, then the personal nature of that engagement will be part of its public import. In this light Hemingway's lifelong quarrel with androgyny becomes our quarrel too, or a paradigm for it that demands serious consideration and is likely to repay it. I shall be trying, then, to present the writings of my Victorian hostages as Hemingway must have read and responded to them, and as they must have reinforced or reminded him of aspects of his own upbringing, and so helped to shape his attitudes and assumptions as a future novelist. My approach will inevitably be speculative, but my speculations will be informed by repeated readings of his works, by critical and pedagogical engagements with them, and by access to old and new information about his life, seen as an acculturation process that continues to impinge in crucial ways upon our own acculturation, our own cultural and literary concerns.

LATE RETURNS

In the second half of this study, in which I follow the curve of Hemingway's adult career through topical approaches to his successive phases, I will again interweave biography with literary and cultural concerns. I will be assuming, in those chapters, that the turning point in Hemingway's adult quarrel with androgyny was his marriage to Pauline Pfeiffer. After her visit with Ernest and Hadley at Schruns in 1925, for instance, Pauline would lament to them in her letters "how I miss you two men"; she would rave over Bumby as if he were her own child and would even propose to make him one of her heirs; and once her affair with Ernest was in the open, she would repeatedly tell him in her letters that "we're the same guy" and would praise him as "a great classic beauty," smart and perfect in every way. The triangulation of her relations with the Hemingways, the appropriation of Hadley's child and of Ernest's identity (as when she returns from a bike race and thinks "of me being Ernest, and how lovely you are, and how we're the same guy"), would be the very substance of *The Garden of Eden* manuscript, as inspired by the similar triangulation of Pauline with Ernest and Mary Welsh Hemingway in 1946. Meanwhile, back in 1926, during the famous hundred-day separation imposed on Ernest and Pauline by Hadley, Pauline had defined their forth-coming marriage in oddly androgynous terms:

> When we see each other . . . we'll find out still more how much we're the same guy. You are very very right in thinking I'd make any one but you a poor wife. I wouldn't make any one else any wife at all. And that's the truth. And of course a lot of people will probably think I make you a funny wife, but maybe you'll like the kind of wife I am because it will perhaps be a little like being your own wife.

Ernest must have agreed since he pressed the same issue with Hadley with mixed results: "She won't admit it but she knows we're the same person—sometimes she has admitted it."[10] That their common insistence on being the same person was founded in androgynous love, or in their fixation with the exchange of sexual identities that each made possible for the other, now seems clear. Pauline will make a funny wife because Ernest will make a funny husband, one who has in effect married himself; she can relate to no other man, and he is more suited to her than to Hadley (with whom he also practiced androgynous exchanges) because that is their essential nature and their common *modus vivendi* or *modus amandi*. The submergence of their peculiar bond by Pauline's steadfast subservience in marriage, by Ernest's systematic absences and masculinist hardenings, and by the supposed cor-ruptions and seductions of Pauline's wealth, could not altogether succeed. By 1946 Hemingway was exploring in his fiction the puzzling basis for his desertion of an essentially balanced union with Hadley, in which both partners retained their independent selfhood, for this plunge into androgy-nous fusion with Pauline.

His betrayal of Hadley, Bumby, and himself was accompanied also by a curious literary betrayal of his early mentors, Sherwood Anderson and Gertrude Stein, through a parodic text called *The Torrents of Spring,* itself a betrayal of his first publisher, Horace Liveright. Interestingly, the betrayal of Liveright proceeded with Pauline's blessing and Hadley's opposition, and allowed for a shift to a new and more substantial publisher, Scribner's, even as his betrayal of Hadley allowed for a new and richer wife. In his recent biography Kenneth Lynn notes the personal cruelty in *Torrents* of Hemingway's satire of infidelity "in Anderson's clodhopper style," his insistence that neither an old nor a new wife can hold a straying husband:

> He and Hadley would not separate for many months, and his union with Pauline would last for years. Nevertheless, the marital doom of both women is written on the wall for all to see in *The Torrents,* along with some insulting reasons why they would be cast off. The parodist portrayed Hadley and Pauline as abjectly anxious to please—as waitresses in the most degrading sense of the term—but then indicated that sooner or later they would have to go, Hadley because she was too old, Pauline because she was too talkative. Given the hopes that both women cherished in their hearts in the fall of 1925, denial must have ruled their minds. *The Torrents* referred to characters in [Anderson's] *Dark Laughter,* not to them. But did either of them fully believe this? It is hard to imagine that they escaped the shadow of doubt so easily.[11]

It would not be the last time Hemingway would satirize someone he was about to leave or marry. But it was, perhaps more importantly, the first time he would destroy or cast off stylistic parents while exchanging wives: for the importance of *Torrents* is its stylistic break with romantic wonderment as a response to changing passions and allegiances, to their imagined primitive embodiments by dark amoral races, to their flightier verbal transmutations into abstract cadences, and to their erotic relevance in the face of modern warfare's bodily mutilations. Here, with a curiously twisted vengeance, Hemingway would herald the ascendency of his own hard-boiled style, his own more appropriate filter for the same postwar materials.

In Part Two of this study I will examine that ascendency, its hardening into the masculinist poses of the 1930s, and its later relaxation into feminine strands of feeling. In "Three Little Savages," for instance, I will explore the registry of maternal suffering in wilderness tales by Marryat, Kipling, and Hemingway, each of whom establishes an imaginative imperial territory in which that oddly Victorian dilemma is witnessed by hardened frontier boys whose reactions indicate their essential guilt and vulnerability and their extraordinary empathy with maternal sufferers. Hemingway's hard-boiled treatment of these inherited as well as personal materials would allow for muted puzzlement, rather than romantic wonderment, and would keep deeper feelings at some distance; yet it would also remain in touch with them, if only by ironic implication and dramatic revelation.

In my next chapter, "Three Wounded Warriors," I will examine two novels, *The Sun Also Rises* and *A Farewell to Arms,* in which young heroes suffer directly from androgynous wounds which are again recorded in hard-boiled prose with deeper implications and which again involve strong identifications with inherited or contemporary female figures—in this case inherited from Craik, Michael Arlen, and Brontë. But now begins a descent into self-pity that borders on self-indulgence, as well as a numbing process that suggests an almost intolerable vulnerability to androgynous self-betrayal for which Duff Twysden (the prototype for Brett Ashley) and Pauline Pfeiffer (the chief model for Catherine Barkley) seem to be the personal catalysts. In "Tough Mamas and Safari Wives" I pursue the deadlier consequences of these betrayals by examining new kinds of female personae, ranging from the feisty old lady in *Death in the Afternoon* through the tough safari wives in *Green Hills of Africa* and "The Snows of Kilimanjaro" and the killer wife in "The Short Happy Life of Francis Macomber," to the proletarian and peasant earth mothers in *To Have and Have Not* and *For Whom the Bell Tolls.* The polarization of Hemingway's male and female characters at this time into killer wives and killer husbands at worst, or into jaded or brutalized men and tough, resilient women at best, has been remarked on. What remains unnoticed is the apparent beginning of that "study of women" that Robert Jordan promises to conduct following the Spanish Civil War and the degree to which Hemingway—like Marryat and Kipling before him—identifies with such women.

In my concluding chapters, "Daughters and Sons" and "Papa's Barbershop Quintet," I pursue into the 1950s Hemingway's emerging sense of identity with adoring daughters or sisters who will either survive his deadlier leanings or preserve him from them, and with devilish and adoring female alter egos who will externalize his inner struggles. His increasing indifference to his three sons, whom he would disinherit at this time, is reflected by the many deaths and defeats his male characters undergo in the fictions of this period, and especially by the rigged demise of the painter Thomas Hudson's sons in *Islands in the Stream.* Hemingway's own disillusionment with his father, which begins to come through in *For Whom the Bell Tolls,* seems for a time to abate, then reemerges with surprising force in *The Garden of Eden,* in the African tales written there by David Bourne. The exception to these male subsidings is *The Old Man and the Sea,* in which the old fisherman provides a fatherly example of stoic courage in the face of significant defeat for the boy on shore who believes in him; but even there the sea itself is seen as a benignly arbitrary woman who gives or withholds great favors. More important in this shift from masculine to feminine concerns is the prominence given to Nick Adams's sister Littless in "The Last Good Country," where the close relations between brother and sister become a paradigm for innocent childhood affections and their redemptive value, and where the children's escape to the woods becomes a benign form of "original sin," or of doing things you would regret not doing that you can repent afterwards.

These signs of new directions and experimental risks are above all present in *The Garden of Eden,* a novel dominated by the painful struggle of the heroine, Catherine Bourne, to define herself creatively in her marriage to a prominent writer whom she controls through androgynous love but who resists her through his own more entrenched creativity. Hemingway's counterpointing technique, his use of the writer David Bourne's African stories about his childhood conflicts with his father to offset David's narrative account of his conflictual life with Catherine and of her approaching madness (all of which parallels Hemingway's account), and his focus especially on David's recuperation of these stories when Catherine burns them because they rival and betray the narrative she shares with David, make for the most strikingly reflexive and easily the most ambitious novel Hemingway ever attempted. This externalized account of a psychic journey into the wilds of androgyny, as inspired by a mysterious Rodin statue of two lesbians making love, and as finally resolved through the conversion of the Bournes' lesbian partner in their *ménage à trois* into the next Mrs. Bourne, the perfect adjunct wife that Catherine has heroically refused to become, is so boldly experimental and so richly different from past work as to demand many-sided study for years to come. The externalization also of the writer's inward struggle with his own feminine traits, his own creative tensions, through his devilish wife and adoring lesbian alter egos, is a development itself worth the price on entry, as is the dominating presence of Hemingway's finest female creation, the conversational artist Catherine Bourne, the talkative waitress of *The Torrents of Spring* (a teller of literary anecdotes!) come back to haunt or "spook" her cruel creator. But most valiant of all is Hemingway's attempt to strike out in a new direction, to make of his own inner conflicts a different kind of novel, as profusely conversational as the later James, as complexly psychological as Woolf or Faulkner, as sexually adventurous as Joyce or Lawrence, and even more boldly androgynous and rebellious than its immediate sources in Fitzgerald and Kipling. That he failed in the attempt is, as E. L. Doctorow argues, almost beside the point.[12] What seems instructive is the degree to which he listened to and learned from the devilish and adoring muses within himself—learned, that is, about what a woman is and suffers and, less consistently, about his own severe dependencies and evasive strengths—and so left us with this lumbering elephant of a book for future hunting.

The gentler Hemingway whom recent critics have found in these late writings is decidedly there, and his presence calls for a major revision of the machismo legend; but Kenneth Lynn is surely right to insist that a more troubled Hemingway also emerges, one unable to resolve the problems that now beset him, and so plagued with physical and mental afflictions, including finally his inability to write, as to take his own life. Lynn's biography seems to me the finest account we have of the origins and recurrences of those inner difficulties that I would call the wound of androgyny, though he tends to see them narrowly as the psychological accidents of childhood and to blame Hemingway's mother especially for them. My own inclination is to place those problems in a wider cultural context than Lynn allows and to rescue Hemingway's mother from further critical abuse—at least until we learn to judge more fairly the interactions between both parents and their famous son that new evidence reveals and to emphasize their positive as well as negative contributions to his development, given their own cultural assumptions—which are again only newly evident. I might also say that a number of my published essays on Hemingway's androgynous upbringing and its relations to his work were available to Lynn while he composed his biography, though he nowhere cites them;[13] and that my own readings of individual works in Part Two, "The Return of the Repressed," were arrived at independently of his work, as no doubt his were of mine. The important thing is that we each take a new look at Hemingway's life and work in terms of his recurrent concern with androgynous problems, that we complement each other's findings even where we differ, and that my particular focus on Hemingway's boyhood readings and on the curve of his career is more consistently guided by a coherent view of a lifelong quarrel between the artist and his secret muses.

Part One

Victorian Keys to the Early Hemingway

Chapter 1

John Halifax, Gentleman

When Ernest Hemingway's maternal grandfather died in 1905, his parents were able to build and move into a larger house at a nearby location. For the first nine years of their marriage Clarence Edmonds and Grace Hall Hemingway had lived with Grace's father, Ernest Hall, in a house that became increasingly crowded as their first four children arrived. Now there would be eight bedrooms for a household of nine: Clarence and Grace; their four children, Marcelline, Ernest, Ursula, and Sunny; Grace's maternal uncle, Tyley Hancock; and a cook and a nursemaid. The servants would again be paid for through Grace's income as a music teacher and concert singer. She had earned as much as $1,000 a month this way before the children came and had helped her husband start his medical practice. He in turn had supervised the cooking and other household chores in his father-in-law's absence and had occasionally himself cooked, as he had loved to do since youthful days as a camp cook in North Carolina. He would continue these chores now that Grace was working again. But as Grace's designs for the new house indicate, her interests were domestic as well as professional. There would be a modern kitchen, the first of its kind in Oak Park, with surrounding cupboards, a high sink, and air drafts for ventilation; and there would be a separate music studio, acoustically perfect, where she could practice her music and give lessons, and where the children could also practice on cello, violin, and piano. Her mother's oil paintings would be placed around the dining room, moreover, as harbingers of the career in painting she would herself begin in her fifties. In the front of the house her husband's medical office, with its bottled fetus and closeted skeleton, would add to this anomalous mixture of professionalism and old-fashioned domesticity, of scientific and artistic bustle, and of oddly androgynous sexual roles. But Clarence's library, which doubled as his waiting room, would provide one of the most telling anomalies. Though it contained sets of the classics— Scott, Dickens, Thackeray, Stevenson, Shakespeare—certain newfangled works, like the novels of Jack London, were excluded from it. As Marcelline reports in her valuable memoir, *At the Hemingways,* "My parents disapproved of the violence and coarseness of [London's] writing. They liked *John Halifax, Gentleman,* much better."[1] Indeed, their third child, Ursula, had been named after the heroine of that novel, which means that the book had become a shaping part of her parents' outlook, at the latest, by April 1902.

The seeming opposition here—between Jack London and a Victorian gentleman named Halifax—was actually between London and the Victorian lady Dinah Mulock Craik whose novel Hemingway's parents admired. London's deplorable "violence and coarseness" would eventually recur, of course, in their son Ernest's writing; but then so would Mrs. Craik's notion of gentility. Her idea of what a Victorian businessman should be—namely, a gentleman and a Christian—was much in vogue in the latter half of the nineteenth century. Grace Hall Hemingway's father and uncle, Ernest and Miller Hall, after whom Ernest Miller Hemingway was named, were businessmen of this order, as was Clarence's father, Anson Hemingway. Ernest Hall ran a wholesale cutlery business in Chicago; Miller's Chicago firm made brass and iron bedsteads; Anson prospered in Chicago real estate. As a travelling salesman for his brother-in-law's firm, Miller Hall and Sons, Uncle Tyley Hancock was decidedly less substantial. He was also something of a tippler, and though Grace was fond of him, she plainly favored her more upright father and paternal uncle, both God-fearing Christian gentlemen like Halifax.

The historic popularity of Dinah Craik's novel helps to explain Grace's admiration for such men. Her son Ernest would later speak contemptuously of the "Christers" in Oak Park, Illinois; but in fact he too admired his grandfathers and granduncles for the mixture of civility and pioneer courage their lives and characters reflected. As he often proudly noted, his grandfathers on both sides had fought in the Civil War; his maternal grandmother, Caroline Hancock, and her brother Tyley had trekked across the Isthmus of Panama at mid-century while on their way to Iowa; and still other members of the family—Hancocks and Edmondses—were early western guides and settlers. Of such sturdy Christian gentlemen and their equally sturdy wives—pioneers, Civil War veterans, western trekkers—Oak Park was originally constituted.

MUSCULAR CHRISTIANS

Dinah Craik's extraordinarily popular novel spoke to this peculiarly adventurous gentility when it appeared in Victorian England in 1856. It was an instant and long-lasting success, a rich Victorian version of the much less substantial Horatio Alger stories Ernest and Marcelline would later devour and which Ernest, at least, would take very seriously.[2] In the 1922 edition of *Halifax,* which appeared a few years before Hemingway's first publications, Gordon Home speaks of the novel's Alger-like appeal "to a large class of readers who at the beginning of life are aspiring to that triumph over adverse circumstances in which Mulock's hero succeeded so well." He locates "the true greatness of the book," however, "in the revelation of the possibility of a life consecrated to the highest ideals being carried on in the midst of everyday perplexities and hampering conditions." The ideals are Christian; the hampering conditions include class biases against the tanner's boy, who, while rising to success as an enterprising miller and philanthropist, single-handedly quells riots, rescues drowning aristocrats, advances fair election laws, improves conditions for the poor, and stems bank panics. Home credits Craik accordingly with striking "a much-needed note of harmony" in the midst of the social disorder of her day and with influencing that greater sympathy between the classes which has since obtained.[3]

The thrust of his comfortable argument is actually well-taken. The book is about the assumption of moral and social leadership by the business classes in the early 1800s, when the industrial revolution first took hold in England, and the solidification of that trend by the 1830s, when the Reform Bill was passed. As the word "gentleman" in its title indicates, it is also about the appropriation of aristocratic virtues and obligations by these same classes—along with aristocratic wealth and privilege. Thus, Halifax marries a dispossessed aristocrat, Ursula March, whose later accession to fortune enables him to introduce a steam engine into his mills, purchase a small country retreat for his family, and move later into a large estate.

The domestic side of the novel was also part of the book's wide appeal. Halifax's Christian virtues are chiefly exercised through close relations with his family and friends, and this intense domestication of Christianity was typically Victorian. What sets this novel off, then, from eighteenth-century precedents like *Pamela,* which signalled the rise of the middle classes, and from later dilutions of that rise like the Horatio Alger stories, is its presentation of a pluck-and-luck success tale within industrial and domestic contexts peculiar to Victorian times. Though other novels of the day would characteristically invoke the domestic pieties as a bulwark against the frightening inroads of urbanism and industrialism, *Halifax* proved to a still receptive age that home and business could be run by the same moral and religious precepts within the old pastoral environs. In suburban Oak Park that message rang true not simply at the turn of the century, but well into the 1920s. As Home said of *Halifax* in 1922: "So wholesome is the story that it should be read by every youth and maiden in the land before the unsatisfactory influence of the decadent school of modern writers can diminish their enthusiasm for the nobility of a life moulded on that of the founder of Christianity." Such pious sentiments would soon be echoed by Ernest Hemingway's parents, for whom the "decadent" qualities of their son's first tales and novels loomed so much larger than the postpioneer courage and post-Christian integrity reflected in them, to say nothing of their son's very evident consecration to his art.

As late as 1964 the *Encyclopaedia Britannica* continued to describe *John Halifax, Gentleman* as "a Victorian best seller . . . still read for its vivid picture of a life regulated by the ideals of philanthropy, hard work and self-discipline," and to ascribe a similar life—one "marked by the domestic virtue praised in her work"—to Mrs. Craik herself. While that entry soon disappeared, by the 1970s Dinah Craik had reemerged for feminist critics like Elaine Showalter as a representative of the first, or "feminine," stage of that three-stage process—feminine, feminist, female—by which British women created "a literature of their own." Showalter argues, for instance, that model heroes created by women novelists of the "feminine" stage are not "fantasy lovers, daydreams of romantic suitors," as male critics tend to see them, but projections rather "of women's fantasies about how they would act and feel if they were men, and more didactically, of their views on how men *should* act and feel"; they are products then "of female fantasies . . . more concerned with power and authority than with romance":

> Many of these heroes are extremely aggressive in bourgeois economic terms. They are successful; they live out the fairy tale of Victorian upward mobility with the single-minded energy that characterized their female creators. John Halifax, for example, the hero of Dinah Craik's 1856 bestseller, *John Halifax, Gentleman,* begins as a beggar, but works hard, subdues fires, riots, and floods . . . , marries an heiress, and buys property. Near the end of his life he has a family estate, a family firm, and a chance to run for Parliament. He might just as well have been called John Bull or Dick Whittington.[4]

Halifax is in fact aligned with Whittington in the novel's second chapter; and in his eventual acquisition of "the fruits of patriarchy" which eluded women writers like Mrs. Craik, he demonstrates how these women writers "identified with the power and privilege of the male world" through paragons like himself, who "enabled them to think out their own unrealized ambitions."

According to Showalter, such heroes also perpetuate doctrines of manliness borrowed from male novelists like Thomas Hughes, the well-known author of *Tom Brown's School Days*, whose belief in "muscular Christianity" proved widely appealing: "The love of sport and animals, the ability to withstand pain, the sublimation of sexuality into religious devotion, and the channeling of sexuality into mighty action are traits the model heroes share. In Hughes' novels, however, manliness is achieved through separation from women; in the women's novels, mothers, sisters, and wives are the sources of instruction on the manly character."[5]

As everybody knows, Thomas Hughes's precedent, that manliness is achieved through separation from women, would be followed by Ernest Hemingway in the century ahead; but as some of us tend to forget, the role of mothers, sisters, and wives as "sources of instruction on the manly character" was one he also favored in works like *A Farewell to Arms, For Whom the Bell Tolls, Across the River and Into the Trees*, and "The Last Good Country." His own mother and sisters had played such roles in his childhood; and as Peter Griffin has persuasively shown, his mother's constant emphasis on the tenets of Christian manliness would profoundly affect his life and work.[6] Grace Hall Hemingway's "model heroes" were her father and uncle, Ernest and Miller Hall, in whose image Ernest was in effect created and duly named and raised. Grace herself had taken Ernestine as her professional middle name when she began her short-lived opera career in New York in 1895. Her decision to abandon that career for marriage was based nominally on the harsh effect of the stage lights on her eyes, which had been weakened in childhood by a severe case of scarlet fever. But her mother's death in the year before her debut had brought her even closer to her father, with whom she shared her love of music, theatre, books, and religion. It seems likely, then, that she had married the young doctor Clarence Hemingway, whom she had come to know during his attendance on her dying mother, so as to better serve her father during his declining years. As Griffin argues, her father and her firstborn son Ernest were the great loves of her life, for which Clarence—like so many Victorian swains before him—served as a useful adjunct.

Thus, from his daughter's marriage in 1896 to his death in 1905, Ernest Hall continued as the dominant figure in his household, leading the family in prayers, presiding over the family table, managing the servants, and providing shelter and a good measure of financial security for his daughter's burgeoning family. In his absence Clarence managed the servants, as he would continue to do after his father-in-law's death. He would also assume control of the family's finances, in keeping with the lines of patriarchal succession; and in fact his loss of control during the Florida land bust of 1928, when he could no longer meet payments on his real estate investments, contributed to his decision to commit suicide. Meanwhile Grace had taken her mother's place beside her father while he lived and had assumed his household dominance after his death. She had been raised by both parents to pursue an independent career in music. Her mother, a concert singer herself, had deliberately kept Grace out of the kitchen on what now seems like an ultramodern premise: "There is no use any woman getting into the kitchen if she can help it."[7] Grace could help it; the family was rich enough to afford servants; she was free to cultivate her voice and to pursue a musical career which would allow her in turn to afford them. Thus her interest in the feminist movement at the turn of the century—Showalter's second stage for "a literature of their own"—was understandably high; and she continued that interest on into the new century, attending feminist meetings on Nantucket Island, for instance, when she summered there with her children.

It was her father's place, then, which Grace more or less assumed in the family after his death. Yet she also nursed and helped to raise six children; her memory books for each of them, along with the memoirs written by her daughters Marcelline and Sunny, testify to her strong concern for them as individuals with their own needs and temperaments. Together with Clarence, moreover, she developed a curious amalgam of old-fashioned and advanced ideas for raising the children androgynously. Grace schooled them in the musical arts and exposed them to literature and painting; Clarence taught the girls as well as the boys how to shoot, fish, boat, swim, and cook. Both parents favored strict moral and religious precepts; both were severe disciplinarians; and both stressed conduct and behavior over patient understanding and active attention to feelings—though Grace's stress on consideration for others was much stronger than her husband's. That she schooled him too in such matters and found him less of a gentleman and a pillar of strength than her father, and less a companion in her love for the arts, was one obvious source for the explosive quarrels which Ernest bitterly records. There is no doubt that she squelched Clarence, or that they both squelched the children when they misbehaved. But it was the combination of swift, harsh, and often arbitrary punishment with loving overindulgence which created so much confusion and resentment in the children and which made Ernest especially suspicious of loving sentiments.

1. Grace Hall Hemingway in concert garb, ca. 1896

Grace's contribution to that dilemma, which has been judged so glibly by an essentially Victorian notion of what a wife and mother should be, can be seen more fairly, I think, with the help of current feminist perspectives on the past. Grace's essentially British upbringing—both parents had migrated from England at mid-century—had instilled in her that evangelical gentility celebrated in Dinah Craik's *John Halifax, Gentleman.* Grace's identification with her father, an enlightened businessman like Halifax, was in this respect not unlike Dinah Craik's identification with her "model hero" in working out her own "unrealized ambitions." But as we have seen, Grace's parents had also encouraged her to pursue her own career as an opera singer. For Grace, then, the possibilities of an independent life in the spirit of the new feminism loomed large and promising; she might well become her own model hero. At the same time, like other young women, she was attracted by the prospects of love and marriage. Her suitor, Clarence Hemingway, was tall, handsome, and devoted. In his love for hunting, fishing, and other outdoor activities, and in his own staunch piety, he seemed an ideal exemplar, moreover, of "muscular Christianity." According to Marcelline, Grace had come to lean on him during the tragic final stages of her mother's illness.

2. The newlyweds Clarence Edmond and Grace Hall Hemingway

By the fall of 1895, when her mother died and Grace left for her long-delayed opera training in New York, they were engaged to be married. The attractions of marriage were thus well-established even before she began her training. After her successful debut that spring in Madison Square Garden, she was offered an opera contract and—like many women—had to decide between marriage and a career. Marriage, of course, meant having children, but as the future mother of six, coming from a family of two, that prospect plainly pleased her. It was during the following summer, while touring Europe with her father, that she finally decided to forego her career and return home to marry Clarence. As the family legend goes, she even passed up a chance to sing before Queen Victoria to keep her marriage date.

Consider, then, the position of a professional singer painfully affected by stage lights and strongly moved by the prospect of continued intimacy with her beloved father. She could continue to give music lessons and perform locally, as she had before her marriage; she could, like other women, marry and raise children; and she could continue to live vicariously, not simply through her father, but through children whom she planned to raise androgynously, as if to work out better fates than her own. But having tasted the professional success she had long prepared for, she entered marriage with a strong sense of her own professional worth. As she told Marcelline in later years, Madame Schumann-Heink had taken the place she might have had in opera.[8] In *Hemingway in Michigan* (1966) Constance Cappel Montgomery responds to that rueful remark as might any male chauvinist: "The irony of the story of this woman who felt she had missed fame and greatness was that she had achieved fame indirectly, but apparently never realized it. Few people today recognize the name Schumann-Heink, but practically any literate person in the world would have been able to recognize the woman introduced as 'the mother of Ernest Hemingway.'"[9]

Montgomery's chauvinist bias is a common one among Hemingway's critics and admirers; but if we reverse her irony and ask the rather pertinent question—which would you rather be yourself, Madame Schumann-Heink or the mother of Ernest Hemingway?—a good many of those same admirers might understand Grace's preference. Initially at least, she did seek vicarious satisfaction through her son's career; and though at first repelled by his writing, she was quite aware of his growing fame and greatness, and—after her husband's suicide—she even *liked* some of his novels (e.g., *A Farewell to Arms, For Whom the Bell Tolls*) and was grateful for his financial help; but in consistently valuing her own personal and professional worth she was many decades ahead of her contemporaries and more truly modern than many of her son's recent critics. Into her late-nineteenth-century marriage, then, Grace brought a sense of personal and professional worth which such critics have variously characterized as utter selfishness, a *grand-dame* manner, monstrous willfulness and self-delusion, frustrated careerism, and castrating Victorian momism.[10] There is, I think, this much truth to all such epithets: like her gifted son, Grace was an extremely narcissistic personality, and with similar good cause. A gifted person herself, she brought the same exorbitant sense of worth and mission into all her activities that he brought into his. As she once wisely told Marcelline, "Ernest is very like me."[11] It is a premise worth pondering if we can agree, in the wake of a resurgent feminism, that wives and mothers have a right to value themselves at least as highly as their career-minded sons and daughters and their prestigious husbands.

John Halifax, Gentleman offers a useful key to such valuations. As Elaine Showalter notes, the woman who wrote it had lost her mother when in her teens and was thus like many women novelists of her day in her "identification with, and dependence upon, the father; and either loss of, or alienation from, the mother."[12] She was also like them in placing wifely and motherly duties above her writing career; for her as for them, the domestic calling was deemed higher than the artistic. She avoided marriage, nonetheless, until she was thirty-eight and well into her successful career, at which time she also adopted a daughter. A dissenting clergyman's daughter herself, her identification with that role seems evident in the very title of her popular tract *Sermons Out of Church* (1875) and in the sermonlike nature of her conservative feminist musings, *A Woman's Thoughts about Women* (1858), on the plights of spinsters, unmarried working girls, and prostitutes. In her paternal identification and maternal loss, in her feminism and evangelicism, in her professional and domestic attitudes, she prefigures and accounts for women like Grace Hall Hemingway.

Consider in this light the following passage from her "sermon" on the "sins of self-sacrifice":

> There is a point beyond which we have no right to ignore our own individuality—that is, supposing we have any. Many people have none. They get the credit of being extremely self-denying, because they really have no particular self to deny. . . .
>
> But to those born with decided tastes, feelings, possibly talents, the exercise of all these is an actual necessity. And lawfully so. If God has given us our little light, what right have we to hide it under a bushel, because some affectionate, purblind friend dislikes the glare of it, or fears it will set the house on fire? . . .
>
> What bitter sacrifices one member of a family gifted with a strong proclivity, perhaps even a genius, for art, music, or literature, sometimes has to make to the rest, who can not understand it!
>
> Now . . . a modern Corinne, with her hair down her back, sitting playing the harp all day long, instead of going into her kitchen, ordering her dinner, and looking after her servants, would be a most aggravating wife for any man to marry. But, on the other hand, a gentleman with no ear for music, married to a wife who is a born musician, may make a very great victim of that poor lady. . . .
>
> We ought always to be chary in allowing ourselves to be forced into sacrifices which do not benefit, but merely gratify the persons exacting them.[13]

Given the eloquence with which Dinah Craik speaks here to issues Grace had to face as the century ended, it is not surprising that she spoke eloquently also to Grace's interests in *John Halifax, Gentleman*.

SETTING AND RISING SUNS

Craik's choice of a lame male character, Phineas Fletcher, as her narrative persona in *Halifax* seems at first glance something less than eloquent; but actually it further supports the notion of working out "unrealized ambitions" through model heroes. As Showalter observes,

It is a commonplace of feminine fiction for the sensitive man to be represented as maimed: Linton Heathcliff in *Wuthering Heights*, Phineas Fletcher in Dinah Craik's *John Halifax, Gentleman*, Charlie Edmondstone in Charlotte Yonge's *The Heir of Redclyffe*, and even such late versions as Colin Craven in Frances Hodgson Burnett's *The Secret Garden* all suggest that men condemned to lifelong feminine roles display the personality traits of frustrated women.[14]

As a frustrated woman in disguise, then, Craik's narrator befriends the novel's hero, John Halifax, in the opening pages. An orphan boy of fourteen, ragged, muddy, miserable, Halifax has been trapped by rain in the same town alley with Phineas and his father. With a strong hand already roughened and browned by labor, he helps to push further into the sheltering alley the little hand-carriage in which the lame Phineas rests. "What would I not have given to have been so stalwart and so tall!" exclaims the envious Phineas; and again, after noting the boy's "serious, haggard face," with its "resolute chin" signalling "character and determination," Phineas expresses his heartfelt envy:

> As I have stated, in person the lad was tall and strongly-built; and I, poor puny wretch! so reverenced physical strength. Everything in him seemed to indicate that which I had not: his muscular limbs, his square, broad shoulders, his healthy cheek, though it was sharp and thin—even to his crisp curls of bright thick hair.
>
> Thus he stood, principal figure in a picture which is even yet as clear to me as yesterday. (2)

Phineas's intensely physical admiration is apparently shared by others, for a few moments later young Ursula March appears in the door of the mayor's house, opposite the alley, offering the boy a slice of bread she has cut from a loaf—until a snobbish servant forces her back inside and (as we later learn) wounds her in the struggle to retrieve the breadknife. Meanwhile her passionate compassion confirms the boy's strong appeal for frustrated women, whether lame, wounded, or disguised. But Phineas's father, Abel Fletcher, has also been impressed. The honest Quaker tradesman hires Halifax to push home the sickly Phineas, who at sixteen is "as helpless and useless to him as a baby," and then takes him on as a driver for his tan-yard. Halifax soon becomes the "able" (i.e., masculine) son the father longs for, and with Phineas strikes up a David-and-Jonathan friendship which lasts throughout his life. They read and discuss books, recite poetry, sneak off to the theatre, and share thoughts, feelings, and troubles, as Halifax works his Christian way upward. Then Halifax marries Ursula March and, when Phineas's father dies, takes over the mill and tan-yard he has since come to manage. Phineas joins the young couple in their new home, becomes the uncle of their children as those children arrive, and continues to share in and record the events of family and business life. By such narrative sublimations, then, Dinah Craik and her female readers work out their own unrealized ambitions.

Given the physical confinement of Victorian women which Phineas's lameness and illness help to codify, the appeal of tallness and physical strength in the young Halifax seems readily comprehensible. Grace Hall's attraction to such qualities is a case in point. A tall, energetic person herself (having grown beyond her short British parents while recovering from another childhood illness), she had always led a physically active life. At twelve she donned a pair of her brother's pants to become the first girl in Chicago to ride the high cycle, which also belonged to her brother. At twenty-four she easily matched her tall, stalwart husband in daily work and bustle. In early matronhood she took calisthenics classes and once surprised her family by kicking as high as the kitchen ceiling. Later she learned to build her own furniture for a second music studio on the family farm at Walloon Lake. She also swam and fished at the lake, and even took lessons in pistol-shooting from her husband, with baby Ernest cuddling against her shoulder when the gun went off. And as her memory book for him attests, she admired his manly little body and his physical exploits, taking obvious pride in accomplishments which, like Phineas Fletcher, she plainly envied. But most of all she admired her daughter, Madelaine "Sunny" Hemingway, for tomboy qualities which spoke to her own energies and convictions:

> She is sometimes caught in innocent mischief and sent to the principal's office . . . but she will not tell on her friends, or get them into trouble. She is quite athletic, a good fellow among the boys and girls, at baseball, basketball, volley and indoor ball. She is game—and to be relied on in an emergency. As genuine a boy as ever inhabited a girl's personality.
>
> She loves to clean fish and chickens, has no squirms like the other girls. The most unusual and interesting child of them all.[15]

This passage from her memory book for Sunny helps to undercut the myth of a maternal tyrant oblivious to her children's needs and natures, squeamish herself before unpleasantness, abhorring nature in the raw. Grace's admiration of Sunny's tomboy abilities suggests, rather, a woman hampered by Victorian conventions but determined to overcome them and to encourage *all* her children to lead active, healthy, outdoor lives. That "genuine . . . boy" in "a girl's personality" tells us much, moreover, about the frustrations of postpioneer women in this country and further explains their easy identification with lame or hearty male protagonists.

Another passage from *Halifax* seems useful in rounding out such split identifications with male figures, weak and strong. Toward the end of chapter 1, when the young beggar boy has pushed Phineas home and said goodbye, Phineas is so moved by the reflection in him "of the merry boyhood, the youth and strength that never were, never could be mine," that he calls out while painfully trying to leave his carriage and mount the steps: "Not good-bye just yet!" Halifax then returns and says it would be great fun to carry Phineas up the stairs: "He tried to turn it into a jest, so as not to hurt me; but the tremble in his voice was as tender as any woman's— tenderer than any woman's *I* was used to hear. I put my arms round his neck; he lifted me safely and carefully, and set me at my own door. Then with another good-bye he again turned to go" (7–8).

Phineas again calls him back, his father arrives, together they coax the boy inside, and Phineas and John enter the house hand in hand, their friendship sealed for life. Like Dinah Craik, both boys have lost their mothers and must now offset the loss with male affection. But more than this, their affection conveys the didactic impulse by which women novelists projected their views "on how men *should* act and feel" onto model heroes. Admiring and identifying with male strength and power, women writers asked that men return the compliment and identify with female powers of tenderness and concern for others. This combination of physically oriented powers, which Dinah Craik and Grace Hemingway seem to have known in their fathers, was to be inculcated in other men by such edifying demonstrations. Thus, what some male critics define as conventional Victorian feminization of men in the genteel tradition seems more obviously a form of outward reaching among frustrated thinking women seeking participatory powers. And that too seems worth pondering as we consider the origin of tough and tender attitudes in the early Hemingway.

Halifax's tender side is shown in other ways. When social obstacles separate him from Ursula March, his health deteriorates and he nearly pines away until she agrees to marry him. When their first child, Muriel, is born blind, he keeps her always by his side and treats her as the family's guardian angel. Of gentle birth himself, he seems to have learned such gentle ways from another Muriel, his mother, who died when he was eleven. But then his real mother is Dinah Mulock Craik, who invests him with these qualities without giving much attention to their origin. Her beggar boy arrives with a Greek Testament whose flyleaf shows only that *"Guy Halifax, Gentleman,"* had married *"Muriel Joyce, Spinster,"* in 1779, and had died a year after his son's birth in 1780. It is enough for Craik, apparently, that young John comes of "gentle" rather than "boorish" blood, for as Phineas now holds, "a gentleman's son has more chances of growing up a gentleman than the son of a working man" (6). So we are back with *Tom Jones* and "the advantages of good descent" and good family stock in shaping democratic heroes, advantages which most of the novel's distinctly boorish aristocrats—Ursula March's relations, for instance—would seem to contradict. But then Christianity is the novel's more plausible democratic solvent, particularly as it figures in the Protestant business ethic. Though offended by the foul-smelling tan-yard, Halifax is not afraid to dirty his hands with honest work, nor to face down aristocrats and working men alike in fair or noble causes; his pride of birth converts readily to middle-class self-responsibility and self-respect; his Christianity, to middle-class righteousness before coarseness, violence, decadence, and injustice of whatever social origin. Our model hero comes fully equipped with these virtues, which are amply tested by recurrent trials. The book's interest lies less in his development, then, than in the application of evangelical gentility to trade and family life—for which women characters will always offer sanction. Thus, Dr. Jessop's wife tells Halifax: "I had heard you were a tradesman; I found out for myself that you were a gentleman. I do not think the two facts incompatible, nor does my husband" (161). And when Halifax sustains a blow from Ursula's boorish cousin and as a Christian refuses to return "blow for blow," Ursula herself completes the moral message: "You have but showed me what I shall remember all my life—that a Christian only can be a true gentleman" (181). For the next seventy years readers like Clarence and Grace Hemingway, who had known such men firsthand, would respond to that message with un-questioning agreement.

There was also a love story, a family romance, to which the Hemingways responded. In 1800, when John and Phineas have reached their twenties, they retreat to a duplex cottage on vacation and there meet Ursula March and her ailing father. Inspired by the pastoral poems of Phineas's ancestral namesake, the young men are in effect looking for a "faithful spouse" and "little son" for John (97–98). Ursula will provide both, but it is her father's death and not her nubile promise which brings her close to Halifax, even as Grace and Clarence Hemingway were brought together by her mother's death. Though Halifax is no doctor, at one point during the father's illness he rides a horse to fetch one; and with Phineas and their landlady he later argues against the same doctor's refusal to tell Ursula that her father is dying, and then gently conveys that difficult truth himself. When death comes, moreover, he recognizes that the stricken Ursula must ease her grief through tears and makes the landlady take her back to her father's bedside. Thus, his relation to the Marches, as to Phineas, is that of healer, rescuer, and comforter, a very Christian but also a very medical role. Indeed, the proliferation of wounds, illnesses, deaths, poxes, and accidents throughout this family romance, with Halifax always at the ready to ease, mend, or avoid them, is rather startling. Ursula's hand—which he later kisses—is wounded during the bread-knife scuffle in the opening pages; a few chapters later he saves her father and cousin from drowning; some five years after that he presides over the father's prolonged death; and by 1812 he knows enough about medical progress to apply Dr. Jenner's vaccine to his children and so save them when smallpox sweeps their neighborhood, sitting up night after night—"patient as a woman"—to nurse their milder cases. Even his first meeting with Ursula, during the cottage episodes, comes after he has leapt through the open window to rescue and bring inside one of the landlady's children, whose cut head is being bandaged as Ursula enters with a request for her ailing father. And a bit later, their courtship is advanced in town by Dr. Jessop and his wife, who are willing to bridge class lines. Neither Dr. nor Mrs. Hemingway would have had much trouble, then, in identifying their courtship and family life with that of John and Ursula. For them as for the Halifaxes, medical and industrial science, business and family life, low and high estate, blended without conflict with Christian gentility.

For Grace the congenital blindness of the Halifaxes' firstborn child, Muriel, her illness during the smallpox episode, and her death shortly after, must have seemed especially poignant. During Grace's severe childhood bout with scarlet fever she had gone completely blind herself, with little hope of recovery. Over the next several months she had learned to play the organ and piano by ear—as Muriel does in *Halifax* just before her death. But one Sunday morning, while her family was at church, Grace had glimpsed the blurred outline of her right hand on the piano keys, had prayed hard with eyes shut tight, then opened them to see clearly both her outstretched hands. When her parents returned from church, she ran to them shouting hysterically that she could see, her tears mingling with her mother's as they joyfully embraced. Grace's sense of being blessed and singled out for a better fate, which she attributed to Ernest too after his recovery from war wounds in Italy, must have begun here.

The Halifaxes too take Muriel's congenital blindness as a sacred sign. She is in fact blessed for being blind by Phineas's father on the night of his peaceful death, in words "spoken with as full assurance as the prophetic benediction of the departing patriarchs of old" (225). That night Phineas too receives his father's blessing and his love—an acceptance long with-held—which he comes to associate with the blind Muriel, the redeeming spirit of feminine confinement and imposed limitation; and for him as for John Halifax, she becomes the family's guardian angel.

Muriel's mother, Ursula, is, by contrast, no angel. When she first appears in the cottage episodes, Phineas takes interesting pains to put that point across:

> A girl, in early but not precocious maturity, rather tall, of a figure built more for activity and energy than the mere fragility of sylph-like grace: dark-complexioned, dark-eyed, dark-haired—the whole col-ouring being of that soft darkness of tone which gives a sense of something at once warm and tender, strong and womanly. Thorough woman she seemed—not a bit of the angel about her. Scarcely beauti-ful; and "pretty" would have been the very last word to have applied to her; but there was around her an atmosphere of freshness, health, and youth, pleasant as a breeze in spring. (108)

The contrast is with domestic dolls and saints in the Dickens tradition, angels in the house too delicate to survive, too ethereal to embrace; but active, energetic, wholesome Ursula is decidedly a substantial survivor, "at once warm and tender, strong and womanly," and therefore a fit mate for strong and tender Halifax. Yet their daughter, Muriel, the fragile essence of dependent father-daughter love, is very much in the Dickens tradition. Like Paul Dombey and Little Nell she is a loving, wizened child who has pre-monitions of death and who in fact dies in her prepubescent years, her sealed eyes opening then only to heavenly light. Grace Hall's early transforma-tions—from blindness to sight after scarlet fever at seven, and from a small to a tall girl after a six-months' illness in her teens—must have made the Muriel-Ursula contrast doubly appealing: she had survived dependent love to become a strong person like her father and a warm and womanly one like her mother. Tall, buxom, and hearty rather than pretty, she gave her whole-some stamp to all her children, who seem uniformly handsome in the Ursula March manner.

Early in their marriage the Halifaxes share a dream of living in the country and of raising a family there, which also meant much to the Hem-ingways. When Ursula receives her withheld inheritance, they are able to establish their pastoral retreat in a place called Longfield. As Phineas makes clear through lyric apostrophe, the family dream is Christian as well as pastoral:

Longfield! happy Longfield! little nest of love, and joy, and peace—where the children grew up, and we grew old—where season after season brought some new change ripening in us and around us— where summer and winter, day and night, the hand of God's providence was over our roof, blessing our goings out and our comings in, our basket and our store; crowning us with the richest blessing of all, that we were made a household where "brethren dwelt together in unity." Beloved Longfield! my heart, slow pulsing as befits one near the grave, thrills warm and young as I remember thee! (243)

Phineas goes on to describe the small farmhouse and the barn, converted into a bedroom for the children, with "windows . . . open all summer round" into which birds and bats would fly. Similarly the farmhouse kitchen is converted into a dining room into which pigeons, doves, and hens walk "at pleasure." Phineas defines this access to natural life as an English family's system of "liberty, fraternity, and equality" (244), and will later contrast it pointedly with the French system.

The young Hemingways similarly set out in 1898 to build a summer cottage at Walloon Lake in northern Michigan with money which must have come from Grace's earnings or her father's investments. Grace called it (and misspelled it) "Windemere," after the Windermere Lake region in England where Wordsworth and Coleridge developed the romantic mythos of country life. Early in 1905, at about the time of Abba Hall's death, a farm on the opposite side of the lake from their cottage was about to be sold for taxes. The Hemingways were able to buy it cheaply and did so in conjunction with plans for their new home in Oak Park following Abba's death. Both the Michigan farm and the Oak Park home were purchased, apparently, out of Grace's patrimony. The *Halifax* precedent for such opportunities must have been very much on their minds, for as Marcelline reports, "Mother named the farm Longfield" and had visions of living there with Clarence "perhaps in their old age."[16]

If Grace's vision was pastoral, Christian, and romantic in the English tradition, Clarence's was more firmly founded in the American romance of pioneer life. There were still Indian tribes in northern Michigan, and Clarence, an avid naturalist, was also a collector of flints and arrowheads. His youthful camp life in the Smoky Mountains of North Carolina, his love of hunting and fishing, testify to his postpioneer nostalgia for the old frontier. But then Grace's family as well as his own had been western guides and settlers. It was easy for them to blend British pastoral and American pioneer traditions into a single dream. Their children would be raised in a healthy

3. Ernest, Grace, Clarence, and Marcelline at Lake Walloon

outdoor environment—like the Halifax children in Dinah Craik's novel, but also like western and even Oak Park children until relatively late in the nineteenth century. Ernest Hemingway would write of how Prairie Avenue led onto the nearby prairies in his childhood and so received its name. But northern Michigan was even more remote and unsettled than suburban Oak Park, and there his parents went in search of lost retreats. Ernest continued that search for the rest of his life, fashioning his own literary dreams out of his parents' British and American bequest. Like the Halifaxes, his parents looked for outdoor health in the vigorously genteel manner; he would go further back to the life of lone frontiersmen for imaginary models, but he would imagine them as being very like his western ancestors, the eventual founders of Oak Park.

The Victorian pastoral dream in Halifax comes to a curious if peaceful end which also must have impressed the Hemingways. On August 1, 1834—with bells ringing as the nation celebrates the freeing of Negro slaves in England's colonies—John Halifax dies. Just two years before, Parliament had also passed the Reform Bill. The connection between such humane advances and the leadership of enlightened Christian businessmen like Halifax is the obvious point. Thus, Phineas overhears John saying to Ursula how he fancied the freeman Paul had stood in the Roman prison on such a day, answering those that loved him with *"I have fought the good fight. I have finished my course. I have kept the faith"* (459). Halifax too has fought the

4. Ernest in a goat-cart on the Oak Park boardwalk

good fight. Lying on a grassy hill with Phineas, looking out westward toward the setting sun, he responds to the news that Abel Fletcher's old house is being converted into an inn and its lawn to a bowling green:

> "What a shame! I wish I could prevent it. And yet, perhaps not," he added after a silence. "Ought we not rather to recognize and submit to the universal law of change? how each in his place is fulfilling his day, and passing away, just as that sun is passing. Only we know not whither he passes; while whither we go we know, and the Way we know—the same yesterday, to-day, and for ever." (461)

The children then troop out from the cottage below, John lies on his back facing the setting sun, pulls his broad straw hat over his face as if to sleep, and—covered by Phineas's protective cloak—dies his peaceful Christian death. When he is brought home and placed in bed, his ailing wife dies the same night while watching over him.

Grace Hemingway would survive her husband's suicide in 1928 by twenty-three years. The ironies of that sequence, given the tenets of muscular Christianity they both lived by, are considerable. They had grown apart as their marriage progressed, and as Clarence's death confirmed, Grace had always been the more muscular Christian and, by that standard, the more likely survivor. But initially they shared a common dream. When they had built their new home in Oak Park in 1905, they had created a family crest

35

5. The Hall-Hemingway family crest: clasped hands joining an *H* with the sun above and a lily below

designed to express family unity to be set in the large glass-topped door between Clarence's office and the living room. As Marcelline tells us:

> It was a large light blue *H*, with the center bar of the *H* formed by two clasped hands standing for the union of Hall and Hemingway. Over it was placed a golden sun with rays extending outward, symbolizing warmth and love, and under the clasped hands was a white lily for peace and purity. My parents had stationery engraved with this symbol, and a few pieces of it remain in some of the memory books my mother kept for each one of her children.[17]

The golden sun suggests the pastoral ideal in *Halifax* and the setting sun under which Halifax completes a life defined by muscular Christianity and close family devotion. The clasped hands suggest the scene in which Halifax refuses as a Christian to return "blow for blow" and is then heralded by Ursula with the novel's moral message: "a Christian only can be a true gentleman": "They grasped hands once more, and gazed unhesitatingly into each other's eyes. All human passion for the time being set aside, these two recognized each in the other one aim, one purpose, one faith; something higher than love, something better than happiness. It must have been a blessed moment for both" (181).

Such blessed handclasps Grace and Clarence could readily accept, along

36

with Ursula March's favorite flower, the arum lily (250), as family symbols. But Halifax's views on growing old and submitting to the universal law of change would prove harder for them to uphold than they realized. The odd thing is how impressed their son Ernest would be with that difficult doctrine. When Gertrude Stein had said—in what must have sounded like censorious maternal accents—"You are all a lost generation," he had responded, in his double epigraph for *The Sun Also Rises*, with a well-known passage from Ecclesiastes:

> One generation passeth away, and another generation cometh: but the earth abideth forever . . . The sun also ariseth, and the sun goeth down, and hasteth to the place where he arose . . . The wind goeth toward the south, and turneth about unto the north; it whirleth about continually, and the wind returneth again according to his circuits. . . . All the rivers run into the sea; yet the sea is not full; unto the place from whence the rivers come, thither they return again.

The inspirational source for Hemingway's choice of this passage, in the Hemingway family crest and the religious tenets it expresses, now seems obvious. But its further inspiration in the closing pages of *John Halifax, Gentleman* is also a distinct possibility, given his parents' emphasis on the value of that novel for themselves. Whether Ernest read it in childhood is of course speculative; but he was invoking in religious accents the universal law of change which Halifax upholds and which his parents at least nominally accepted; and as his choice of a rising rather than a setting sun confirms, he was also emphasizing the ascendancy of his own generation. The striking point here is that his faith in the abiding earth, rather than in the heaven in which the fulfilled Halifax believes, is a minimalized form of the same religious vision. The earth's circling winds, the rivers Ernest cherished, the sea he came to love, are muted aspects of his parents' bygone faith, signs of certainty in changing times, and therefore answers to the predicament of lostness. He was taking what he could of his parents' religious heritage into the life ahead and was understandably disturbed by their initial misconception of his thrust. How much he was taking, and on what basis, can be better understood by still other aspects of *John Halifax, Gentleman*.

FLOATING HEDONISTS

Ursula March's cousin, Richard Brithwood, Esquire, is married to Lady Caroline Brithwood, a friend of the notorious Lady Hamilton, Lord Nelson's mistress. According to Phineas's father—who describes Brithwood as "a fox-hunting, drinking, dicing fool"—Lady Caroline has been "brought up in the impious atrocities of France, and the debaucheries of Naples" (167). The marital disharmonies of such decadent aristocrats—against whom the Victorian middle classes would eventually react—are an important part of the novel's subplot and of its social theme. The spread of French impieties at the turn of the century—through scandalous novels as well as scandalous aristocrats—was one of the causes for the Victorian taboo on sexuality. The white lily in the Hemingway family crest goes back to such historic conflicts, and Lady Caroline's fictive role in this one may well bear on the reversal of the Victorian taboo by such as Lady Ashley "in our time." "Brett." and "Brithwood" have their sonic similarities, no doubt coincidental; yet the subplot of *Halifax* suggests otherwise. Thus, Lady Brithwood is designated from the first as a handsome, charming hedonist hell-bent on adultery. She is also in her own way irresistible. As Phineas sums her up:

> Even if not born an earl's daughter, Lady Caroline would have been everywhere the magic centre of any society wherein she chose to move. Not that her conversation was brilliant or deep, but she said the most frivolous things in a way that made them appear witty; and the grand art, to charm by appearing charmed, was hers in perfection. She seemed to float altogether upon and among the pleasantnesses of life; pain, either endured or inflicted, was to her an impossibility. (175)

Hemingway's floating hedonist, Lady Ashley, will endure and inflict her share of pain; but if he read about this early floater, this "magic centre of any society wherein she chose to move," he would have been drawn to her as in fact John Halifax's firstborn son, Guy, is drawn to her when she appears ten years later at Longfield. Like Ernest, Guy is named after his grandfather, *"Guy Halifax, Gentleman,"* from the family Bible flyleaf, and is thus characterized as "a little gentleman from his cradle" (247). When Lady Caroline arrives in a coach and four at Longfield, Guy is the first to announce her. "Isn't it a pretty view?" he boldly asks her as they approach the house; and having touched her green gown (his mother favors gray), he thereupon installs himself as "her admiring knight attendant everywhere." All through dinner he fixes "his admiring gaze upon the 'pretty lady'"; and afterwards he takes her down to the garden and gathers for her "a magnificent arum lily" (250). His conversion of her into a new romantic mother seems obvious enough. At bedtime he even lifts up his face to her for a goodnight kiss, and next day is disappointed to learn he is not likely to see his "pretty lady" again.

Ernest, if he read the novel, would not have been disappointed with the melodrama that has meanwhile transpired. Nominally Lady Caroline has come to secure John Halifax's vote for a candidate her father favors—Mr. Gerard Vermilye—as a Member of Parliament for their district. Actually she has an assignation with Vermilye, her secret lover, with whom she will eventually run off to Paris. But Halifax is aware of the affair and for the time being thwarts it by escorting Lady Caroline safely back to her churlish husband. There is a passionate exchange, which young Ernest would have relished, between the Halifaxes and Lady Caroline on the dread sin of adultery, which she confesses she has committed and which she defends vigorously on the grounds of her husband's brutality and her lover's kindness and devotion; and there is much play on her waning beauty and her desire for lost youth—*"la liberté et ses plaisirs, la jeunesse, l'amour"* (254)—which tends to sensualize her earlier democratic embrace of "the rich flesh-and-blood life of the people. *Liberté—fraternité—egalité"* (175) and thus to challenge the Halifax version of those words. Yet when young Guy, "who had lingered out of his little bed most unlawfully—hovering about, ready to do any chivalrous duty to his idol of the day," comes up for his goodnight kiss, Lady Caroline is unable to kiss him and moves from hysterical laughter at her sinful condition to "a passion of tears" (253).

Young Ernest would have loved that thwarted kiss from a sinful lady, and an older Ernest might even have found its modern analogue. But an earlier exchange, between Lady Caroline and Phineas, on the Arcadian nature of family love, might have impressed young Ernest even more profoundly:

> After tea we all turned out, as was our wont on summer evenings; the children playing about; while the father and mother strolled up and down the sloping field-path, arm in arm like lovers, or sometimes he fondly leaning upon her. Thus they would walk and talk together in the twilight, for hours.
>
> Lady Caroline pointed to them. "Look! Adam and Eve modernized; Baucis and Philemon when they were young. *Bon Dieu!* what it is to be young!"
>
> She said this in a gasp, as if wild with terror of the days that were coming upon her—the dark days.
>
> "People are always young," I answered, "who love one another as these do."
>
> "Love! what an old-fashioned word. I hate it! It is so—what would you say in English?—so *déchirant*. I would not cultivate *une grande passion* for the world."
>
> I smiled at the idea of the bond between Mr. and Mrs. Halifax taking the Frenchified character of *"une grande passion."*

"But home-love, married love, love among children and at the fireside; —you believe in that?"

She turned upon me her beautiful eyes; they had a scared look, like a bird's driven right into the fowler's net.

"*C'est impossible—impossible!*" (251–52)

Earlier, Lady Caroline had confessed to Ursula that she was "sick of courts sometimes" and "would turn shepherdess myself, if we could find a tolerable Arcadia" (247). But faced with this tolerable Arcadia, she confesses its impossibility for herself, even as Brett Ashley will confess to Jake Barnes in *The Sun Also Rises:* "I couldn't live quietly in the country. Not with my own true love." Brett's unhappy life with the British aristocracy, her hedonistic response to it, her freewheeling ways, may well originate in Lady Caroline's oddly modern pre-Victorian dilemma. "Isn't it pretty to think so?"—the modern novel's famous concluding line—may well originate there too.

The predictive nature of *John Halifax, Gentleman,* as to Ernest's future life, adds an even greater irony to his parents' admiration for this novel. The boy who prefers Lady Caroline to his mother inevitably gets into trouble. A governess named Miss Silver, who turns out to be the daughter of a notorious French Jacobin, comes to live with the family at their new estate, Beechwood Hall. Both Guy Halifax and his younger brother Edwin fall in love with her and quarrel violently when she turns down Guy for Edwin. With the family peace thus broken, Guy leaves for Spain, ostensibly on his father's business. Two years later he is in Paris, associating with the decadent British aristocrats in Lord Luxmore's set. Lord Luxmore is Lady Caroline's father; she has since run off with and been abandoned by Sir Gerard Vermilye, whose political and erotic schemes John Halifax had long ago foiled. While drunk at a gaming-house, Guy strikes Sir Gerard for insulting his father and—fearing he has killed him—flees to America. As if to underscore the relation between thwarted loves and deadly blows, Guy's farewell note reaches the family on the wedding day of Edwin and Miss Silver.

This Victorian anticipation of knight-errant Robert Cohn, battling on foreign strands for Lady Ashley's honor, is intriguing enough; but it is the theme of family disgrace, and of the separation from his family of a rebellious son, which prefigures Hemingway's postwar quarrel with his family, his flight to Paris and Spain, his "disgraceful" novels and divorces. Still, *Halifax* is a Victorian novel, not a modern life. In its closing pages Guy returns to the family after eight years of perilous ventures. Stronger and wiser, he furthers a marriage between his business partner, Lady Caroline's brother, and his younger sister Maud, which his father had once forbidden, and himself rejoins the family firm. Meanwhile Lady Caroline turns up, withered, rouged, senile, and is also taken in by the compassionate Halifaxes, who nurse her through her final year.

This acceptance of wayward sinners by staunch Christians is, I think, curiously wistful in its generous forebearance. In Lady Caroline especially Dinah Craik creates a complex and decidedly appealing character, kind to her servants, attracted by John Halifax's manliness, drawn to his children, vocal in her attack on marital abuse, charming and vital in her supposed sensual decadence. She also comes from a Catholic family and, like Halifax, favors the Catholic Emancipation Bill. Such points might have bemused the young Ernest Hemingway, who grew up in a suburb of Chicago where, as he later told Harold Loeb, "The Catholic children used to pity the Protestant children because of their strict regimens."[18] Hemingway's religious impulses would eventually draw him to Catholicism and to a Catholic second wife, Pauline Pfeiffer, as he continued his own waywardness. Thus Craik's fusion of Catholic lenience with French license might have seemed to him, as perhaps it seemed to her, secretly attractive.

His parents had admired this novel for its Christian blend of strength and tenderness, its pastoral warmth and vigor, its reminders of their own medical courtship and of Grace's triumph over childhood illness. The success of its hero, a staunch Christian businessman who had weathered many adversities, confirmed their faith in their own gentlemanly fathers, and therefore in themselves; its portrait of a strong, active, womanly wife, especially in contrast with fragile dolls and sensual decadents, confirmed their evangelical view of love. Indeed, the family romance in this novel gave them a pattern for marriage so compelling that they worked it into their family crest. Even its blend of science, literature, theatre, and music with love of nature and the Protestant work ethic seemed exactly suited to their varied interests. For Ernest, their firstborn son, their transmission of the pastoral idyll to family life in northern Michigan, and its fusion there with the family's pioneer heritage, proved enormously rewarding; the mixture of toughness and tenderness in his makeup would reflect that fusion; nor was he entirely unmindful of this and other uses of his mother's patrimony and professional earnings, after the example of Ursula March, for he would himself accept such bounties from his first and second wives. His interest in the universal law of change and its necessity would become a permanent part of his outlook and of his quarrel with his parents' passing ways, and yet it would also reflect their faith in the religious context of all such generational cycles. Finally, his attraction to Catholic lenience and European license, in combination with his family's pioneer heritage, would result in a stoic hedonism by which he felt his generation might survive. Whether or not he read *Halifax,* then, his outlook was profoundly shaped by its inspirational effect upon his parents and his own early life.

Not the least part of that effect was its confirmation of the harsh moral regimen, in paradoxical combination with loving overindulgence, which his parents had imposed on all their children. But that too was characteristic of evangelical gentility in many turn-of-the-century homes. As Vineta Colby observes in *Yesterday's Woman,* "The fact is that evangelicism in all its forms stressed punishment and suffering, obedience and humility. Family love was on the one hand sentimentalized into an ideal of sweetness and tenderness, but the other hand was an iron fist for instilling discipline and distributing punishments."[19] Like Samuel Butler and many others before him, Ernest received this double message from both parents. Added to its confusion was his father's weaker position in an androgynous household in which his mother, vicarious identifier with Halifax and other Christian gentlemen, exhibited such muscular strength. Yet he would himself follow her example, in his mid- to late twenties, by taking on the role of "Papa," after "Abba" (meaning "Father") Hall, and thereafter adopting many adoring "daughters."

Chapter 2

✿

Fauntleroy and *Finn*

As child is father to the boy
I find Al Capone's pan to find [in] Hemingway
The other face of Fauntleroy

F. SCOTT FITZGERALD,
Fitzgerald Papers, Princeton

When his second collection of stories, *Men Without Women,* appeared in October 1927, Ernest Hemingway was six months into the second of his four serial marriages. On February 14, 1927, he had written to Maxwell Perkins at Scribner's to explain his title. He had chosen "Men Without Women" because in almost all the stories "the softening feminine influence through training, discipline, death or other causes" was "absent."[1] Apparently the presence of such influences in his own life was troubling him. His divorce from Hadley Richardson had become final only a few weeks before he wrote to Perkins. As if to gain time for himself between marriages, he had postponed his wedding to Pauline Pfeiffer until May. His nominal excuse was a trip with a friend, Guy Hickok, through fascist Italy. Pauline had called it his "Italian tour for the promotion of masculine society" with some justice.[2] From 1921, when he married Hadley, to his death in 1961, the new proponent of male independence would be serially dependent upon four wives. In his life as in his fiction, his pretensions to bachelor freedom were always more imaginative than real.

Hemingway himself was aware of other ironies in his chosen title. As he wrote to Scott Fitzgerald on September 15, 1927, he had "called the book Men Without Women hoping it would have a large sale among the fairies and old Vassar Girls."[3] He was, it seems, jokingly edgy about men who identify with women, yet also live without them, as do women (by his logic) who identify with men. In an essay review that fall, one such androgynous reader, Virginia Woolf, would complain aptly enough that the writer— though otherwise courageous, candid, and highly skilled—was "self-consciously virile" and had contracted rather than expanded his talent. Turning Hemingway's bullfight metaphor against him, she would accuse him also of faking his closeness to reality: for "the true writer stands close up to the bull and lets the horns—call them life, truth, reality, whatever you like, —pass him close each time."[4] When Perkins sent on the review in November, Hemingway found it "damned irritating"; he felt that his artistic honesty was being impugned by "Bloomsbury people"—all over forty—who cultivated their own reputations and resented young intruders on the modernist preserve. What upset him most, however, was the theft of his bullfight metaphor. Thus, with something close to rattled virility and small-boy talent, he admitted to Perkins that he "would have enjoyed taking the clothes off Virginia Woolf this noon and permitting her to walk down the Avenue de l'Opera letting every one, truth, reality, whatever she liked—pass her close each time."[5]

To such literary insults domestic injuries were soon added. While he was on a winter alpine trip with his second wife, a sore throat worsened into grippe; his son Bumby sleepily poked him in the eye one night, cutting the pupil; a tooth began aching; hemorrhoids flared; and with Pauline presiding, he took to his bed for six days to recover. Then came a copy of the *Oak Park News* containing a feature article about his mother. As Carlos Baker reports,

It was headlined LAUNCHES NEW CAREER AFTER RAISING FAMILY, and told of Grace Hall Hemingway's recent success as a landscape painter at the advanced age of fifty-two. "One might suspect," wrote the reporter, Bertha Fenberg, "the mother of Ernest Hemingway, author of *The Sun Also Rises,* to be something of a harsh realist, but this very jolly woman laughs at the pessimism of 'these young writers' and expresses the sane belief that the pendulum is swinging back to normal. 'God's in his heaven, all's right with the world' is her way of expressing her own happy life." No doubt, said Ernest sourly, Grace wished that her son Ernie were Glenway Wescott or some highly respectable Fairy Prince with an English accent and a taste for grandmothers.[6]

Ernest's pessimism would soon be vindicated. A year later his father would commit suicide, partly in reaction to real estate losses in the Florida land bust preceding the stock market crash of 1929; and for the time being at least, his chastened mother would abandon her jolly outlook. But where she had invoked Browning's *Pippa Passes* in defense of her outworn views, Ernest had harped on their effeminate implications for himself. Grace wanted him to be like his fellow expatriate, Glenway Wescott, whose prize-winning tribute to American matriarchy, *The Grandmothers,* had appeared in 1927 and whom Ernest himself had satirized in 1926, in *The Sun Also Rises,* as a "rising novelist" from "New York by way of Chicago" with "some sort of English accent" and a great many feminine affectations. Worse yet, she wanted him to be like that "highly respectable Fairy Prince," little Lord Fauntleroy, another American boy from New York who acquires an English earldom, if not an English accent, and shows a decided taste for elderly relatives. In the late nineteenth century Fauntleroy had won the hearts of millions by charming his gruff, aristocratic grandfather into kinder senti- ments and actions, including the making of much-needed improvements for his neglected tenants. He had charmed him, moreover, by being very much his widowed mother's boy and was thus a young literary hero shaped through training, discipline, and death by "the softening feminine influ- ence." Hemingway's sharp denial of such influences makes his "Fairy Prince" remark all the more intriguing, given his iceberg view of his own creations, and may well suggest some contraction of outlook, if not talent, in his devotion to male independence. The Fauntleroy lead to his past is accord- ingly worth puzzling over at some length.

LOST CONNECTIONS

"As soon as it was safe for the boy to travel, they bore him away to the northern woods." So Carlos Baker begins his standard biography, omitting with iceberg aptness the reasons why "they"—Hemingway's parents— proceeded with such undue haste to expose their firstborn son to outdoor life and concentrating instead on the fact of early exposure. So Hemingway himself would concentrate on Nick Adams's early years in Michigan without explaining how and why he got there. Thanks, however, to newly available papers and letters, and to information which Baker and other biographers supply but underplay, we can now attend more directly to such iceberg omissions. We can say, for instance, that Hemingway's parents belonged to pioneer families—Halls and Hancocks, Hemingways and Edmondses— going back through western settlement and the Civil War to the American Revolution; and that outdoor life was accordingly an imaginative extension of their common family dream. We can say, further, that the dream was British as well as American, that the names "Windemere" and "Longfield," which Grace—born of British parents—had given to their Michigan cottage and farm, invoke the British pastoral vision of Wordsworth and Dinah Mulock Craik, respectively, by which children might be raised in accord with God and Nature as decidedly muscular Christians. We can say, then, that the dream explains those radical experiments in childrearing in which both parents concurred; for if Grace and Clarence Hemingway were in many ways conventional suburbanites, one of the peculiar ways in which they extended their combined family heritage was through childrearing. The cottage they bought in northern Michigan soon after their marriage was for the wholesome outdoor upbringing of muscular Christian postpioneers. There Clarence would teach his wife and four daughters, as well as his two sons, how to shoot, fish, boat, and swim; and as the founder of the local Agassiz Club back home, he would also teach his children the naturalist lore his own mother had first taught him. The raising of tomboy girls as well as manly sons was part of the family plan, and active, energetic Grace, at twelve the first girl in Chicago to ride the high cycle, was as keen for it as her vigorous husband. Indeed, her favorite daughter in this regard was Sunny, the most athletic tomboy of them all, and she reveled as much in the manly exploits of her first infant son as in the smocks and tresses she favored for his infant wear.

Her twinship experiments, in which she tried to match Ernest with his sister Marcelline, his elder by a year, have long been misunderstood as attempts to feminize or sissify her son after the popular notion of Fauntleroy. But androgynous dollhood comes closer to her apparent intention. Ernest and Marcelline were her twin Dutch dollies, boy and girl, and the Dutch length of their hair and their matching dresses were androgynous features. As Peter Griffin shrewdly observes, it was *her* infant dresses—preserved from her own childhood—that Ernest wore, as if to emphasize her vicarious stake in his future.[7]

After infancy, accordingly, it was the male side of the androgynous mixture that Grace endorsed. If Ernest had to wait until he was six for his first boy's haircut, Marcelline had to wait an extra year in kindergarten so that she and Ernest could enter first grade together. In the following summer, moreover, Marcelline's hair was cut short to resemble Ernest's. Her suffering from that tonsorial reversal must have deeply impressed her brother, who would later imagine a heroine raped and cropped by Spanish fascists. Marcelline was in fact recropped by an obliging older girlfriend when her summer haircut grew out unevenly. As punishment for that

6. Ernest and Marcelline in twin baby dresses, 1900

embellishment, her disenchanted mother made her wear one of her sister Sunny's baby bonnets to school until her hair grew out again. After two mortifying weeks, however, Marcelline's second-grade teacher intervened and convinced Grace to relent; a week later the teacher promoted Marcelline to the third grade, where she belonged, and so for a time foiled the twinship plan. But not for long. Between seventh and eighth grades both parents agreed that Marcelline should stay out of school for another year to avoid being "rushed through strenuous routines during the difficult maturing time of the early teens."[8] So again Ernest caught up with her, and they finished high school together. An observant boy, Ernest must have noted how each of his sisters spent a quiet year out of school during that "difficult" time when pubescent girls first menstruate. Neither he nor his baby brother Leicester would suffer that particular female shame.

The edge Grace gave to maleness was not uncommon among turn-of-the-century women with advanced ideas. We have already seen, following Elaine Showalter's lead, how women novelists in nineteenth-century England tended to project their desire for power and freedom onto model male heroes, like Dinah Craik's *John Halifax, Gentleman,* whose pluck-and-luck progress "enabled them to think out their own unrealized ambitions."[9] We have also seen how staunchly Grace admired *Halifax,* and how the traits exhibited by his kind—"The love of sport and animals, the ability to withstand pain, the sublimation of sexuality into religious devotion, and the channeling of sexuality into mighty action"—were those she hoped to inculcate into her firstborn son, even as "mothers, sisters, and wives" in

47

7. The Hemingways—Marcelline, Madelaine, Clarence, Grace, Ursula, Ernest
(in Dutch dolly haircut)

Victorian women's novels were always the inculcators and definers, "the sources of instruction" for the hero's "manly character."[10]

It was a character, moreover, which combined feminine with masculine propensities, as in Halifax's strong and tender ways and their influence on his children. But Halifax himself we do not see before his fourteenth year. For an even younger model hero, one more likely to have influenced Ernest Hemingway's infant years, we must turn to Frances Hodgson Burnett's famous novel of 1886, *Little Lord Fauntleroy*. Anyone familiar with the author's life and with the plot of her best-selling book will recognize the same projected fantasy as in Dinah Craik's bestseller: an American boy (a younger Halifax) is raised by his widowed mother to be "brave, just, and true" like his dispossessed British father and to make the world a better place to live in; he is open and sympathetic, affectionate and loving, but also fearless and (in several dramatic instances) able to withstand pain; a charming boy who calls his mother "Dearest," he is also possessed of "a fine, strong, straight little body" that his mother and his nanny much admire; he loves sports and animals, helps the poor and unfortunate, and is remarkably considerate of others; at seven he becomes the legal heir to his British grandfather, the earl of Dorincourt, with a great deal of future power for good or ill; and so great is his charm that he persuades the crusty, ill-natured

8. The Hemingways—Ernest (after boy's haircut), Ursula, Clarence, Madelaine, Grace, Marcelline

earl to accept and love his widowed mother as well as himself. The novel and the play based upon it enjoyed enormous popularity in the late nineteenth century, especially with American mothers, who for a time dressed their sons in black velvet suits with lace collars and neck ribbons and arranged their hair in shoulder-length curls, even as they had dressed them earlier in "gal's clo'es" like Fauntleroy's when he was "knee high to a grasshopper," and had favored lengthy hair.[11]

Grace Hall Hemingway was one such mother in 1899, when her first male child was born. Indeed, even before he was born, she had dedicated him to making the world a better place to live in—quite possibly a place like England![12] Both her parents were British citizens, like Frances Hodgson Burnett, who had emigrated to America in mid-century, and she shared the American fantasy of a triumphant return to royal favor. As her daughter Marcelline reports, one of the near-triumphs of her brief career in grand opera was the invitation to sing before Queen Victoria which conflicted with her travel plans. Though she would never return to England, she had visited there twice before with her parents and had been raised in an essentially British household. Thus, Marcelline describes her mother's father, Ernest Hall, as "a typical British gentleman" with pink cheeks, thick black eyebrows, and mutton-chop whiskers, wearing elegant dark clothes, immaculate gray gloves and a black derby or top hat, and walking the streets with his small white Yorkshire terrier. Soft and gentle in speech, affectionate but reserved in manner, sincerely religious, he shared with the family his love of animals, music, opera, and theatre, but seldom spoke of such gruesome matters as his Civil War experience. According to Marcelline, her mother's "close, congenial friendship" with her father and her maternal uncle, Tyley Hancock, made for "a very happy and loving household"; and she speaks warmly also of the "similar sense of humor and a certain British deliberate-ness and neatness" which they shared, and of the "family jokes and light-hearted conversation and . . . good-natured teasing" which characterized their table-talk.[13] Her description of this domestic milieu comes so close in tone and quality to that of the American-British household in *Fauntleroy*, and of the prose used to describe it, as to make it fairly clear where Ernest got his aversion to affected English accents. The speech in surrounding house-holds would have sounded very different to his childish ears. Though he himself would later subscribe to British reserve and understatement, the American-British patois in *Fauntleroy* must have come all too close to home for comfort.

Little Lord Fauntleroy is, of course, a children's novel; but it appeared at a time when children's novels were written, as the saying then went, "for children of all ages," and when they appeared without distinction on the same bestseller lists with adult novels. As Ann Thwaite points out in her fine biography of Mrs. Burnett, *Waiting for the Party*, children's books actually dominated the bestseller lists in England and America in the 1880s. Thus, in 1884 the best-selling books were *Heidi* and *Treasure Island;* in 1885, *A Child's Garden of Verses* and *Huckleberry Finn;* in 1886, *Little Lord Fauntleroy*, *King Solomon's Mines*, and *War and Peace*.[14] If *War and Peace* seems an anomaly in this sequence, that is chiefly because we have since come to

9. The Hall family—Abba Ernest, Leicester, and Grace

distinguish—as the Victorians did not—between children's literature and the literature of childhood. By that distinction *Heidi* and *Treasure Island* might appeal to "children of all ages," but *Huckleberry Finn* gives full and serious attention to distinctly adult interests and to that extent belongs in a class with *War and Peace*. Oddly enough, so in its much more modest way does *Little Lord Fauntleroy.* A slighter and less demanding book than *Finn,* more fairy tale than novel, it deals nonetheless with adult interests with wide cultural implications. As its sensational reception suggests, it essentialized certain assumptions of the genteel tradition about women and children which were then in jeopardy—assumptions which *Huckleberry Finn,* for example, appearing in the previous year, was more or less designed to reverse. What that reversal amounts to can be briefly indicated by Huck's famous decision, at the end of Mark Twain's novel, to avoid being civilized by Aunt Sally by lighting out for the territory. Since we still read *Huckleberry Finn,* we think we know what Huck's decision encompasses; but since we have stopped reading *Little Lord Fauntleroy* and other genteel works, we don't really know how much it overlooks. Let me quote a key passage from the opening chapter of *Fauntleroy* which will help to show what I mean:

When he was old enough to walk out with his nurse, dragging a small wagon and wearing a short white kilt skirt, and a big white hat set back on his curly yellow hair, he was so handsome and strong and rosy that he attracted everyone's attention, and his nurse would come home and tell his mama stories of the ladies who had stopped their carriages to look at and speak to him, and of how pleased they were when he talked to them in his cheerful little way, as if he had known them always. His greatest charm was this cheerful, fearless, quaint little way of making friends with people. I think it arose from his having a very confiding nature, and a kind little heart that sympathized with everyone, and wished to make everyone as comfortable as he liked to be himself. It made him very quick to understand the feelings of those about him. Perhaps this had grown on him too, because he had lived so much with his father and mother, who were always loving and considerate and tender and well bred. He had never heard an unkind or uncourteous word spoken at home; he had always been loved and caressed and treated tenderly, and so his childish soul was full of kindness and innocent warm feeling. He had always heard his mamma called by pretty, loving names, and so he used them himself when he spoke to her; he had always seen that his papa watched over her and took great care of her, and so he learned too to be careful of her.

So when he knew his papa would come back no more and saw how very sad his mamma was, there gradually came into his kind little heart the thought that he must do what he could to make her happy. (16–17)

The passage goes on to describe how the child, following his genteel father's example, tries to comfort his mother through small acts of affection and sharing, and how he overhears her telling the servant one day, "He is such a little man, I really think he knows."

What Frances Hodgson Burnett omits here that Mark Twain includes I need not elaborate. What seems more striking, a century afterwards, is the overlap between what she affirms—indeed, idealizes—and what Twain and his modern successor, Ernest Hemingway, working in a far more realistic tradition, might also to be said to affirm. Mrs. Burnett's little paragon is "strong," for instance, as well as tender, and nothing less than "fearless" in his attempts to make friends. His mother calls him "a little man" for his thoughtful efforts to comfort her as she grieves her husband's death. Before and after this passage, moreover, there are repeated references to his "strong back" and "sturdy legs" (16) and to his "strong, lithe, graceful little body" and "manly little face" (30). Even when likened to a "fairy prince," in later pages, he is called "rather a sturdy young model of a fairy" (61). His athletic drive is stressed in chapter 2 when he wins a race in the New York streets. Similarly, his ability to withstand pain is stressed when he lets his gout-stricken grandfather lean on him as he walks, or when he learns to ride a jolting pony. But the emphasis here is on manly concern for others, on fearless friendliness. If his manly sphere is at this point domestic, his sensitivity to feelings, his ready sympathy, his wish "to make everyone as comfortable as he liked to be himself," remind us of yet another domestic context, that of Jim and Huck on their Mississippi raft, their floating home, where "free and easy and comfortable" relations prevail, and where sensitivity to feelings and sympathy for suffering is also much in evidence.

I do not mean to ignore the more serious problem of race relations Twain confronts, nor the range of riverfront violence and depravity he explores; but Burnett too in her genteel way exposes the poverty and squalor ignored by British aristocrats and the illness, unemployment, and victimization among New York's working poor. She was in fact a social realist of sorts in her adult novels, and her attempt here to join American democracy with British aristocracy was no more wishful than Twain's similar attempt in *The Prince and the Pauper,* nor more outmoded than his satire on slavery two decades after its abolition or on medieval darkness after a thousand years of evolving light. The crucial difference between them, in this passage at least, is the young boy's fearless friendliness with *women,* his manly concern especially with his mother's feelings. This is what is lost or reversed by Twain and Hemingway. Their tenderest relations and their manliest acts are, characteristically, between men without women, as with Jim and Huck on the raft or Jake and Bill on the fishing grounds at Burguete, and they are both rather hard on real or substitute mothers.

Plainly, Frances Hodgson Burnett belongs with Dinah Mulock Craik and other women novelists of the last century in projecting upon her young model hero her fantasies of how *she* would act and feel if she were him, and her views on how he *should* act and feel. They are power fantasies, then, and their didactic call for male courage in pursuing tender relations, particularly with women, strikes an especially plangent note. Burnett herself was only three years old, like Fauntleroy, when her father died of apoplexy and the family fortunes changed. A prospering ironmonger and silversmith in Manchester, he had moved the family the year before to ampler and more comfortable quarters backing onto fields belonging to the earl of Derby, with the lake and beautiful grounds of Temple House close by. With his death in 1853, however, the Hodgsons had to move to a seedier section of Manchester, where the children were exposed for the first time to backstreet glimpses of the urban poor. Her mother then courageously took over her husband's business and ran it until the 1860s, when the American Civil War cut off the cotton supply to Manchester's thriving mills, causing shutdowns and bankruptcies which depressed her trade. Responding to an unduly optimistic letter from an American uncle, the Hodgsons moved to Tennessee in 1865, when Frances was fifteen—and suffered outright poverty for the next few years. Though her brothers could get jobs, the only way Frances could help out was by writing tales for *Godey's Lady's Book* and other journals. By 1870, when her mother died and Frances was twenty, she had begun to write her way back toward the lost prosperity of early childhood and the lost glimpse of aristocratic bounty. Her identification with young Fauntleroy at the time of his father's death, and with his ascension from depressed to princely circumstances, and with his mother's eventual enjoyment of those circumstances, speaks eloquently enough to her desire for male power and privilege and to her toughness and determination in pursuing it.

She was, in short, a woman whom Ernest Hemingway might have admired—as Mark Twain actually did—if he had looked more closely into the genesis of fairy princes. Indeed, her two failed marriages, her long association with Scribner's, and her novel about a self-willed Spanish lady who comes to love a bullfighter, *The Pretty Sister of José,* suggest an odd affinity with Hemingway. But then my whole point in hammering at the lost aspects of the feminine genteel tradition is to suggest that affinity. Burnett—a plump, square-faced, determined woman, self-driven, extremely active, and frequently ill—was as exemplary in admiring male powers as was Dinah Craik in admiring Halifax, or Grace Hall in admiring her muscular husband

and precociously manly son. In one marvellous letter Burnett describes the "superb arms and divine antique legs" and the "exquisite pure bronze" sunburn of a local swimming instructor; in another she defends the theory by which her "two strong, manly, robust boys" find clothing unnecessary; in a third, she admits in her zest for gardening that she would have liked to have been "at least two strong men in one."[15] Perhaps the wild, oath-swearing heroine of her next novel, *A Lady of Quality*, who strikes and inadvertently kills a man with her whiphandle, was an expression of that wish. For Clorinda Wildairs, an eighteenth-century hoyden who prefigures recent feminist rompers like Erica Jong's Fanny Hackabout-Jones, was in Frances's view "a magnificent creature who rides over laws as she leaps fences." She was implicit, moreover, in all Burnett's previous heroines, not a new departure but a spirited example of what Burnett had "cared for most all [her] life—from the time [she] was eight years old," the time perhaps when, in apparent envy of white male powers, she was herself found furiously whipping a black doll in emulation of Simon Legree after reading *Uncle Tom's Cabin*.[16] There was obviously a great deal of frustrated frenzy behind Burnett's gentility. Within twelve years of *Fauntleroy* she would triumphantly purchase a large estate, Maytham Hall at Rolveden in Kent, in order to play Lady Bountiful herself. In the light of such actions, her use of Hawthorne's feminist heroine in *The Blithedale Romance*, Zenobia Fauntleroy, as the source of her model hero's name seems a telltale transmission of feminist desires into more publicly acceptable forms.[17] The fairy prince and his mother speak in genteel terms to a whole complex of frustrated energies.

Whether they speak in realistic terms is another question. The wishful aspects of *Fauntleroy* can be read as a conventional return to that royal favor we all enjoyed when our parents read us fairy tales. But as the long opening passage on "manly" qualities suggests, the wish originates also in genteel feminist desires. The aspiration toward masculine strength and vigor shows that Frances, Dinah, and Grace stood squarely behind their real or imagined sons as envious admirers. Similarly, the didactic call for male tenderness shows that such genteel mothers also sought reciprocal treatment, courageous acknowledgment of participatory powers, and androgynous equality with their sons. They were not interested in feminizing young boys, but in sharing with them a fuller range of human possibilities than their own limited spheres allowed. Frances Hodgson Burnett, who failed at so much else and who often neglected her sons in pursuing male perquisites, succeeded nonetheless in winning that reciprocal regard. So, in her early motherhood at least, did Grace Hall Hemingway.

In the passage already quoted from *Fauntleroy*, consider the continuing

10. Ernest, Abba Ernest Hall, Marcelline, and Ursula at Lake Walloon

account—hitherto excluded—of the model hero's "manly" desire to make his grieving mother happy:

> He was not much more than a baby, but that thought was in his mind whenever he climbed upon her knee and kissed her, and put his curly head on her neck, and when he brought his toys and picture books to show her, and when he curled up quietly by her side as she used to lie on the sofa. He was not old enough to know of anything else to do, so he did what he could, and was more of a comfort to her than he could have understood.
>
> "Oh, Mary," he heard her say once to her old servant. "I am sure he is trying to help me in his innocent way—I know he is. He looks at me sometimes with a loving, wondering little look, as if he were sorry for me, and then he will come and pet me or show me something. He is such a little man, I really think he knows." (17)

According to Ann Thwaite, Frances Hodgson was just such a thoughtful child at the time when her mother grieved her father's death. So too in after years was Burnett's own son Vivian, the overt model for Fauntleroy, who seems to have sensed her marital distress and her need for comforting. So too, in the happy British years when his parents lived with Grandfather "Abba" Hall, was Ernest Hemingway. Thus, in her memory book for Ernest, Grace early notes his "easy contented disposition" and cuddly ways: "He is a little love baby, delights to pat Mama, and snuggle up close"; "He sleeps with Mama and lunches all night"; "He is *so* strong and well and loves Mama *so* tenderly. He pats my face in the night and squeezes up close."

She records his extraordinary sympathy, as when he cries bitterly "over the death of a fly he had tried to revive on sugar and water"; his sensitivity to feelings, as when he comforts his sister Marcelline on their parents' absence: "Don't cry, Mockme, Daddy and Sweetie be home pretty soon"; and his endless delight in identifications: "He loves to play kitty and be the baby kitty, and Mama be the mama titty and stroke him and purr"; "He loves to play circus and be different animals"; "He loves to play that he is a 'ports-man,'" an "onward tistian Soldier," an Indian-fighter like Pawnee Bill; and most aptly in this context, "He can imitate a fairy with his little flying hand."

But, like Fauntleroy, Ernest too was a sturdy little fairy, fearless and strong, though sometimes a bit obstreperous—an ungenteel quality which, at this point in his life, his mother took in stride.

> He storms and kicks and dances with rage, when thwarted, and will stand any amount of rough usage when playing. Has good "grit." He comes and slaps you when you don't suit him, and kisses you when he's sorry.

> He has wonderful courage, and endurance, will stand a severe injury, if you will just "tiss it."

> He is perfectly fearless after the first time bathing in the lake—in fact, will creep out so far in the water, that he has to be brought back.

> He has fine nerve and endurance. . . . He is a little man, and a good hard worker delighting to share in the work and privations of sports-men or working men. His father's own boy.[18]

But also his mother's, who plainly admires and encourages his tough and tender ways. His early sense of manliness was as much infused with the Fauntleroy ideal she favored as with the pioneer ideal she also furthered, but which his father especially advanced. Like Fauntleroy, then, he was an affectionate, tender-hearted, considerate child who wore Dutch locks and infant dresses and called his mother "Fweetie." At two he learned how to sew and loved it; at a month short of three he also learned to load, cock, and shoot a pistol; at four years and eight months he could even hit the bull's eye "quite frequently" in target practice; and yet at five he was still "a very loving boy" who cuddled around his mother's neck and said: "I'm Mama's little mink, ain't I? Will you be my Mama Mink?" A lover too of sports and animals, a boy who shouted "'fraid of nothing' with great gusto," he was

11. Ernest as Huck Finn with a toy gun, Lake Walloon

also much admired by his mother for his courage and endurance, his ability to withstand pain, and his manly little body.

If Grace had imagined her "little man" after the literary model of Fauntleroy, and of his older predecessor, John Halifax, her husband Clarence had imagined him after frontier models like Pawnee Bill and Huckleberry Finn. In the early years, while "Abba" Hall was still alive, there was no essential conflict between these models. Grace's androgynous ideal blended readily with her husband's pioneer ideal in the childrearing experiments they conducted together in Oak Park and northern Michigan. But Ernest was like other American boys. He would eventually prefer Huckleberry Finn, whose frontier antecedents were at least secure, to Fauntleroy, the "Fairy Prince" whose undeserved reputation as a prig and a sissy he spent a lifetime dodging and denying. In her memory book for Ernest, Grace records her son's childhood wish to follow his father's lead: "Ven I det to be a big boy I do-in to de moakey mountains wif Daddy, and I take a big dun an sute bears and lions, an evry-sing." His father's youthful camping trip in the Great Smoky Mountains of North Carolina had become a family legend. It was a geological expedition for which Clarence served as the camp cook, and he often told his children stories about it: how he had been alone in camp one day and had shot a giant mountain lion in a tree crotch overhead; how he had killed and fried some partridge and a few squirrels, garnered honey from a beehive, baked biscuits and cooked a blackberry pie when camp provisions were running low. The trip became his pioneer idyll, connecting him with ancestors who had actually lived on the frontier. Marcelline records, in this vein, how her father spent his free hours after school as a boy delving into Indian mounds along the Des Plaines River, and how on summer vacations he took his younger brothers there and pretended they "were members of a mythical tribe of Indians, whom he christened the Skowhegans."[19] In 1928, the year he committed suicide, he wistfully tried and failed to get Ernest to join him on a return trip to the Smokies.

But Clarence too had been raised in the genteel Christian tradition. He had chosen the medical profession because he wanted to heal, save, and nurture human lives in the Christian manner of John Halifax. He too was very much his mother's boy; and in fact his early interest in botany and nature lore had been stimulated by his mother, who had studied botany and astronomy at Wheaton College in Illinois. In his book on Hemingway, Scott Donaldson unquestioningly accepts the judgment of Ernest's younger brother, Leicester, that their paternal grandmother, Adelaide Hemingway, was a "'dedicated intense woman who absolutely' controlled her family of six children, while on the other side of the family Caroline Hancock Hall 'also dictated the lives of her husband and two children.'" From which Donaldson concludes that, in ruling her own family roost, Grace Hall Hemingway was merely emulating "the pattern of matriarchy which had been established by both of Ernest's grandmothers."[20] It makes no difference to Donaldson, apparently, that Caroline Hall was dead, and therefore unobservable, long before Leicester was born; or that Adelaide Hemingway died when Leicester was eight years old; or that Marcelline—who knew her paternal grandmother for twenty-five years—describes her in a far more sympathetic light as the confidante, friend, and teacher of her children and grandchildren; or that she worked her way through college and earned a degree when few women had them; or that Caroline Hall was similarly a professional concert singer like her daughter and encouraged her daughter's career in opera. That the frustrated ambitions of such women might be diverted into shaping domestic roles rather than dictatorial matriarchy does not occur to Donaldson, who sees in Grace's "early taste of musical success," for instance, only a clublike "advantage over the husband she returned to Oak Park to marry."[21] Such comfortable chauvinism, alive and well in the late 1970s, helps to show how thoroughly the legend of Huckleberry Finn has wiped out a saving grace of the genteel tradition, which directed manliness as well as womanliness at healing and nurturing relations and mutually supportive roles.

Like Huckleberry Finn, Dr. Hemingway also wanted to light out for the territory. As Donaldson reports, throughout his young manhood Clarence "had wanted to be a medical missionary" in China "like his brother Will"; and because of his love for the outdoors he had later "planned to move to Nevada as an escape from city life." But in Donaldson's chauvinist script, "Grace said no to both proposals, and so he stayed in Oak Park . . . as something less than the head of his household."[22] Apparently Grace's professional work in Oak Park, which would have been rather hard to pursue in China or in thinly settled Nevada, had no bearing on the conflict.

Another Hemingway critic who thinks along these lines is Jackson Benson. In *Hemingway: The Writer's Art of Self-Defense,* Benson sees the "Victorian-feminine mind" and the "civilized-feminine environment" it engendered as the great obstacle in Hemingway's world to "masculine independence":

> Although Papa was strict and ruled at times with an iron hand, it was always Mama who set the patterns, and it is from Mama that the spiritual, moral, and cultural energy of the household radiated. The gentility of the Hemingways, like the gentility of the Oak Parks of America, was based largely on female-inspired standards of conduct. Typically, in the youth of Ernest Hemingway, all those aspects of masculinity associated with aggressive male behavior were either held in abeyance or transferred to other more "appropriate" locations. All the basic aspects of living—birth, sex, and death—are discovered in the Michigan woods by Nick, the young, semiautobiographical protagonist of the Hemingway short stories . . . , and Nick's initiation to the masculine role and male activities—hunting, fishing, drinking, and the problems of courtship—takes place in the woods also.[23]

In a later passage Benson continues to argue from the early Michigan tales:

> Hunting and fishing are continual symbols for the attempt of the Hemingway boy to identify himself with the father, attempts to return to the primitive family structure based on masculine authority and power which was destroyed by the Victorian-sentimental spiritualization of love, elevation of the woman to wisdom and authority, and reduction of the male to worse than the devil. The male was an ineffectual and misguided child who must be always watched, fre-

quently scolded, and in general directed away from the base natural tendencies of malehood. Animals, the object of the hunt, in their natural and direct behavior become linked in the Victorian-feminine mind with all that is to be avoided and all that is base in human nature. It is rather natural, according to this line of thinking, that men should enjoy chasing them and, in part, emulating them in the chase.[24]

Alas for Benson and his devilish chasers, the Victorian-feminine mind was never that simple. Like a great many genteel ladies before her—e.g., Dinah Mulock Craik, Frances Hodgson Burnett, and, indeed, Adelaide Edmonds Hemingway—Ernest's mother admired and encouraged the love of sports and animals in her son and husband. Given her British pastoral ideal and her evangelical view of muscular Christians, she had no quarrel with manly strength and vigor nor with natural environs and natural species; in fact, she spent more summers in Michigan with the children than did her husband, who had to attend to his medical practice in Chicago. Thus, the lines of cultural conflict as Benson sees them are much too neatly drawn. Though they accord with Hemingway's tales and with their origins in *Huckleberry Finn,* they do not accord with the lives and times behind these fictions.

As with mothers, moreover, so with sons. Nick Adams, the hero of these early tales, may well be a version of "Huck Finn in our time," as Philip Young has argued,[25] and therefore another seeker after lost male freedom; but he is also as much a projection of the author's wishful fantasies as Huck was. When Mark Twain lit out for the territory, for instance, he faithfully wrote back long letters to his mother; later he married a genteel wife who pointedly called him "Youth"; and he pursued gentility—indeed courted it—quite as avidly as he rebelled against it. As critics have long held, he was closer to Tom Sawyer in outlook and conduct than to Huckleberry Finn, whom he only wished to emulate. So too was Ernest Hemingway closer to Tom than Huck. With some justice his mother gauged his boyhood conduct by Booth Tarkington's genial novel, *Seventeen.*[26] It seems fair to say, then, that he only *wished* to emulate Nick Adams as a boy who runs away from home, sleeps with and impregnates an Indian girl, and goes to war as a combat soldier: for by most accounts Hemingway never did such things. The wishful projections of these male authors, whose efforts to define themselves independently seem to me as real as current feminist efforts, cannot be taken at face value. They are, as Leslie Fiedler would argue, duplicitous projections which life and history tend to belie.[27] So too perhaps with feminist projections, old and new. It seems important, therefore, that we try to sort out as best we can their historical basis as myths of aspiration with valid and invalid aspects.

NEW DIRECTIONS

According to Ann Thwaite, Fauntleroy's reputation as a prig and a sissy was partly the result of the book's illustrations, which were based on a photo of Burnett's son Vivian taken in 1884:

> He was wearing his best black velvet suit and his hair was long and curly—the sort of length lots of boys have it now, but at that time long hair was rapidly going out of fashion and anyone over five was expected to have it cropped, as Vivian himself did, soon after the photo was taken. That black velvet suit caused a lot of trouble and made a great many boys hate the name of Fauntleroy. Mothers somehow got the idea that, if they dressed their sons in black velvet and lace collars, they would miraculously become as clever, courteous and charming as Fauntleroy himself.[28]

In later years the American humorist Irvin S. Cobb recalled the Fauntleroy clothing mania that had laid hold of American mothers in his childhood, a catching lunacy "which raged like a sedge fire and left enduring scars upon the seared memories of its chief sufferers." In Britain Sir Compton Mackenzie would recall "the confounded *Little Lord Fauntleroy* craze which led to my being given as a party dress the Fauntleroy costume of black velvet and Vandyke collar." Though such clothes had been worn by children before *Fauntleroy* appeared, they "became identified with the book and the play," Thwaite notes, "and lots of boys hated them all. They preferred to dress like Tom Sawyer and Huckleberry Finn."[29]

Thwaite speaks here to the American preference, the opposing craze for bare feet, straw hat, ragged pants and shirt that followed the Tom Sawyer books—the costume Ernest Hemingway wears, for instance, in several childhood photographs. But Hemingway's graduation from Fauntleroy clothes and locks in infancy to cropped hair and Sawyer clothes in boyhood was one which many American sons underwent as the century turned. It is the suppression of the Fauntleroy impress which demands explanation and which goes beyond the reaction of frontier-minded boys to the attempt to impose genteel manners on them through genteel costumes.

Thwaite's second argument, that *Fauntleroy* is a male Cinderella story which appealed chiefly to girls and their parents, comes closer to the point.[30] The novella speaks to women's aspirations and parental wishes at a time when the genteel tradition was clashing with new realities. In the play version of the book the hero's part was acted by girls or young women. In the first film version twenty-seven-year-old Mary Pickford played both son and mother. Even in the 1930s version the hero's role was performed by an English boy, Freddie Bartholomew, whose accent seemed effeminate to American ears. The feminization thesis, to which Benson and others still respond, seems at stake here; and in fact the feminine notion of achieving success through charm and consideration helps to account for the book's initial appeal to girls and mothers. In regenerating his aristocratic grandfather by assuming charitable intentions where none exist, Fauntleroy shames the grandfather into middle-class decency and wins himself an earldom. He seems like Richardson's Pamela in this respect, winning status and privilege not through sexual virtue but through generous consideration of others. What makes for decent human relations and improvements for the poor makes also for princely rewards.

But for maturing middle-class boys thrust by patriarchal tradition into competitive sports and business ventures, even into war, such pathways to success began to seem unreal in modern times. If their own grandfathers, living in genteel suburbs, had managed to trek westward, survive wars, and conduct business ventures with their integrity as honest Christian gentlemen more or less intact, changing conditions made for changing assumptions. For one thing, integrity was much harder to preserve in a standardized world where charm itself had been commercialized; for another, the sheer possibilities for adventure by which masculine identity might be defined— what Benson calls "those aspects of masculinity associated with aggressive male behavior"—had been sharply reduced. Indeed, they had virtually disappeared with the disappearing frontier, with the triumphant spread of commercial sameness, and with the conversion of wartime gallantry into random slaughter. It was these radical changes, and not the Victorian-feminine impress, that would destroy "masculine authority and power" in modern times, whether in its "primitive" or genteel family forms.

Hemingway's aversion to gentility must be seen in this broader context. His portraits of sportsmen and soldiers, rum runners and runaways, were part of a last-ditch attempt to revive the lost frontier and the possibilities of male self-definition it seemed to offer. The attempt went hand in hand, moreover, with his suppression of the rival female emphasis on manly strength and tenderness in his childhood, a suppression which seems all too clear in his satiric portraits of genteel Christian mothers. He could not admit to the "softening feminine influence" which had helped to shape his manliness. Like Mark Twain before him, he blamed such influential mothers for stifling qualities which they actually nurtured. Though the real problem lay in changing conditions in a rapidly changing world, where male self-definition was increasingly difficult, he blamed mothers also—and fathers only incidentally—for their failure to anticipate those conditions. The "big world out there" was harder for men to thrive in than Dinah Mulock Craik or Frances Hodgson Burnett or Grace Hall Hemingway had imagined. And yet, ironically enough, under the guise of a tough exterior shielding the extreme vulnerability of tender feelings, Hemingway continued to evade those conditions himself, or to confront them only through that postfrontier stoicism by which he first became famous, and to define himself meanwhile in an imagined world of men without women as his shortsighted mother might have wished. More ironic still, in his own shortsighted denial of his mother's influence, he continued to deny also those emotional resources— fearless friendliness with women, manly courage in domestic relations— which might have strengthened his own relations with women, enriched and expanded his art, and preserved his life and sanity in old age. It seems no accident, then, that he kept coming back to those resources, as if to revive them too, and that he actually prized them as the female complement or corrective to male self-definition. But what he came back to, always, was their impossibility "in our time." Thus, *A Farewell to Arms, For Whom the Bell Tolls, Across the River and Into the Trees,* "The Last Good Country," and *The Garden of Eden* are all concerned with courageous but failed attempts, by adult or adolescent heroes, to retrieve lost edens. What they fail to retrieve, essentially, is the androgynous happiness of the Fauntleroy phase of childhood—"the happiness of the Garden that a man must lose"[31]—when Grace and Clarence and their children lived with "Abba" Hall in genteel harmony.

Chapter 3

Captain Marryat

I pretended to think no more of my disappointment, nevertheless, I found myself constantly dwelling on the size of my lost fish, and lamenting my being obliged to abandon him to his more voracious brethren of the deep. These thoughts so filled my mind that at night I continued to dream over again the whole incident, beginning with my patient angling from the rock, and concluding with my disconsolate swim to shore—and pursued my scaly antagonist quite as determinedly in my sleep as I had done in the deep waters.

CAPTAIN MARRYAT,
The Little Savage (1848–49)

During the Christmas season of 1925 the Hemingways—Ernest, Hadley, and Bumby—were wintering at their favorite mountain resort, the Hotel Taube, in Schruns, Austria. With them for the holidays was a friendly American guest, Pauline Pfeiffer. Ernest had just sent off the manuscript of his parodic novel, *The Torrents of Spring*, to his first publisher, Horace Liveright. As his friends then suspected, the book was a deliberate contract-breaker, a satire of Liveright's best-selling author (and Ernest's first literary mentor), Sherwood Anderson, which Liveright would be forced to turn down, leaving Ernest free to publish with Scribner's. Significantly, Ernest had sent the manuscript off at Pauline's urging. Within the coming year he would follow his own urgings for Pauline and would similarly force Hadley to release him from their marriage contract. A few days before Pauline arrived, however, he seemed blissfully free of all such passive aggressions and was relaxing in bed, nursing a sore throat and chest, writing long letters, and reading up a storm. As he informed Archibald MacLeish on December 20:

> I've been reading all the time down here. . . . Just finished Buddenbrooks, Thomas Mann, ½ of it's a pretty good novel. The Moonstone by Wilkie Collins much more enjoyable. Have another fine one by Wilkie Collins to read: Jezebel's Daughter. Also 9 vols. of Trollope. Also 2 Capt. Marryats. Capt. Marryat, Turgenieff and the late Judge [Henry] Fielding are my favourite authors. Schruns is the place to read. Last year ran out of Literature and Kriminal Romanzen and read 21 vols. of Nat Gould. He, at least, wrote much better about horse racing than Sherwood Anderson.[1]

So too did Hemingway, of course, in "My Old Man," a horse-racing tale written in the Anderson manner in 1922. But it was one thing to surpass an old friend and mentor through emulation, quite another to humiliate him through satire. In his cover letter to Horace Liveright Hemingway had tried to argue otherwise. *The Torrents of Spring,* he said, was directed chiefly at Anderson's latest novel, *Dark Laughter:* it was in this respect like Fielding's parody of Richardson's *Pamela* in *Joseph Andrews;* both books were classics now, probably because no writer "with any stuff can be hurt by satire"; it was in any event to Liveright's interest to contain the controversy and have both writers under the same roof.[2]

Was it to Ernest's interest, meanwhile, to have Pauline and Hadley under the same Austrian roof? He had taken the title of his parody, *The Torrents of Spring,* from a lyric novel by Turgenev about first love in Frankfort ending in shameful separation and leading to lifelong bachelorhood when a strong-willed rival seduces and enslaves the passive hero and carts him off to Paris— even as Ernest would soon leave Schruns and Hadley to follow the strong-willed Pauline to Paris. Ernest still greatly admired Turgenev and in the letter to MacLeish had called him "the greatest writer there ever was"—if not the writer of the greatest books. Yet as he often held in later years, he felt that he had already beaten Turgenev in his "first fight," meaning his first book, *In Our Time,* a collection of ironic, deadpan tales which Liveright had originally published and which roughly matches Turgenev's *A Sportsman's Sketches* in design and manner.[3] Now, in his second "fight," *The Torrents of Spring,* he was beating Fielding—whom he similarly admired—at the game of satire, and treating his contemporaries Anderson and (in passing) Gertrude Stein as something less than worthy opponents. As he later admonished Faulkner, you should never compete with living writers but "should always write your best against dead writers" whose stature is known "and beat them one by one."[4]

What, then, was Captain Marryat doing at the head of this otherwise distinguished list of dead favorites worth surpassing, this winter assemblage of authors live or dead treated like discardable wives and mistresses, dispensable friends, outgrown parents, filial or sibling rivals? And who indeed was Captain Marryat, that Hemingway should so admire him? One answer to these questions came a few days later, on December 24, 1925, in a letter to Scott Fitzgerald:

> Am reading Peter Simple by Capt. Marryat. Haven't read it since I was a kid. Great book. He wrote 4 great books. Frank Mildmay or the Naval Officer. Midshipman Easy. Peter Simple and Snarleyow [sic] or the Dog Fiend. He wrote a lot of kids books in later life and people get them mixed up. You ought to read Peter Simple.
>
> If you want to read about war read any of those 1st 3.
>
> Pauline Pfeiffer gets here tomorrow to stay for Christmas and New Years.[5]

The conjunction of Pauline Pfeiffer with Captain Marryat's novels about British naval warfare in the early nineteenth century is a happy one. With Pauline, Ernest would in 1934 purchase a cruiser, named *Pilar* after Pauline's secret nickname from the beginning of their affair; and some eight years later, during the Second World War, having left Pauline for Martha Gellhorn, he would arm *Pilar* for secret antisubmarine patrols of the Gulf Stream in the manner of Marryat's adventurous British frigates; then in his closing years, during his fourth marriage, he would fashion similar adventures in one of his last major novels, the posthumously published *Islands in the Stream*. But more interesting still than these long-delayed naval maneuvers, *Frank Mildmay; or, The Naval Officer*—first on his list of Marryat's "great books," presumably best by its placement there, and quite possibly the second of the "2 Capt. Marryats" reserved for winter reading in 1925—was among other things about a young man's simultaneous involvement with two women he loved, a situation that Hemingway knew firsthand with Pauline and Hadley and would later write about at great length in *The Garden of Eden* manuscript (1946–58). The interconnections between Hemingway's crowded life and changing loves, his prodigious winter reading, and his own rivalrous writings were indeed prophetically profound that holiday season in Schruns. They were also a long time coming, as his childhood reading of Marryat's novels well attests.

IMPERIAL REBELS

Captain Frederick Marryat's reputation as a children's novelist was fortunate for the young Hemingway. His parents had strongly disapproved of the similar adventure novels of Jack London, then in his prime; but the safely dead and supposedly harmless Marryat was fair game for Christian readers—and was in fact a Christian by persuasion. *Frank Mildmay* ends with a conversion scene, and there are Christian sentiments and repentance themes through all the novels, whether written for adults or children. But there is also in the adult novels open recognition of the heterosexual side of naval life, the penchant for heavy drinking and brawling, and the frequent recourse to ungentlemanly oaths and insults, which must have delighted the young Hemingway. One way he was able to circumvent his parents' narrow Oak Park outlook, then, and break through toward his own modern horizons, was by reading about such gamey matters in Marryat's tales of pre-Victorian naval warfare.

As two recent scholarly collations help to show, Hemingway seems to have read at least six Marryat novels in childhood: the four "great books" listed in the letter to Fitzgerald—*Frank Mildmay, Midshipman Easy, Peter Simple,* and *Snarleyyow*—which he apparently groups himself as boyhood reading; and two others, *Jacob Faithful* and *Masterman Ready,* which, along with *Midshipman Easy,* are listed in his Key West Book Inventories for 1940 and 1955, and which were probably bought at random as childhood favorites he wanted to reread. All six of these novels appear, for instance, among the twenty-four Marryat titles on the Oak Park Public Library "FICTION-AUTHOR LIST" for 1904, which means that Hemingway might have read them during the school year in boyhood or, more probably, during the vacation months when he and his family used to take out thirty or forty books on summer loan for their stay at Walloon Lake in northern Michigan. Between the ages of eight and seventeen, then, Hemingway had access to some three or four hundred library books during the summer months alone. Given his habit from boyhood onward of reading the authors he liked in depth, we can assume that he read a fair number of the library's Marryat holdings.[6] But let us concentrate for the time being on the six novels which, in effect, he calls to our attention.

Five of the six feature or contain the basic Marryat plot of the young boy who leaves or runs away from home to join the British navy, and four of those five are strongly antiparental in outlook. In *Peter Simple* the clergyman father is so obsessed with the material question of his son's elusive inheritance, and so oblivious to all else, that he goes mad when his son is defrauded and imagines himself at various times a nursing child, a pregnant woman, a magazine full of gunpowder, and a gas balloon. In *Frank Mildmay* the wife of a schoolmaster is singled out, *in loco parentis,* for her suspicious and covetous nature, which inspires the young hero to lie and steal and so obliterates all previous moral training. In *Mr. Midshipman Easy* the father is satirized throughout as a foolish philosopher who instills in his son his blind belief in equality and the rights of man; he too goes mad as his more fortunate son learns through harsh naval experience how and when to temper or discard these otherwise admirable doctrines. In *Jacob Faithful* the father is similarly satirized for his oversimple stoical doctrines—"It's no use crying, what's done can't be helped"; "Take it coolly"; and "Better luck next time"—which become his son's chief inheritance; and both parents are literally done away with when the mother's excessive gin-drinking leads to her death by spontaneous combustion and to her husband's death by drowning as he flees the appalling conflagration. Such imaginatively vengeful parental fates—madness, spontaneous combustion, drowning—are sometimes mixed with softer filial sentiments, even in the adult novels; and in children's novels like *Masterman Ready,* written when Marryat had been for some time a parent himself, there are lessons in consideration and concern for a mother's fears and tears and respect for a father's wisdom. But plainly, the more prevalent stress on freedom from foolish parental views and ways, and on rebellious flight from the parental nest, would not have escaped the young Hemingway.

Marryat's novels were reissued by Everyman's Library in 1906 and 1907 with brief introductions to each volume by R. Brimley Johnson. In his introduction to *Peter Simple* Johnson develops at greater length an account of Marryat's life and works as "an admirable sailor, and an admirable writer." Hemingway read this introduction in 1925. If he also read it in childhood, or the similar account by W. C. Courtney for the Dana Estes edition of 1896, he would certainly have been impressed by the example of a brave, experienced naval officer who turned his early adventures into the stuff of fiction. Hemingway's respect for men of action who became writers must have begun, then, at an early age. When on December 24, 1925, he advised Fitzgerald "if you want to read about war read any of those 1st 3" novels by Marryat, he was stressing again an advantage over Fitzgerald he had touched on in a previous letter from Schruns, dated December 15, 1925, on "The Importance of Subject": "The reason you are so sore you missed the war is because war is the best subject of all. It groups the maximum of material and speeds up the action and brings out all sorts of stuff that normally you have to wait a lifetime to get."[7] Like Marryat, in whose novels he early found such grouped materials and stepped-up revelations, Ernest had himself experienced war, had written stories about it, and would in a few more years write his first war novel. Marryat's leading place in that trio of favorites—Marryat, Turgenev, Fielding—reflects, then, his importance for Hemingway as a martial man turned writer. Sportsman Turgenev and Judge Fielding were similarly experienced men, writing about male or patriarchal pursuits; but they were not experienced in "the best subject of all."

Perhaps more important, for the young Hemingway, was the example in Marryat's life and work of a boy breaking away early from parental bonds and outlook into a male world where masculine identity and selfhood were defined by other men. The British naval world in the early nineteenth century, as described by Marryat, was just such a world. The American frontier, as defined by family and public legend and by the fiction of Cooper, Twain, Wister, and Harte, was another such world. But as Michael Reynolds has discovered, Hemingway read relatively little American literature in childhood. His chief models of excellence were British.[8] Though in Upper Michigan, and to some extent in Oak Park, he was steeped in the family version of the American frontier dream, his reading during those years was chiefly among classic British novelists like Fielding, Smollett, Austen, Thackeray, Dickens, and the Brontës, and adventure novelists like Kipling, Stevenson, and Marryat; and Marryat especially seems to have defined for him his boyhood version of a world of men without women.

The imperialist origins of that world connect it historically with the emergence in America in the late nineteenth century of male definitions of masculinity, as in Twain's novels of the vanishing frontier, which clashed with the implicitly feminine definitions of masculinity in the genteel tradition. As I have earlier shown, the overlap between muscular Christian manhood in the genteel tradition and frontier masculinity has been lost in American literature and culture, undercut in fact by literary mythologists like Twain and Hemingway.[9] Marryat's novels were in many ways harbingers of that muscular Christian tradition. The question of what constitutes a gentleman at sea is endemic to all of them, and Marryat's answers to that question are often at least quasi-Christian in substance. Hemingway's tolerance for those Christian answers can be explained, I think, by their largely male devising. He might reject or suppress maternally endorsed heroes like Fauntleroy and John Halifax, but he could only applaud and embrace Frank Mildmay, Peter Simple, Jack Easy, and even young Jacob Faithful and old Masterman Ready, as men of action whose lives and values were defined by other men of action.

The great British imperialist novel of the nineteenth century—the novel by which the new masculine ethos was most purely and strongly defined—was, of course, *Tom Brown's School Days* (1858), a copy of which is listed in Hemingway's Key West Book Inventory. As Thomas Hughes triumphantly affirms, British public schools like Rugby were designed to train boys for service to God and Empire. The emphasis on group sports and group discipline, on manly skills like boxing and wrestling, the indulgence of manly larks like poaching and coaching adventures, the stress on physical courage and endurance—"the consciousness . . . so dear to every Englishman, —of standing out against something, and not giving in"—were strategies for producing muscular Christians who would preserve and extend the greatness of the British nation.[10] There is a marvellous passage on fighting near the beginning of part 2, chapter 5, in which Tom wins the now-traditional schoolyard battle against a bully, which Hemingway must have relished:

> After all, what would life be without fighting, I should like to know? From the cradle to the grave, fighting, rightly understood, is the business, the real, highest, honestest business of every son of man. Every one who is worth his salt has his enemies, who must be beaten, be they evil thoughts and habits in himself, or spiritual wickedness in high places, or Russians, or Border-ruffians, or Bill, Tom, or Harry, who will not let him live his life in quiet till he has thrashed them.
>
> It is no good for Quakers, or any other body of men, to uplift their voices against fighting. Human nature is too strong for them, and they don't follow their own precepts. Every soul of them is doing his own piece of fighting, somehow and somewhere. The world might be a better world without fighting, for any thing I know, but it wouldn't be our world; and therefore I am dead against crying peace when there is no peace, and isn't meant to be. I'm as sorry as any man to see folk fighting the wrong people and the wrong things, but I'd a deal sooner see them doing that, than that they should have no fight in them.[11]

The blending of imperialist wars against Russians and Border-ruffians with the thrashing of schoolyard bullies and with internal struggles against masturbation and other bad habits, the easy equation throughout of spiritual with physical combat, and with the way things are, makes this paean to fighting a classic of its kind; but it was a kind which did not come to the fore until the 1860s in England and the 1880s in America. As Philip Collins points out in an aptly titled pamphlet, *From Manly Tears to Stiff Upper Lip: The Victorians and Pathos,* there was a shift in sensibility in England in the latter half of the century as Public Schools deemphasized "godliness and good learning" and preached instead "the hearty enjoyment of physical pursuits" and game-playing. Excessive displays of emotion, as in the previous sentimental phase, became bad form; "patriotism and doing one's duty to country and Empire became the main sentiments which the new system sought to inculcate."[12] The stiff upper lip, in service of the new imperialism, replaced the old manly display of tender feelings for social or personal sufferings; and a new masculine ethos emerged, independent of those "softening feminine influences" of the waning genteel tradition against which Hemingway still rebelled in the mid-1920s.[13]

Marryat's novels of naval warfare, written in the 1830s and 1840s, were precursors to this trend, and it is no accident that Tom Brown himself reads them at one point in his school days. So too did Hemingway in his adolescent years. Indeed, the equivalent American literature and legend of the vanishing frontier, which he absorbed largely as a private family tradition in his childhood, was then less fully articulated for him as a purely masculine ethos than the British imperialist version he found in Marryat, Hughes, Kipling, and Stevenson. His early stoicism and fighting spirit were in large measure British in origin, in keeping with the British contours of his early Oak Park life, wherein muscular Christian gentility combined such virtues with more "feminine" considerations. Marryat allowed him to begin that separation and repression of the feminine which marks his adolescent years and which eventually characterizes his adult stances. But with Marryat, as with the later Hemingway, there were lingering ambivalences, as we shall see, which point up the limitations and hazards of all such manly rigor.

DRINKERS AND CROSS-DRESSERS

Another admirer of Marryat, Joseph Conrad, aptly defined him as "the enslaver of youth, not by the literary artifices of presentation, but by the natural glamour of his own temperament. . . . His novels are not the outcome of his art, but of his character, like the deeds that make up his record of naval service."[14] Marryat's young naval heroes seem in this regard like variant aspects of their creator. At least three of them—Frank Mildmay, Peter Simple, and Jacob Faithful—write first-person accounts of their youthful adventures, as would two of Hemingway's somewhat older heroes. Along with Mr. Midshipman Easy, whose tale is recounted in the third person, these young adventurers offer versions of youthful trial and error with striking relevance for the early Hemingway. Peter Simple, as the fool of the family who proves to be brave and resourceful under fire, is the most attractive of the four. As a boy Hemingway could relate easily to this dramatic disproof of an original family judgment, especially given his penchant for getting into minor scrapes and his growing resistance to family strictures. Jack Easy and Jacob Faithful help to frame his attitudes in this regard toward parental judgment. Jack is the indulged son of a foolish philosophical parent, Nicodemus Easy; he is sent to the navy as the one place where his father's beliefs in equality and the rights of man may be put to fair use in an otherwise harsh world, and he quickly learns the folly of that assumption. But his captain is in debt to his father, and along with other surrogate parents, he too indulges Jack, gives him leeway to work through for himself the practical limitations of his father's philosophy. This kind of indulgence of youthful errors was a condition Hemingway sorely desired in a family given to sudden and often arbitrary punishments. A related attitude, his strong dislike of his parents' arbitrary ways, would be given its fictional expression by Jacob Faithful, a Thames waterman by trade who receives such judgments unforgivingly, nurses his resentments, and only after long separation and hardened feelings finally learns to yield and forgive the elders who have been quick to find him wanting. Between the indulged Easy and the resentful Faithful—whose last name itself suggests the author's ironic view of parental misjudgments—Hemingway could play out his own feelings about growing up misjudged.

But Marryat's first naval hero, Frank Mildmay, in some ways his most autobiographical creation, comes closer to the actualities of Hemingway's early life and, indeed, those of most resentful children. Mildmay is himself a proud, impudent, willful young man who creates as many predicaments as he suffers from unjustly. He is forever picking fights, testing limits, bridling into difficulties, getting away with as much as possible, repenting and forgetting learned lessons with equal ease. Of these four figures he comes closest to the portrait of Marryat which emerges from Brimley Johnson's introduction to the Everyman *Peter Simple* and—in more piecemeal fashion—from W. C. Courtney's general and specific introductions to the Dana Estes editions.

Impulsive, generous, quick-tempered, outspoken, energetic, Marryat was in many ways a prototype of the kind of man of action, man of letters Hemingway would become. Along with his brave exploits at sea Johnson records his sorrier conduct on land during his editing days in London. Indeed, the account reads almost like a blueprint for Hemingway's future conduct during his own editing days in Paris. Thus, editor Marryat writes abrasive letters to his publishers, challenges one fellow author to a duel and treats others as rivals trying to steal his jokes, threatens to flog a persistent questioner when he runs for Parliament, and jockeys aggressively with American critics when he visits this country. One incident Johnson fails to record, a public scuffle with a former protégé, amply reported in the Sunday papers, seems all too predictive of the future Hemingway.[15]

It seems no accident, then, that one of the major themes of Marryat's books is vengeance. The plot of *Snarleyyow; or, The Dog Fiend* is nothing more than a series of vindictive reprisals, double, triple, and quadruple crosses, in keeping with the treasonous support of James II, circa 1699, which constitutes its political intrigue. Similarly, each of Marryat's young naval heroes engages in shipboard reprisals against bullies who need thrashing, in the Tom Brown schoolyard manner; and with Marryat, as with Hughes, there is a zest for thrashing as endemic to the fighting spirit. Frank Mildmay is an especially good indicator, then, of what Marryat's "temperament" must have meant to the early Hemingway, if only in terms of sheer pugnacity. For Hemingway, as for many other readers, Marryat turned vitriol and unforgivingness into attractive aspects of the male ethos.

Hemingway's adherence to that ethos, and his awareness of its possible consequences, seems to have been well-established by the time he was ten. Thus, on June 19, 1909, in one of his earliest letters, he reports the latest masculine news to his sister Marcelline:

> Dear Marc,
> Our room won in the field day against Miss Koontz room. Al. Bersham knocked two of Chandlers teeth out in a scrap and your gentle Miss hood had Mr. Smith hold him while she <u>lickt</u> him with a raw hide strap.
>
> Lovingly, Ernest[16]

As the equation of love and venom here suggests, the female of the species early seemed to him deadlier and more treacherous than the male. The captains of Hemingway's own ships were schoolmistresses and mothers whose "soft sentiments" were often mixed with harsh punishments, and he was ruefully aware of their punitive powers. He persisted nonetheless in his strictly male adherences. Thus, on July 17, 1915, when Ernest was nearly sixteen, he begins and ends a letter to a friend called "Carissimus" with a progress report on the manly art of swearing:

> I got your catalogues thanks hellish much. Honest that ———— of a ———— of a boat of mine is ————. I use these dashes because I swore so much this afternoon at the thing that It could Break my head wide open to invent any more. . . . Gosh but its lonesome here. . . . Nobody to swear with a while. When I am stuck out in the lake somebody will come by and yell "What's the matter?" Boy you should here me then. I get off some deuced eunique ones.[17]

Such early nautical displays of the language of male identity, expressed always out of parental earshot, suggest one reason why *Peter Simple* proved so appealing. One of the comic leitmotifs of that naval novel is the language of the boatswain, Gentleman Chucks, which proceeds from genteel remonstrance to inventive invective whenever Chucks reprimands an errant seaman—as in the following instance:

> "Allow me to observe, my dear man, in the most delicate way in the world, that you are spilling that tar upon the deck—a deck, sir, if I may venture to make the observation, I had the duty of seeing holy-stoned this morning. You understand me, sir, you have defiled his majesty's forecastle. I must do my duty, sir, if you neglect yours; so take that—and that—and that—(thrashing the man with his rattan)—you d——d hay-making son of a sea-cook. Do it again, d——n your eyes, and I'll cut your liver out." (ch. 12)

The passage from the language of gentility to the "language really used by men" (to alter Wordsworth) was one that Ernest early wanted to make, if only as an assertion of youthful independence from parental strictures. Then, too, he had himself long endured his parents' verbal pieties during punishments, and may well have resented them more than the actual thrashings. Here, then, was the beginning of a literary style devoted to the explosion of genteel euphemisms.

Prominent among those early strictures was a strong prohibition against drinking. His father was adamant on the subject, and had even fired a jolly Irish maid who was especially fond of Ernest and had always brought him presents for twice coming home drunk at night after her day off. Indeed, she was forced to leave the premises without giving Ernest the last of her many presents for him. Ernest would eventually become a heavy drinker himself, and the pleasures of Italian liqueurs were among the gifts of liberation he would bring to his sisters on his return from World War I. Imagine then his response to the similarly liberal view of drinking in Marryat's novels. In *Jacob Faithful* especially, Marryat develops a festive view of drinking. Though the death by spontaneous combustion of Jacob's gin-swilling mother is early posted as a lugubrious warning against excess, Jacob is soon exposed to the more genial views and habits of his Thames lighter companions, old Tom Beazeley and his son, young Tom. The father, who has lost his legs at the Battle of Trafalgar, now stumps about the riverboat on eight-inch wooden legs. He is given to singing sea ballads at every opportunity and to drinking grog at night to comfort himself for his lost limbs. His son Tom, Jacob's peer and counterpart, sneaks his share of grog when he can, and there is much banter aboard the boat about how much he should imbibe. When Jacob's large-nosed Latin teacher, Domine Dobbs, comes aboard the lighter, much effort is devoted to getting him drunk on grog while old Tom sings ballads and spins yarns—a session which ends with the two boys, Jacob and young Tom, putting their drunken elders to bed and standing sober watch. When the elders wake next morning, Domine suffers from a hangover and a swollen nose. He is ashamed and repentant, but when he tries to argue the wrongfulness, indeed sinfulness, of intoxication, old Tom refutes him:

> "Nonsense, old gentlemen; why make a fuss about nothing?" said old Tom, . . . "You had a drop too much, that's all, and what o' that? It's a poor heart that never rejoiceth. Rouse a bit, wash your face with cold Thames-water, and in half an hour you'll be as fresh as a daisy."
>
> "My head acheth!" exclaimed the Domine, "even as if there were a ball of lead rolling from one temple to the other; but my punishment is just."
>
> "That is the punishment of making too free with the bottle, for sartain; but if it is an offence, then it carries its own punishment, and that's quite sufficient. Every man knows that when the heart's over light at night, that the head's over heavy in the morning. I have known and proved it a thousand times. Well, what then? I puts the good against the bad, and I takes my punishment like a man."
>
> "Friend Dux, . . . thou lookest not at the offence in a moral point of vision. . . . I would point out that intoxication is sinful."
>
> "Intoxication sinful! I suppose that means that it's a sin to get drunk. Now, master, it's my opinion that as God Almighty has given us good liquor, it was for no other purpose than to drink it; and therefore it would be ungrateful to Him, and a sin, not to get drunk —that is, with discretion."
>
> "How canst thou reconcile getting drunk with discretion, . . . ?"
>
> "I mean, master, when there's work to be done, the work should be done; but when there's plenty of time, and everything is safe, and all ready for a start the next morning, I can see no possible objection to a jollification." (ch. 14)

Plainly the young Hemingway could find ample sanction here for his own future appreciation of life's liquid jollifications. As he must have seen, the passage corresponds with the example of the generous Irish maid and of his maternal uncle Tyley Hancock, another yarn-spinner and tippler whom he also loved and admired. From Marryat, then, came a further rationale for directions he was already taking, if only in his mind.

Still another direction seems evident in Hemingway's letter to "Carissimus" previously cited. After the opening passage on swearing Ernest abruptly turns to his father's discovery of the old "female" ice-cream cutter who spread typhoid in the school lunchroom, then goes on to discuss similar female infections:

> I have got some good news for you cuspidoriac. I was reading Marcelline my sweet sisters' mail as usual trying to find out what the dames think of me when I saw a letter and I read it and it was from your friend Dorothy Hollands. I copped it and will enclose it in this letter. Gosh but it is mushy. I tell you guy *beware*! all females are alike. She wrote me a letter and I will send it to you too. Why don't you write to some females? It is fun—all you do is say "I am having a fine time. Do write and tell me about all the news of Dear old Oak Park." You send this and get a sixteen Page letter to laugh at. Try it very soon.

The last phrase is blurred and may read "my son," which better suits the air of feigned superiority. The letter turns next, at any rate, to masculine news of the porcupine Ernest shot and skinned, of the buck and doe he sighted ("They go along in long jumps with their white tails sticking up"), and of plans to shoot the buck when his father arrives. Then, after noting three squirrels and a sapsucker he shot the day before, he delivers the closing passage on swearing.

As such manly discourse suggests, Ernest was then trying to distance himself—none too successfully—from the growing pressures of sexual socialization. His intense interest in "dames" and "females"—whatever their mushy poisons—is quite transparent. Nor were all females inevitably alike. A year later, on July 13, 1916, in an unclaimed letter to a classmate named Emily Goetsmann, then enviably visiting a ranch in Montana—a girl with whom he shared literary as well as outdoor interests—Ernest again defensively mocks "The marvel of the Feminine mind." Thus, after citing his sister Marcelline's unfathomable interest in a freshman at Illinois named Horace, a wearer of tortoise-shell glasses whose "sole interest is Mathematics" and who "believes fishing is an idle waste of time," he tells Emily of a visit from his "old Ojibway pal and woodcraft teacher Billy Gilbert," who had "relapsed into a state of matrimony three years ago":

> The last time I saw him he was a part of the forest, one of the last of the old woods Indians. Now he lives in a cabin and raises vegetables and cuts cord wood.
> "My Woman," said Bill, "she no like the woods."
> Do you remember this fragment from Kipling? It seems to apply to Billy.

"Through the nights when thou shalt lie
Prisoned from our mother sky,
Hearing us, thy loves, go by,
In the dawns when thou shalt wake
To the toil thou cans't not break
Heartsick for the Jungles sake."

The rest of it doesn't matter; that is the part that applies to Bill. You remember that piece don't you? It is what the animals say to Mowgli when he leaves the Jungle to be married.

If the Lad Horace is what they turn out at Illinois me for Cornell. Just think how pleased my family would be if they would civilize me and inculcate a taste for Math and a distaste for Fishing.

Your sincere Friend
Ernest Hemingway[18]

The use of Kipling to define Billy's predicament as a displaced male American Indian and the closing allusion to Twain's uncivilizable character, Huckleberry Finn, are instructive—as is the sharing of such sentiments with a young female devoted to the male outlook. The opposition at seventeen of fishing to matrimony, and to family and civilization, would continue, of course, for many years—as would the opposition between male-oriented and mushy females. And Marryat, Kipling, and Twain, in these early years, would provide fuel for both oppositions.

Marryat's contribution in this regard was considerable. In *Frank Mildmay*, for instance, he created opposing types of heroines like those that intrigued the young Hemingway. Thus, the hero falls in love in the same night with genteel Emily Somerville, the "perfect beauty" and fount of virtue he eventually marries, and with the "fascinating actress" Eugenia, who meanwhile becomes his mistress, bears his child, and arranges her life for his pleasure and advancement. Indeed, her selfless devotion to the hero includes the "libertine" French notion that marriage is a contract to be broken at the wish of either party. She accordingly withdraws from Frank's life when their illicit union threatens his professional prospects, returns at his convenience, and just as conveniently dies (as does her child) when the hero finally seems ready, through religious conversion, to marry virtuous Emily. Hence Mildmay is able to lead a richly adventurous seaman's life, one which includes liaisons with Spanish prostitutes, Nova Scotian nymphs, and a West Indian mistress, before giving in to marital piety. Between his affairs with women who selflessly devote themselves to him and his final pious devotion to the marriageable Emily, he fulfills most of Ernest's boyhood dreams about adoring and forbidden sweethearts.

Hemingway's sudden "reconversion" to Catholicism, which he used to annul his first marriage to Hadley Richardson and to sanction his second marriage to Pauline Pfeiffer, and the selfless Hadley's "libertine" willingness to free him from their marriage contract, suggest how oddly life would imitate manly art in the mid-1920s. *Frank Mildmay* was certainly on Ernest's mind during those winter months at Schruns when his first marriage began to break up; but then so was Turgenev's *Torrents of Spring*, and there is no way of knowing how much the renewed force of childhood reading might have affected his personal conduct. Still, like Mildmay, he easily gave way to the prolonged dilemma of being caught between opposing loves, and probably did find sanction for that choice in Marryat's fictional precedent.

In his own fiction the adult Hemingway would slightly alter Marryat's example and would combine genteel heroines with selfless mistresses to produce hybrid types like Catherine Barkley and Countess Renata. In *Snarleyyow; or, The Dog Fiend* Marryat creates in some abundance a third type of heroine who would influence the youthful Hemingway much more emphatically. Indeed, the number and variety of "tough" women who appear in this historical novel is rather staggering. Though all of Marryat's marriageable heroines have a certain amount of grit, they remain passive and undeveloped as characters; their chief function is either to help the hero out of scrapes or to be rescued by him. In *Snarleyyow*, by contrast, the women either put men into scrapes or get them out of them; they are the active and largely effective figures in a world where men seem hopelessly embroiled in endless vendettas. A covetous old crone, Captain Vanslyperken's mother, is a retired murderess who valiantly tries to incite her ineffectual son to commit murder and other vengeful crimes, and who is herself murdered when she takes over her son's duties and nearly kills his resilient nemesis, his shipboard servant Smallbones. The widow Vanderloosh, who runs a Lust Haus, or pleasure house, for sailors, proves much more effective in leading on the foolish Vanslyperken; and her substantial weight, along with that of her resourceful maid Babette, is sufficient to bring down her ample bed on the captain's vicious dog Snarleyyow, trapped for a time beneath it and finally dispelled by the outraged pair. Among the more attractive heroines, Moggy Salisbury stands out as the defender of her short-legged husband, seaman Jemmy Ducks, meeting ridicule of his low stature with sharp invective and vigorous assault, boxing ears and brandishing knives and cleavers as needed, outfacing and outwitting threatening males like Vanslyperken. Moggy and her husband become allied, halfway through the novel, with the band of smugglers' wives who occupy and later defend successfully against military assault a cliffside cave on the Isle of Wight—the youthful precedent, I am going to argue, for the guerrilla cave dominated by Pilar in *For Whom the Bell*

Tolls. Prominent among these women is the famous former courtesan, Nancy Dawson Corbett, now a smuggler's wife who functions as their watchful agent in Portsmouth and, in the process, detects a male betrayer who is promptly executed, dupes Vanslyperken into self-betrayal, and "disarms" attacking militia by informing them that the smugglers' cave they seek is occupied solely by women. Leading the women is the gallant Lady Alice Barclay, wife of a Jacobite leader plotting to restore James II to the English throne. Her last name suggests Barkley, but it is her dominant position in a rebel cause that matters here. For all the smugglers, male and female, are enlisted in this cause, and when the militia attacks they are all dressed as women, male and female alike, so as to disconcert their male attackers. The tactic succeeds when the soldiers refuse to fight women and are nearly wiped out by the male smugglers' deadly fire. Here, it seems to me, the fiercely militant Pilar and her domestic predecessor, Marie Morgan, the smuggler's tough wife in *To Have and Have Not,* were born (or at least implanted) in Ernest's youthful mind.

Interestingly, the spectacle of men dressed as women occurs at least three times in Marryat's novels. In *Peter Simple* the young hero dresses in girl's clothes to avoid discovery when he and his older friend and protector, Terence O'Brien, escape from a French prison and begin their adventurous trek across enemy countryside. In *Mr. Midshipman Easy* the hero persuades the pompous Mr. Hicks, vice-consul at a Moorish port, to dress in Hicks's sister's clothes as part of an elaborate ruse to prevent her elopement with a British captain, whereby the vice-consul, the British captain, and the hero's ardent friend Gascoigne (who thinks the disguised "woman" is the Moorish girl he hopes to marry) are all comically foiled. The more serious stratagem in *Snarleyyow* may serve as a useful key to all these strange occasions. It begins when the hapless Smallbones is rescued at sea by the smugglers and left with their women in the island cave. Having lost most of his shirt and the back of his trousers during the rescue, he is forced to wear women's clothes, which, as Nancy Corbett says, are "the regular uniform of the cave." The same uniform is adopted as a disguise by the local male smugglers who come from Portsmouth to the cave's defense, and is then adopted also by Sir Robert Barclay and his men when they arrive by sea from France and Holland. Meanwhile Nancy Corbett has "disarmed" the approaching militia by calling them "lady-killers," an epithet which nicely opposes male gallantry and its deadly results with the deadly female vengeance which follows.

Not that Marryat was overly mindful of such ironies. More probably he was attracted by the prospect of comic relief from the tensions of sexual separation which his fictions otherwise advance. Mark Twain would similarly dress Huck Finn in skirts, five decades later, as a ruse for gathering information on shore as to Huck's supposed murder. When a shrewdly observant country woman detects the ruse by the way Huck threads a needle, throws lead at a rat, and catches yarn in his lap, we get Twain's view of behavioral differences between the sexes. But more pertinent, for Twain as for Marryat, is the sharp social division which generates such border-crossing comedy, and the male ethos, which, by insisting on that division, probably betrays an inordinate fear of female powers. At least twice in Marryat's fiction—in *Peter Simple* and again in *Snarleyyow*—gangs of women overpower and rout daunted males in quasi-comic scenes. His willingness to adopt a female-oriented outlook in *Snarleyyow* is a curious tribute to the kind of warlike women he evidently both feared and admired, as would Hemingway in his wake.

There is, of course, no male transvestite comedy in Hemingway's fiction; but as in Shakespeare, there are women who dress like men, and as I have argued elsewhere, there are androgynous situations in at least five published and three posthumously published novels, in one of which—*The Garden of Eden*—the question of sexual identification with women is seriously explored.[19] Plainly Hemingway must have been given pause by these odd relapses from the male ethos in Marryat's "war" novels, if only in response to his own androgynous impress during those "twinship" years in childhood, when he and his sister Marcelline were dressed in look-alike smocks and frocks. For him as for Marryat, the more immediate and decidedly more paramount appeal of the treatment of naval warfare had its hidden sexual agenda.

IMAGINED WARS

In his introduction to *Peter Simple* Brimley Johnson remarks that Marryat was "never present at a great battle" but "had seen much smart service and knew from others what lay beyond his own experience." Thus he often wrote in his novels about battles he had never seen, adapting written or oral accounts by others to his own uses. In *Frank Mildmay,* for instance, he presents the central episode of the Battle of Trafalgar, which had occurred the year before he joined the navy. As Oliver Warner observes, he views the battle not from a ship of the line "but from a frigate whose duty was to repeat signals of flag officers."[20] Such tangential approaches allowed him to present naval warfare from the inside, as seen by petty officers engaged in special tasks, the nature of which he could fill in from his own experience. At Trafalgar, then, Mildmay presents his own initiation into battle by describing first the layout on the flagship's decks, "the shot and wads prepared in ample store," the powder boys on their boxes, the carpenter waiting to plug up shot-holes, the surgeon ready with "knives, saws, tourniquets, sponges, basins, wine and water." Next, he tells how his own feelings shift from fear to shame to clinical detachment as the action progresses, until he is able to behold "a poor creature cut in two by a shot with the same indifference that at any other time I should have seen a butcher kill an ox": "Whether my heart was bad or not, I cannot say; but I certainly felt my curiosity was gratified more than my feelings were shocked, when a raking shot killed seven and wounded three more. I was sorry for the men, and, for the world, would not have injured them; but I had a philosophic turn of mind; I liked to judge of causes and effects; and I was secretly pleased at seeing the effect of a raking shot" (ch. 3).

Hemingway's affinity for this kind of honest response is behind his advice to Fitzgerald to read Marryat about war. As he evidently saw, Marryat's "philosophic turn of mind" corresponded with his own naturalistic and clinical outlook as a doctor's son trained to observe nature and anatomy with equal coolness; and in fact Marryat himself defines Mildmay's interest at Trafalgar in just these terms:

> I attended the surgeon in the steerage, to which place the wounded were removed, and saw all the amputations performed, without flinching; while men who had behaved well in the action fainted at the sight. I am afraid I almost took a pleasure in observing the operations of the surgeon, without once reflecting on the pain suffered by the patient. Habit had now begun to corrupt my mind. I was not cruel by nature; I loved the deep investigation of hidden things; and this day's action gave me a very clear insight into the anatomy of the human frame, which I had seen cut in two by shot, lacerated by splinters, carved out with knives, and separated by saws! (ch. 3)

Four years later, at a battle off the Isle d'Aix, Mildmay shows the same medical detachment:

> While this was going on, a very curious instance of muscular action occurred: a lad of eighteen years of age was on the forecastle, when a shot cut away the whole of his bowels, which were scattered over another midshipman and myself, and nearly blinded us. He fell—and after lying a few seconds, sprang suddenly on his feet, stared us horribly in the face, and fell down dead. The spine had not been divided; but with that exception, the lower was separated from the upper part of the body. (ch. 11)

An observer of operations at his father's hospital, himself splattered at eighteen by the shellburst which caught him in the Italian trenches during World War I, Hemingway could well relish the matter-of-fact description of such morbid events. They are always carefully framed in Marryat's novels by precise accounts of general naval strategy and of specific battle movements, all of which also fascinated Marryat as much as they would later fascinate Hemingway. Thus inside views of action are placed in broader perspective by a knowledgeable observer, an experienced guide to naval battlefronts often never seen. The example which Hemingway follows in *A Farewell to Arms,* in the retreat from Caporetto which occurred a year before he reached the Italian front, was first set by Marryat in *Frank Mildmay, Peter Simple,* and *Mr. Midshipman Easy.* And in all these novels the coast patrols for "prizes," the legitimized piracy by which British men-of-war preyed on the merchant and naval ships of Spain, France, and America, established fictional precedents too for the antisubmarine hunts along Gulf coasts in *Islands in the Stream.* Finally, there are many instances of personal heroism, based on Marryat's actual exploits—as when Frank Mildmay saves fellow seamen from drowning or rides a fireship into the heart of the French fleet off the Isle d'Aix—which anticipate the more grimly heroic actions of characters like Robert Jordan.

As Oliver Warner shrewdly notes, Marryat began his career "as delineator of the naval wars against Napoleon, as describer of the world about which Jane Austen knew something from her sailor brothers, but which she excluded from the forefront of her stories."[21] Writing in the 1830s and 1840s, at the beginning of the Victorian age, Marryat was accordingly filling in a broad range of neglected experience for the British reading public, educating them in the terms of imperialism and of the male ethos it generated— terms which gradually took hold in the 1860s in the crucial shift in national sensibility which then occurred. His forthright accounts not simply of naval warfare and piratical adventure, but of impressments, floggings, executions, brawls, songfests, and mutinies; his shrewd estimates of courage and resourcefulness under fire or during storms at sea; his sensible views on fairness and good leadership in establishing the discipline necessary to successful combat and low casualties, were absorbed as a kind of national heritage. He would influence English and American writers for generations to come; and if Hemingway was especially drawn to his descriptions of warfare and to his repeated concern with the courage, skill, and humanity in some captains and the lack of it in others, he was not alone in drawing on the wealth of experience—of grouped and maximized materials and stepped-up revelations—which the many-sided Marryat provided for his literary heirs.

Consider, among a wide variety of precedents, the jerky shorthand speech of the apothecary, Mr. Phineas Cophagus, in Marryat's "shore" novel, *Japhet in Search of a Father*, which Dickens seems to have transferred without thanks to the scapegrace Alfred Jingle in *The Pickwick Papers;* or the bite given to his tyrannical grandmother's bottom by the young hero of *Percival Keene*, news of which follows him to school, and the similar biting sequence in *David Copperfield;* or the many collaborative ventures on sea and land of "equality Jack" Easy and his African counsellor and helpmate Mesty, an escaped slave from America with filed teeth and pointed chin, who claims the lost rank of Prince in Africa, and whose full name—imposed by a British enlistment officer steeped in German scholarship—is Mephistopheles Faust—as Melville surely noted in pairing Ishmael with Queequeg and Fedallah with Ahab in *Moby Dick,* and as Twain too may have noted, more selectively, in pairing Huck with Nigger Jim as raft-borne freedom-seekers. Or consider the historical sea-novels of C. S. Forester as they draw on Marryat's example, or the ironic turn-of-the-century tales of youthful romance at sea and of imperial decline on land and sea by Joseph Conrad. Consider too Joyce's use of the title phrase from *Japhet in Search of a Father* in chapter 1 of *Ulysses,* where Malachi Mulligan early taunts Stephen Dedalus with that well-placed epithet; or T. S. Eliot's use of the Thames boating scene in *Jacob Faithful* in which a Shakespearean actor intones, "The barge she sat in, like a burnish'd throne, Burned on the water" while colliers' women in a nearby boat banter about the sexual implications of such language;[22] or, more poignantly, Virginia Woolf's use in "The Captain's Death Bed," of Marryat's serene death in a mirrored room with a sky-blue ceiling and reflected birds and roses as a kind of literary antidote for the many grim and pointless deaths in her own stricken family and for her own deathward leanings.

Hemingway was in good company, then, in partaking of Marryat's bounty, which he did with some freedom from childhood onwards. Indeed, even the children's tales—which he dismissed so easily in adulthood—were an important part of that early bounty, especially as they provided him with an overall fund of nature lore and practical knowledge—as when the old seaman in *Masterman Ready* and the old forester in *The Children of the New Forest* teach shipwrecked or outlawed boys how to cope with wilderness conditions and, above all, how to plan ahead to avoid disastrous consequences and insure benign ones. Young Ernest must have enjoyed such tales, having been raised himself in a pioneer tradition, and with the same British twist. In his later fictions his code heroes would be fashioned along the same pragmatic lines; and at least two of his more grizzled heroes would show the same grandfatherly concern for children, and the same honest piety, which

Marryat's old men display and which Ernest first knew with his own British grandfather, "Abba" Hall. Whether he first learned about icebergs from *Jacob Faithful* (ch.21) in those years, or was first exposed to African perils in *Masterman Ready*, seems less important than his absorption of such "wilderness" models. In this honorific light his Michigan, African, and Caribbean tales may be said to begin with children's stories like *The Little Savage*, *The Settlers in Canada*, *Scenes in Africa*, *The Privateer's-Man*, and *The Travels of Monsieur Violet*.

EARLY RETIREMENTS

In 1843 Marryat had retired to a farm property called Langham, where he wrote most of his children's novels. He had separated from his wife and was now surrounded by their seven surviving children, who had all come to live with him. In the August 1867 issue of *Cornhill Magazine,* in an essay called "Captain Marryat at Langham," an anonymous contributor describes Marryat's idyllic retirement as witnessed during friendly visits in the 1840s.[23] Interestingly enough, "Cornhill Magazine 1867" is listed in Hemingway's Key West Book Inventory, along with "Cornhill Magazine 1883"; but as the more precise Cuban inventory of 1962 indicates, the 1867 volume runs only from January to June. Whether Hemingway owned and lost the next volume, containing the essay on Marryat, is of course wholly speculative. But internal evidence alone suggests that he might well have read the essay (or one of its biographical reprises) by 1925, when he began writing *The Sun Also Rises.* Consider the following passage—in which Marryat proudly marches the *Cornhill* writer off to a decoy lake, "where a new pipe was being made and a new trench dug"—as it bears upon that novel:

> This was an interesting sight, even to the uninitiated. The decoy man, a great rough-looking fellow in a fur cap, was a reclaimed poacher, and he looked entirely his original character. Marryat always held that reformed blackguards made the most honest servants. He had a very unmagistrate-like leniency for poaching, and having convicted this man, Barnes, of the offence, he had placed him as his gamekeeper and decoy man; and I know that he never had reason to repent his trust in him. When, years later, Marryat's son Frank went to California, Barnes declared his resolution of going with him, the which he did, and remained with him the whole time of his sojourn there.[24]

Hemingway would have liked Marryat for his leniency to poachers. He had himself fled game wardens for shooting a protected bird, the blue heron, when he was sixteen, and had then returned at the advice of elders to admit his crime and pay his fine. He would save that episode for his later unfinished novella, "The Last Good Country," written in the 1950s, in which his early grudge against game wardens is still rabid; and he would frequently tell versions of it to his wives and friends. He would have enjoyed thinking of himself as a reclaimed poacher and reformed blackguard, and his decision to attach the name Barnes to a character much like himself in *The Sun Also Rises* probably begins here. Jake Barnes—whose first name derives from a Revolutionary war ancestor, Jacob Hemingway, and perhaps also from another misjudged Marryat character, Jacob Faithful—is something of a gamekeeper and decoy man himself, as Hemingway devises him, being partial to bulls and fishes, and having lost part of his male organ in the war; he may also be said to serve as a decoy for attracting other men to Lady Ashley. But we can only guess that Hemingway consciously entertained such private ironies; or that he read further about the actual Barnes, as he might have done in young Frank Marryat's book about his experiences with the ex-poacher in the California gold rush; or that he read by then still other relevant books— *Joseph Rushbrooke; or, The Poacher* and *The Children of the New Forest*—by the elder Marryat. We can be reasonably sure, however, that he read *Jacob Faithful*, where in chapter 19 Jacob and young Tom Beazeley are caught poaching on Wimbledon Common, and the incensed Jacob stands off the common-keeper with a gun and wants to shoot him—as does the incensed Nick Adams during his similar ordeal in "The Last Good Country."

But of course all such nominal links are unimportant in themselves; they simply help to establish an ongoing, indeed a lifelong, affinity. Early in 1922, when he first arrived in Paris, Hemingway would spend his mornings in a corner of Sylvia Beach's bookshop "reading magazines and Captain Marryat and other books." In 1935, in his *Esquire* column, he would begin his long list of novels which aspiring writers should read with two by Tolstoy and three by Marryat *(Mildmay, Simple,* and *Easy)*. During his Cuban years (1939–60) he would acquire a biography of Marryat and a complete set of his works. As late as 1958, moreover, in his *Paris Review* interview with George Plimpton, he would still list Marryat (before Shakespeare!) among those who had influenced his "life and work."[25] The inclusion of "life" with "work" seems appropriate in this context, since Marryat is the only writer he admired whose work lacks high artistic status, but whose life seems to have enriched his work, at least for Hemingway. Thus he speaks in 1958 of "the good Kipling" as having influenced him, but makes no such apology for Marryat. Whatever further slants he may have drawn from the *Cornhill* essay on Marryat's life (or from its recurrence in biographies) are accordingly worth pursuing.

The essay opens with the question of why Marryat retired to the country after leading such an exciting life in literary and social circles in London and on the Continent, wherein, as "the merriest, wittiest, most good-natured fellow in the world," he "had kept up a round of incessant gaiety and a course of almost splendid extravagance." The essay closes with two answers to that question. This "spoilt man of the world" had "abandoned society prematurely" and had "put aside fame before it had had time to pall" because he wanted to "watch the green buds coming out in the quickset hedges" in spring. At first the anonymous writer finds this answer unsatisfactory: "This was what the popular novelist and wit had come down to!" But after Marryat's death he begins to question "whether it was a 'coming down' after all, or a return to the childlike simplicity of all true genius; or perhaps the beginning of an awakening to that better child-likeness of which we have all been told, and which Marryat fully experienced before he died."

The body of the essay supports this second answer. Marryat had left the intellectual and social world behind not simply because he loved nature more, but because he wanted to create for himself and his children the kind of childhood world he had always wished for himself. In actuality, he was intensely unhappy in childhood and had twice run away from school, nominally because he was "bent upon going to sea," but more immediately and more tellingly "because I didn't like having to wear my brother J———'s breeches. You see, I came just below him, and, for the sake of economy, my mother used to give me his outgrown clothes. I could stand anything else, but I could not stand the breeches."[26]

Readers of Hemingway's "Fathers and Sons" will remember how much Nick Adams dislikes wearing his father's underwear, the smell of which makes him feel sick, and how he puts it under two stones in a creek and is whipped for lying when he says he has lost it. Hemingway obviously must have shared in Marryat's refusal of such submerged identity and in Marryat's decision—as the second son whose elder brother, Joseph, stood between him and his father's favor and fortune—to seek his own attire. In this light the adoption of female dress in Marryat's fiction might well imply identification with other submerged identities—and particularly with their anger. Be that as it may, he did eventually inherit liberal sums from his father and a wealthy uncle, and from another brother who died young; but meanwhile as a second son he had found his own breeches, first as an outstanding naval officer, then as a popular novelist and social dandy. He had spent money as freely as he made or inherited it, however, and was always forced to enhance his fortune by his pen—a condition Hemingway could well appreciate in 1925. Marryat was disappointed, moreover, by the failure of the Admiralty to reward him for his services with the usual sinecure, and by the similar failure of the Conservative party to find him employment, and of the king to grant him knighthood. It looks accordingly as if by 1843 he considered himself misjudged, like Jacob Faithful, by the world's elders, and so returned from whence he came, to a childhood world where he could live more comfortably as the sole reigning elder. Hemingway's similar flight from the literary circles in Paris, after the fiasco of his divorce from Hadley and his marriage to Pauline, is the interesting parallel here. For at Key West and in Cuba, in Africa and Spain and Idaho, he too recreated childhood worlds, akin to the woods and lake in northern Michigan, where as "Papa" (a title, the *Cornhill* essay tells us, that the much more formal Marryat intensely disliked) he too reigned supreme in newfound comfort.

The image of Marryat at Langham, absorbed by 1925, may well have served Hemingway then as a predictive model. For the anonymous *Cornhill* writer not only refers to "Barnes," "breeches," and "Papa"; he also presents Marryat as a kind of retired sportsman and gentleman farmer who writes as and when he pleases, without the stimulus of intellectual circles, and in the full vigor of his middle years. In Langham cottage there are "capital pictures," "first-rate bronzes and marbles," and "a splendid library." In the fields outside, Marryat moves surrounded by a virtual menagerie of tame birds and animals and by adoring children:

> I can think I see him now, as I look back at the time [writes the *Cornhill* visitor], sitting about on his dun-coloured Hanoverian pony, called Dumpling, —a name he very well deserved, —dressed in that velveteen shooting-jacket I have spoken of, which he used to boast of as having cost only twelve and sixpence; with a hole in the rim of his hat, through which . . . he could thrust his eye-glass . . . in order to save the trouble, when out shooting, of raising his glass each time he fired.[27]

The casual hunting clothes, the helpful eye-glass, would have appealed to the roughly dressed Hemingway, who worried always about his hunter's vision. The stories of Marryat's indulgent treatment of his children, whom he also urged to attempt new things, refusing incapacity as an excuse, suggest also the attempt by bachelor father Thomas Hudson, in *Islands in the Stream*, to create indulgent learning situations for his three sons on the tropical island of Bimini, where the painter lives in a house likened to a ship—and from which he eventually leaves to captain a boat in search of submarines. The *Cornhill* version of Marryat's farm retreat, during what Oliver Warner calls "his *Tempest* period,"[28] is more serene than the one

Hemingway would imagine during his last decade, partly because it excludes the drowning at sea of Marryat's elder son Frederick in 1847; but it does contain the tale of his "poor little boy Willie," the original for the ship's boy Willie in *The King's Own*, whom Marryat had taken to sea with him in the 1820s, but who died at seven of diabetes—a sequence Hemingway may have filed away for his own future account of the deaths of Hudson's sons. As Carlos Baker notes, Hemingway had taken his own boys as apprentices on the *Pilar's* antisubmarine patrols in World War II, "believing that the experience would give them the same sort of education that cabin boys had profited by on British men-of-war in Captain Marryat's time."[29] By the 1950s, however, he seemed less sanguine about such training and could only imagine his sons' early deaths.

Hence his own Prospero would prove less magical, more vulnerable to the inroads of violence, than Marryat seemed at Langham. But the model was there, and Hemingway's resurgent Catholicism may even have insured his sympathy with the childlike faith in Christianity which sustained it, and which the dying Marryat openly expressed. Indeed, those famous last words—dictated to Marryat's daughter in that mirrored room with its sky-blue ceiling and painted birds and roses—offer fitting testimony to the gentling effect of Marryat's faith in his final year, and to the softening or feminization of the male ethos which then occurred:

> 'Tis a lovely day and Augusta has just brought me three pinks and three roses, and the bouquet is charming. I have opened the window and the air is delightful. It is now exactly nine o'clock in the morning, and I am lying in a bed in a place called Langham, two miles from the sea, on the coast of Norfolk. . . . To use the common sense of the word I am happy. I have no sense of hunger whatever, or of thirst; my taste is not impaired; my intellect, notwithstanding the narcotics, is this morning, I think, very pure; but the great question is, "How do I feel . . . as an isolated Christian, towards God?" I feel that I love Him, and were my reasoning powers greater, could love Him more. . . . After years of casual, and, lately, months of intense thought, I feel convinced that Christianity is true . . . and that God is love. . . . It is now half past nine o'clock. World, adieu.[30]

The contrast with Hemingway's self-inflicted death by shotgun blast, after months of mental and physical illness, is startling, and suggests how closed he had become by 1961 to his own "feminine" resources. But certainly in 1925 he could have understood Marryat's "great unselfishness" in concealing his final illness "lest those about him should be distressed on his account; so that only by accident was it discovered by his son that that painful organic disease which in the end killed him, had commenced."[31] For about facing death bravely, if not serenely, both writers could at least agree with the stoic Shakespeare. As Major Carbonell says in *Japhet in Search of a Father* of the risk of another duel: "After all, what is it? . . . we all owe Heaven a death; and if I am floored, why then I shall no longer be anxious about title or fortune."[32] So too, in "The Short Happy Life of Francis Macomber," the hero says of the resumed risk of hunting lions: "After all, what can they do to you?" To which his British guide replies: "That's it. . . . Worst one can do is kill you. How does it go? . . . 'By my troth, I care not; a man can die but once; we owe God a death and let it go which way it will he that dies this year is quit for the next.' "

As Hemingway must have known, these stoic sentiments from Shakespeare occur elsewhere in Marryat. In *Percival Keene,* for instance, which is on the Oak Park Public Library list for 1904, variations on the lines appear three times. In the same novel, moreover, a cowardly clerk runs screaming before a charging cow in one comic chapter, even as Hemingway's hero runs wildly before a charging lion in the Macomber tale; and in the next chapter, Marryat's hero is shot in the back of the head in a hunting "accident" which later proves intentional, even as Hemingway's hero is shot there "accidentally" in the Macomber story.[33]

Of course, Percival Keene survives while Macomber expires; but the narrative sequence is one of a number of strikingly suggestive models for his later fiction which Hemingway early found in Marryat. More important still, he also found a British literary guide and father whose turbulent lifelines he could follow, whether in fiction or in fact, and whose idyllic retirement he could emulate in his own more strenuous and competitive manner, but whose serene death he ultimately could not beat.

Chapter 4

The Kipling Impress

In her autobiographical memoir, *How It Was*, Mary Welsh Hemingway notes in passing "a verse of one of his favorite women-defying songs" that Ernest had sent to Harvey Breit early in 1953 as consolation for romantic troubles:

> If you don't love me, Mama
> Then I don't care at all
> Cause I can get more womens
> Th[a]n a passenger train can haul.[1]

When Ernest first discovered this popular verse is unclear, but the notion conveyed of transferred love as a kind of revenge on an originally unloving "Mama" seems plain enough and may serve here as a paradigm for his romantic conduct from boyhood onward. As he entered adolescence, his affections began to shift from his mother to his three younger sisters. His enforced closeness to his older sister Marcelline had by this time become irksome. The "twinship" scheme, which had kept them together from infancy through high school, had given way to that need for separate identity which supposedly distinguishes male from female development.[2] Tall, handsome Marcelline, who sang well and could not be dominated, was too much like his mother to please Ernest;[3] and though his androgynous ties with her in infancy had shaped his feelings about edenic love and had virtually guaranteed the fictional recurrence of those feelings, he was moving now toward estranged independence. The priorities of separation were very much in force; but then, so too were the priorities of connection with his younger sisters, Ursula and Sunny, who served as adoring companions in the northern woods and to whom he now turned for the affection and admiration his mother had once supplied. By seventeen his paternal and protective instincts were also strong, and as his sister Marcelline attests, he even liked to pick up another favored sister, baby Carol, "and dandle her on his knee."[4] Though still a dutiful son throughout these years, he had failed too often to meet his mother's high expectations to remain her altogether devoted admirer. And as he moved more confidently into the male provinces of hunting, fishing, hiking, and boxing, he would become increasingly critical of her cheerful pieties.

MOWGLI IN NORTHERN MICHIGAN

In Hemingway's adolescent years the writings of Rudyard Kipling served more obviously as a model for such leanings than those of Captain Marryat. Kipling's works were included among the sets of British classics in his family library, and he had access to additional works at the Oak Park Public Library. Kipling was also taught in school, and Ernest's interest in the Mowgli stories—as indicated in a letter to a high school classmate, Emily Goetsmann—was probably reinforced by his teachers. In 1915, about the time that he began to imitate Ring Lardner, he nonetheless listed Kipling and O. Henry in his high school notebook as his favorite authors.[5] The four works by Kipling which seem to have influenced him most in boyhood were *The Jungle Book, Stalky & Co., The Light That Failed,* and *Soldiers Three.* In different ways each of them confirmed or helped to shape his definitions of male independence and his emerging attitudes toward women as they served or threatened that independence.

As the Goetsmann letter shows, his feelings about Billy Gilbert, "one of the last of the old woods Indians," had been defined for him by a verse from *The Jungle Book* in which the animals lament the fate of Mowgli "when he leaves the Jungle to be married." Thus, his "old Ojibway pal and woodcraft teacher" had once been "a part of the forest." But now, having married a woman who dislikes the woods, he "lives in a cabin and raises vegetables and cuts cord wood." Confined by that toil, "Prisoned from our mother sky," he seems like Mowgli "Heartsick for the Jungle's sake." Marriage to a domestic or civilizing woman, as opposed to an outdoor girl like Emily, has cut him off from his former life and "loves," the animals who define his fate. Sharing in that Jungle sadness, Ernest sees a similar threat to himself ahead: "Just think how pleased my family would be if they would civilize me and inculcate a taste for Math and a distaste for Fishing."[6]

The fusion here of ideas drawn from Twain and Kipling suggests another

12. High school classmate and literary correspondent Emily Goetsmann

early paradigm. Fisherman Huckleberry Finn, who refuses to be civilized, and wild boy Mowgli—raised by wolves, educated by his Jungle friends, and deserting them finally through marriage—were united in Ernest's youthful imagination by a common predicament. Mowgli, the product of a British imperial imagination, and Finn, an imagined extension of the American pioneer impulse, were in effect one person. Hemingway's British-American heritage had allowed him to imagine their fusion and to equate them also with the American woods Indian, Billy Gilbert. In a very real sense, Mowgli was alive for him in the northern Michigan woods, and so helped to convert those woods into grounds for male self-definition.

Though Kipling's animal stories appeal to children of both sexes, they are predominantly male-oriented. Animals are a subordinate species with whom children—male or female—find it easy to identify; but Kipling's animals are chiefly concerned with hunting and territorial rather than domestic problems. As powerful and untamed creatures they are fine outlets for childhood aggression; but since they are chiefly male animals—Baloo the bear, Bagheera the black panther, Akela the leader of the wolf pack—their appeal to young boys is especially strong. Since the Romantic Revolution, legends of wild boys, nurtured by animals, have flourished anew, partly in response to the disappearance of wild regions as industrialization and urbanization took hold; but there have been few legends and fewer tales about wild girls, perhaps because of the early impress of the imperial imagination on romantic themes.

As Roger Lancelyn Green has observed, Baden-Powell, founder of the Boy Scouts, used the Mowgli stories as the basis for establishing the Wolf Cubs as a unit for his youngest charges.[7] The imperial value of Boy Scout training has often been noted, and it seems no accident that Mowgli himself eventually becomes a forest guard under British imperial direction. Even Tarzan of the Apes—a Kipling offshoot, as Edgar Rice Burroughs has himself noted—would preserve such connections in his role as Lord Greystoke.[8] Captain Marryat's *Little Savage* (1848–49), which Hemingway seems to have read by the late 1920s, is an early instance of the same impress: a tale of shipwreck survivors from a British vessel who soon die off, leaving only an adult sailor to raise a child born on the island. When the sailor also dies, the boy is left to his own devices. He catches and tames a baby seal and two migratory birds for company, cultivates his own garden, and kills birds and fish for food. From the sailor he had learned something about natural history and the Bible. Later, when a missionary's wife is left stranded with him, he learns something more about Christianity and about the far-flung reaches of the British Empire in which that religion supposedly thrives; but aside from survival measures and a few fishing and boating exploits, he does little to insure himself a place in children's literature—except perhaps for the early Hemingway. Kipling's Mowgli would enlist Ernest and other children much more actively in adventures along imperial frontiers.

Enlistment may be the appropriate word for Kipling's youthful readers. In his imperial largesse he liked to imagine for them heroic children performing quasi-military deeds. Thus, in "Wee Willie Winkie" a lisping boy— a future colonel—outbluffs an Afghan band to save a fair but foolish lady; and in "The Drums of the Fore and Aft," two fourteen-year-old drummer boys manage to get themselves killed while rallying retreating troops. The adolescent nature of Kipling's adult soldiers—enlisted to defend the Empire—has been remarked upon, as has his belief in the educational value of schoolboy pranks for future military strategists.[9] Though Mowgli is no future soldier, his education seems no less imperial in design, especially as his animal mentors teach him how to survive, how to live in accord with Jungle laws and in harmony with its denizens. For the Jungle is a veritable mini-Empire: its laws involve predatory and territorial rights and powers; and struggles for dominance, as with Shere Khan the tiger, or struggles for survival, as with the routing of the Red Dog pack, are very much in order there. Mowgli's great advantage over his animal brothers in these conflicts is his superior human intelligence, an asset which allows identifying readers the comfort of animal brothers to whom they too are eventually superior, and yet also sets them off in opposition to the Man-Pack, the adult Indian world outside the Jungle, to which, through Mowgli and the animals he controls, they again prove superior. Doing in adults is one of the cheerful pastimes of much children's literature, and when Mowgli lets in the Jungle on the villagers who treat him badly and destroys their compound, we have a fine example of the infusion of childhood revenge-fantasies with imperial designs. For the villagers are not real adults—they are only superstitious natives—and though Mowgli is one of them by birth, his allegiance is with the Jungle world of animals and children until such time as he can join with the imperial guardians of such realms, the British Forest Officers, to whom all lesser breeds owe ultimate allegiance. The "outcaste" Mowgli may emerge then as a pagan wood-god with a good measure of prideful independence; but he serves nonetheless as an enlisted deity, a forest guard for the Department of Woods and Forests whose imperial function—Kipling pointedly tells us—is to tend "the huge teak forests of Upper Burma; the rubber of the Eastern Jungles, and the gall-nuts of the South."[10]

When in 1918 Ernest Hemingway was wounded and received a medal of valor, his father would write him glowing letters, addressing him as "Old

Scout" and expressing how glad he was that his own ideas for his son's "early training as a woodsman and real scout" had "worked out" in the war.[11] His view of the eighteen summers Ernest had spent in northern Michigan as a training period, preparing him for the rigors of war service with the American Red Cross ambulance corps, was not unlike Kipling's view of his years at United Service College in England and his similar view of Mowgli's forest years as preparation for service to the British Empire. In his Nick Adams stories Ernest himself would focus on those early years in the northern woods and would connect them with Nick's war service in tales like "Now I Lay Me" and "Big Two-Hearted River." Nick's return to those woods after the war would reflect his own return to the "good place" he had known in childhood, the training ground for his future life as a woodsman, sportsman, ambulance corpsman, and war correspondent. Kipling's account of Mowgli's acquisition of self-discipline and Jungle lore and law was an early imaginative confirmation, then, of the training in wood lore and outdoor skills and responsibilities that a younger Ernest was receiving from his father, and its imperialistic implications blended readily with the Hemingway family's patriotic stake in past and future wars.

Like Mowgli, who marries a Muslim girl at the edge of his beloved Jungle and lives within its folds, Ernest too would arrange to be married in northern Michigan and to spend his honeymoon at the family cottage on Walloon Lake. He had brought his bride to the "good place," and would later bring her and all subsequent wives along on hunting, fishing, bullfighting, and other sporting or warring expeditions. Literary-minded outdoor girls like Emily Goetsmann, summering in 1916 on a ranch in Montana, would be his solution to the dilemma posed by Huckleberry Finn, as he lights out for the territory, or by Billy Gilbert, as he marries an Indian woman who dislikes the woods. Mowgli seems to have provided that solution by marrying a docile girl willing to live with him in the forest, close to his former "loves" and in fact in touch with them in his work. Mowgli's attitude toward his beloved animal brothers suggests also that love which Hemingway's sportsmen bear toward the animals and fish they kill. Though Hemingway would never personify such creatures in his serious fiction, and would in the Macomber story mock the society columnist who pictures the Macombers on *Safari* in *Darkest Africa* "pursuing *Old Simba* the lion . . . [and] *Tembo* the elephant," he would himself put his readers into a wounded lion's head in the same story and criticize Macomber for failing to know "how the lion felt"; and in *The Garden of Eden* manuscript he would go even further and create an African story of a young boy's heartfelt sympathy for a hunted elephant who has lost his closest friend.[12] Kipling's Jungle romance, a childhood adven-

ture with imperial implications, had impressed Hemingway more profoundly than he ever quite acknowledged. But then how *could* he acknowledge that his beloved bulls and fishes, who unfailingly exercised and more
often than not affirmed his superior human skills, did something for him
that his wives and sweethearts often failed to do?

STALKY IN OAK PARK

If *The Jungle Books* helped to define the life Hemingway cherished in northern Michigan, *Stalky & Co.* spoke secretly and savingly to the life he never
wrote about—the submerged part of his boyhood—in Oak Park, Illinois. In
an earlier letter to his high school classmate Emily Goetsmann, he had
recommended *Stalky & Co.* as well worth reading, presumably because it
spoke to their common view of high school life.[13] Kipling's schoolboy novel
was a fictional version of his own adolescent years at United Service College,
a premilitary training school in northern England. One of many successors
to *Tom Brown's School Days,* the novel follows the established formula of
schoolboy triumphs over masters, bullies, toadies, townies, and other outsiders. As the arch-planner of such escapades, Stalky is the future military
strategist *par excellence,* and the novel ends with the narrator's praise of the
extensions of his academic pranks to the battlefields of India and Europe:

"India's full of Stalkies—Cheltenham and Haileybury and Marl-
borough chaps—that we don't know anything about, and the surprises will begin when there is really a big row on."
"Who will be surprised?" . . .
"The other side. The gentlemen who go to the front in first-class
carriages. Just imagine Stalky let loose on the south side of Europe
with a sufficiency of Sikhs and a reasonable prospect of loot. Consider
it quietly."[14]

The imperial design, considered quietly, is plain. Adolescent rebels who
are smart enough to make fools of peers and elders will eventually outwit
enemies afield and dubious friends in first-class carriages. Their schoolboy
pranks should be indulged, tacitly encouraged, if the Empire is to survive the
stupidities and blunders of those other peers and elders, the "gentlemen"
who nominally run the show. The young Hemingway's assent to such
extensions of adolescent life into future situations seems evident in a letter of
June 22, 1952, written to the biographer of his reporting years in Kansas
City and Toronto, Charles Fenton. Fenton had offended Hemingway by
reaching back for material to his years at Oak Park High School. Since

Hemingway himself had never written about those years, he considered them out of bounds to literary critics. But what chiefly troubled him was the false view of his early life that Fenton would uncover. All his good friends in Oak Park were dead or gone. Only the "Christer element" was left, people who did not like him or his friends and who would only mislead Fenton about his past. Indeed, Oak Park itself had changed so drastically that the "true gen" about it was no longer available. On June 22, nonetheless, Ernest proceeded to provide Fenton with the "true gen" about Oak Park:

> It used to have a North Prairie and a South Prairie. The North Prairie ran from a block beyond your house as far out as the Des Plaines river which then had plenty of pickerel in it up to Wallace Evans' game farm where we used to poach. Where you see an apartment building now there was usually a big old house with a lawn. Where you see subdivisions and row after row of identical houses there used to be gypsy camps in the fall with their wagons and their horses.
>
> Oak Park had its own artesian water supply and some of us kids used to bring pickerel from the Des Plaines and put them in the reservoir. We caught gold fish out at the creek and breeding ponds on the game farm and brought them back in minnow buckets and stocked the reservoir to make feed for the pickerel. In the deep water the gold fish all turned silver or silver and black mottled. . . .
>
> They had a thing in High School called the Inner Circle. These were morally certified youths and leaders in the school who were informers for the principal[,] a man known as Pussy-foot McDaniell's or Gum-Shoe Mac who had been given the job primarily to stamp out the fraternities. They used detectives to get evidence on the fraternities who at worst only drank a little and used to meet up over the barn of the Mills boys house. The school board hated Mr. Mills who was a fine man and manufactured, among other things, slot machines. He was a Catholic, which was ill-regarded in school board circles and he had served, I believe, a year in the Penetentiary [sic]. He was a fine father and a good husband and we used to go down to the factory to study how the machines work. All the Mills boys were good athletes and fine swimmers and divers. Actually there was only one fraternity and when the school had kicked them out we other kids who had been too young to belong to it formed a sort of underground. The nonsense of the Greek letters meant nothing to us and we could see why fraternities were bad even then. But the resistance to the police control of Gum-Shoe Mac, so called because he wore rubber soled shoes and always

appeared noiselessly, was a sacred, well-organized and secret thing and we hunted down the inner circle as though they were Darland's police. Since you would never come in contact with other than Inner Circle characters I doubt if you would get a very favourable reading on me.[15]

The ingenuity with which Ernest and his poaching friends convert the town reservoir into their private fishing pond is like the ingenuity of Stalky and his friends in converting a nearby estate, nominally off-limits to students, into a private pleasure ground for smoking and reading and special treats at the keeper's cottage. The hunting down of Inner Circle types is like the vengeful triumph of Stalky & Co. over obtuse masters and their student disciples; and the phrase Hemingway applies to the hunting process—"a sacred, well-organized, and secret thing"—comes straight out of Kipling and suggests that the "underground" as he recalls it has acquired a rather bookish gloss. Finally, the related admiration for the Mills boys and their ill-regarded father, the reformed gangster and slot-machine maker, as against Gum-Shoe Mac and his police patrol, is like the allegiance given by Stalky and his friends to the few elders who move them—their military fathers whose professions they will follow, the Head of the College who sees through cant and indulges but also disciplines their pranks, and a few fine teachers.

Elsewhere in the letter Hemingway specifically commends to Fenton Margaret Dixon and Fanny Biggs as his two best English teachers, but dismisses "Old Platt" as "a friendly fool." This speaks to the fine discrimination of Kipling's young heroes as to their elders' faults and virtues, and to that moment early in the novel when they discuss "the inequities of their elders with a freedom, fluency, and point that would have amazed their parents" (72). Their later objection to married house-masters who leave their work to student prefects is another fine discrimination, one which bears more obviously on their military future (162). For Kipling as for Marryat, marriage and the military life do not mix well. Thus Kipling's future soldiers never indulge romantic leanings. Their one prankish deviation is to pay a shopmaid to kiss a pursuing prefect so as to embarrass him before his peers.

Nor do they display their deepest patriotic feelings. When a fatuous M.P. addresses the college on the glories of service to the Empire, they are appalled by his sacrilege:

> Now the reserve of a boy is tenfold deeper than the reserve of a maid, she being made for one end only by blind Nature, but man for several. With a large and healthy hand, he tore down these veils, and

trampled them under the well-intentioned feet of eloquence. In a raucous voice, he cried aloud little matters, like the hope of Honour and the dream of Glory, that boys do not discuss even with their most intimate equals, cheerfully assuming that, till he spoke, they had never considered these possibilities. He pointed them to shining goals, with fingers which smudged out all radiance on all horizons. He profaned the most secret places of their souls with outcries and gesticulations. He bade them consider the deeds of their ancestors in such a fashion that they were flushed to their tingling ears. Some of them—the rending voice cut a frozen stillness—might have had relatives who perished in defence of their country. They thought, not a few of them, of an old sword in a passage, or above a breakfast-room table, seen and fingered by stealth since they could walk. He adjured them to emulate those illustrious examples; and they looked all ways in their extreme discomfort.

Their years forbade them even to shape their thoughts clearly to themselves. They felt savagely that they were being outraged by a fat man who considered marbles a game. (256–57)

Kipling's sexist observation here about maids "being made for one end only by blind Nature, but man for several," helps to place this turn-of-the-century passage for us. Under the new imperial sway, boys and men no longer reveal their feelings publicly. Their duties to country as well as home give them a tenfold edge over maids in emotional reserve, and require not only a stiff upper lip, but also contempt for blabbing politicians who fail to grasp the depth of their unspeakable, hence unspoken, commitment to the Empire. The M.P. is dismissed accordingly as "a Jelly-bellied Flag-flapper" from the lower classes—"born in a gutter, and bred in a board-school, where they played marbles" (259). And the depressed and disgusted Stalky proceeds to disband the volunteer cadet corps he had organized with secret pride a few weeks before.

The genesis of Hemingway's famous dismissal of patriotic rhetoric in World War I, in *A Farewell to Arms,* seems evident in this imperial lament. Though Kipling was staunchly devoted to the Empire, and something of an admiring toady to its wiser heads, his fictional—hence "real"—allegiances were with Tommies, gentlemen rankers, minor officers, and loyal natives—the "ordinary" men who did the actual fighting and kept the peace. Indeed, his affinity with raffish but heroic types would prove particularly appealing to Hemingway, who would also focus on mixed moral types from lower orders—boxers who throw fights on their own terms, second-rate bullfighters with integrity, lone smugglers, honest prostitutes—all working at odds with corrupt societies. Kipling was not unmindful of those odds, but his faith in the social fabric was still very much intact. The "inside" outsiders of *Stalky & Co.*, the mischievous sons of colonial officers and administrators who nonetheless keep well within imperial and schoolboy lines, would eventually become the minor officers and officials who keep the Empire going. Kipling's similar origins had put him at fictional odds, however, with "gentlemen who go to the front in first-class carriages," and should those gentlemen altogether betray the Empire and its real preservers, the next logical step—for him as for Hemingway—might well have been a separate peace. The distance between Kipling and Hemingway, given their stiff-upper-lip mentalities and their tenfold emotional reserves, was only as extensive, then, as the possibilities for faith in martial enterprises would allow. Hemingway's grounds for disillusionment with the military life were, in World War I at least, much greater than Kipling could imagine as the century turned, or even—from his home-front perspective—when the great war occurred. But the appeal to imperial humility in poems like "Recessional" (1897) was not without its predictive value; and the concurrent distaste in *Stalky* (1899) for imperial rhetoric suggests Kipling's similar fear of the betrayal of "sacred" and "secret" things—like the integrity of those who put their lives on the line for public causes. The ebullient young Hemingway—already disillusioned with parental pieties—must have derived much comfort, accordingly, and some food for future thought, from the ebullient Stalky's disillusionment with the M.P.'s "profane" rhetoric.

DICK HELDAR IN KANSAS CITY

Kipling's early romantic novel, *The Light That Failed,* had even more widespread implications for the youthful Hemingway. It begins, for instance, with a scene straight out of his childhood and ends with a glorified version of his own blind seeking after death. Between those related events, fictive and real, the novel speaks also to his boyhood fears about weak eyesight, to his early ambitions as a reporter and creative writer, and to his early self-pity as a rejected wartime lover. It was from this book too, one conjectures, that he learned to comb the range of English verse for titles and quotations. If Kipling could allude to Herrick's "Nightpiece to Julia" and Marvell's "To His Coy Mistress" in his text, so could Hemingway. And in fact, the lines from Marvell which Kipling's hero quotes to his dog Binkie would inspire Lieutenant Frederic Henry, along with T. S. Eliot, to quote likewise: "Were there but world enough and time, This coyness, Binkie, were no crime. . . . But at my back I always hear—."[16]

Dick Heldar, knowing that he will shortly go blind, declaims these lines while seeking inspiration for his final painting, "the Melancolia that transcends all wit" (198). The melancholy lady in question will combine the cold career woman who rejects him, his beloved Maisie, with the reformed tart Bess who poses for him. Eliot would study that combination carefully as a precedent for his own neurasthenic and pub versions of modern melancholia, and Hemingway's lieutenant would reverse the sequence, moving from Italian whores to slightly addled British nurses. He would also bow in passing to the "sound of horns and motors" in Eliot's *Waste Land* before repeating Marvell's lines ("But at my back I always hear / Time's winged chariot hurrying near") at midpoint in *A Farewell to Arms;* but it was Kipling's precedent that moved his maker first, and perhaps most, in his adolescent years.[17]

As Kipling's novel opens, two orphans are about to engage in illicit pistol practice on a lonely British beach. Dick Heldar and Maisie, his companion of four years, are under the guardianship of a religious widow, Mrs. Jennett, who, as Kipling puts it, "was incorrectly supposed to stand in the place of a mother to those two orphans" (2). Dick has been with her longest and, since his provision is less than Maisie's, has suffered most from her loveless discipline:

> The many hours that she could spare from the ordering of her small house she devoted to what she called the home-training of Dick Heldar. Her religion, manufactured in the main by her own intelligence and a keen study of the Scriptures, was an aid to her in this matter. At such times as she herself was not personally displeased with Dick, she left him to understand that he had a heavy account to settle with his Creator; wherefore Dick learned to loathe his God as intensely as he loathed Mrs. Jennett; and this is not a wholesome frame of mind for the young. Since she chose to regard him as a hopeless liar, when dread of pain drove him to his first untruth he naturally developed into a liar, but an economical and self-contained one, never throwing away the least unnecessary fib, and never hesitating at the blackest, were it only plausible, that might make his life a little easier. The treatment taught him at least the power of living alone—a power that was of service to him when he went to a public school and the boys laughed at his clothes, which were poor in quality and much mended. (3)

Kipling has drawn this situation from his own boyhood bondage with his sister Trix at Lorne Lodge in Southsea, England. His Anglo-Indian parents had placed the two children under the care of a retired sea-captain and his wife, Pryse and Sarah Holloway, following the common practice of sending colonial children home so as to preserve their health and insure their proper education. Kipling never seems to have resented this decision openly, and his lifelong reverence for his mother admittedly contrasts with Hemingway's later hatred for Grace Hemingway. But Kipling's hatred for Mrs. Holloway, who became the children's sole guardian when her kindly husband died, may well have served as a convenient displacement for resentment. In the memorable tale "Baa, Baa, Black Sheep" (1888), in *The Light That Failed* (1890), and again in his autobiography, *Something of Myself* (1937), he fashioned her into a figure whom Hemingway could readily connect with his pious mother. Thus in the above passage Mrs. Jennett's religious severity leads Dick to loathe rather than love his Creator and to develop into a defensive liar so as to avoid being "disciplined." Hemingway's resentment of his parents' severe strictures and punishments, accompanied by easy pieties, would guarantee his sympathy with Dick's responses, which were much like his own in early boyhood. He too had learned the value of protective lying, and had observed with envy the leniency of the Catholic faith enjoyed by other children. He was even embarrassed by having to wear knickers to school long after other boys had been shifted to trousers and in a heartfelt letter pleads with his mother to let him change.[18]

Pistol practice was another matter. For Dick and Maisie revolvers were sensibly prohibited. But for Hemingway and his sisters target practice was not only encouraged and abetted by his parents, but initiated—for Ernest at least—at a shockingly early age. Indeed, his conditioning began in infancy as his mother held him against her shoulder while firing the old Smith and Wesson revolver which her husband's father had used in the Civil War—and which her husband would eventually use to shoot himself. Baby Ernest, oblivious of such consequences, would then giggle with each recoil, and would soon assume an even more active role. Thus at two years and eleven months Grace wrote in his baby book: "He shoots well with his gun and loads and cocks it himself"; and at four years and eight months: "He is a good pistol shot. Hits the bull's eye quite frequently in target practice." An exceptionally robust, sizeable, and active child by age three, "broad and squarely built," able to catch fish by himself and walk for miles, Ernest was apparently physically ready for such training.[19] But his parents' postpioneer naivete, if not madness, in putting such life-and-death responsibility upon him has to be acknowledged. Though Clarence Hemingway would train all his children to handle weapons safely, he apparently had no conception whatever—nor had Grace—of the emotional burden such responsibility entails. Part of the shock of Clarence's suicide came from the abrogation of gun-safety laws drummed into Ernest and the other children; and Ernest's own long-delayed decision to commit suicide might be said to begin here, with the life-and-death options thrust upon him in infancy, like a much-enshrouded moral incubus.

He found ample romantic support for such deadly options, however, in Kipling's early novel. Though Kipling's children are adolescents when they discover "that their lives would be unendurable without pistol practice," their adventure as the novel opens is a predictive one. Once on the beach, Dick fires a shot at the breakwater to see how far the bullets carry, then hands the gun to Maisie. But while Maisie is firing out to sea, her pet goat Amomma begins eating some of the cartridges in the box behind them. Maisie turns sharply at the disturbance and fires the gun inadvertently near Dick's face. "Oh, Dick!" she exclaims, "have I killed you?"

> Then she heard him sputter, and dropped on her knees beside him, crying, "Dick, you aren't hurt, are you? I didn't mean it."
>
> "Of course you didn't," said Dick, coming out of the smoke and wiping his cheek. "But you nearly blinded me. That powder stuff stings awfully." (7–8)

Blindness was Kipling's fictional substitute for the poor eyesight from which he suffered at Lorne Lodge and for which he received several beatings at school, and several more at the lodge, for supposed delinquencies, before the fault was discovered and corrected by glasses. Eventually his hero Dick Heldar will go blind because of damage to his optic nerves from a saber cut on his forehead. But Maisie's early role as the near-initiator of blindness is much more to the novel's psychic point. The rejected lover, whether blinded by saber or gunpowder, seeks his own destruction as punishment for the cold beloved who fails to see his merits clearly and to devote herself to him. It is she (with some help from her lower-class double Bess) who denies the primacy of his vocation, or "vision," over hers and who callously neglects him.

Behind that denial there is, of course, Kipling's mother's well-intentioned neglect and Mrs. Holloway's studied callousness. But more overtly, for Kipling, there was the indifference to his early love of another child boarded with Mrs. Holloway, Flo Garrard, a pale, slender, pretty girl one or two years older than himself, self-contained and aloof, like Dickens's Estella, and apparently just as heartless. Though Flo is the nominal model for Maisie, she had actually arrived at Lorne Lodge a few years after Kipling had left it (though his sister Trix had not)—which means that his memories of events suffered through with his sister, and not with Flo Garrard, were the basis for the life endured there by Dick and Maisie. But in 1880, when he was fourteen and a half, Kipling had returned to the lodge to bring his sister away and was immediately smitten by the new girl he met there. Over the next two years he managed to see her several times, and at sixteen, when he left England for India, he considered himself engaged to her. Two years later he was apparently shattered when she broke off the engagement by mail. Though he would go on to other loves, he would never forget her. A chance meeting in 1890, when he was back in England, was sufficient to destroy a new engagement (with Caroline Taylor) and to send him on the double rebound, as it were, into the arms of Carrie Balestier, whom he would marry in 1892. But even in marriage he continued to cherish his initial love, and in poems like "The Virginity" (which Hemingway much admired) and "The Vampire," he would aggrandize his "folly" while at the same time castigating the heartless maid who had failed to "understand."[20]

Hemingway's early relish for such feelings must have been considerable. He would eventually undergo the same experience himself with his wartime sweetheart, Agnes Von Kurowsky, and would consider himself her hapless victim, though there is every reason to believe that he too was emotionally primed for rejection. As with Kipling, he had already received some initial priming through his more obvious disaffection with his mother, which like many adolescents he attributed to her supposed disregard of his worthiness rather than to his own need for independence. An extremely dependent person all his life, never able to leave one woman without leaning on another, and therefore consecutively married for forty years, he nevertheless imagined himself as a man able to live without women, though somehow always involved with them and always in one way or another betrayed by them. The conversion of his wives from adoring "sisters" into betraying "mothers," as his own inability to sustain self-regard and affection changed his view of them, is a pattern much remarked upon by recent biographers.[21] And certainly the pattern was there in his boyhood as he turned from his mother to his younger sisters for affection, and for the first time figuratively sang: "If you don't love me, Mama / I don't care at all." But he did care intensely, both for his mother and his sisters, and later for his wives and sweethearts, and there is much poignance accordingly in the early appeal for him of a sister-mother-sweetheart mixture like Kipling's Maisie. He would have been deeply touched by that first kiss on the beach when Dick learns that Maisie will be sent away to a school in France, declares his love for her, and exacts from her a somewhat reluctant promise to care for him indefinitely. And he would have rejoiced and shivered too when, fortified by that pledge, Dick defies the gasping Mrs. Jennett on reaching the lodge, refuses ever to be beaten again, demands his tea—and that night dreams "that he had won all the world and brought it to Maisie in a cartridge box"—which she then turns over with her foot and, "instead of saying 'Thank you,'" accuses him of selfishness for not bringing her goat Amomma the grass collar he had promised (16). For Ernest too would soon exact his pledges, defy his Mrs. Jennett, and then dream and live that curiously selfish dream, to the neglect of everybody's goat except his own.

More immediately, however, he would be moved by the daring life of modern war correspondents which Kipling was one of the first novelists to record. This relatively recent trade, born in the imperial years of the late nineteenth century, was one Hemingway would follow in the Balkans after the First World War, and again in the Spanish Civil War and the Second World War. His decision to become a reporter in Kansas City at eighteen, rather than go on to college, was probably much influenced, then, by his reading of Kipling's account of the war-front escapades of Dick Heldar and his friends. Dick's vocation as an artist who paints war pictures and draws battle sketches for illustrated magazines was based on that of R. Caton Woodville in the days when photography was still in the long-exposure stage. Dick's friends Torpenhow and the Nilghai—special correspondents for the new syndicates that supplied the British masses with picturesque accounts of military campaigns throughout the Empire—were invested with the lore and experience of Kipling's schoolboy friends like Lionel Dunsterville, the original of Stalky, who had given Kipling detailed accounts of desert warfare in Egypt during the siege of Khartoum, and with Kipling's own knowledge and experience as a reporter in India. The second chapter of *The Light That Failed* opens with Dick drawing a sketch of Torpenhow as the latter sews himself a new pair of breeches out of a sacking canvas in a desert camp in Egypt. Dick shows him the sketch, along with others he has done while knocking about the world, and Torpenhow promptly arranges to hire him to do battle sketches for Torpenhow's syndicate:

> So it came to pass that . . . Dick was made free of the New and Honourable Fraternity of war correspondents, who all possess the inalienable right of doing as much work as they can and getting as much for it as Providence and their owners shall please. To these things are added in time, if the brother be worthy, the power of glib speech that neither man nor woman can resist when a meal or a bed is in question, the eye of a horse-coper, the skill of a cook, the constitution of a bullock, the digestion of an ostrich, and an infinite adaptability to all circumstances. But many die before they attain to this degree, and the past-masters in the craft appear for the most part in

dress-clothes when they are in England, and thus their glory is hidden from the multitude. (24–25)

This knowing description of the rough-and-ready life of the new profession must have deeply impressed the young Hemingway. His own weak eyesight might keep him out of the army if he tried to enlist, but like Kipling and Kipling's fictional heroes he could always see action by entering the reporting fraternity. The qualities of war correspondent and battle-sketcher were those he already aspired to. As Robert Moss observes in *Rudyard Kipling and the Fiction of Adolescence,* they were "spartan virtues . . . uncomplaining toil, devotion to duty, fearlessness in battle, constant stoicism." Thus, "Dick and the newspapermen essentially adopt the code of the soldier; in order to file their stories they live under difficult conditions, endure privation when necessary and display courage in the face of the enemy. When it is required, they even join in the fighting themselves, as do Torpenhow and Dick in Chapter II."[22]

So too would Hemingway in World War II, when his reconnaissance activities while approaching Paris put his professional standing in some jeopardy. But more important than such Kiplingesque liberties, he had gleaned from his early reading of the novel a "masculine code" derived from military experience which—by Kipling's "law"—would then be applied to the artist's development of his craft. As Moss further expounds,

> The "law" may be defined as a brief series of universally applicable commandments which one must follow in order to avoid folly, mediocrity or evil; they are the moral givens in Kipling's cosmos, rules from which any shade of ambiguity or equivocation has been withdrawn. Dick enunciates the code in connection with painting, but Kipling obviously intends it to have far wider resonances: ". . . you must sacrifice yourself, and live under orders, and never think for yourself, and never have real satisfaction in your work. . . . There's no question of belief or disbelief. That's the law, and you take it or refuse it as you please." The phrase "under orders" was not idly chosen; the paradigmatic exponents of the law are, for Kipling, nearly always the soldiers and civil servants of the Empire.[23]

Hemingway would embrace this logic and seek from disciplined soldiers and sportsmen the "rules" by which his art might eventually prosper. As an artist-reporter he would live their lives, adopt their codes, and eventually "paint" what he saw. His interest in the novel's action-oriented view of art was accordingly very strong. When Dick Heldar comes to London to peddle his sketches and paintings, he and his reporter friends are contemptuous of the dilettantism and fashionableness which govern the London art world. No one has yet seen the kind of action-oriented art he has to offer, and there is much danger of his giving in to his own fashionable success. Hemingway's predicament in Paris in the 1920s was of a similar order, but in several ways his reading of *The Light That Failed* had prepared him for it. "There are few things more edifying unto Art than the actual belly-pinch of hunger," writes Kipling when his hero deliberately starves himself, on arriving in London, rather than admit to the syndicate that he can't wait till the end of the month for money they still owe him (41). Hemingway would work variations on that hunger theme throughout his writing career. His nostalgia for his own "starving years" in Paris (where he could always rely, of course, on Hadley's nest egg) was grounded in Kipling's view of the exigencies and discipline needed for "true" creative effort. Similarly Dick's satiric description of the London artists who give teas and talk about "Art and the state of their souls" would sanction later contrasts of his own hardworking ways with those of fellow writers in Paris. And Dick's self-satire of his own artistic yieldings, when straight-man Torpenhow asks him "What is Art?" would serve as a working model for how not to do it:

"Here's a sample of real Art [Dick tells Torpenhow]. It's going to be a facsimile reproduction for a weekly. I called it 'His Last Shot.' It's worked up from the little water-colour I made outside El Maghrib. Well, I lured my model, a beautiful rifleman, up here with drink; I drored him, and I redrored him, and I tredrored him, and I made him a flushed, dishevelled, bedevilled scallawag, with his helmet at the back of his head, and the living fear of death in his eye, and the blood oozing out of a cut over his anklebone. He wasn't pretty, but he was all soldier and very much man. . . . I did him just as well as I knew how, making allowances for the slickness of oils. Then the art-manager of that abandoned paper said that his subscribers wouldn't like it. It was brutal and coarse and violent, —man being naturally gentle when he's fighting for his life. They wanted something more restful, with a little more colour. . . . Behold the result! I put him into a lovely red coat without a speck on it. That is Art. I polished his boots, —observe the high light on his toe. That is Art. I cleaned his rifle, —rifles are always clean on service, —because that is Art. I pipeclayed his helmet, — pipeclay is always used on active service, and is indispensable to Art. I shaved his chin, I washed his hands, and gave him an air of fatted peace. Result, military tailor's pattern-plate. Price, thank Heaven! twice as much as for the first sketch, which was moderately decent. (55–56)

Hemingway's parents had similarly objected to the novels of Jack London as being "brutal, coarse, and violent." In his adolescent view they preferred "pretty Art" instead, though melioristic would have been more to the point, since they obviously accepted Kipling. Nevertheless, the acceptable Kipling gave him a vocabulary and an outlook for combating such views. It was, moreover, an "insider"'s outlook, founded on firsthand knowledge of things bloody, coarse, and fearful, as Dick Heldar here demonstrates by his knowing account of the actual details of military life.

Not surprisingly, then, Hemingway would later fashion some of his own more somber accounts of artistic and heroic predicaments out of Dick's artistic trials and errors. Thus, when Dick yields to the allurements of the London art world ("I like the power; I like the fun; I like the fuss; and above all I like the money," 52), we have the makings of Harry's yielding to the allurements of the rich in "The Snows of Kilimanjaro," at the expense of artistic talent and integrity; and there is even a lament for the lost love who turned him down (i.e., Agnes Von Kurowsky) to complete the parallel. More telling perhaps is Dick's attempt to die in accord with the artistic principles by which, at his best, he has tried to live. Thus, when he leaves London, blind and loveless, for the Egyptian battlefield, and then parleys his way to redeeming death at the front, we have a preview of the dying Harry's attempt, while on African safari, to defy his fate by writing stories in his mind—and a romantic literary sanction, as well, for his Kiplingesque dream-flight to glory when a British pilot, Old Compie, arrives from the world of Torpenhows and Stalkies to fly him out.

Kipling's portrait of Maisie offered the young Hemingway still another kind of preview. As a career woman—one of the first in fiction—she would confirm some of his worst fears about deadly females. But though many of Kipling's commentators would take a similar view, Kipling himself was more evenhanded than they allowed. At the end of chapter 1 he makes the point that Dick may well be selfish, or at least wrongheaded, in what he expects from Maisie. He repeatedly shows her telling Dick that she cannot give him what he wants, that her own career in painting comes first. And he shows dramatically that the destruction of Dick's finest painting, the *Melancolia*, is poetic justice for his attempt to beat Maisie at her own subject, to break her will by doing a better version of it than she—being a mere woman—can achieve. But each of these concessions is undercut by male chauvinist assumptions which are even more pronounced, and which themselves easily account for the critical consensus on her character.

Like Flo Garrard, Maisie is a would-be painter who wants to study in Paris with a famous master. Like Flo, she lives in London with another woman painter; and again like Flo, she rejects her childhood sweetheart when they meet again by chance, so as to continue her artistic life. In that sense the book was plainly designed by Kipling to avenge himself on Flo Garrard. It is a wish-fulfillment fantasy in which self-destructive feelings engendered by rejection are glorified while hostile feelings are given ample play. Hemingway would similarly indulge himself in the mean-spirited tale "A Very Short Story," in response to his rejection by Agnes Von Kurowsky. But it was another man's attractiveness, and not her career in nursing, that deprived him of Agnes. His fascination with Kipling's Maisie would have begun rather with his mother's aborted career in grand opera, and with her subsequent activities as a concert singer and teacher in Oak Park. Grace Hemingway never let her children forget the brilliant career she had abandoned when she married their father. Ernest, who often wanted to forget it, would have enjoyed the debunking of that sacrifice through the undermining of a young woman who refused to make it.

In *The Light That Failed*, accordingly, Kipling told him what he wanted to hear. "Give 'em what they know," says Dick Heldar to Torpenhow in his discourse on fashionable Art, "and when you've done it once do it again." For all his attempts at evenhandedness, Kipling follows his own satiric advice in his larger dealings with Maisie. Thus Dick can confidently say to Maisie, "You aren't a woman," because she doesn't accept the traditional woman's role—doesn't devote herself, that is, to his own needs and desires (124). It is she, then, rather than Dick, who is truly selfish, and the case seems dramatically proven when she learns of his blindness, late in the novel, and is unable to step forward and take care of him—as a "real" woman would and, indeed, as the lower-class Bess is willing to do, albeit to her own advantage. Meanwhile, Maisie is engaged in what Dick contemptuously calls "Woman's Art," which apparently means art with no real experience of the world behind it (83). She avidly seeks success, for instance, as a display of her own magnificence and must therefore be diminished by experiencing "the size of the world"—which Dick will show her—and by sacrificing herself to the "law" as already indicated. Dick admits that he no longer obeys the law himself, in his own pursuit of success; but then he has already seen the world and understands his folly. His friends Torpenhow and the Nilghai have also attacked his love-and-marriage folly, arguing that marriage will ruin *his* career, that wives and action-oriented art do not mix well. But that chauvinist contradiction is all right for men to uphold, side by side with the notion that marriage to Dick should be Maisie's true career when Dick goes blind.

The deadly relation between women and art is further demonstrated when the ex-tart Bess destroys Dick's masterpiece (an early precedent, apparently, for the burning of David Bourne's African stories in *The Garden of Eden* by his mad wife Catherine Bourne). Her motive is revenge, not simply because he continues to bait her as she poses for the painting, but because he has deprived her of Torpenhow's love in the past, and now she is unable to recapture him. So, when the painting is finished, she smudges and scrapes it out with turpentine and a palette knife. "Only a woman could have done that!" says the chastened Torpenhow, who feels guilty for bringing "gutter-devils" like Bess into their bachelor haven. But expiation comes when he discovers that Dick is now blind and afraid, and he must wrestle him down in his frenzy, hold his hand, calm his fears, and—when sleep comes at last—kiss him lightly on the forehead "as men do sometimes kiss a wounded comrade in the hour of death, to ease his departure" (215).

In the wake of female viciousness, then, male camaraderie triumphs in a tender way. Whether on the battlefield or in bachelor quarters, it proves to be man's best and most durable form of love. Thus, when Torpenhow takes Dick to the park to be near a regiment of guards as they drill, Dick responds with lyric poignance: "Oh, my men! —my beautiful men! . . . I could draw those chaps once. Who'll draw 'em now?" (219–20). The as-yet-unborn answer to that question is, of course, Ernest Hemingway, Kipling's modern heir, who would find in this bliss-before-blindness sequence still another source for "The Short Happy Life of Francis Macomber." As Hemingway must have seen, Dick Heldar's brief happiness comes with the completion of his masterpiece. When it is wiped out by the vengeful Bess, he dies in effect to his happy life, as we learn through Torpenhow's farewell kiss and through Dick's complaint, as the next chapter opens, of being "dead in the death of the blind" (222). His later death on the battlefield is merely the heroic completion, then, of these predictive events. So too at the end of the Macomber story the British guide Wilson and the newly brave Macomber will share a moment of blissful male tenderness while on African safari, before his "accidental" shooting by a presumably vengeful wife as he faces a charging buffalo; and here, Maisie's near-blinding of Dick by gunpowder as Kipling's novel opens, Bess's midway destruction of his painting, and Dick's glorified death as the novel closes, will find their "true" literary connections.

Hemingway's interest in Maisie would have other literary extensions. In his Spanish Civil War play, *The Fifth Column* (1938), he would create the only career woman in his canon. Though Dorothy Bridges—a former Junior Leaguer and Vassar graduate—is now a war correspondent in Madrid, she seems as naive about her profession as Maisie often seems about hers. But secret agent Philip Rawlings, with whom she falls in love, is there like another Dick Heldar, ready to dramatize the extent of her ignorance of espionage and betrayal in the besieged city and to point up the super-ficialities and follies of her female outlook. When in the concluding scene he tells her that she's a useless, uneducated, lazy fool, at best a handsome sexual commodity, he is presumably trying to make her dislike him so as to continue his bloody trade without the further complications of love. But in fact he has just offered a fair summation of the character Hemingway presents throughout the play, in reaction to his own mixed feelings about his wartime sweetheart and fellow correspondent in Madrid, Martha Gellhorn. Hemingway's need to disparage Martha—who was actually too diligent, smart, and capable to please him, and too physically attractive not to—was like Kipling's need to disparage Flo Garrard; and Kipling's disparagements were much on Hemingway's mind when he wrote the play.

On May 5, 1938, for instance, in a letter to his editor, Maxwell Perkins, he took Kipling's format for publishing his Anglo-Indian play, *The Story of the Gadsbys,* as a possible model for publishing *The Fifth Column:* "How would it be to publish the three unpublished stories and the play in one vol? Might be fine. Remember the Gadsbys by Kipling. Was a vol of plays and stories. One of his best books of stories. Successful too. Would be a good length."[24]

The Story of the Gadsbys had appeared with "The Courting of Dinah Shadd" and other stories in an undated New York edition; it would also appear in a single-volume selection of Kipling's works (1931) and in various collected editions in company with *Soldiers Three* and *In Black and White.* Originally published in 1889, a year before *The Light That Failed,* its theme of the unsettling effects of a marriage between an older officer and the young daughter of the woman he was ostensibly courting would have intrigued Hemingway, who in 1938 was about to abandon his second wife, Pauline Pfeiffer (then forty-seven) for his third wife, Martha Gellhorn (then thirty). Captain Gadsby is in fact made unfit for war, as the play ends, by the hold on his imagination of domestic obligations to his young wife and child. This is the fate that Philip Rawlings manfully avoids at the end of Hemingway's play by severing romantic ties with Dorothy; but Hemingway himself would prove less manful. In an earlier work, *Green Hills of Africa* (1935), his epithet for Pauline had been P.O.M., or "Poor Old Mama," a locution which takes on added interest in the light of act 1 of *The Gadsbys,* called "Poor Dear Mamma," in which the aggressive young heroine steals her captain away from P.D.M. It looks very much as if Hemingway wrote *The Fifth Column* in order to prevent himself from making the "colossal mistake" with Martha that Rawlings fears and avoids, and that Kipling had warned him about through Dick Heldar's deadly fascination with career-girl Maisie and through Gadsby's unmanning by a younger woman. But of course P.O.P., or Poor Old Papa, was too weak to follow his own literary leads, or too primed by early rejections, and wound up reenacting his own live version of Kipling's admonitory tales.

That he had been trying to learn from Kipling seems evident in his deliberate inversion of Dick Heldar's attempt to win Maisie's heart, in *The Light That Failed,* by his glowing description of the exotic foreign places he can show her. Thus, in *The Fifth Column,* when Dorothy Bridges tries to share with Rawlings her playgirl fantasies of a glamorous life of expensive clothes and foreign travel by his side, he responds by sardonically debunking all the exotic places he has known where the idle rich may gather.[25] Similarly, when Rawlings finally avoids Gadsby's fate by discarding Dorothy and consorting with a Moorish whore, he reverses Dick Heldar's progress from his youthful amours, while knocking about the world, with "a sort of Negroid-Jewish Cuban, with morals to match," to his later deadly relations with Maisie (149–50). Thanks to Kipling, then, the man of action may have his disreputable playgirls but knows better than to marry those with respectable careers.

Hemingway too knew better, but as his four marriages attest, he was much more susceptible than Rawlings to professional and economic charms. Hadley, the least professional of his wives, had been a pianist with a nest egg like his mother. Pauline had written for *Vanity Fair* before stealing him away from Hadley. She was also rich enough to devote herself to Ernest at her own expense and still help him out financially, as Grace had often helped his father. Martha was a novelist and war correspondent, callings she pursued fiercely throughout her rocky years with Ernest so as to pay her share of expenses, as Grace had done before the children came. Mary Welsh was also a war correspondent and reporter; but wisely or unwisely she decided to subordinate such interests and devote herself to Ernest—at his expense. That none of these eco-marital strategies worked for very long is a testament perhaps to the precariousness of Hemingway's easily wounded, indeed self-wounded, self-regard, and to the short-lived nature of his intense affections. But more to the point, it is a testament to the ongoing power of his original relations with his mother, the first professional woman in his life, the first to support herself and help her husband, and therefore the first to challenge the primacy of his own male "vision," or vocation. For like Kipling's Maisie, Grace had often failed to see Ernest's merits clearly and to devote herself to him, and had even made a point of throwing him out of their summer cottage after his twenty-first birthday, for passive-aggressive revilements and other forms of grossly adolescent behavior. He reenacted this early dilemma most fully with his third wife, Martha Gellhorn, who spent too much time away from home, diligently earning her keep, to suit his dependent needs and desires, and who also rejected him first for his abusive ways, before he had quite managed to replace her. In marrying Martha, then, he had not only managed to make that "colossal mistake" which Rawlings fears and avoids in *The Fifth Column;* he had also managed to marry Kipling's Maisie, a career girl whose sizeable ego he might diminish, that is, by showing her the war-torn world—wrapped, no doubt, in a Spanish cartridge box—but without any provision whatsoever for her cartridge-chewing goat, Amomma.

MULVANEY IN MILAN

In March and April of 1951, in a series of irate letters to his publisher, Charles Scribner, Hemingway had fumed away at a rival war novelist, James Jones, whose best-selling novel, *From Here to Eternity,* had just been published by Scribner's. In one letter he had called Jones a "psycho" who would "probably commit suicide" and whose novel was a "bowl of scabs" and would do "great damage to our country." In another, after calling Jones a "psycho," "coward," and "whimpering neurotic" and giving a few modest instances of his own greater courage under stress, he had asked that several references to himself in the novel be deleted since Hemingway was "a good fighting name back to 1700's in the states and long before that elsewhere" and should not be sullied. Then, as an apparent afterthought, he had accused Jones of two kinds of professional stupidity:

> If he had any brains he would have known how many professional soldiers have had syphilis, as he would have known the origin of his title and the name of the man who wrote the ballad he took it from, and also a short story by Kipling called "Love O' Women." I could write from now until the end of next week case histories of soldiers and bull fighters I have known (also boxers) who had what we called the old rale (a name for it that goes back nearly to Chaucer's time). From the time I was a kid I had to distinguish between soft and hard chancres and courageous Jones comes along and says *he* has had the clap and it was horrible.[26]

Hemingway is responding here to an almost gratuitous insult in chapter 35 of Jones's novel, where the defiant hero, charged with disorderly conduct, glibly undercuts the argument of his defense counsel, Lieutenant Culpepper. The lieutenant has just told him that the military court will excuse him if he admits to being drunk and "feeling his oats," since most commanding officers know that "wild and woolly boys" with their "devil-may-care attitude" make "the best soldiers"; indeed, "getting drunk and running wild is not only a soldier's nature, it's almost his sacred duty; just like the way Ernest Hemingway said that syph was the occupational disease of bullfighters and soldiers. It's the same damn thing." To which Private Prewitt replies that neither he nor the lieutenant has ever had syphilis; but he has had the clap (gonorrhea) himself: "And if syph or the clap are the occupational diseases of soldiers, then I'll get out and be a garage mechanic." "Besides," he adds, "I aint begging none of them for nothing."[27]

As Hemingway rightly understood, Jones's hero has gone out of his way to challenge Hemingway's authority on military matters: he is not merely defying court and counsel here, he is also defying Hemingway and, in effect, Hemingway's predecessor Kipling, the latter for his cheerful view of drunken rapscallions, the former for his grim view of professional stoics. Against these outworn versions of the good soldier, then, a new contender has risen: the stubbornly defiant individualist who loves the army so much he lets it kill him—as the AWOL Prewitt literally does when he tries to return to his battalion after the attack on Pearl Harbor and is shot down by an overzealous night patrol.

Hemingway's discomfort with this perversely cocky rival was further aggravated by what he knew about Jones's literary ignorance. From Charles Scribner, apparently, he had heard the story of Jones's letter to Maxwell Perkins, back in 1946, citing the Yale drinking song as the source of his title phrase "from here to Eternity." When Perkins gently replied that Kipling's ballad about gentlemen rankers was the original and more fitting source, Jones promptly read *Barrack-Room Ballads,* then added not one but two epigraphs from Kipling to his title pages, including the appropriate refrain from "Gentlemen Rankers."[28] Hemingway himself had read Kipling in some depth in boyhood, and Chaucer too, and had learned something also of that long line of fighting men from which he had descended. Though we may discount his first-hand knowledge of sexual diseases in his youth, he evidently did look them up in his father's medical library, probably because he had heard much street talk about them and had read about them in Kipling's "Love O' Women." What outraged him most about Jones, accordingly, was that Jones lacked such credentials—had no knowledge of the long literature of war, no martial or medical ancestry, and was by his own testimony on his return from Guadalcanal a neurotic and a deserter, and therefore no "real soldier";[29] yet he had the upstart nerve to make literary capital of those professional hazards, psychosis and syphilis, which better men than he had dealt with in the established manly fashion.

A territorial squabble, then, involving questionable passports, points of entry, and rights of domain, with suicide as the projected—indeed, projective—resolution. It would be Hemingway, and not Jones, who would take his own life, some ten years later, when he could no longer compete along such literary frontiers. Already he felt crowded out of his invented and inherited space as the world's foremost war novelist.

Kipling had preceded him, of course, in that capacity. In *Soldiers Three* and related tales about his "three musketeers" from the lower ranks—Mulvaney, Ortheris, and Learoyd—he had done for the British soldier what Captain Marryat had done, much earlier in the century, for the British sailor: brought his life and ways into public consciousness, that is, as an imperial heritage. He was extremely sensitive, in this regard, to popular prejudices as to the unsavoriness and debauchery of enlisted lives, and in redeeming tales like "Love O' Women" he deliberately tried to overcome them. Thus, in this unusual story, which originally appeared in a collection called *Many Inventions* (1893), Mulvaney tells the unnamed narrator about an incorrigible roué named Larry Tighe, a stray-lamb gentleman ranker like those in the Kipling ballad borrowed by knowing Yale song writers as the century turned and more recently by ignorant James Jones. For his many amorous exploits Private Tighe had acquired the nickname, "Love O' Women," from which the story takes its resonant title. He has also acquired syphilis while wronging his many female victims and is now trying to get himself killed in battle before losing mental and bodily control. But Kipling accords him an even more glorious demise, along the lines of Antony and Cleopatra, by allowing him to totter valiantly through a rough campaign and then rise from his deathcot to confront silently the bawdyhouse woman he has chiefly wronged. "Time was whin you were quick enough wid your words, —you that talked me down to hell," says that "fine big woman," now called "Di'monds-an-Pearls"; but when the living corpse before her replies, in Mulvaney's Irish brogue, "I'm dyin', Aigypt—dyin'," she opens her arms to embrace him, holds him up through his death-rattle, and then—lacking Cleopatra's asp—shoots herself with a handy pistol so as to join him in death. The doctor fetched by Mulvaney calls it "a double death from naturil causes, most naturil causes"; he then decides to bury the pair at his own expense in the Civil Cemetery, with a Church of England service, and is so moved by their example that he runs off himself with a major's lady later that year. A cooler man, Private Ortheris steps in and closes Mulvaney's tale with a ballad about the wise advice that "the Girl told the Soldier": namely, "don't try for things that are out of your reach."[30]

That womanizing can lead to scandalous and deathly consequences seems to be the moral wisdom of the tale; but the romantic nature of these tragicomic deaths lends them a dignity and point that Hemingway would find missing in Jones's novel. In Hemingway's somewhat hysterical view, Jones was a coward with "the psycho's urge to kill himself" and would do so, hopefully, as soon as it would not damage Scribner's sales.[31] Apparently Hemingway preferred the death-urges of those who try to die valiantly in battle, like Private Tighe and perhaps himself, to those of Jones and his hero. All of which lends a self-destructive and perhaps even a romantic edge to his own active courage, and to the accrued damages to mind and body of his many wounds and accidents, before he would yield to his own "psycho's" urges late in life. The method he would employ for his own self-destruction occurs, not incidentally, in chapter 38 of Jones's novel, in which a successful but self-isolated army boxer named Private Bloom puts the muzzle of a loaded rifle into his mouth and pulls the trigger with his big toe. Perhaps that published precedent explains, more than any other factor, Hemingway's overdetermined reaction to Jones's novel.

Meanwhile, Kipling's glorification of military life had given him an early model for his own active courage and its literary extensions. *Soldiers Three* (1887) was originally a collection of six tales involving one or more of the "three musketeers," plus a seventh tale, "In the Matter of a Private," which one of them might have told to the unnamed narrator. Nine other tales which belong under this title would appear in other Kipling collections, however, and would then be added to the 1898 edition of *Soldiers Three*. Hemingway would follow the same pattern with his Nick Adams stories— seven in *In Our Time* (1925), included with five later Adams stories in *The First Forty-Nine Stories* (1938); and editor Philip Young would include all twelve stories with unpublished fragments of varying lengths in the posthumous collection, *The Nick Adams Stories* (1972). As we shall see, Hemingway's lone serial hero would take a dimmer view of war than that of Kipling's serial trio; but the author's more ebullient boyhood sentiments about war, as imbibed from Kipling's musketeers, were nonetheless durable and would resurface in later years.

In many ways, for instance, Kipling's musketeers foreshadow the three schoolboys Stalky, M'Turk, and Beetle, with whom Hemingway had early identified. They are dedicated soldiers who never talk about their deepest feelings; they use elaborate stratagems to defeat obtuse superiors, villains, peers, and outsiders; they like to drink and they like to fight; and they are all wary of women and of the hazards of womanizing for military life.

Interestingly, though never bound by mere regulations, they have designed most of their stratagems to keep the social and military systems going. Thus, in five of the first six tales the problem is to preserve some facet of social or military order. In "The God from the Machine" Mulvaney prevents a blackguard captain from eloping with the colonel's daughter. In "Private Learoyd's Story" Learoyd foils a snobbish woman who wants him to steal for her the colonel's lady's dog. In "The Big Drunk Draf'" Mulvaney comes out of retirement as a civilian to help an inexperienced officer gain control of a wild regiment which has served its time and is returning home. In "The Solid Muldoon" he persuades an angry soldier that his wife is faithful. And in "Black Jack" he prevents a dozen "Black Irish" barracks-mates from killing their color-sergeant and pinning the crime on him.

In all these tales, moreover, shrewd schemes, high spirits, and justified revenge are the adolescent keynotes. These notes recur in combat stories like "The Taking of Lungtungpen," where a company of British troops, having just forded a stream at night, are forced to fight naked while taking a native town and, seized with jubilant laughter, proceed to kill seventy-five natives while remaining unhurt themselves. The same manic approach to enemy lives characterizes "With the Main Guard," wherein the Black Tyrone, having seen their dead mutilated by "Paythans," are allowed to take over hand-to-hand fighting from Mulvaney's company so as to achieve their revenge, before the solid press of men breaks up and the fleeing natives are slaughtered by gunfire from Mulvaney's company.

The telling of this tale is designed to rouse a morose and sweltering Learoyd from the death-dumps, and accordingly, it contains such cheerful designations as "Silver's Theatre" in Dublin for the gut between two hills where the close combat takes place. The designation follows from a Black Tyrone's remark, when a captain counts his losses: "'Captain dear,' sez he, 'if wan or two in the shtalls have been dishcommoded, the gallery have enjoyed the performences av a Roshus.'"[32] If "Roshus" is the great Roman actor Roscius, a synonym for emotive actors since Shakespeare's time, then his performance against the "Paythans" must have been ferocious. *Ferocious* seems to be the word, at least, for the Black Tyrone, a company like the Italian Arditi whom the young Hemingway would praise in still another theatre—the Oak Park High School auditorium—while lecturing on his recent war experiences and displaying his battle trophies to former school-mates. The tale concludes, at any rate, with Learoyd's recovery as the relief guard arrives and with the rescue of a two-year-old army child who has wandered toward the parapet and who now holds up her lips to be kissed by the three musketeers. Presumably it is for her sake that these teary veterans have slain so many "Paythans" in the past.

In "Chapter VI," one of the inserted paragraphs between the stories of *In Our Time*, a wounded Nick Adams lies with his back against a church wall and speaks to the wounded Italian lying beside him: *"Senta Rinaldi. Senta. You and me we've made a separate peace."*[33] Such an idea would not be unthinkable for one of Kipling's musketeers: Ortheris wants desperately to go home, for instance, in "The Madness of Private Ortheris," and Mulvaney asks, "Fwhat the divil possist us to take an' kape this melancolious counthry?" in "With the Main Guard." But to follow through on such rebellious sentiments, as Lieutenant Henry does in *A Farewell to Arms,* would be—for Kipling's three—unthinkable. Nor would Hemingway think or feel this way as an ambulance corpsman in World War I, not even after being wounded. But during his early Paris years, after absorbing the antiwar sentiments of literary friends and of poets and novelists like Owen, Sassoon, Dos Passos, and Ford, he would begin to approach the war from a different angle and would become one of the most famous advocates of "a separate peace." Thus, in two war tales, "Now I Lay Me" and "A Way You'll Never Be," we see Nick Adams suffering badly from shell shock, afraid to sleep without a light, and inclined to rave wildly when he revisits the front lines in his new American uniform. There is no uplift here; the effect is of deadly disillusionment under which Nick bears up as well as he can. In "Big Two-Hearted River" he will finally return to the "good country" of his youth so as to regain some sense of the order, health, and beauty the war has swept away.

Plainly Hemingway had abandoned the patriotic dedication of his Kiplingesque youth. But as we can see from a related tale from *In Our Time,* called "Soldier's Home," he had not altogether abandoned his earlier outlook. Harold Krebs, the protagonist of the tale, had enlisted in the Marines in 1917, coming straight from a Methodist college in Kansas, and had remained in Europe until the summer of 1919. Having returned home too late to be considered a hero, he begins to lie about his experiences "in order to be listened to at all." But it is the lies he tells, and not his war experiences, which are the source of his subsequent disillusionment:

> A distaste for everything that had happened to him in the war set in because of the lies he had told. All of the times that had been able to make him feel cool and clear inside himself when he thought of them; the times so long back when he had done the one thing, the only thing for a man to do, easily and naturally, when he might have done something else, now lost their cool, valuable quality and then were lost themselves.[34]

The Kiplingesque sentiment is clear: World War I had been the occasion for doing "the only thing for a man to do," and Krebs had done it "easily and naturally." The difference from Nick Adams's reaction to the war is striking.

There is an admission here that the battlefields of World War I were "the good place" for Krebs; he feels no need for "a separate peace," nor for that "last good country" in northern Michigan to which Nick returns for therapeutic relief. Krebs has even appropriated attitudes about women from his war experience. He does not want to court American girls, to have to work to get them and then to suffer consequences. He will avoid such consequences now. The army has taught him that he does "not really need a girl," for "sooner or later you always got one," when you were ripe for it, and therefore "did not have to think about it." He prefers, accordingly, the French and German girls he has known, with whom it "was simple and you were friends" and there "was not all this talking."[35] The Kipling note seems strong on several counts: Krebs has been "a good soldier," like Mulvaney, Ortheris, and Learoyd; he has the same wariness about women; and if he can no longer fight the "good" fight, he can at least look forward to reading about it in war histories, as Hemingway did in the 1920s and after.

It seems clear from this story, and from Hemingway's renewed dedication to social causes in Spain in the late 1930s and to the allied cause in World War II, that war had always been for him a Kiplingesque occasion, at least when faith in the larger enterprise allowed for it—and in Krebs's case, even when it didn't. Hemingway's early relish for Kipling's war stories had not only helped to catapult him into World War I; it had also helped him to extend his own imagination as to what constitutes a "good soldier" and what does not, and to fashion stories and novels which pursue that basic theme.

As with Kipling, moreover, the connections between love and war—as well as the disconnections—were always prominent in his fiction. In "With the Main Guard" Mulvaney remarks of close combat that "Each does ut his own way, like makin' love . . . the butt or the bay'nit or the bullet accordin' to the natur' av the man." And again he speaks of "the fog av fightin' . . . that, like makin' love, . . . takes each man diffirint."[36] Hemingway's fusions of erotic with martial actions would become similarly pronounced in *For Whom the Bell Tolls*, and have often been noted by his critics.[37] In *A Farewell to Arms* and elsewhere he would also deal with the loss of love as somehow endemic to the rigors of combat, a theme Kipling broached eloquently in "On Greenhow Hill." In that haunting tale a troublesome deserter makes Learoyd recall his own reasons for enlisting, since there's always "a lass tewed up wi' it," whether a man deserts or enlists. Learoyd's sweetheart was a miner's daughter in Greenhow Hill named 'Liza Roantree. His rival for her hand was a preacher and friend, but Learoyd in his jealousy was ready to throw him down a mine shaft until told by him that 'Liza is dying and would soon elude them both. Sparing his friend's life, Learoyd enlists in the army to forget his sweetheart, who assures him in a last visit that she loved only him. As his sad tale ends, however, Ortheris spots the lovesick deserter some seven hundred yards across the valley and kills him with a single shot. "Happen there was a lass tewed up wi' him, too," says Learoyd once more. But Ortheris, refusing to reply, merely stares "across the valley with the smile of the artist who looks on the completed work."[38] Since this is the last line of the tale, we must assume that Kipling also smiled upon completing it, that his martial art was, among other things, a kind of compensation for the lost "love-o'-women" like Flo Garrard. With Hemingway the lost love was Agnes Von Kurowsky, Grace Hemingway's heir as the rejecting woman whose failure to understand seemed endemic to enlistment or desertion. For both writers, accordingly, the "good soldier" is defined as either a spurned or spurning lover, one who in some sense gives up love for war. Otherwise, like Private Mulvaney and Lieutenant Henry and Captain Gadsby, he is forced to retire from active combat.

Meanwhile, there are those easy French and German girls. In his seminal essay, "Hemingway: Gauge of Morale," Edmund Wilson devotes a long footnote to the chapter which might be written "on the relation between Kipling and Hemingway, and certain assumptions about society which they share":

> They have much the same split attitude toward women. Kipling anticipates Hemingway in his beliefs that "he travels the fastest that travels alone" and that "the female of the species is more deadly than the male"; and Hemingway seems to reflect Kipling in the submissive infra-Anglo-Saxon women that make his heroes such perfect mistresses. The most striking example of this is the amoeba-like little Spanish girl, Maria, in *For Whom the Bell Tolls*. Like the docile native "wives" of English officials in the early stories of Kipling, she lives only to serve her lord and to merge her identity with his; and this love affair with a woman in a sleeping bag, lacking completely the kind of give and take that goes on between real men and women, has the all-too-perfect felicity of a youthful erotic dream. One suspects that *Without Benefit of Clergy* was read very early by Hemingway and that it made on him a lasting impression. The pathetic conclusion of this story of Kipling's seems unmistakably to be echoed at the end of *A Farewell to Arms*.[39]

In *The Good Kipling*, which takes its title from a qualification made by Hemingway while listing literary forebears, Elliot Gilbert follows up on Wilson's closing comments. After analyzing Kipling's story of a common-law marriage between an Anglo-Indian civil servant named Holden and his devoted native "wife," Ameera, and after noting Ameera's clear-sighted courage in facing her child's death and her own, and the religion of love that sustains her ("There is no God but thee, beloved"), he notes also how torrential rains obliterate the lovers' former home and how the hero "hurries away through the rain at the end of the story, leaving his dead wife behind," in anticipation of the final scene in Hemingway's novel. Gilbert concludes from such foreshadowings that "Lieutenant Henry and Catherine, the central characters in Hemingway's *A Farewell to Arms,* are in many ways the doubles of Holden and Ameera":

> Both couples find love outside the arbitrary bounds which society has established for it, and both nurture that love in a precarious world which threatens them at every moment with separation and death. Both find an almost idyllic happiness in the midst of a holocaust, both are tantalized for a brief moment with the hope, which they never quite permit themselves to believe in, of a normal existence, and in both cases the women die, leaving the men to face life alone.[40]

In such bleak romantic tales Kipling had indeed sounded plangent chords to which the youthful Hemingway would in due time respond. But Wilson to the contrary notwithstanding, Hemingway's first "submissive" heroine, Catherine Barkley, would be Anglo-Saxon without the "infra." Her Britishness might derive from Kipling, but more probably it began with the quasi-British nature of the Hemingway household while "Abba" Hall still lived, and with the muscular Christian gentility therein that made for adoring sisters. The Indian girl Trudy in "Fathers and Sons," who initiates Nick Adams into sexual mysteries, comes closer to the Kipling precedent, but proves far from submissive when she also bestows her favors on another boy in "Ten Indians." Both writers were reacting, nevertheless, to liberated women like Maisie, Brett Ashley, and Dorothy Bridges, by preferring less threatening partners; and it is a point of some interest that Edmund Wilson's footnote on the Kipling impress follows from a discussion of the brutal rejection of Dorothy Bridges, in *The Fifth Column,* and the hero's subsequent reversion "to a little Moorish whore." This is the "split attitude toward women" which, in Wilson's view, Hemingway shares with Kipling.

But then neither writer can be reduced to such easy oppositions. Kipling admired tough army wives like Dinah Shadd, whom Mulvaney courts and marries, and "Ould Pummeloe," who dies while helping to save Mulvaney's regiment from cholera and bequeaths her daughter to their care. He created also the Jamesian Mrs. Hauksbee, a woman of wit and insight who enlivens and broadens her small corner of Anglo-Indian society. And in "Lispeth" he even created a rebellious native girl who spurns the deceitful Chaplain's wife who had encouraged her devotion to a faithless Englishman. Hemingway too was ambivalent; he admired and perhaps even identified with tough, rebellious, or courageous ladies, and was far more attracted to liberated types like Brett Ashley in *The Sun Also Rises* and Catherine Bourne in *The Garden of Eden* than the split theory allows. He departs from Kipling, moreover, in his grimmer outlook toward the inevitable failure of romantic love. For Kipling, who remained married to one woman for a lifetime, lasting romantic happiness was at least conceivable, as in tales like "The Brushwood Boy"—which, not incidentally, Hemingway and his first wife Hadley much admired.[41]

Perhaps the chief source of Kipling's optimism was his mother's return to England, in his early boyhood, to rescue him from the bondage of Lorne Lodge. She then became his supportive confidante and the model thereafter for the many benignly approving "mothers" in his fiction. In "The Brushwood Boy," for instance, where a young officer and the girl next door discover they have independently dreamed the same adventurous dream from childhood onward, the ensuing marriage between them has been arranged by the hero's beloved mother. Grace Hemingway was no less approving of her son's first marriage. Indeed, her admiration for red hair and her passion for music seem to have influenced his choice of a red-headed pianist some eight years older than himself. At their wedding in northern Michigan, moreover, the orphaned Hadley had only Grace to look to for maternal sanction. But during the previous summer Grace had thrown Ernest out of the Michigan cottage where Ernest had thrived in boyhood and where the wedding now took place; his wounded feelings were only superficially healed, and his passive resentment would soon harden permanently into adolescent hatred. Hadley too, given her all-too-sheltered life while her overprotective mother lived, had no further desire for maternal sanction. For these opposite reasons, the family ties that bound them at that northern wedding were tenuous at best. Both Hadley and Ernest were ready to break away to Paris, where, some six years later, even the ties that bound them to each other would dissolve. Ernest's passive aggressions against his mother would be repeated with all future wives and sweethearts and would virtually guarantee the grimness of his romantic outlook.

It was the grimmer Kipling, accordingly, whom he looked to for sustenance in his early writings and whom he took as a model for his shorter fictions. His *New York Times* obituary, on July 3, 1961, quotes him as having said that such Kipling stories as "At the End of the Passage" and "The Strange Ride of Morrowbie Jukes" had been very influential in the forming of his style. What these stories have in common is their bleak premodern

outlook. In each tale Kipling creates paradigmatic situations which anticipate those in Hemingway's "A Clean, Well-Lighted Place" and "A Natural
History of the Dead," to say nothing of Kafka's "In the Penal Colony" and
Conrad's *Heart of Darkness*. In "The Strange Ride," for instance, the setting
is a leper colony in which, after a feverish midnight ride and a sudden tumble
down an unseen slope, an Anglo-Indian civil engineer seems to be entrapped
for life. The sand slope is unclimbable; the river semi-circling the colony is
made impassable by rifle fire and quicksand pockets. Jukes seems destined to
join the living dead, feeding on crows and sleeping in sandholes, until
fortuitously rescued by a faithful servant with a long rope. The situation in
"At the End of the Passage" is less allegorical, less Kafkan, but no less
paradigmatic. Four Anglo-Indian civil servants—a surveyor, a political ad-
visor, a doctor, and an engineer—meet each weekend to play whist at one of
their widely scattered stations. All under thirty, they have nonetheless come
to understand "the dread meaning of loneliness" which their isolated work
entails. Exposed to dust storms, unrelenting heat, frequent epidemics, political intrigue, and widespread suffering, they are often unable to sleep, and
they play whist and sing nostalgic hymns to keep from breaking down or
committing suicide. At the end, one of them dies with horror-struck eyes
wide open. The doctor who photographs that effect then tears up the film.[42]

Leprosy, suicide, insomnia, psychotic breakdown, and the appropriate
situations to convey their larger implications as modern fates—this seems to
be the form and substance which influenced the style of Hemingway's
shorter fictions. Kipling's penchant for such gloomy paradigms was itself
roused by a long romantic poem, "The City of Dreadful Night" (1874),
written by the doomstruck Victorian poet James Thomson, upon which
Kipling would draw for Dick Heldar's painting *Melancolia* as well as for his
own fulsome sketch of an insomniac's walk through a corpse-strewn, heat-
struck Indian metropolis, called "The City of Dreadful Night," wherein
thousands lie dead or prostrate under a pitiless moon. It seems only too
appropriate that Thomson was a dipsomaniac and insomniac, an army
teacher and sometime journalist who once reported on a civil war in Spain
for the *New York World*, as well as a misogynist whose first great youthful
love—much mourned and never replaced—died in her teens. The line from
this Victorian "laureate of pessimism," through the darker Kipling, to such
modern laureates of pessimism as T. S. Eliot and Ernest Hemingway, seems
founded in such experiential patterns. As end-products in that lugubrious
line, *The Waste Land* and "A Natural History of the Dead" were a long time
in the making.[43]

Chapter 5

Wuthering Heights

When you have been lucky in your life you find that just about the
time the best of the books run out (and I would rather read again for
the first time *Anna Karenina, Far Away and Long Ago, Buddenbrooks,
Wuthering Heights,* . . . and a few others than have an assured income
of 2 million dollars a year) you have a lot of damned fine things that
you can remember.

ERNEST HEMINGWAY,

Esquire, February 1935

In 1949, two years before her death, Grace Hall Hemingway had sent to her
son Ernest—then fifty years old—the five "baby" books she had compiled
during his first eighteen years. The last of these books contains a letter Ernest
had left for her shortly after his sixteenth birthday. He had shot a blue heron
in violation of the game laws; the game warden's son had discovered the bird
in Ernest's boat, and when the warden himself came after Ernest, he had fled
first to family friends in Horton Bay, then to his Uncle George's summer
home in Ironton. In the letter Ernest is very much his mother's son: he tells
her how he had stolen back to the family farm at night to kill a chicken and
pick some beans and dig some potatoes for her, assures her that the farm will
be all right, and asks how long he should continue to hide at Uncle
George's.[1]

The game warden episode in Hemingway's adolescence had a curious resonance for him. He told several embellished versions of it to friends over the years, and his sisters Marcelline and Sunny, his brother Leicester, and his fourth wife, Mary, have since provided four different versions of it in their books.[2] In January 1952 Hemingway began to write his own fictional version of the episode. He worked on it sporadically until 1958, then set it aside to complete his novel about androgynous couples in France in the 1920s, *The Garden of Eden*. "The Last Good Country" (1973), as the unfinished novella is now called, is also about an androgynous couple, a brother and sister, who like Hansel and Gretel run off to the woods together when the brother—Nick Adams—is pursued by game wardens.[3]

The story of their flight is an odd mixture of western melodrama and childhood fable. Some critics call it puerile and sentimental, but even in its flawed and unfinished state, it may be the most genuinely tender and personally revealing story Ernest ever wrote. Nick Adams is a protective and caring brother; his sister Littless is similarly caring, and the intimacy between them is freshly rendered. The two siblings characterize themselves as "criminals" who love each other and do not love "the others" in their family (57–58); they are "different from the others" in that they take risks and get into trouble (99); they have a capacity for what their friend Mr. Packard calls "original sin" (84)—doing things worth repenting and therefore having to cope with consequences; and as they flee through the northern Michigan woods, they cope rather well, as did Hemingway's pioneer ancestors. They are frontier throwbacks, then, and the bond between them—the wellspring of childhood affections—flows fresh and clear like the roadside spring they sit by as the story opens and the similar spring they later camp by in the forest.

On the second afternoon of their encampment, at the point where the long manuscript breaks off, Nick agrees to read to his sister from one of the three British novels she has brought along in her pack, *Kidnapped, Lorna Doone*, and *Wuthering Heights*. He has already told her that *Lorna Doone* and *Wuthering Heights* are "too old" for her (67), but since he has just chosen to read *Wuthering Heights* to himself, he agrees now that it is "not too old to read out loud" (114). Whether read aloud or silently, *Wuthering Heights* is an appropriate choice for this fable of adolescent flight into "the last good country," the disappearing northern wilderness, and of early rebellion against the binding, "civilizing" ties of the world left behind. It seems even more appropriate, however, for the "iceberg" world from which this story rises, in which Oak Park and northern Michigan translate rather obviously into the opposing grounds of Emily Brontë's famous Victorian novel— sedate Thrushcross Grange and the wild moors and craggy heights beyond.

OAK PARK AS THRUSHCROSS GRANGE

When Ernest received his baby books back in 1949, he had read them with some absorption and sent a rare appreciative letter to his mother. Apparently the appreciation cost him some effort since he also included in the letter an acerbic paragraph threatening to cut off his contribution to her support if *McCall's* magazine published a proposed interview with her about his childhood.[4] As the tension between those opposing sentiments suggests, the question of preserving his privileged access to his own childhood was beginning to cause him acute discomfort. He was willing to make his own disclosures, and to risk his own embarrassments, with Malcolm Cowley in *Life* magazine (January 10, 1949) and Lillian Ross in the *New Yorker* (May 13, 1950); but these professional journalists were his friends and gave him at least the illusion of control over the making of his own public mythology. To allow Grace's views to become public would not only be more embarrassing; it would be like putting his life into her hands once more. By 1951, moreover, he was beginning to feel even more threatened by academic poachers on his early years, like Charles Fenton and Philip Young, who took his reporting stint in Kansas and his war wounds in Italy as fair game for scholarship.[5] It was like being dead before his time, or at the very least, deprived of his own past and of the imaginative resources stored there for his own future fictions. Thus in 1952, with his mother safely dead and *The Old Man and the Sea* behind him, he began to develop into fiction one of the last of those private resources, the blue heron story which his early letter to his mother had probably recalled.

In his own mind the story had grown to represent (among other themes) the first independent thrusts of boyhood, the very opposite of his devoted actions in the early letter. Nick Adams would never ask his mother for instructions, nor return at night to help her with provisions from the farm. In 1915, however, Ernest himself had good reasons to want to help his mother and to abide by her decisions. When not one but two game wardens came to the family cottage in search of him, Ernest was working on the family farm across the lake. When the men proceeded to question his mother about him, but without at first revealing their business, she had not only dressed them down for impudence, but had then driven them off (in Sunny's version with a shotgun!) and had sent two of the girls across the lake with explicit instructions for flight.[6] Her decisive actions and her obvious concern for his welfare could not have escaped him. She had stood by him in an emergency, and he was scared and grateful enough to pay his night-time tribute. In "The Last Good Country"—after some thirty-odd years of well-nurtured hostility—he would reverse that tribute and convert her courage, caring, and resourcefulness into their exact opposites. Thus, Nick Adams's mother proves completely helpless in facing the emergency: she allows the fictional game wardens to encamp in her cottage, retires with a sick headache, and leaves the details of flight and safety to her abandoned children. Nick and Littless then plan their escape in terms closer to the author's wishful thinking about his own lost boyhood opportunities.

Mrs. Adams's character conforms, of course, with her first appearance in the early tale "The Doctor and the Doctor's Wife" (1924). There too, in the same northern Michigan cottage, she rests in a room with drawn blinds while others are left to cope with harsh realities; but far from being helpless in her blind passivity, she unmans her cowardly husband by insisting on the validity of her benign Christian Science outlook over and against his medical and pragmatic views. The tale itself is now so ingrained in the early modern mythology of castrating wives and mothers—one thinks of Lawrence's Mrs. Morel, Thomas Wolfe's Eliza Gant, and James Thurber's cartoon harridans—that we scarcely think to question its likelihood. What stands out in the story is the clever juxtaposition of Mrs. Adams's Christian Science journals on her bedside table with her husband's medical journals, still unopened in their wrappers "on the floor by the bureau" in his separate bedroom. But how in fact did that juxtaposition—and that unlikely pairing of wholly contradictory outlooks—come about?

Though Grace Hall Hemingway became something of a mystic and a spiritualist in later life, she was not originally a Christian Scientist. She was raised as an Episcopalian and had become a Congregationalist by the time she married Clarence Hemingway. Clarence had been raised as a Congregationalist and continued to teach Sunday School classes in that church long after his marriage there. Grace directed the choirs. They shared between them that muscular Christian gentility then common in both England and America. It was an outlook that could and did accommodate medical and natural science, and that postpioneer life in northern Michigan in which all the family engaged in summer months. There was no sharp discrepancy in their beliefs; both parents were mainstream Protestants, active churchgoers, and pious disciplinarians at home. As we have seen, moreover, Grace had actually helped to support the family while her husband built his early medical practice, and in 1908 she had even covered his apparent fear of a nervous breakdown by treating him (ostensibly) to a four-month refresher course in obstetrics at a New York hospital.[7]

The idea of opposing Christian Science to medicine must have come, then, from Hadley Richardson's tales about her mother's interest in theoso-

13. Abba Ernest Hall, Grace Hall Hemingway, and Marcelline
on the Oak Park Lawn

phy and mental science, which had led to experiments with ouija boards, automatic writing, and seances conducted in darkened rooms.[8] Because of a back injury Hadley had sustained in a childhood fall, her mother had also treated her as an invalid and had forced on her a sheltered life. The atmosphere of the home was high-minded, serious, and gloomy, in keeping with her mother's odd religious interests. Her father was by contrast a gentle, ineffectual man who had entered the pharmaceutical house founded by his own more forceful father, had eventually failed badly, and had committed what Ernest later saw as a cowardly act of suicide when Hadley was twelve. The opposition between mental science and pharmaceuticals, dominant wife and cowardly husband, must have reminded Ernest of his own parental constellation. Indeed, these similar constellations seem to have brought Ernest and Hadley closer together in their early courtship, as when the sheltered Hadley aptly exclaimed, "The world's a jail and we're going to break it together."[9] It seems evident—if "the world" refers to early environs—that they saw themselves as spiritual inmates of parental jails from which, with luck and Hadley's nest egg, they might soon escape. Ernest listened to her stories, fled with her to Paris, and there infused his characters

129

Dr. and Mrs. Adams with Richardsonian as well as Hall and Hemingway traits. When his own father later committed suicide, it simply confirmed the wisdom of that fictive fusion.

The step from darkened seances to darkened bedrooms was an easy one, since Grace Hall Hemingway had weak, overly sensitive eyes, damaged by scarlet fever in childhood, and was afraid that too much light would hurt them. As Marcelline reports, "She was often bothered with headaches because of bright lights" during her early musical career and had given up grand opera because of that reaction.[10] It seems reasonable to suppose, then, that she would often retire to her room to rest her eyes or to recuperate from light-induced headaches while the children were growing up; and perhaps also she suffered from time to time, like other women, from menstrual headaches. Whether her two sons, Ernest and Leicester, have deliberately misconstrued such problems to settle scores with her is hard to determine. Leicester confidently asserts, in his biography, that his mother found it so hard to handle six children that she would rush to her room, draw the shades, and declare that she had a sick headache "whenever there was a serious emotional crisis."[11] Ernest too, in his stories, invents a devastating mother who uses dark religious meditations and psychosomatic headaches as domineering or evasive ploys. It is, of course, quite possible that Grace Hemingway did behave this way, and that only her two sons—who had never suffered from bright lights, nor menstruated, nor tried to raise six children—saw her truly. But two of her daughters, Marcelline and Madelaine, fail to recall or invent such tales in their biographies. Indeed, by their accounts—which are by no means uncritical—Grace Hemingway was by and large an energetic, outgoing, cheerful woman with a keen eye for human foibles. Her religious outlook—which by any account was often cloying and unrealistic—was apparently also buoyant, elastic, and sustaining, and did not altogether blind her to life's many difficulties. Indeed, her inveterate optimism comes through as neither more nor less a shield against such difficulties than her son's inveterate pessimism. We can understand, however, how his early need to break with such religious optimism—and to arrive at his own new sense of things—might lead him to create a reductive version of his mother's outlook and to pare his father down to those neglected medical journals.

Something of that struggle between old and new perspectives seems to have governed also his reductive approach to other parental traits. At the end of "The Doctor and the Doctor's Wife," for instance, young Nick chooses to go off into the woods with his father rather than return at her request to his mother's darkened room. But meanwhile, Nick has been sitting in those woods "with his back against a tree, reading"—a privileged activity which links him oddly with his resting mother. Perhaps that is why his father now pockets the book for him as they go off together to one of the last male preserves. This casual pocketing of the world of art, music, and literature—the world, that is, which Grace Hemingway had opened to all her children, back in Oak Park, but which Mrs. Adams has reduced to Christian Science—is instructive. The books which Littless brings with her to "the last good country" are part of a late attempt to do more justice to that heritage, and may help to open up the problem.

Every summer (as noted earlier) the Hemingway family borrowed from thirty to forty books from the Oak Park Public Library to take with them to northern Michigan. Because we never see the Adams family except in northern Michigan in summer months, we cannot say that they did likewise; we don't know how or where they live at other times. But in this late, unfinished novella, the children are nonetheless drawn as literary and cultural travelers as well as frontier throwbacks. As they move through the vaulted aisles of an ancient virgin forest, for instance, Littless is so impressed by the religious atmosphere that she asks her brother if they "can go to Europe some time and see cathedrals" (75). When Nick says they will go there once he gets past this trouble and learns to make some money, they begin to discuss his future career as a writer and the present reception of his early stories by his mother and his friends. In one of her more fanciful moments, moreover, Littless tells Nick that she had learned from a Bible story how she might drive spikes through the heads of the game warden's son and the two game wardens "while they slept" (98–99). And, as already indicated, Nick later agrees to read from *Wuthering Heights* to his sister as the manuscript breaks off. Their flight to the woods can be seen, then, as a quest for that "ideal blend of wilderness and civilization" that Hemingway and Hadley had found at a pension in the mountains near Montreux in 1922, and that Hemingway had kept on seeking all his life.[12] It is not so much a rebellion from civilization as an attempt to fuse it with the wilderness.

Nevertheless, the denial of parental sources of culture—and particularly of maternal sources—is part of that attempt. When Littless asks about cathedrals, for instance, she invokes Wordsworthian views about the religious aura of vaulted forests and genteel views about touring Europe which originate with Grace Hemingway. For Grace was twice taken to Europe by her parents and had toured there a third time with her father in the summer preceding her marriage to Clarence Hemingway; it was her impression of European cathedrals—or her books about them—which probably registered them first in her children's minds. Whether she also visited the Lakes Region in England, where Wordsworth dwelled with his sister, or simply read about it in romantic literature, is uncertain; but as we have seen, she named and misspelled the family cottage on Walloon Lake in northern Michigan "Windemere" in 1900 because it reminded her of that romantic ground; and in 1905 she named the newly purchased farm across the lake "Longfield," after the pastoral retreat of the Halifax family in Dinah Mulock Craik's *John Halifax, Gentleman*. Her pastoral, Christian, and romantic view of nature would have been impressed upon her children's minds long before they read romantic literature in school and, like Littless, learned that solemn hemlock forests can make you "feel awfully religious" (74). "That's why they build cathedrals to be like this," says Nick to his awe-struck sister at this juncture; and then, explaining that he "has read about them" and "can imagine them," though he has never seen one, he calls the forest "the best [cathedral] we have around here" (75).

Allusions to forest cathedrals are rare in Hemingway's fiction. His view of nature is sometimes benignly universal, as in *The Old Man and the Sea*, which reaches for "mysterious" effects; but generally nature remains a secular if much-prized refuge from wasteland society: it is "the good place," the last imaginative frontier, where men may still affirm health, beauty, order, and integrity as they test themselves against primitive conditions. In "The Last Good Country," however, a religious view of nature emerges as a kind of youthful prelude to such adult ideas. Nick and his sister have, as it were, a right to their religious feelings; they have earned them by striking out at night across hills and farms, on through the slashings of an old logging camp, to a smooth brown forest floor from which ancient hemlocks rise sixty feet high before branching. Here Nick confesses to Littless that he "always feels strange. Like the way I ought to feel in church"; and he urges her to enjoy rather than fear the solemn scene and the strange feelings it evokes. "This is good for you," he adds. "This is the way forests were in the olden days. This is about the last good country there is left" (74).

Nick's reaction to "the last good country" is like Robert Jordan's reaction, in *For Whom the Bell Tolls*, to the two headquarters in Madrid for volunteer brigades from abroad during the Spanish Civil War:

> At either of those places you felt that you were taking part in a crusade. That was the only word for it although it was a word that had been so worn and abused that it no longer gave its true meaning. You felt, in spite of all bureaucracy and inefficiency and party strife something that was like the feeling you expected to have and did not have when you made your first communion. It was a feeling of consecration to a duty toward all of the oppressed of the world which would be as

difficult and embarrassing to speak about as religious experience and yet it was authentic as the feeling you had when you heard Bach, or stood in Chartres Cathedral or the Cathedral at León and saw the light coming through the great windows; or when you saw Mantegna and Greco and Brueghel in the Prado.[13]

As with Nick Adams's church at home, crusader Jordan's first communion had failed to move him as expected. He finds substitutes for it now, however, in military dedication to the antifascist cause in Spain, in classical music and art, and in medieval cathedrals. These sources of "authentic" feeling are all familial in origin. They go back to ancestors from both sides of Hemingway's family who fought for freedom and against slavery in American wars, and to his mother's stress on music, art, and literature in the home, especially as they minister to religious ends. On the other hand, the source of Jordan's fear of worn and abused words is also familial. Hemingway had begun his literary life by resisting the religious rhetoric that dominated his household—the easy pieties and homilies for all occasions, and the unearned optimism (as he came to see it) from which they sprang. He knew from the drift of such rhetoric what church and communion were supposed to make him feel. He also knew—or soon discovered—how to find such feelings elsewhere. In art, music, and literature, and in the great forests, the great battlefields, and the great cathedrals served by them, he would find his equivalent feelings.

Like a good many sons, however, he would seldom recognize or acknowledge the parental basis for those equivalents. The source of the cathedral episode in "The Last Good Country" is a case in point. In 1927 his sister Madelaine "Sunny" Hemingway had written to ask if she might visit him and Hadley in Paris. She was unaware at the time that Ernest had just left Hadley and was about to marry Pauline Pfeiffer. But Ernest was touched by her request. In 1915, when the game warden episode occurred, Sunny had been his closest companion. She went with him on family errands and forest walks, on hiking and boating expeditions. She was with him in the boat when he shot the blue heron; she was with her mother when the game wardens appeared at the family cottage and her mother called for the shotgun. Feeling again the need for her support in 1927, Ernest immediately cabled to urge her to join him in Paris for a trip to Spain. When lack of funds and parental disapproval held her back, he was sorely disappointed. As Sunny then informed him, his cable itself had upset their parents: "Oh, Ernie, if you only had said 'Cathedrals' instead of 'Fiesta' it might have been better. They have a horror for Fiesta and Spain in general—ever since your book [*The Sun Also Rises*]. They can't believe that I would become anything

133

but a prostitute if I even visited such a place. They're afraid of all the drinking etc. Your book was too vivid on the life that is led. They never should have seen the cover even."[14]

As it turned out, Sunny would sail to France with Ernest and Pauline in 1929, a few months after their father's tragic suicide. Though Ernest would never quite assimilate that tragedy, he loved his father much and could forgive him many things. But his bitterness about his mother's disapproval of Sunny's trip, and its basis in her disapproval of his life and writing, stayed with him. In the 1950s he would draw upon these episodes from the 1920s for the forest conversations between Nick and Littless in 1915.

Thus, when Littless learns that seeing cathedrals in Europe will cost money and that Nick must learn how to make it by his writing, she asks a provocative question: "Couldn't you maybe make it if you wrote cheerfuller things?" "That isn't my opinion," she hastens to add. "Our mother said everything you write is morbid" (75). While Grace Hemingway *might* have said this about Ernest's juvenalia, she knew and he knew that it was often quite lighthearted; it seems more likely then that he has transposed her objections to his early *published* writings back into his hero's adolescent years. In a variant version of the unfinished novella's final page, for instance, Nick reminds Littless that Mr. Packard had liked his "story about the whore," which probably refers (anachronistically) to Nick's experience at seventeen in "The Light of the World" (1933). Packard's preference and his earthy tolerance suggest still another story, "Up in Michigan," in which Hemingway had borrowed the first names (but not the age and characters) of his prototypes for the Packards, Jim and Liz Dilworth of Horton Bay, for a seduction tale which horrified his parents when it appeared in *Three Stories and Ten Poems* (1923), but which pleased the Dilworths when they read it.[15] These later responses help to determine, I think, what Littless tells Nick in 1915—namely, that she and Mr. Packard "are the only ones who like what you write."

It was to the Dilworths' home at Horton Bay that Ernest had fled from the game wardens, following his mother's instructions. The Dilworths, who were old settlers in the region, had become close family friends of the Hemingways during their early summers there. Jim Dilworth ran the local blacksmith shop; his wife Liz managed a lakefront restaurant for which Ernest—like Nick Adams—may have provided trout caught in and out of season. All the Hemingway children called Liz Auntie Beth; and for Ernest at least Jim seemed like a prize Dutch uncle. In later years, accordingly, Ernest would be reminded of the Dilworths by the German Swiss family who ran the pension in the Swiss Alps which offered such an "ideal blend of wilderness and civilization"; and while travelling in the Spanish Pyrenees he would express his admiration for the Spanish people by calling them "good guys" like Jim Dilworth.[16]

In "The Last Good Country" the Packards seem to reflect these "ideal" Dilworth qualities. Mr. Packard is a seasoned pioneer who has owned saloons and farms and now owns the general store and the local hotel. He talks frankly with Nick, gives him good advice, helps him to escape, and stymies the game wardens when they appear in his store. Mrs. Packard, whom the Adams children call Aunt Halley, is a handsome, homespun woman who manages the hotel, smells wonderfully of the kitchen on baking day, and still prides herself on being "all the woman" her husband can handle—even after "change-of-life." She also loves culture in an earthy way, as her husband loves good whiskey (83); and the cheerful badinage between them seems designed to reflect a happier blend of culture with frontier earthiness than Nick's parents offer. "I wish Mrs. Packard was our mother," says Littless in a variant passage; and in the printed text Nick turns to Mr. Packard as a fatherly confessor—someone he need never lie to, someone (in an excised passage) who can advise him on those puzzling sexual matters which—in "Fathers and Sons" (1933)—his own father dismisses as "heinous crimes" (236–237).[17] The Packards are the "good frontier parents," then, who assist Nick and Littless in escaping the game wardens to "the last good country." They are versions of the parents Ernest would have liked for himself, in place of the strict, sober, and essentially suburban parents who actually raised him.

WINDEMERE AS WUTHERING HEIGHTS

When Mrs. Adams retires with a sick headache, in "The Last Good Country," she writes her husband a letter which the hired girl mails on the following day. This is the only reference (64) to Dr. Adams in the published manuscript. We are not given his present address; nor do we ever see the contents of the letter—though presumably it concerns Nick's troubles with the game wardens. In Leicester Hemingway's biography, however, we do see the game-warden letter written by Grace Hemingway to her husband, then tending his practice in Oak Park, with its very different account of the actual troubles. In it Grace tells her husband of the impudent interview and her strong reactions to it; she then adds an account of the wardens' previous visit to a neighbor's farm, and of their disappointment there on learning that Ernest was, after all, only a minor.[18] The letter is a characteristic report of a current emergency and, in effect, a request for aid and advice. She had preceded it with a special delivery letter after the wardens had left her doorstep, and had gone to the neighbors "to see how the land lay." On the basis of her reports, Clarence would soon write to Ernest, then at his Uncle George's farm, supporting the uncle's view that Ernest should turn himself in, confess to the shooting (if not the crime), and pay the fine for his offense. This Ernest did, without any apparent threat of reform school or prison for his punishment.

Grace's faithful account of the northern crisis and her reliance on her husband's assistance were typical of their relations in these years. She was always willing to take strong stands, but wanted his advice and support before taking them. If there was a rift between them as man and wife, as many argue, they were still a working team as parents. Perhaps the need to attend to his medical practice in Oak Park and Chicago was a marital as well as an economic strategy for Clarence. As of 1908 he had begun to spend less time at the summer cottage, where he presumably longed to be. Vacations can be arranged, however, even for busy doctors, and he had always gone north for the full summer in previous years. The decision to keep apart as much as possible, whether open or tacit, may well account for Dr. Adams's conspicuous absence in "The Last Good Country." There are oblique references to "fights" among "the others" in the family which reinforce this view. "Haven't we seen enough fights in families," says Littless to Nick when they begin to quarrel (70). Parents as well as siblings may be included in such remarks.

A less obvious explanation for Dr. Adams's absence may be his eventual suicide. In "Fathers and Sons," when Nick in his thirties drives through the Southwest with his son, he remembers that tragic event. In the 1950s, some thirty years after his own father's suicide in 1928, Hemingway may have felt unable to resurrect him as a character. It seems interesting, in this light, that the three novels Littless brings with her to the forest all begin with a father's death and the abrupt launching into life of a "son" who must reclaim or establish his missing patrimony. In Stevenson's *Kidnapped* David Balfour is instructed to seek out a distant uncle when his father dies; his adventures thereafter—once he is kidnapped by his uncle's henchmen—include a long "flight through the heather" with his Jacobite friend Alan Breck of the Stewart clan, a kind of political version of the forest flight of Nick and Littless. In Blackmore's *Lorna Doone* the young hero's father is slain by the Doone clan, aristocratic brigands who prey on local travellers and farmers. When the hero, young John Ridd, is taken from school, he first undergoes the obligatory schoolyard fight with an older student. Later he fishes his way up a forest stream and is revived by the captive heroine, Lorna Doone, when he collapses at the top of a water-slide inside the Doone Glen. He meets her secretly thereafter, whenever possible, and eventually speaks his love in terms which must have fascinated the young Hemingway: "Have I caught you, little fish? Or must all my life be spent in angling after you?"[19] The hero's sister Annie is, however, a close second to Lorna in his strong affections, and the bond between them seems more suitable to the book's allusive place in "The Last Good Country." The allusions are in any case much muted. When Nick tries to read *Lorna Doone* on his first forest morning, he feels that "it did not have magic any more" and "was a loss on this trip" (102).

Originally Littless had intended to bring with her "Lorna Doone and Swiss Family Robinson" (58), as if to emphasize the theme of family survival in the wilderness. But as her actual choices suggest, the problem for this escaping pair is how to survive without parental guidance. As we have seen, David Balfour and John Ridd have just lost their fathers and must face the world without them. In *Wuthering Heights* too, the father of the Earnshaws dies in the early pages, after bringing into their midst an unrefined orphan from Liverpool who soon becomes his favorite "son." Indeed, he is named "Heathcliff" after a previous son "who died in childhood," and some critics even see him as the father's bastard child.[20] He is in any case raised as one of the family before the father's death some six years later, and only afterwards shunted aside by the jealous older brother Hindley Earnshaw. By then he is well on his way to reclaiming his briefly endowed patrimony.

Meanwhile he has enjoyed with young Cathy Earnshaw an idyllic childhood companionship on the moors and fields outside the Earnshaw home. The odd thing about this companionship is that we almost never see them together on the moors. Our vivid impression of their childhood eden is conveyed obliquely, and by retrospection. Thus, when Cathy becomes ill in later years, after her attempt to placate Heathcliff and her husband Edgar Linton ends in a bitter brawl, she pauses in her mad reverie over a lapwing's feather from her pillow:

"Bonny bird; wheeling over our heads in the middle of the moor. It wanted to get to its nest, for the clouds touched the swells, and it felt rain coming. This feather was picked up from the heath, the bird was not shot; we saw its nest in the winter, full of little skeletons. Heathcliff set a trap over it, and the old ones dare not come. I made him promise he'd never shoot a lapwing after that, and he didn't. Yes, here are more! Did he shoot my lapwings, Nelly? Are they red, any of them? Let me look." (105)

Trapper Heathcliff, restrained from shooting lapwings by his tender-hearted foster sister, reminds us of poacher Nick Adams, killer of forbidden birds, beasts, and fishes in Hemingway's novella, and of Littless's determination to keep him from committing even more serious crimes. But there are few such recollected moments in *Wuthering Heights*. Our impression of vital childhood life on the moors comes, rather, from Cathy's sense of entrapment and loss during her married rages, as when she dreams of being home again and wishes she were a girl once more, "out of doors . . . half savage, and hardy, and free; and laughing at injuries, not maddening under them!" (107); or when the servant Nelly early tells us how Heathcliff and Cathy "promised fair to grow up rude as savages" under Hindley's neglect after his father dies, and how "one of their chief amusements was to run away to the moors in the morning and remain there all day" (46). The theme of childhood rebellion is also strong, and much is made of Cathy's bold, mischievous ways, even while her father lives. But in fact her idyllic life with Heathcliff is more largely a shared state of mind than a dramatic or descriptive presentation; and this seems to me precisely why it had such an impact on the young Hemingway. Like Nick Adams, who had grown too old at sixteen for the "magic" of mere adventure stories like *Kidnapped* and (with more fulsome complications) *Lorna Doone,* he was ready then for an intensely romantic distillation of his own childhood conflicts.

Catherine's famous declaration, "I *am* Heathcliff" (74), is the keynote here. When she is about to marry Edgar Linton, she explains to Nelly that in her soul and heart she is convinced she is wrong (71), for there Heathcliff resides: "He's more myself than I am. Whatever our souls are made of, his and mine are the same, and Linton's is as different as a moonbeam from lightning, or frost from fire" (72). Heathcliff, she continues, is "always in my mind—not as a pleasure, any more than I am always a pleasure to myself—but as my own being" (74). Heathcliff similarly sees her as his "existence" (133); asks angrily when she is dying, "Would *you* like to live with your soul in the grave?" (135); and cries out when she is dead: "I *cannot* live without my life! I *cannot* live without my soul!" (139). Nevertheless, he does live on, consumed by his twin desires for revenge against those who have kept him from Catherine and for reunion with her in death.

Their shared state of mind—founded in their childhood life on the moors, expressive of the wild spirit of Nature which governs the hardy Yorkshire character and makes it superior to the effete, "civilized" ways of the frame narrator, Mr. Lockwood of London, and more centrally, to the nervous, sickly, effeminate gentility of nearby Thrushcross Grange—is very much what the novel is about. Hemingway would find an analogy for it, during his courtship of Hadley Richardson, in Kipling's "Brushwood Boy," where the hero and heroine discover as young adults that they have traversed the same dream-landscape since childhood and have shared the same nocturnal adventures there.[21] But the internalized and obsessive kinship in *Wuthering Heights*, which Ernest had first read in adolescence, seems to have made the more lasting impression. In *A Farewell to Arms* he would borrow Catherine Earnshaw's Christian name, her pagan passion, and even her death in childbirth, for his British heroine, Catherine Barkley, and would invest his narrator, Lieutenant Henry, with a muted version of Heathcliff's need to rehearse and mourn his loss long after the heroine's death. Even more importantly, when Catherine Barkley tells Lieutenant Henry, "There isn't any me any more. I'm you" (115), and he later agrees "We're the same one" (299), we have a modern version of merged identity like that which Emily Brontë introduced in Victorian times; and when our modern Catherine further insists, "You're my religion. You're all I've got" (116), we have a modern instance of Cathy Earnshaw's sacrilegious preference for life on the moors with Heathcliff over life in heaven (72), and of the satanic Heathcliff's insistence on being buried beside her without religious rites (263). Hemingway's purported view of *A Farewell to Arms* as an "immoral" book[22] is probably founded in this antireligious notion, with its origins in the eleventh-century opposition between the chivalric "religion of love" and Christianity; and the illicit or common-law marriage between his unmarried pair follows the similarly illicit (if unconsummated) marriage between Catherine and Heathcliff in that tradition.

Similarly, the love affair between Robert Jordan and the Spanish girl Maria, in *For Whom the Bell Tolls*, is like that in Brontë's novel, not only in its assumption of fused identities ("I am thee" and "You are me," etc.), but also in its romantic mystique of the earth moving when the lovers copulate. Though at least one critic has tried to apply the term *agape* to such selfless fusions,[23] their grounding in the pagan religion of love, on the one hand, and the wild spirit of Nature, on the other, removes them from the Christian purview and suggests, rather, their romantic origin in Emily Brontë's novel. Even the curiously diffident, offstage, and largely unsensuous nature of sexual love in Hemingway's fiction seems to match well with the preadolescent origins of passion in *Wuthering Heights* and its unconsummated if charged development in young adulthood. The passionate fusions in Hemingway's novels are similarly asexual in tone and texture, for all the dangling lyric participles and virile references to *cojones* which accompany them.

Another point of correspondence is that of male orientation. Like Hemingway's high school correspondent, Emily Goetsmann, Emily Brontë seems to have been the kind of outdoor literary girl Hemingway secretly wanted for himself. Feminist critics have recently remarked on the androgynous outlook of Brontë's heroine—her childhood conversion of the outcast Heathcliff into the whip her father had promised her on going off to Liverpool but had lost while returning with his orphan surprise.[24] Cathy had asked for a whip because, though "hardly six years old . . . she could ride any horse in the stable" (38). Such tomboy propensities continue over the next six years, when she romps on the moors with urchin Heathcliff before being gentrified at Thrushcross Grange. In these several ways she sets an early precedent for Frances Hodgson Burnett's whip-wielding "lady of quality" some five decades ahead, who also moves from strenuous equestrian delights in childhood to the sadder strains of adult gentrification.[25]

Brontë's tomboy emerges, of course, as more imperiously male in her demands on life than Hemingway might have liked; and the young man with whom she identifies is—like Charlotte Brontë's Rochester—too much the Byronic hero-villain to match well with Hemingway's stoic sufferers. But looking at Cathy and Heathcliff as an impressionable youth, Hemingway seems to have found an early model for the kind of romantic rebellion he would later tone down with his own stoic modifications. For current feminist critics like Sandra Gilbert and Susan Gubar, Heathcliff is an androgynous extension of Cathy Earnshaw's being—a male completion who guarantees her wholeness and power in a world where women are otherwise kept subservient; and we can see in Heathcliff's later revenge against both Wuthering Heights and Thrushcross Grange the vengeful application of that unified power against the forces which have thwarted them both: the patriarchal crudeness of Hindley Earnshaw and the patriarchal gentility of Edgar Linton.[26] But for the young Ernest Hemingway Cathy must have appeared rather differently: as a strong-minded outdoor girl who admires a rough-hewn, virile outcast much like himself or like those imagined versions of himself who would populate his later fictions, minus the Byronic fireworks. And in fact, Heathcliff in his early years is more stoic sufferer than Byronic hero-villain. As we shall see, moreover, he is succeeded by a modified version of himself—Hareton Earnshaw—with whom Hemingway could more readily identify, even as the spirited and demanding Cathy is succeeded by a daughter who comes closer to the adoring outdoor literary girls whom Hemingway both admired and desired.

The sibling nature of the bond between Brontë's pair is also relevant here. In the 1950s Hemingway would model the flight of Nick and Littless, in "The Last Good Country," on that of Catherine Barkley and Lieutenant Henry in *A Farewell to Arms*. In rowing across Lake Maggiore to reach

Switzerland, deserter Henry and his common-law bride may be said to attempt the forbidden union which Brontë's foster siblings avoid—though death in childbirth is the common punishment for both forbidden unions. Ostensibly, Hemingway's literally adolescent rebels attempt no forbidden union; but they do consider themselves "criminals" in their flight, as did Catherine Barkley and Lieutenant Henry. Littless goes Catherine one better, moreover, by actually cutting her hair short to resemble her brother's, and not merely suggesting it. She also banters about whores and whiskey in ways suggestive of Catherine's probing interest in Henry's other women; and she even proposes to become Nick's common-law wife when they grow up, and to bear his children. As such playful testing of limits suggests, she is certainly old enough to hear him read aloud from *Wuthering Heights* as the manuscript breaks off.

Interestingly, *Wuthering Heights* too plays fast and loose with the incest question. Indeed, from a Freudian point of view, incest figures as the unstated basis for the frustration of romantic love between Heathcliff and Cathy, and for her marriage to another man. The successive marriages of Cathy's daughter to two first cousins continue this flirtation with nearly incestuous unions. And yet Brontë overrides such easy Freudian formulations by insisting on the wildly innocent nature of childhood bonding and by investing her passionate rebels with a kind of fierce asocial purity. They are, finally, uncontainable creatures, victims of a world which refuses their large demands for asocial and asexual recognition as one person.

Hemingway seems to have entered into that recognition at an early age. As the strong infantile bond with his mother and his older sister Marcelline relapsed, deteriorated, indeed, collapsed in gradual disillusionment, he took ease and comfort from the love of adoring younger sisters. This shifting of affections kept his tenderest feelings alive and fresh and may well be said to have kept him going through the rough romantic years ahead. His twinship in infancy with his older sister Marcelline was the bridge, I think, or the mode of transfer, from one bonding to the others. What Grace had first ordained Ernest would pursue for his own later advantage—and, as I shall be arguing shortly, for his own emotional health.

The sibling relationship in "The Last Good Country," to which he returned only towards the end of his life, seems to me the important literary and biographical clue to this transfer, especially as mediated through *Wuthering Heights*. As a young writer in Paris, Hemingway would begin to compose stories about an apparently sisterless Nick Adams who is forced to choose between his mother's falsely benign Christian Science outlook and his father's empirical views as a backwoods doctor and naturalist who loves to hunt and fish. He would also send Nick out on runaway expeditions, exposing him to backwoods and urban versions of the corruptions, fantasies, and grotesqueries of the boxing world. Finally he would take him though the First World War and its aftermath, returning him to the woods and streams of northern Michigan for recuperation, exhibiting also his uncertain stance between marriage and the life of men without women. All this is well in keeping with D. H. Lawrence's view of Nick Adams, in his early review of *In Our Time,* as "the remains of the lone trapper and cowboy."[27] Though from time to time Nick has a few male friends and at one point a girlfriend named Marjorie, he does grow up chiefly as a loner, a vestigial frontiersman, and continues in this role even in marriage. He also dreams, in one war story, about the rivers he has fished and remembers them more clearly than the girls he has known. After the war, moreover, he returns to those dreamed-about rivers to recover the health, order, and integrity they offer as internalized frontiers—states of mind and heart where the lonely trapper feels most at home.

It comes as something of a surprise, then, to learn that he shares those imaginative conditions with a sister in "The Last Good Country." The only references to a sister in previous tales had come in "Fathers and Sons," published in 1933, where Nick remembers how his eagle-eyed father could see his sister Dorothy on the dock across the lake, and recalls also his own youthful anger when his Indian friend Billy Gilby said that Gilby's half-brother Eddie would "come some night sleep in bed with you sister Dorothy" (239). Though Nick himself has been sleeping with their Indian sister, Trudy Gilby, Nick threatens to kill Eddie for wanting to return the compliment. As his intense reaction suggests, Dorothy may also be the "one person in his family that he liked the smell of, one sister. All the others he avoided all contact with" (243). Of course, we do not learn who "the others" are, nor why they offend his nasal sensitivity; nor do we learn how deeply he values this or any sister until "The Last Good Country," where, interestingly enough, he actually prefers Littless (in an excised passage) to the Indian girl Trudy, now pregnant by him.[28]

Whether Dorothy and Littless are the same sister is another puzzle. As in "Fathers and Sons," there are references here to "others" in the family (57, 70) and to "the other kids" who have gone to visit friends in Charlevoix (79). But since Nick and Littless "loved each other and . . . did not love the others" (57), we can assume that Littless is the "one person in his family" Nick likes the smell of back in "Fathers and Sons," and that may be Dorothy. But then again maybe not. The most frequently cited prototype for both Dorothy and Littless is Madelaine "Sunny" Hemingway, whom Ernest did in fact protect with some vehemence from amorous admirers and who was indeed his eleven-year-old companion and his favorite sister in his sixteenth year.[29] Yet at one time or another all his sisters were his favorites. In the light of his changing affections, our best bet is to consider Littless as an invention, as Ernest would have himself insisted. She is the essence of beloved sister-hood, a composite of all his favorites, and we need not dwell on her origins beyond noting that all his sisters appealed to Ernest's tender feelings at different times in his early years.[30]

The derivation of Littless's name from one of the cats Hemingway owned in Cuba in the 1950s helps to underscore the point. That feline female appears with a male cat named "Boy" in *Islands in the Stream,* and her catness may itself be the essence of early tenderness, as the name "Cat" for Catherine in *A Farewell to Arms,* or the story "Cat in the Rain," or the nickname "Feather Kitty" for Ernest's first wife Hadley, or the game of baby and mama kitty that Ernest loved to play with his mother in infancy, all suggest. In adolescence his sisters had come to represent such feline tender-ness in ways I shall presently develop, and sharing in their outlook was a crucial experience in the life at Walloon Lake. The lone trapper and cowboy was in fact extremely close to and fond of one or more of his sisters in these years, and therefore ready for the kind of sibling rebellion Emily Brontë champions in *Wuthering Heights.*

WUTHERING HEIGHTS AS ADOLESCENT REBELLION

In *The Female Imagination* Patricia Spacks argues that Catherine Earnshaw, in spite of her defeat and death, represents "some triumph of adolescent over adult standards, articulating a kind of social criticism." Defining Catherine and her imaginative extension, Heathcliff, as "transcendent narcissists," she claims that the novel's "emotional commitment" is not to maturity but to "the ghosts of those too bound in their narcissicism to grow beyond it." The adults in the novel—Nelly Dean, Lockwood, Joseph, the mature Hindley Earnshaw and his wife, and the mature Edgar Linton and his sister—lack the "grand passions" which characterize the protagonists and are in various ways faulted for their inadequate standards. The theme of "justification by feelings" which "permeates the lovers' statements about themselves and one another" is thus the measure of the book's power and of its troubling meaning.[31] What Faulkner might call the "significant defeat" of adolescent rebellion is the paradox the novel poses. Its appeal to another champion of significant defeat, Ernest Hemingway, may be found in that paradox: for Hemingway too was in many ways a transcendent narcissist who seems to have discovered, in the supposedly selfless union of Heathcliff and Catherine, a way of easing the tensions of his own adolescent drives. His tactic was to reverse the gender formula by converting his Catherines into imaginative extensions of his Heathcliffs—completions, as it were, of the male's female incompleteness. Thus, Catherine Barkley, Maria in *For Whom the Bell Tolls,* and Countess Renata in *Across the River and Into the Trees* are adoring, sisterly women whose devotion to their lovers curbs their selfishness and at the same time provides a selfless standard from which to judge the world's inadequacies; and Maria even *becomes* Robert Jordan's certified extension, his female completion, just before his death: "I go always with thee wherever thou goest," Jordan then tells her. "Whichever one there is, is both" (463). Interestingly, in *The Garden of Eden* manuscript (ca. 1946–58), where the androgynous nature of such selfless loves becomes explicit, Hemingway comes remarkably close to the Gilbert and Gubar version of the gender formula in *Wuthering Heights;* he creates two flamboyant heroines, Catherine Bourne and Barbara Sheldon, who are strikingly like Catherine Earnshaw Linton in their demonic suffering and frustrated creativity, but who destroy themselves (again like Catherine) when they attempt to convert their passive artist-husbands into male extensions of their aggressive female selves.

But if Hemingway's transcendent narcissists, whether male-oriented or female-oriented, are like Brontë's romantic lovers in their assorted self-completions, they are also like them in their defiance of the world's restrictions. More positively, they are like them in valiantly defending their loving selves against the world's apparent need to maim and limit the young, and ultimately to deprive them of their love.[32]

The critique in *Wuthering Heights* of this maiming process accounts for a large part of its appeal for the early Hemingway. The novel's surprising use of "coarse" language as an antidote to false pieties and gentilities is one example of that critique. In her preface to the second edition of her sister's novel (1850), Charlotte Brontë actually cites the problem of harsh language for the novel's early readers:

Men and women who, perhaps, naturally very calm, and with feelings moderate in degree, and little marked in kind, have been trained from their cradle to observe the utmost evenness of manner and guardedness of language, will hardly know what to make of the rough, strong utterance, the harshly manifested passions, the unbridled aversions, and headlong partialities of unlettered moorland hinds and rugged moorland squires, who have grown up untaught and unchecked, except by mentors as harsh as themselves. A large class of readers, likewise, will suffer greatly from the introduction into the pages of this work of words printed with all their letters, which it has become the custom to represent by the initial and final letter only—a blank line filling the interval. I may as well say at once that, for this circumstance, it is out of my power to apologize, deeming it, myself, a rational plan to write words at full length. The practice of hinting by single letters those expletives with which profane and violent persons are wont to garnish their discourse, strikes me as a proceeding which, however well meant, is weak and futile. I cannot tell what good it does—what feeling it spares—what horror it conceals.[33]

Charlotte Brontë's spirited defense of her sister's earthy language strikes a distinctly modern note. In the same year, in her "Biographical Notice of Ellis and Acton Bell," she also notes that the Brontë sisters had chosen "positively masculine" names "without at that time suspecting that our mode of writing and thinking was not what is called 'feminine'" (4). The assumption of male privileges as to coarse language by women writers "in our time" suggests one of the basic ways in which Emily Brontë prefigures current trends. That Ernest Hemingway should be among the first to follow her example (along with Marryat's) is not without its androgynous ironies, though his own recourse to filler words—for instance, "I obscenity in the milk of thy obscenity" in *For Whom the Bell Tolls*—involves an almost more diffident use of expletives than the one she challenges. But there can be no question of his adolescent delight in Emily Brontë's brave language. On the novel's opening page Mr. Lockwood records in euphemistic terms Heathcliff's implicit imprecation—"Go to the Deuce"—on inviting him to "walk in" to Wuthering Heights (13). In the third chapter he records, in Catherine's narrative, the pious Joseph's reference to "'owd Nick" (27) and the impious Heathcliff's "Oh, God confound you, Mr. Lockwood" (31) upon discovering Lockwood in Catherine's room; his "God! he's mad to speak so!" when Lockwood attempts to explain his conduct (32); and his employment of "an epithet as harmless as duck, or sheep, but generally represented by a dash" when addressing his daughter-in-law as "you worthless ——" (34). In chapter 6, moreover, after Nelly Dean takes up the narrative, the language issue is joined through Heathcliff's boyhood account of his fateful visit with Catherine to Thrushcross Grange and of the bulldog episode in which his curses become an early signal for the social rift ahead: "The devil had seized her ankle, Nelly; I heard his abominable snorting. She did not yell out—no! She would have scorned to do it, if she had been spitted on the horns of a mad cow. I did, though; I vociferated curses enough to annihilate any fiend in Christendom" (48).

Such language does not go unnoticed by the servant who in rescuing Catherine calls Heathcliff a "foul-mouthed thief" (48), nor by the roused parents of the Linton children, who call him "a gypsy . . . a little Lascar, or an American or Spanish castaway": "'A wicked boy, at all events,' remarked the old lady, 'and quite unfit for a decent house! Did you notice his language, Linton? I'm shocked that my children should have heard it'" (49).

Heathcliff—the "American or Spanish castaway"—is then thrust out by the servant while Catherine is taken inside, but he remains long enough to observe through the window how Catherine "was a young lady and they made a distinction between her treatment and mine" (50). As the future creator of another American "castaway," young Nick Adams, Hemingway must have been impressed by that distinction and its verbal basis. Given his own early responses to Oak Park pieties and gentilities, his sympathies with "the naughty, swearing boy," as the "old lady" later pointedly calls him (52), must have been unusually strong.

Although the gentrified Catherine who returns from Thrushcross Grange never wholly abandons her "unfeminine" outlook, neither she nor any other woman in the novel is given to profane language. That gift is bestowed by the female author only on her male characters. Thus, it is Hareton Earnshaw—Heathcliff's adopted "son" after Hindley dies, and the supposed object of his revenge on Hindley—who continues the language problem even unto the third generation. For Hareton too is a "naughty, swearing boy." Indeed, his "devil daddy" Heathcliff has won his regard by teaching him to swear at his real father, Hindley Earnshaw (95). Such training bears fruition when Catherine's daughter, Cathy Linton, strays at thirteen across the moors to Wuthering Heights, is finally apprehended by negligent Nelly, and then mistakes the degraded Hareton for a servant:

> "Now, get my horse," she said, addressing her unknown kinsman as she would one of the stable-boys at the Grange. "And you may come with me. I want to see where the goblin hunter rises in the marsh, and to hear about the *fairishes,* as you call them—but make haste! What's the matter? Get my horse, I say."
>
> "I'll see thee damned, before I be *thy* servant!" growled the lad.
>
> "You'll see me *what?*" asked Catherine in surprise.
>
> "Damned—thou saucy witch!" he replied.
>
> "There, Miss Cathy! you see you have got into pretty company," I interposed. "Nice words to be used to a young lady! Pray don't begin to dispute with him. Come, let us seek for Minny ourselves, and begone." (160)

A moment later Miss Cathy is even more shocked to learn from a house-keeper that Hareton is her cousin, though initially she had befriended him and made him her guide on the moors. Nelly's summary of the double insult is nicely focussed on the verbal basis for such reactions:

> I could gather . . . that her guide had been a favourite till she hurt his feelings by addressing him as a servant; and Heathcliff's house-keeper hurt hers by calling him her cousin.
>
> Then the language he had held to her rankled in her heart; she who was always "love," and "darling," and "queen," and "angel," with everybody at the Grange, to be insulted so shockingly by a stranger! She did not comprehend it; and hard work I had to obtain a promise that she would not lay the grievance before her father. (162)

Once Cathy agrees *not* to consult her father, and so expose *Nelly's* negligence, Nelly too calls her "a sweet little girl"—a telling distinction in this novel about tough little girls and boys who never quite grow up.

The emphasis on rough male language continues, in these later chapters, as when Heathcliff reclaims his effeminate son Linton and calls his mother "a wicked slut" for failing to waken his filial regard (169), or shouts "damn it" at Cathy when she tries to kiss him, a few years later, on learning he is her uncle (176). He then tells the degraded Hareton, whom he claims is "damnably" fond of him (178), not to "use any bad words" when showing Cathy and her other cousin, Linton, about the farm (177); but the bedevilled Hareton soon says "devil" (179), to the amusement of his gentrified peers, and will later tell Cathy to "go to hell" (235).

These "devils," "damns," "sluts," "hells," and "Gods" without the dashes seem mild enough today; but Emily Brontë is always careful to point up their significance as forbidden social and masculine terms which characterize her hardy Yorkshire types and set them off from the weak, effeminate gentry at Thrushcross Grange. Her masculine vocabulary for Wuthering Heights, reinforced in the opening pages by references to "silver jugs and tankards" and "villainous old guns" and pistols on the inner walls, and by the violent feelings and actions of all who live there, must have rung freshly enough on Ernest Hemingway's youthful ears. Here was a male-minded woman writer whom he could admire and desire and even emulate.

Of course, the language of "profane and violent persons" in this novel is not always profane; more often it is merely violent, or better still, constructed so as to praise whatever is strong and masculine, and so capable of violence, and to condemn whatever is weak or effeminate, and in that sense

feminine. This juxtaposition of "manly" against "womanly" traits and virtues occurs with surprising frequency, and with obvious appeal for the early
Hemingway. When the gentrified Catherine returns from Thrushcross
Grange, for example, and laughs at Heathcliff's grimy clothes and unwashed
hands and face (51–52), a rift develops between them which is never wholly
mended. Servant Nelly Dean then becomes sorry for Heathcliff and urges
him to let her clean and dress him smartly. When he finally agrees, she makes
the first of many telling contrasts: "I'll steal time to arrange you so that
Edgar Linton shall look quite a doll beside you: and that he does. You are
younger, and yet, I'll be bound, you are taller and twice as broad across the
shoulders—you could knock him down in a twinkling. Don't you feel that
you could?" (54).

The contrast between the "doll" Edgar Linton and the already manly
Heathcliff is one Catherine herself soon takes up. Thus, when Edgar inadvertently remarks of Heathcliff's newly "elegant locks," that they look like
"a colt's mane over his eyes" (55), Heathcliff throws a tureen of hot ap-
plesauce into his face, and Edgar begins wailing. When his sister soon wails
too, and wants to go home, Catherine attacks them both: "'Well, don't cry!'
replied Catherine contemptuously. 'You're not killed. Don't make more
mischief—my brother is coming—be quiet! Give over, Isabella! Has anybody hurt you?'" (56).

As her contempt suggests, Catherine has returned to attitudes shared
with Heathcliff when they first observed this wailing pair through the
windows of Thrushcross Grange and despised and "laughed at the petted
things" (48). From this point onward she will be torn between such attitudes and her newly acquired gentility. It is out of this self-division that she
aligns her soul and Heathcliff's with lightning and fire, and Edgar Linton's
with moonbeams and frost, or compares her love for Edgar with changing
foliage and her love for Heathcliff with "the eternal rocks beneath" (74)—
even as Nelly sees Heathcliff as "a bleak, hilly coal country" and Edgar as "a
beautiful fertile valley" (64). That Cathy sides with rock and coal and the
wilder elements becomes painfully evident when Heathcliff reenters her life,
a few years later, and she is again torn between him and the gentler Edgar.
Indeed, the full measure of her contempt flares out when Edgar breaks down
emotionally, in "mingled anguish and humiliation," because Catherine too
wants him to fight Heathcliff fairly, and refuses to let him call the servants for
assistance:

He leant on the back of a chair, and covered his face.

"Oh, heavens! In old days this would win you knighthood!" exclaimed Mrs. Linton. "We are vanquished! We are vanquished! Heath-cliff would as soon lift a finger at you as the king would march his army against a colony of mice. Cheer up, you shan't be hurt! Your type is not a lamb, it's a sucking leveret." (99–100)

To this wifely insult Heathcliff adds his own full measure:

"I wish you joy of the milk-blooded coward, Cathy! . . . I compliment you on your taste: and that is the slavering, shivering thing you preferred to me! I would not strike him with my fist, but I'd kick him with my foot, and experience considerable satisfaction. Is he weeping, or is he going to faint for fear?" (100)

Under these provocations Edgar strikes Heathcliff a surprise blow on the throat "that would have levelled a slighter man" (100) and then leaves to fetch the servants. Ironically, this is the only actual blow in the battle between them that both Nelly and Catherine have oddly desired. In the larger battle for "justification by feelings," however, Heathcliff wins hands down. Thus, Heathcliff's fire is directed not only at Edgar's limited courage, but also at the quality and depth of his love:

"If he loved with all the powers of his puny being, he couldn't love as much in eighty years as I could in a day. And Catherine has a heart as deep as I have; the sea could be as readily contained in that horse-trough, as her whole affection be monopolized by him. Tush! He is scarcely a degree dearer to her than her dog or her horse. It is not in him to be loved like me: how can she love in him what he has not?" (126)

Similarly, he despises Edgar's sister Isabella for picturing in him "a hero of romance, and expecting unlimited indulgences from my chivalrous devotion" (126). The satire here of Isabella's "cherished" preconceptions in the face of Heathcliff's deliberate coldness—"She cannot accuse me of showing one bit of deceitful softness" (127)—reminds us of Robert Cohn's romanticism, in *The Sun Also Rises,* in the face of Brett Ashley's coolness, and helps us to place *Wuthering Heights* as one of the earliest reactions to the sentimental love tradition, then at its height. Again and again Heathcliff deprecates these and other sentimental virtues prized by the age, and with Brontë's apparent connivance. He is brutal to women, at one point boxing the second Catherine's ears repeatedly (215) and shoving Nelly aside (216), at other points shaking up Isabella (147), flinging a knife at her (150), and hanging her dog (110), and at different times imprisoning Cathy and Isabella and Nelly Dean at Wuthering Heights. He is brutal also to children, terrorizing his ailing, peevish son by Isabella, Linton Heathcliff, scorning his weakness with wry epithets like "puling chicken" (169) and "whey-faced whining wretch" (170), and so reinforcing the general view of Linton (Nelly's, Joseph's, Hareton's) as ill-spirited and effeminate, "more a lass than a lad" (163, 169, 179). In degrading Hareton, moreover, by raising him as a caricature of his own youthful persecuted self, he invokes what seems to be his governing principle: "I've taught him to scorn everything extra-animal as silly and weak" (178). It is this principle, certainly, which governs his scorn of Edgar Linton's "paternal" virtues—carefulness and kindness (219)—or of that *duty* and *humanity* and *pity* and *charity* with which Edgar tends his ailing wife, imagining "he can restore her to vigour in the soil of his shallow cares" (129).

That Heathcliff lacks what others call "common humanity" might seem to damn him in our eyes, and there are indeed frequent invocations of his "demonic" or "monstrous" or "infernal" nature. But in fact the running contrast with Edgar Linton confirms the primary strength and value of Heathcliff's violent and destructive passions. When he asks Nelly Dean of Edgar Linton, "Can you compare my feelings respecting Catherine, to his?" (125), the novel's method of comparing characters by the force and kind of their feelings, or by the kinds of feelings on which sheer *being* is best sustained, is tellingly invoked. By such measurements all the adult characters, but especially Edgar Linton and his sister Isabella—except for her brief conversion to male vengefulness (143, 149) and to knives and pistols as the agents of male power (119)—are found wanting. Only those high-powered adolescents Heathcliff and Catherine measure up, because only they are true to the range, depth, and intensity of their emotions. It is on these grounds that Hemingway and many other writers (e.g., Lawrence) are drawn to them; and here Heathcliff's supposed villainy, like Frank Mildmay's pugnacity in Marryat's sea novel, becomes part of his total appeal for "manly" readers like Ernest Hemingway.

But the novel's ongoing argument is scarcely confined to Heathcliff's long revenge. It extends, rather, to the next generation, and to the marriage of Catherine's daughter to Heathcliff's adopted "son" Hareton. It is here that the blend of "wilderness" and "civilization"—on which Hemingway must have focussed—finally occurs. Thus, Cathy Linton seems to inherit the best aspects of both her parents. As Nelly describes her in childhood, she has "the Earnshaws' handsome dark eyes" and "the Lintons' fair skin, and small features, and yellow curling hair." Her spirit is "high" but not "rough"; her heart is "sensitive and lively to excess in its affections" and with a "capacity for intense attachments" like her mother's; but she can also be soft, mild, gentle, pensive, like her father. Consequently, "her anger was never furious; her love never fierce; it was deep and tender" (155). To this happy combination Nelly adds "faults to foil her gifts": her propensity to sauciness and perversity, which she attributes to parental indulgence, but which we are meant to see, I think, as signs of her demonic heritage (155). Like her demonic mother, moreover, she is a wall-climbing, tree-climbing, straying girl whose idea of heaven consists of rocking in a rustling tree while the wind blows and the moors, woods, and waters "sparkle, and dance in a glorious jubilee"—in contrast with her genteel cousin Linton's idea of lying "half-alive" on the sunny heath "in an ecstasy of peace" (198–99).

Similarly, the inarticulate and supposedly "dumb ox" Hareton is seen by Heathcliff and others as a healthy, handsome, outdoor lad, in sharp contrast with the ailing Linton, and therefore as a more likely subject for future transformation. In this light, his schooling in animality by his "devil daddy" seems like the best possible preparation for his future schooling by his "genteel" cousin Cathy. And indeed, the enmity between Hareton and Cathy is quickly dissolved over the pages of the books she gives him (249); they become close allies, and his features brighten visibly as his mind and heart respond to her tutelage (254). Nelly sees them as *her* children now (254), and when Heathcliff finds them chatting by the fire, he suddenly sees himself and Catherine as young allies and recalls (through Hareton) his youthful pride, happiness, and anguish (255). It is at this point that he forgoes further revenge and wills to die, as if recognizing the completion of his thwarted dream in these newly allied descendants of warring households.

The importance of reading for this new alliance cannot be overemphasized. When Mr. Lockwood first decides to leave the Grange, he visits the Heights and witnesses a quarrel between Cathy and Hareton over the books which Heathcliff has forbidden her, and which Hareton has in fact stolen from her in an attempt to reach her by learning how to read. When Cathy continues to mock his clumsy attempts at self-education, he hurls the books upon the fire (239). When Lockwood returns to the Heights some months later, however, he sees Cathy teaching a transformed Hareton how to read, dealing him playful slaps and kisses as alternate punishments and rewards (243). When Cathy and Hareton leave for a stroll on the moors, Lockwood learns from Nelly Dean the tale of Heathcliff's last days, and of the reconciliation between Cathy and Hareton which broke his desire for revenge. The tale takes some twenty pages in the telling (245–65), and only when it is ended do these newly betrothed lovers return from their stroll. Lockwood's response to their return is interesting: " '*They* are afraid of nothing,' I grumbled, watching them approach through the window. 'Together they would brave Satan and all his legions'" (265–66). He is referring to Nelly's closing remarks about legends of ghosts walking the moors after Heathcliff's death, and about the proposed shift from the possibly haunted Heights to the Grange; but readers of Hemingway biographies will catch also the resonant similarity to his own infant response, *"fraid a nothing,"* when asked by adults "What is he afraid of?"[34] We may legitimately ask, ourselves, how much weight these dauntless lovers had for him in the face of those wilder ones whose "unquiet slumbers" are pondered in the final lines (266). Certainly the idyllic alpine retreat of the lovers in *A Farewell to Arms* and the idyllic forest camp of the siblings in "The Last Good Country" come closer to what Cathy and Hareton enjoy than to the haunted, stormy world of Heathcliff and his spectral bride; and the same may be said of the union of Marita and David Bourne at the end of *The Garden of Eden* manuscript, as compared with the earlier destructive union of David with his own mad Catherine Bourne.

One last word on the satire of religious severity as it affects these bookish outdoor lovers. The satire begins with Lockwood's early discovery of Catherine's diary account of a three-hour Sunday sermon, some time after her father's death, and of Heathcliff and Cathy hurling religious pamphlets into the fire on being discovered playing rather than praying by the pious Joseph (26–27). Lockwood turns next to another religious pamphlet, "Seventy Times Seven, and the First of the Seventy-First," and then dreams, not unnaturally, of becoming himself an antireligious rebel like Heathcliff and Catherine (28–29). Joseph's religious zealotry, which the pamphlets underscore, punctuates most of the narrations that follow, and is last observed (in present narrative time) when he condemns Cathy for bewitching Hareton as the lovers leave for their "framing" stroll on the moors (243; see also 249, 251–52). His opposition of the Bible to the kind of "satanic" reading which unites these moor-rambling lovers would not have been lost on the early Hemingway, for whom his parents' Christian gentility had come to represent arbitrary discipline, outmoded restrictions (as against dancing, gambling, smoking, swearing, and drinking), and those cheerful pieties, homilies, and proprieties against which he would forge his own blunt style. Though the family library and his mother's incisive letters played an obvious part in that literary rebellion, he would attribute it himself in later years to his two "real friends" at Oak Park High School, teachers Fanny Biggs and Margaret Dixon, who first encouraged his writing and engaged him deeply with English literature.[35] It was here that his own Hareton-like conversion to a "manly" role in the world of letters probably began.

SISTERLY LOVE

On June 2, 1950, Ernest Hemingway wrote what seems to have been an unsent letter to Arthur Mizener, then teaching at Carleton College. The letter was one of a series in which Hemingway offered Mizener advice about his work in progress, a biography of Scott Fitzgerald, and threw in occasional anecdotes and judgments about Scott and his writing. One of his running themes was how wrong Edmund Wilson and Maxwell Geismar were about Fitzgerald, and also about himself. Wilson's "hidden wound" theory, in *The Wound and the Bow*, was particularly gravelling, and in this letter he offers a counterargument which begins with the beneficent effects of sisterly (as opposed to motherly) love:

> My sister Ura went to your college and now lives in Hawaia (misspelled) and an irrevelant fact. When I came home after the first war she always used to wait, sleeping, on the stairway of the third floor stair-case to my room. She wanted to wake when I came in because she had been told it was bad for a man to drink alone. She would drink something light with me until I went to sleep and then she would sleep with me so I would not be lonely in the night. We always slept with the light on except she would sometimes turn it off if she saw I was asleep and stay awake and turn it on if she saw I was waking. At that time I could not sleep without a light on and this shows you how much Wilson and Geismar know and what a fine girl you had at your college.
>
> Hell this love or hate your mother thing is too simple. What if you've been in love with two of your sisters, five dogs, maybe twenty cats, 4 different airplanes, two cities and five towns, three continents, one boat, the oceans, and Christ count them, womens. So it was your mother. That's much too simple any way one plays it. Also I love my children, writing, reading, pictures, shooting, fishing, ski-ing, and various people in Venice. Also love my wife Mary. Also love the 4th Inf. Div. and the 22nd Regt. of Inf.
>
> Get off your couch Hemingstein and give the professor a rest. I also love Fats Waller who is dead and the Normandie which was burned by idiocy and sold for scrap. Also love Hong Kong and the New Territories. Two girls in Venice and one in Paris. Love them true and good.[36]

Having warmed up on his many loves, Hemingway proceeds to his many visible (as opposed to hidden) wounds ("22") and his many killings ("122 sures"). Then he tells about the one killing which made him feel the worst, a young boy on a bicycle dressed in a German soldier's uniform. After which he concludes: "No; I think how we are is how the world has been and these psycho-analitic versions or interpretations are far from accurate." Turning next to his own biographical fate, he further concludes: "No. It will get all fucked up like always and I figure to have all my papers and uncompleted Mss. burned when I am buried." On August 29, 1950, he adds a postscript: "Don't know why I never sent this. Probably thought it was too violent."[37]

Of course, none of his letters and manuscripts were burned. He meant them to be pondered in spite of many protests to the contrary. And indeed, the implicit argument in this convoluted letter seems worth pondering. He seems to be saying not simply that his loves were multiple and various, and not reducible to the love-hate relationship with his mother and such hidden wounds as that might reveal; but also that sisterly love had proved more supportive to him, and more therapeutic, than motherly love, and that he valued it more highly. His younger sister Ura, or Ursula, born in 1902, would have been about seventeen when he came home from the war. In one way he oversimplifies psychoanalytic theory himself by trying to present her comforting actions as lovingly innocent. We could easily take this sleeping arrangement with his sister as a neurotic attachment, replacing an original fixation with his mother. But his covering statement—"That's much too simple any way one plays it"—should be heeded. Our Freudian preconceptions do rule out the possible beneficence of love, along with its variety and multiplicity, in favor of its possibly neurotic origins. The sisterly love Hemingway admires here does seem more like an innocent adolescent "crush" than an incestuous fixation; and in "The Last Good Country" there is every evidence that Hemingway—like Emily Brontë before him—was trying to secure its legitimacy.

I shall leave the full proof of this for a later chapter. For the moment I want to concentrate on the first night Nick and his sister spend together in their forest camp, and on its connections with the Mizener letter. Here is the relevant passage:

> In the night he was cold and he spread his Mackinaw coat over his sister and rolled his back over closer to her so that there was more of his side of the blanket under him. He felt for the gun and tucked it under his leg again. The air was cold and sharp to breathe and he smelled the cut hemlock and balsam boughs. He had not realized how tired he was until the cold had waked him. Now he lay comfortable again feeling the warmth of his sister's body against his back and he thought, I must take good care of her and keep her happy and get her back safely. He listened to her breathing and to the quiet of the night and then he was asleep again.

It was just light enough to see the far hills beyond the swamp when he woke. He lay quietly and stretched the stiffness from his body. Then he sat up and put on his moccasins. He watched his sister sleeping with the collar of the warm Mackinaw coat under her chin and her high cheekbones and brown freckled skin light rose under the brown, her chopped-off hair showing the beautiful line of her head and emphasizing her straight nose and her close-set ears. He wished he could draw her face and he watched the way her long lashes lay on her cheeks.

She looks like a small wild animal, he thought, and she sleeps like one. How would you say her head looks, he thought. I guess the nearest is that it looks as though someone had cut her hair off on a wooden block with an ax. It has a sort of carved look.

He loved his sister very much and she loved him too much. But, he thought, I guess those things straighten out. At least I hope so. (101)

The sibling roles in the Mizener letter are reversed in this passage. The wakeful Nick pledges himself to "take care of" his sister. He contemplates her beauty as she sleeps with the visual appreciation of a verbal artist. He pauses over the question of "too much" sibling love—*hers* rather than his—then leaves it wisely for the future. In the paragraphs that follow he worries about feeding her better, decides not to wake her up, again notes her facial beauty as she smiles in her sleep, and quietly prepares breakfast.

One reason for this role reversal is the fictional sister's age: like Sunny at the time of the blue heron incident, she is eleven years old. Her chopped hair reminds us also of Marcelline's fate at the age of six, and therefore of the combined nature of this loving portrait. In this light her "small wild animal" gameness for this venture, now in repose, fits all the Hemingway sisters: Marcelline, who once ran away to Chicago; Ursula, who, according to Constance Montgomery, once ran off to Petoskey to be with Ernie; Sunny, who hiked with him in the northern woods; and even baby Carol, who was probably the second of the two loved sisters in the Mizener letter, and whom Ernest considered "the most beautiful" until she eloped in 1933 against his wishes. Still, the features of the sleeping sister probably belong to Ursula, whom Ernest thought of as his "lovely sister" as late as 1949, and whose wakeful concern in the Mizener letter Nick now emulates.[38] As with Ernest's mother, the reversal of "how it was" allows him to reconstruct the scene to Nick's advantage and to emphasize his protective responsibility as an older brother. In this mythic flight of runaway siblings Nick is to retain his "natural" superiority in a situation which allows *him* to protect, nurture, and appreciate his vulnerable partner. He will always be the older, wiser brother; and if he benefits from the check to his vengeful and destructive passions which Littless—the littlest sister—provides, and from her companionship in his otherwise lonely exile, his dominant position remains intact. Here is the clue to the recurring problem of sisterly or adoring, selfless love in Hemingway's fiction—and, indeed, his life. We shall see later what sad things happen when, in *The Garden of Eden,* which he was then also writing, the hero gazes lovingly and aesthetically upon another sleeping Catherine, another "wild" girl whose androgynous actions truly threaten his hegemony.

What seems more important, at this juncture, is the genuine tenderness and loving care displayed here. There is nothing like it elsewhere in the whole Hemingway canon. As we shall see, even the concern for "too muchness" helps to place it as a healthy stage of emotional growth for Nick as well as for his sister. The "crush" is playfully and respectfully rendered; the adolescent love at stake is the kind that enables adult love to prosper. The return to it in fiction is an attempt—like Emily Brontë's—to discover what went wrong, why adolescent flight and rebellion ultimately failed, or why this second version of "the garden of eden"—beyond that of infancy with Marcelline and his mother—had to be abandoned. Among its several meanings, the theme of "original sin" in the tale is about that dilemma and its essentially innocent basis. Which means that—however long the repayment was in coming—the debt Ernest repays here to his several loving sisters was considerable. Fortunately for him and for us, at one time or another, he did love them all "very much."

Chapter 6

John Masefield

In March 1916, in the first of his two known letters to his high school literary correspondent, Emily Goetsmann, Hemingway had responded with delight to her remarks about the British poet, John Masefield: "Your friend Masefield is certainly great. As soon as I received your letter I went to the library and got 'The Story of a Round House.' . . . Read all the ones you recommended and at the same time got another volume—Sea Ballads, or some such name. Hope you read Stalky and Co. You'll like it."[1]

"Sea Ballads"—actually named *Salt-Water Ballads*—follows Marryat in dealing with deaths at sea, shipwrecks, battles, pirates, and drunken sailors. *The Story of a Round House* contains two long narrative poems—"Dauber" and "Biography"—and a selection of shorter poems. Among the latter are a number of poems—a ballad about "the old bold mate of Henry Morgan," a requiem for a dead knight, the famous "Sea Fever," and a few memorial poems for dead ladies—which must have impressed the young Hemingway.[2] Indeed, he even memorized one of the *carpe diem* poems, "Laugh and Be Merry" (266–67), for recitation at school in June 1917, possibly for its stirring references—at graduation time—to drinking wine in the face of life's brevity.[3] But it was the long poem "Dauber," from which the book's title "story" derives, that seems to have roused him most. "Dauber" is about a would-be artist who wants to paint the sea and the great clipper ships that sail there. When at almost twenty-two he enlists as lampman and painter on one such ship, he is "Bullied and damned" by his mates for his desire to paint and to know his subject "From the inside" (5). To the seamen he seems a "daubing, useless article" (9), "always late or lazing" (8) for the work that matters. Even the ship's boys play tricks on him and, in a device borrowed from Kipling, erase his "stinking" canvases (9) when he tries to hide them under the long boat on the deck (15–16). What seems most striking, however, is his desire to "win his mates' respect, / and thence, untainted, / Be ranked as man, however much he painted" (106–7). Thus he reasons:

> That was what going aloft meant, it would be
> A training in new vision, a revealing
> Of passionate men in battle with the sea
> High on an unseen stage shaking and reeling,
> And men through him would understand their feeling
> Their might, their misery, their tragic power,
> And all by suffering pain a little hour,
> High on the yard with them, feeling their pain,
> Battling with them; and it had not been done.
> He was a door to new worlds in the brain,
> A window opening letting in the sun,
> A voice saying, "Thus is bread fetched and ports won,
> And life lived out at sea where men exist
> Solely by man's strong brain and sturdy wrist."
> (108–9)

He decides accordingly to "endure it all, endure and learn" until he acquires "the power to show / All he had seen" and "the power to know" (110).

This manly artist's credo, as Masefield presents it, seems even more plausibly articulated than in Kipling's *The Light That Failed*. The new seaman and would-be painter must overcome his shipboard fears, for instance, if he is "To share man's tragic toil and paint it true" (110). He gets his chance when ordered aloft to pull in sails during a series of storms off Cape Horn. At which time

> Painting and art and England were old tales
> Told in some other life to that pale man
> Who struggled with white fear and gulped and ran.
> (120–21)

Once the long ordeal is over, however, he feels he has "had a revelation of the lies / Cloaking the truth men never choose to know." Having "beheld in suffering," he can "bear witness now and cleanse their eyes" (146). For he has "done with fear" now, "endured the worst," "got manhood at the testing place" (159, 160); and when a bosun voluntarily shows him how to tie a complicated knot, he feels "promoted into man" and able to "compass his life's scheme" (161).

The mate too confirms his Cape Horn wisdom:

"You've had your lesson: you're a sailor now.
You came on board a woman ready to faint.
All sorts of slush you'd learned, the Lord knows how.
Well, Cape Horn's sent you wisdom over the bow.
If you've got sense to take it. You're a sailor.
My God, before, you were a woman's tailor."
(166)

But the "dauber" is still a would-be artist, and in that conditional sense still "a woman's tailor." Unwilling to throw away his paints, as the mate wishes, he persists in his artistic dream until a new storm arises and he again goes aloft, this time slipping to a death mourned by all his shipmates. His last enigmatic words are "It will go on" (176), meaning presumably that other artists will learn such manly trades in order to bring them to life for us.

Meanwhile, he has been in this pursuit his mother's—not his father's—son. For the interesting tale he tells a shipmate, before his testing, is about his mother's desire to become a painter, back on the farm where he was raised, and how his father thwarted that desire and later tried to thwart him too.

"My mother came from under Meon Hill;
She died when I was only ten, poor woman!
I know my memory of her's living still,
And will, I hope, as long as I'm a human.
For no man had a mother like her, no man.
She wasn't like my father: rose and oak.
It wasn't marriage, but the Devil's joke."
(65–66)

Masefield's mother had died in 1885, when he was six and a half. One suspects that if Ernest Hemingway's mother had died when he was that age, he too might have fashioned such a tribute. In March 1916, some nine months after the blue heron episode, he was at any rate still sufficiently his mother's son to take the above passage in stride while calling Masefield "great." But since he was also aware by then of rifts in his parents' marriage, he would have been especially mindful of the line—"It wasn't marriage, but the Devil's joke."

Of course, the oppressor in Masefield's fictional marriage is the father, a farmer who clings to the land his forefathers have tilled before him and who

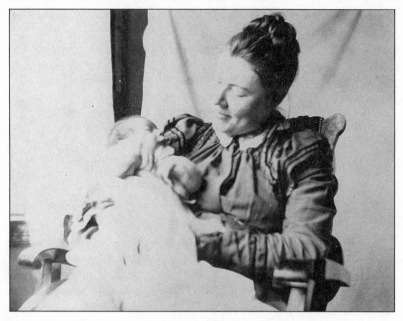

14. Mother and son; Grace Hall and Ernest Miller Hemingway, 1899

wants his only son to follow in that agricultural tradition. Hemingway's father had no such immediate heritage; but he was in fact a zealous amateur farmer in the summers at Longfield, the property across the lake from Windemere cottage that had been bought in 1905 (as I have argued) with Grace's patrimony; whereas Ernest was, like Masefield's protagonist, a reluctant worker on that farm. He too would have preferred not to learn that trade—"the farm to me / Was mire and hopeless work and misery. . . . The farm was prison" (68–69)—and to follow instead his "straying" thoughts (69). As Masefield's narrator puts it:

> "I could forget the farm by wandering out,
> Tracing the little brooks and trying to find
> A gravelly stretch with belly-rubbing trout. . . .
>
> That's what I loved, water, and time to read."
> (70–71)

So, instead of farming, the narrator follows his Hemingwayesque delight in books and trout streams. But eventually his desire "to be near water flowing" (72) earns his father's wrath—and leads to an important discovery. One day, when his father whips him for a building a small ship model, he climbs upstairs to recover in the "flat" (73), a dusty attic given over to the family cat and her recent brood of kittens—those familiar links (for Hemingway as for Masefield) with tender childhood feelings. Watching the kittens play about a hole between the beams in the attic floor, smiling at their games, he puts his hand into the hole and pulls up a leathery, spider-nested book:

> "It was my mother's sketch-book; hid, I fear
> Out of my father's sight: he couldn't bear
> For her to do a thing he couldn't share.

> "There were her drawings, done when she was a girl. . . .
> She'd leisure then for drawing, mother had.
> She hid them in the roof like something bad,
> Something she dare not show or felt a shame of,
> For fear of being chid or made a game of." (75)

Grace Hall Hemingway scarcely hid her artistic talent in this manner from her husband's chiding. But in subordinating her career in music to marriage she was responding to social pressures that put marriage and family before careers for women; and in this subordination her husband and her sons, Ernest and Leicester, certainly acceded—as to a great degree she did herself. We know, however, that Ernest would ignore her struggle and would reverse the domestic conflict found in Masefield's poem in a military tale, "Now I Lay Me" (1927). In this story, Hemingway's shell-shocked protagonist cites as his earliest memory "the attic in the house where I was born" and the items stored there, including (besides his parents' wedding cake) "the jars of snakes and other specimens that my father had collected as a boy and preserved in alcohol"; then, almost parenthetically, he notes that his mother had burned those specimens in the backyard when his grandfather died and the family moved to a new house. Her thoughtless villainy is further compounded by a similar memory of her burning his father's Indian relics, while he was away on a hunting trip, when cleaning out the basement of the new house.[4]

In his recent biography, Jeffrey Meyers contends that these memories are not autobiographical, as many critics believe, but invented, since Hemingway's father "retained his treasures until the end of his life."[5] Though Meyers gives no evidence for the latter claim, the Masefield precedent certainly supports it. It may be, of course, that Ernest was reminded of some such incidents while reading Masefield's poem, and stored them up for future use; but it seems more likely that he invented them while reversing

Masefield's remembered precedent in later years. In any case, he plainly sides with the fictional father in these domestic mishaps, in which the lost boyhood treasures suggest a lost manly calling.

One wonders, nonetheless, what Ernest thought, at almost seventeen, when presented with Masefield's story of the link in artistic talent of a mother who had hidden her creations for shame and of a son who had found them and in doing so had found himself.

> "That was a find for me, that was a treasure,
> I didn't heed my cart-whip weals a scrap.
> And most the valley pictures gave me pleasure,
> With fields like counties in a printed map,
> Or Bredon Hill in cloud wearing his cap. . . .
> And one of Bristol."
> (75–76)

As a yellow playbill in his mother's sketchbook attests, the boy's parents had gone to Bristol on their wedding day to see two plays (which may explain the attic wedding cake in "Now I Lay Me"). After noting that initial sharing and a sketch done "Before she stopped being Queen or father chid" (76), he then observes the dates pencilled on each picture, including that on the last unfinished sketch—March 1863—smeared by tears (77).

> "That was a holy afternoon to me,
> That book a sacred book, the flat a place
> Where I could meet my mother face to face."
> (77)

From then on the flat becomes his "secret room" or "lair" where he spends "many a golden time" learning to draw by sketching the valley below, visible through an attic peephole, on the blank pages of his mother's book (78). Then, as drawing becomes his "joy," he branches out to draw everything he sees and tries (in diction Ernest would later echo)

> "*To see the thing distinct and get it true,*
> *And catch the very motion,* as when grass
> Or corn is ruffled when the flurries pass."
> (78; my italics)

Indeed, he cares for nothing else, spends all his time and money on his attic passion, until his exasperated father delivers an ultimatum: "Either I took to farming, like his son, . . . / Or I must go" (78–79). As we shall see, the ultimatum is not unlike that which Hemingway received in the summer of 1920, first from his father, then from his mother; but Masefield treats his fictive situation with considerably more fairness and balance than his literary heir could muster then or afterwards. Thus, Masefield's narrator understands and appreciates his father's position. As his sister tells him, he is "breaking father's heart," helping to kill him, "giving him our mother over again": "It's wearing him to death, Joe, heart and brain. / You know what store he sets on leaving this / . . . to a son of his. / Yet you go painting all the day" (81).

On the other hand, he also knows that he loathes farming and feels unfit for it, and must therefore choose whether to "spoil [his] father's life or spoil [his] own" (82). He decides to accept his father's option and break away clean, then goes to live with a maternal uncle—who also lives in a dream of a dead woman he has loved (84–85)—and takes up house-painting for a living. Even then he envisions his father and sister sitting desolate, the farm run down and ready for auction, and his sister reprimanding him like a bitter ghost: "Joe, you have killed your father: there he lies. / You have done your work, you with our mother's ways" (87). One day, however, seeing a "skysail-yarded clipper" towed through the local sea-gates (87), he is inspired "to see the sea and ships and what they meant" (90), and soon enlists on another clipper as its "dauber." By following his "mother's ways" he may have killed his father; but he can at least pursue his own artistic dream.

Masefield's version of those disputed ways is somewhat fanciful. He had actually been raised in a middle-class household. His father was a solicitor—not a farmer—and though the father sometimes neglected his children, he had no objections when his wife sang songs and recited poetry to them, as she loved to do. She did not sing sea chanties, however, nor was Masefield himself especially drawn to the seafaring trade. In 1886, about a year after his mother's untimely death, his paternal grandfather also died and the family moved into his rambling townhouse. There the young boy had the run of his grandfather's ample library and could satisfy his growing love of literature. He began to retell to his younger brothers the adventure tales he had read and was soon writing poems himself about ponies and Red Indians. Then, in 1891, when Masefield was thirteen, his father also died and the six Masefield children were adopted by a childless couple, their paternal Uncle William and Aunt Kate, who considered the arts such a waste of time that they removed his grandfather's library.

Aunt Kate especially scorned his love of books and was determined that he should go to sea as a merchant mariner. At first that practical fate seemed harsh to the bookish Masefield; but his spirits rose when a kindly governess described her brother's happy lot as a cadet on the school ship *M.M.S.*

Conway, then permanently moored in Liverpool harbor. For the next two years Masefield went to school on that anchored vessel, then in April 1894 shipped out as an apprentice seaman on what proved to be his first and only voyage on a clipper ship. Though often seasick and once prostrated by heat, he ultimately performed well—particularly during the long Cape Horn ordeal—and may be said, like "Dauber," to have gained his manhood. Yet oddly, when his ship reached its destination in Chile, he soon fell victim to a combination of sunstroke and nervous breakdown and—after hospitalization in Valparaiso—was shipped home by steamer as a Distressed British Seaman. His early sailing career had lasted only thirteen weeks.[6]

One thinks, of course, of Ernest Hemingway's equally limited war service in Italy and how much he made of it. He had spent less than two weeks as a Red Cross canteen worker at the front when he was wounded by shell fragments and machine-gun fire and sent back to the American Red Cross Hospital in Milan. Out of that brief sequence came his great war novel, *A Farewell to Arms,* half a dozen war stories, and the background for *The Sun Also Rises* and other tales of postwar disillusionment. Masefield too would create sea ballads, verse narratives, stories, and novels out of his brief experience as a merchant seaman. He would later extend that experience in World War I, when—like Hemingway—he served as a British Red Cross orderly in France for a year, then transferred to the motorboat ambulance service during the disastrous campaign in the Dardanelles—out of which came his popular epic account of gallant defeat, *Gallipoli,* in 1916.[7] Hemingway too would extend his early range, notably as a war correspondent in the Balkans in the 1920s.

But whatever the extent of their experience, and however much they made of it, it seems evident that both would rather write than fight, and that at least one of them—Masefield—could imagine maternal sources for that happy choice. By contrast Hemingway would align himself with his inartistic father and with those "men without women" whom he most admired. Masefield's "Dauber" admires them too, but insists on the female origins of his desire to depict their lives. His ancestral muse, like Masefield's, is feminine; whereas Hemingway's is—not simply masculine—but oddly *sui generis*. Yet, still more oddly, it was Hemingway, not Masefield, whose talents derived from a mother steeped in all the arts—an extremely promising opera singer in her youth, a self-taught painter and popular lecturer in later years, a cogent correspondent at all times. Only that famous tag line, "grace under pressure," betrays suppressed awareness of how "manfully" she fought to keep her talents alive and functioning against social and familial odds her son would never face. What happened, we may well want to ask, to make him deny this maternal heritage, and to ignore or perhaps deliberately reverse this early revelation from Masefield: that even manly art may and perhaps *must* proceed from womanly ways?

OUR MOTHER'S WAYS

One thing that happened was a change for the better in literary taste. In 1923, when Yeats won the Nobel Prize for Literature, Hemingway would compare the Irish poet's "subtle genius" to "vintage champagne," whereas that of contenders like Robert W. Service, Bliss Carman, Alfred Noyes, and John Masefield was more like "coca-cola."[8] His own fondness for Coca-Cola would continue, nonetheless, albeit in a different generic form. As his Key West library listings attest, he would acquire four Masefield novels over the next two decades: *Sard Harker* (1924), *The Taking of the Gry* (1934), *Victorious Troy; or, The Hurrying Angel* (1935), and *Dead Ned: The Autobiography of a Corpse Who Recovered Life Within the Coast of Dead Ned and Came to What Fortune You Shall Hear* (1938).[9] The first two novels deal with mythical Latin American countries, after the manner of Conrad's *Nostromo,* and with British seamen caught in their political toils; the third novel is about one of the last clipper ships, *The Hurrying Angel,* and its rescue by an apprentice seaman when its drunken captain is disabled and all senior officers are lost during a cyclone; the last novel is about a doctor's apprentice falsely accused of murder, in eighteenth-century London, then revived from hanging by medical friends for a second chance at life. All four are melodramatic adventure tales that Hemingway must have read as a stay against insomnia; but at least three contain suggestive minor precedents for his fictions. Thus, *Sard Harker* begins with a boxing match between black and white opponents which the black boxer throws—an incident not unlike the Vienna match described in *The Sun Also Rises* (1926) and the thrown matches also at stake in "The Killers" (1926) and "Fifty Grand" (1925); similarly, *Victorious Troy* opens with a brief account of a merchant captain's longed-for chance to sink a U-boat by gunfire in World War I, and of the drinking habits he acquired while hunting submarines—which eerily predicts the submarine hunts of World War II in *Islands in the Stream* (1970); and finally, *Dead Ned* contains a gypsy fortuneteller's glimpse of the hero's deadly fate which prefigures Pilar's glimpse in *For Whom the Bell Tolls* (1940). Hemingway's interest in boxing, sailing, medicine, and Latin America may have been fed by these novels, then, but aside from these few suggestive episodes (and another just ahead from *Victorious Troy*) nothing much came of this reading.

With Dauber's attic vocation the case seems otherwise, perhaps because of the kindred spirit detected there. Born in 1878, Masefield was only six years younger than Hemingway's mother; his lifespan—like hers—would extend from Victorian well into modern times and would embrace some of the same genteel traditions. Indeed, the family resemblances behind this poem are rather striking. There is a photograph taken of Masefield at about age three, for instance, dressed in a child's smock and with finger curls at his forehead. This is how Grace Hemingway would dress her son Ernest in infancy. Again like Ernest, Masefield came from a family of six children, with an older brother and sister before him, and two younger brothers and a sister who came after. He was especially close, moreover, to his older sister Ethel in childhood, and began an intimate correspondence with her during his lonely New York years as a bar-boy and millworker (1894–97). He had gone there to accept a berth on another clipper ship, at Aunt Kate's insistence, but at the last minute deserted her, having grown to hate the trade he would later celebrate in his poems. He wanted instead to become a writer, and to Ethel he began sending his early attempts at poetry. Their correspondence lasted until her marriage in 1899, by which point he had returned to England and had begun to publish some of his poems in British periodicals. He then turned to his younger sister Norah as a literary correspondent whom he might educate in the arts.[10]

There is a scene in *Victorious Troy* in which Masefield celebrates genteel sibling relations like those Hemingway enjoyed with his several sisters. There, apprentice seaman Dick Pomfret, after doing all he could to save his ship on the first night of the cyclone, falls into an exhausted sleep, then awakes after a time oddly refreshed:

He had fallen asleep half-frozen, but woke with a kind of sticky warmth all over him, thinking of his sister at home. She was a jolly good sort of chap, he thought; he didn't know why he should think of her now; but he did, with much approval. She was a year and more older than he. She was very like him in many ways, tall, straight, very dark, with almost black eyes and thick smudges of eyebrows. She was fond of riding, and deft at crafts, a neat carpenter and clever silversmith: she made good beltclasps and rings: she had a good voice and could sing: she danced well. In fact, she did most things well. He called her Charles, from some fancied suggestion in her face of Charles the Second. She called him Dog, or The Dog. They were very good friends, and when together spoke a nursery language, which they had perfected in childhood, and now spoke with ease and speed. It was made up of words of their own invention, contractions and interchangements agreed upon, and much slang twisted from its original meaning. It was pronounced always "in the manner of the governors"; the "governors" being the rustics of their neighborhood. He went over some of her remarks to him: —

"Where hast mut der cat, Dog? Her'llt be bun gobbed."

"Thoust a bison. Duck her tuddies and ging did a splodge."

They were incomprehensible to any but their selves, no third in the world knew what they meant, yet to themselves the one meant:

"Where have you put your hat, Dick? You'll be sunstruck," and the other:

"You're a wise one. Chuck your lessons and come and bathe."

He thought of these things now with a great deal of pleasure. He liked her; she was a good chap. He did not know the depth of her love for him. He wondered vaguely if she were thinking of him in her bedroom at home in England.[11]

Masefield's personal stake in this passage is considerable. An apprentice seaman much like himself in 1894 has just done his best, in 1922, to rescue one of the last clipper ships whose drunken captain—called at various times "the Old Man" and "the ship's father" (261)—has failed her. Pomfret has lost his hat before the cyclone strikes, and his memory of his sister's private reference to sunstroke (which he has been fearing all day) is a reminder of how his instincts have helped to pull him through. It is also a reminder, for Masefield, of that combination of sunstroke and nervous breakdown that ended his first and only clipper voyage much less gloriously than Dick's will end. But the important point is the association of Pomfret's best instincts and manliest actions with his sister's supporting love. Freudian readers will be quick to note his warm, sticky feeling as he awakes "thinking of his sister at home," the desexualizing references to her as that good chap Charles, the alternative to lessons and sunstroke of bathing together, and that last bedroom image of her in England, hopefully thinking of him. But such patronizing treatment excludes the refreshing tenderness of the passage, its affectional straightness as an androgynous tribute to a loved person who has helped to make possible such confident strength and wisdom as Pomfret has been able to exercise during the storm. Hemingway would have felt these qualities, I think, when he read the passage in 1935 and found echoes in it of his own early loves: for his older sister Marcelline, with whom he first knew androgynous love in infancy; for his baby sister Carol, who looked exactly as he did in early boyhood; for his favorite sister Ursula, who kept him bedcompany after the war to ease his loneliness; and for his tomboy sister Sunny, who did well in all sports and with whom he shared a private language much like this one in his adolescent years, and special nicknames too.[12]

Even the songs and crafts and family bathing were typical of the Hemingway household, where music and making things well received almost equal emphasis, and where "skinny dipping" in Walloon Lake was a common practice every summer. Perhaps that is why the line "He did not know the depth of her love for him" reminds us of the passage in "The Last Good Country" where Nick thinks: "He loved his sister very much and she loved him too much. But . . . I guess those things straighten out. At least I hope so" (101). Or why "Charles" and "The Dog" recall the name reversals of the androgynous couples in the posthumously published novel, *The Garden of Eden*. Or, going backwards, why the "good chap" motif recalls a forerunner of those couples—Brett Ashley in *The Sun Also Rises*. In the midst of those family resemblances, then, Masefield seems to have planted a few tender seeds, as late as 1935, which would bear literary fruition two decades later.

An important difference emerges if we conclude that Masefield's maternally inspired vocation in "Dauber" had been reinforced by sibling love rather than divorced from it, as with Hemingway. Masefield could and did love mothers as well as sisters (particularly his older sister), and apparently relied on older women with some understanding of the connection. Thus, on his return to London in the late 1890s he turned chiefly to his godmother, Ann Handford-Flood, for emotional support. Miss Flood was a maiden friend of his mother, had been kind to him in childhood, and now became a trusted confidante. Within the next few years, moreover, he would meet and marry Constance de la Cherois Crommelin, his senior by eleven and a half years. At one point he would even become enamored for a year with an actress "old enough to be his mother," who wisely kept him at arm's length until his ardor cooled. And in America, during his wartime lecture tour in 1916 (which took him often to Chicago), he would meet a wealthy patron of the arts, Florence Lamont, another older woman who would become a lifelong friend.[13]

As we have seen, Hemingway too was much attracted to older women. His first sweetheart, Agnes Von Kurowsky, and his first two wives, Hadley and Pauline, were all seven or eight years older than himself. His Paris mentor, Gertrude Stein, was also "old enough to be his mother," and his bookshop friend Sylvia Beach was twelve years older. Masefield would stand by most of his older women friends, however, and would remain married to Constance until her death at ninety-three. His instinct was to be loyal to the women he relied on, not to rely on them—as Hemingway often did—until betrayal seemed expedient.

Hemingway felt, of course, that women were the great betrayers. From childhood onward he knew that older women could be punitive, hard to please, and inclined toward independent ways which he construed as dominance. Indeed, he had gradually shifted his affections from his mother and older sister to his more pliable younger sisters so as to avoid such difficulties. On going off to war, moreover, on what might be seen as his first real flight from the parental nest, he had curiously misled his parents and a few friends into believing he was getting married in New York to the actress Mae Marsh. His mother especially was shocked by the unexpected news and wrote for further explanation, at which point the hoax dissolved;[14] but it seems to have been his first rebellious attempt to hurt her for not loving him enough, and perhaps his first invocation as well of that misogynous rationale for his many divorces and infidelities in later life: "If you don't love me Mama / Then I don't care at all / Cause I can get more womens / Th[a]n a passenger train can haul." Yet it was not his mama, but rather his wartime sweetheart, Agnes Von Kurowsky, who first confirmed his latent views on women as betrayers.

In "A Very Short Story" (1924), Hemingway records the disillusionment of a young soldier like himself who becomes engaged to a nurse while recuperating in an Italian hospital, returns home at her behest expecting her to follow, receives a letter from her calling their love a "boy and girl" affair now over, and takes out his anger by catching gonorrhea from a salesgirl in a Chicago taxi.[15] As my colleague Robert Scholes has amply demonstrated, it is a revenge story in which our sympathies are directed toward the twice-wounded soldier (first by Mars, then by Eros) and against his treacherous sweetheart.[16] The revenge, of course, is Hemingway's, on Agnes Von Kurowsky, for betraying their wartime love. We are very much into the soldier's point of view, accordingly, and when the lovers quarrel before parting "about her not being willing to come home at once" (240), we are forced to conclude that she has always wanted to get rid of him, while professing otherwise. Since we know that Hemingway's ardor for Agnes was at least equal to hers for him, the unbalanced stress on *her* professions of love and on *her* conditions for marriage, becomes suspect. Indeed, even the solid grounds for her reluctance—his extreme youthfulness, his newfound drinking habits, his playboy tendencies—are oddly present in the story only as groundless female admonitions: "After the armistice they agreed he should go home to get a job so they might be married. Luz would not come home until he had a good job and could come to New York to meet her. It was understood that he would not drink, and he did not want to see his friends or any one in the States. Only to get a job and be married" (240).

Without knowing Luz's point of view—or her age and experience as compared to his—we have no idea as to why she sets such strange conditions. She is made to sound prim, shallow, and dishonest instead of honestly troubled about marrying such a dubious partner. It is she, moreover, who is made to seem romantically naive when her subsequent love affair with an Italian major—the nominal cause of the breakup—fails to end in marriage. One wonders, finally, why our truehearted soldier ever fell in love with her. Was it possibly because he *wanted* to be rejected?

In *Prisoners of Childhood* Alice Miller writes about a common pattern among narcissistic types who feel insecure about their mother's love: a compulsion "first to conquer and then to desert" the women they desire; a need to "quit women as soon as [they] feel essential to them."[17] It seems evident enough that Hemingway felt similar compulsions during his four consecutive marriages and recurrent infidelities. Indeed, his misogynistic theme song—"If you don't love me, Mama"—speaks directly to them. The memoirs of his sisters further confirm that Grace Hall Hemingway expected much of her children and was hard to please. And her admiration for her father and uncle, Ernest and Miller Hall, in whose idealized image she had tried to raise her son *Ernest Miller* Hemingway,[18] further explains her desire to impose on him expectations which he often failed to fulfill. Not incidentally, then, Ernest's wartime sweetheart, Agnes Von Kurowsky, also had expectations which Ernest found it hard to fulfill. When he returned home from the war, he did nothing about finding work, began drinking secretly at night—and waited for the axe to fall. As he emotionally understood, Agnes was rejecting him when she refused to come home with him to get married. She was doing what they both knew he wanted her to do—setting in motion that delayed rejection they both wanted to occur. Their quarrel, then, was over his passive role in the game plan—his refusal to take responsibility for his own part in the break ahead. Two years later he would repeat that refusal during his long-delayed attempt to break with his mother—to whose disturbing ways we now return.

As I have argued in earlier chapters, Grace's expectations for Ernest were more complicated than her many critics have allowed. Through him she could herself be like the men she most admired, Ernest and Miller Hall, and could enjoy vicariously their freedom to pursue cherished goals. Thus, her stake in her son's behavior involved not only an imposed admiration for his elders but also identification with them and, through them, with him. When he disappointed her, accordingly, she was more deeply disappointed than with her other children. This may explain why all her daughters were able to make relatively stable and lasting marriages.[19] But it is an oddly one-sided explanation, a familiar Freudian dumping on the mother, only slightly relieved by my neofeminist modification as to her own entrapment and her own need for vicarious satisfaction. The unasked question here is what and how much did Ernest contribute to his own future troubles? The answer seems to be a sense of his own potential importance which matched his mother's. A horrendous clash between these two extremely narcissistic personalities seems to have been inevitable, given the different nature of their artistic gifts and the necessity on Ernest's part for some kind of adolescent rebellion.

As we now know in abundant detail, the clash took place in the summer of 1920 at the cottage in northern Michigan which Ernest considered his truest home. Until recently the mythic version of the event has been that Grace threw him out of the cottage on or directly after his twenty-first birthday by writing her famous "bank account" letter, the heartless economic drift of which condemns the vicious sender rather than the innocent receiver. It now seems evident, however, that Grace was reacting—albeit harshly—to a delayed adolescent rebellion of a familiar kind, one which left her far more emotionally bruised and flayed than has ever been acknowledged. She was reacting, moreover, in concert with her husband, who had seen for himself how Ernest was behaving and who had then twice written asking him to leave—before Grace even put pen to paper. Max Westbrook's account of these matters, in "Grace under Pressure: Hemingway and the Summer of 1920," is surely the *locus classicus* of scholarly adjudication, and the point of departure for all future discussion of this apparently crystallizing episode in a great writer's youth.[20]

As Westbrook amply documents, Ernest had responded to his father's "kick out" letters through a series of passive aggressions against his mother. Thus, at 9 P.M. on the night he received the second letter he insulted her gratuitously for preferring "moron literature" and sampling better work only for approval. That same night he slipped out of bed at midnight to attend a secret island picnic on Walloon Lake with his younger sisters, Ursula and Sunny (then sixteen and fifteen, respectively), his wartime friend Ted Brumback, and two thirteen-year-old neighborhood girls. It was, in Ernest's view, an innocent occasion, but when the mother of one of the neighborhood girls arrived at Windemere Cottage at 3 A.M., asking where the missing girls were and wanting to know what those "grown men" wanted with them, the occasion became—from a parental point of view— outrageous. Grace was offended not only by the deception but by its irresponsible, alarming, and provocative nature—its apparent defiance not of severe restrictions but of reasonable adult expectations. And indeed, the defiance seems as deliberate as the insults which preceded it. "One could even argue," writes Westbrook, "that in responding to his father's dismissal by insulting his mother and leading a midnight escapade Ernest was insisting on his own eviction."[21]

That argument seems to me exactly right. As early as 1917, Dr. Hemingway had found Ernest "just as headstrong and abusive and threatening as ever" and had complained also of how the six children together took advantage of him whenever possible. By 1920 Ernest's ringleader role as an adolescent rebel, even after his return from the war, was a parental byword. Indeed, when the girls returned from Michigan in the fall Clarence would write to Grace that he too could see "Ernest's teachings" in their still rebellious behavior.[22]

Thus, Grace's review of Ernest's failings in her famous "bank account" letter was a point on which both parents agreed. During the "trying time of adolescence," she wrote, "when the mother must make constant excuses for overwrought nerves," the child she has lovingly raised "turns and tongue thrashes her, sneers at her advice and precautions, considers her quite out of date." Ernest's dinner-time insults in 1920 were part of a long pattern, then, and had been preceded that summer by his refusal to do chores on the cottage and farm while loafing with his wartime friend. His part in the midnight escapade was a continuation also of earlier instigations of his sisters' rebellious conduct. His harassed parents, caught between their absolute sense of right conduct and their indulgent affections, coping strenuously against changing and more modern expectations among their children, found him guilty of familial breaches of conduct on reasonable as well as outmoded grounds. In writing her own eviction letter, accordingly, Grace was merely bringing to a head a long-standing family crisis and giving Ernest the severance he wanted and needed and was too weak and irresponsible to take upon himself. The repetition of the same pattern in his four marriages confirms its early origins. Of the four wives who suffered from his passive aggressions, only Mary Welsh had the courage and good sense to demand that he leave by his own decision—which may explain why that marriage lasted the longest and was terminated only by another and more tragic choice.

What Grace wanted from Ernest, interestingly, was very much in keeping with the genteel tradition he was trying to cast off. "A Mother's love seems to me like a Bank," her famous letter begins. "Each child that is born to her enters the world with a large and prosperous Bank Account, seemingly inexhaustible." During the first five years the child draws upon her resources: "physical labor and pain, loss of sleep, watching and soothing, waiting upon, bathing, dressing, feeding, amusing: the Mother is practically a body slave to his every whim." Over the next ten years "the Bank is heavily drawn upon for love and sympathy, championship in time of trouble or injustice, nursing through illness, teaching and guiding, developing the young body and mind and soul at all and any expense to the often exhausted parents." Then, after the adolescent period already described, comes full manhood:

> The Bank is still paying out love, sympathy with wrongs, and enthusiasm for all ventures; courtesies and entertainments of friends, who have nothing in common with Mother, who unless they are very well bred, scarcely notice her existence. But the Bank goes on handing out understanding and interest in budding love affairs, joy in plans of every sort.
>
> The account needs some deposits, by this time, some good sized ones in the way of gratitude and appreciation. Interest in Mother's ideas and affairs. Little comforts provided for the home—a desire to favor any of Mother's peculiar prejudices, on no account to outrage her ideals. Flowers, fruit, candy, or something pretty to wear, brought home to Mother, with a kiss and a squeeze. The unfailing desire to make much of her feeble efforts, to praise her cooking, back up her little schemes. A real interest in hearing her sing, or play the piano, or tell the stories that she loves to tell—a surreptitious paying of bills, just to get them off Mother's mind.
>
> A thoughtful remembrance and celebration of her birthday and Mother's Day. The sweet letter, accompanying the gift of flowers, she treasures it, most of all. These are merely a few of the deposits which keep the account in good standing.
>
> Many mothers, I know, are receiving these and much more substantial gifts and returns from sons of less abilities, than my son.[23]

Over the next several years Ernest would indeed give his mother the Fauntleroy treatment she desired. Though the chilling effect of his eviction never thawed, there was a semblance of family harmony. During his first marriage he would write birthday letters and send or bring occasional gifts. But his mother's condemnation of his earliest published writings widened the already deep cleavage between them, and his portrait of "the doctor's wife" in one of those tales—though only nominally based on Grace—indicated clearly enough how he felt about her cheerful pieties. Indeed, one wonders if she was altogether blind to the implications of that portrait. The woman who asked him to favor "her peculiar prejudices, on no account to outrage her ideals," could not have been unmindful of the personal animus behind that selective view of spousely narrowness; her objections to the immorality of his writings must have come from a personal sense of their provocative implications for herself—a point which her many biographical detractors have always conveniently overlooked. Her "whipping boy" had a "whipping mother" to draw on from time to time, and his penchant for that kind of vengeance was evident enough from early times. When Grace demanded that he leave the cottage, when she accused him of having overdrawn the Bank of motherly love, he responded by accusing her of trying to cover up her guilt in putting money into the music studio on the farm across the lake that might have gone for her daughters' college education—and in one late version of the event, for his own.[24] His own blindness, here and elsewhere, to her rights as an artist and an individual seeking seclusion from family demands so as to do her work and be herself, is instructive. Though the money for the studio was her own, though she earned it through music lessons and concerts, her only possible role in her son's eyes was still that of the Bank to be drawn on for moral, spiritual, and educational support. Yet paradoxically it was her approval that he most desired, her recognition of his writings and himself, whether at twenty-one or later—an unacknowledgeable desire since she remained his most obvious rival throughout his life—the artist he most wanted to equal in confidence and maturity, the person he most feared to confront, to the point of being afraid to attend her funeral in 1951, from which he abjectly stayed away. And yet his famous tag line for courageous and aesthetic conduct—"grace under pressure"—echoes her name and indicates his ongoing acknowledgment of the force and value of her example. He knew that she had championed him in times of youthful trouble or injustice, though he wrote otherwise; he knew that she, and not his father, was the survivor and champion he must try to emulate; and he also knew that his father's failure to match her in these roles might be his own. As Peter Griffin has observed, it was Ernest, and not his father, who could not stand up to Grace under the several pressures of his early manhood.[25] His rearrangement of the terms of parental conflict in Masefield's attic was the first of many future evasions of that ongoing problem.

Part Two

The Return of the Repressed

Chapter 7

Three Little Savages

The adult Hemingway would draw upon Captain Marryat's life and work in a variety of ways, but most obviously he was influenced by his novels of naval warfare, smuggling, and privateering—all written in the 1830s and '40s—which would affect his own novels of the 1930s and after about smuggling, deep-sea fishing, and anti-submarine patrols. Less obviously, but no less intriguingly, Marryat's novels and tales of wilderness survival would anticipate Hemingway's own tales of backwoods life in Upper Michigan and big-game hunting in Africa. The first critic to detect such connections seems to have been Allen Tate, for upon meeting him in Sylvia Beach's Paris bookshop in late September 1929, Hemingway had "without preliminary" said that Tate was "wrong in a review to attribute to him the influence of Marryat and Defoe."[1] Oddly, Tate had made no such attributions about Marryat in his reviews of Hemingway's early work for *The Nation,* but he had indeed made much of Defoe as one of Hemingway's several eighteenth-century forebears, referring to him obliquely as "the author of 'Moll Flanders' and 'Captain Singleton,'" ending his first review with a line from *Captain Singleton* to demonstrate its similarity with "the method of Mr. Hemingway's prose," and citing him along with Swift, in his next review, as forerunners in that "sustained satire" for which Hemingway's "indirect irony, the irony of suppressed comment," was "pre-eminently fitted."[2] A tough-minded critic himself, the future hatchet-man for the New Critical movement, Tate plainly admired Hemingway for his hard-boiled modern realism. In dubbing him "the best contemporary author of eighteenth-century prose," he was calling attention not simply to his "integrity" as a careful prose stylist like Swift, Sterne, Fielding, or Defoe, but also to his straightforward attitude toward experience, his translation of objects and events into immediate life, his verbal mastery of the new/old worlds of criminal lowlife and wilderness survival which Defoe especially had mastered before him. Thus, in reviewing *In Our Time,* it was the wilderness theme and its verbal mastery that captured Tate's attention:

> Most typical of Mr. Hemingway's precise economical method is the story Big Two-Hearted River, where the time is one evening to the next afternoon and the single character a trout fisherman who makes his camp-fire, sleeps all night, gets up and catches a few trout, then starts home; that is all. But the passionate accuracy of particular observation, the intense monosyllabic diction, the fidelity to the internal demands of the subject—these qualities fuse in the most completely realized naturalistic fiction of the age. This sentence has much the method of Mr. Hemingway's prose: "When we saw the creature killed, I had a great mind to have the skin of her, and made signs to the prince that he should send some of his men to take the skin off"—and it would convey more of its quality had it not been written in 1720 by Daniel Defoe.[3]

Tate draws this sentence, as indicated, from the remarkable African trek of a stranded band of mariners in *The Life, Adventures, and Piracies of the Famous Captain Singleton.*[4] The trek in question begins early in the novel, at a point when the young British hero first assumes command over the Portuguese sailors who have joined him in mutinous separation from their parent ship, and begins to direct their cross-continental progress from East to West Africa. That Tate finds similar qualities at work in that early imperial venture as in Nick Adams's therapeutic fishing trip in northern Michigan seems to me an historically brilliant *aperçu.* Nick does have much in common with young "Captain Bob," even as Captain Bob has much in common with the several heroes of Captain Marryat (e.g., Peter Simple, Midshipman Easy, Percival Keene) who are similarly orphaned, stranded, and/or abandoned, and for whom the problem of cross-country survival is a problem also of ritual ascent into manhood and of physical mastery of an ever-dwindling wilderness, an ever-shrinking imperial frontier. Thus, Defoe's eighteenth-century precedent, as developed by Marryat in the nineteenth century, had apparently reached Hemingway by circuitous readings; and if he confused Captain Singleton with Captain Marryat when accosting Tate in Sylvia Beach's bookshop, his error is understandable—and remarkably revealing. Though he had read *Robinson Crusoe* in boyhood in a children's version, he was not really familiar with Defoe when he first read Tate's reviews in 1926. Later—perhaps at Tate's instigation—he would acquire copies of *Moll Flanders, Captain Singleton, Memoirs of a Cavalier,* and *Roxana* in his Key West and Cuban libraries.[5] But his early readings in Marryat—whether in Oak Park and northern Michigan in boyhood, or in Sylvia Beach's bookshop in the early 1920s—had prepared him for Tate's educated guess about wilderness and lowlife fictions; and so, in his heated response at being almost found out, he gave himself away. Captain Marryat, if not Defoe, was indeed a profound influence on his early tales of diminished frontier life in northern Michigan.

Still another reviewer of *In Our Time,* D. H. Lawrence, had shrewdly described Nick Adams as "a type one meets in the more wild and woolly regions of the United States. . . . the remains of the lone trapper and cowboy."[6] Lawrence was more articulate than Tate about the grimness of the hero's outlook, his last-ditch bitterness as the modern inheritor of a diminished and devalued world. But neither he nor Tate had much to say about the hero's youth, his painful passage from boyhood into bitter early manhood within the wilderness sequence—"Indian Camp," "The Doctor and the Doctor's Wife," "The End of Something," "The Three Day-Blow," "The Battler," and "Big Two-Hearted River"—from *In Our Time.* Marryat's precedent in using the wilderness to develop such ritual passages seems most relevant to these tales. Thus, in novels like *Masterman Ready, The Children of the New Forest, The Settlers in Canada, Scenes in Africa,* and *The Travels of Monsieur Violet,* a familiar pattern appears as older men teach boys or younger men how to cope with wilderness conditions, and above all, how to plan ahead to avoid disastrous consequences. In *Masterman Ready,* moreover, there is even an African subplot in which three foolhardy British boys, having escaped a Dutch prison in Capetown, trek northward and—in another familiar sequence—fear roaring lions at night, run from one in daytime panic, and inadvertently wound one who exacts deadly vengeance. Their Defoe-like exposure to wilderness perils becomes, in Marryat's hands, a learning experience, a lesson in survival tactics for outcast children, as old Masterman Ready tells this story of his youth to still other shipwrecked children, and so helps to inculcate that grit, resourcefulness, and stoicism by which future generations of British imperialists would colonize the world. Hemingway's American colonist, a latter-day Adam(s) nicked by passing time and populated space, seems to have settled permanently with his family into a diminished frontier setting. His physician father serves the local Indians and backwoodsmen and Nick himself develops proprietary relations with an Indian girl and a waitress. Eventually we learn that he has one or more sisters, poaches fish and game for a local restaurant, and seduces summer guests. His relations with his mother, a pollyannish Christian Scientist, seem distant. Though his father teaches him to love the outdoor life, Nick is often disillusioned with him, with good reason, and at one point considers blowing off his head with his own shotgun. Nick is certainly like Marryat's naval heroes in having such difficult parental relations, and like his outcast children too in having them in wilderness settings. The most obvious precedent for this unusual pattern comes from an unfinished Marryat novel called *The Little Savage,* which was completed and posthumously published by Marryat's son Frank in 1848–49.

FRANK HENNIKER

Strictly speaking, "the little savage," Frank Henniker, was never at odds with his parents, both of whom had died in his infancy. Instead, he was raised by their survivor, the last man alive of the shipwrecked company that had come ashore on the guano island off Peru where Frank was later born; and his relation to this man, in Marryat's naively Freudian terms, was rather like that of Hamlet to his uncle, that is to say, his father's murderer and successor and his mother's lover. Thus, Edward Jackson and Frank's father had worked for the same master and wooed the same woman, their master's daughter; but Edward had fallen into dissipation and disgrace, while Frank's father had risen in favor and won the daughter's hand. Later the three would meet on the ill-fated ship on which Jackson was a lowly sailor and Henniker and his wife were privileged passengers. After the shipwreck Jackson had exiled himself from the rest of the party when Henniker was elected leader, but had soon returned, bided his time, and with the number of survivors greatly reduced, had murdered Henniker and the ship's captain, his two remaining rivals. Mrs. Henniker survived another six months, and though she abhorred Jackson, he succeeded in Marryat's veiled prose in forcing her sexual submission by withholding food from her and from her infant child (chap. 13). Thus Jackson repeats the surrogate functions of Hamlet's oedipal uncle and becomes, inevitably, young Frank Henniker's retributory, if not expiatory, victim.

This oddly burdened children's story begins, then, *in medias res,* with the narrator Frank Henniker announcing his "very curious history" as "the first instance of a boy being left alone upon an uninhabited island." His first recollections, however, are of being in company with a man upon this island when he is about five years old, walking often along the seashore, being dragged by this older companion over dangerous places:

He was very unkind to me, which may appear strange, as I was the only companion that he had; but he was of a morose and gloomy disposition. He would sit down squatted in the corner of our cabin, and sometimes not speak for hours, —or he would remain the whole day looking out at the sea, as if watching for something, but what I could never tell; for if I spoke, he would not reply; and if near to him, I was sure to receive a cuff or a heavy blow.[7]

The mistreatment of children, which Dickens and Charlotte Brontë would develop into a fine domestic art by mid-nineteenth century, is here in the wilderness enisled; but the tables are turned so rapidly that we have no time to muse upon the years between his mother's death and Frank's first memories—the years, that is, between two and five. We know only that Frank and the man in question, Edward Jackson, call each other Master and Boy, that they live on a rocky island three miles round, without beach or landing place, but with a forest of underwood and bushes near its summit. The seabirds who deposit guano there are a seasonal source of food; the climate is warm; the two estranged companions live in a cabin built by the original band of survivors, broiling dried birds or fish, or frying eggs to keep alive.

Then, when Frank is twelve or thirteen, a ship approaches in a gathering squall, the storm worsens as the two islanders try to light a guiding fire, and suddenly the man is struck and blinded by lightning at about the same time as the ship is destroyed by the developing tornado. From this point on "Boy" becomes "Master," and in his newfound love of power and superiority he exacts a sometimes brutal vengeance.

Thus, having been treated as a slave, Frank proceeds to act the tyrant, depriving Jackson of water, tossing rocks at him, then using the knives he has discovered from the wreck of the ship to slash Jackson's wrist when Jackson tries to choke him to death as he feigns sleep, and—finally—leaving Jackson's wound untended while he in fact goes to sleep. Later he binds the wound with feathers, but the ligatures have been slashed and the arm is useless. Such horrendous actions, so vividly described, seem so brutal and deliberate that the narrator pauses to explain them:

> The reader may exclaim—What a horrid tyrant this boy is—why, he is as bad as his companion. Exactly—I was so; but let the reader reflect that I was made so by education. From the time that I could first remember, I had been tyrannised over; cuffed, kicked, abused, and ill-treated. I had never known kindness. Most truly was the question put by me, "Charity and mercy—what are they?" I never

heard of them. An American Indian has kind feelings—he is hospitable and generous—yet, educated to inflict and receive, the severest tortures to, and from, his enemies, he does the first with the most savage and vindictive feelings, and submits to the latter with indifference and stoicism. He has, indeed, the kindlier feelings of his nature exercised; still, this changes him not. He has been from earliest infancy brought up to cruelty, and he cannot feel that it is wrong. Now, my position was worse. I had never seen the softer feelings of our nature called into play; I knew nothing but tyranny and oppression, hatred and vengeance. It was therefore not surprising that when my turn came, I did to others as I had been done by. (20)

Here, then, is "the little savage" upon whom Nick Adams may be said to have modelled at least some of his antiparental feelings. It is not simply that Jackson's blindness reminds us of the cultivated blindness of Nick's Christian Scientist mother, resting in her darkened room in "The Doctor and the Doctor's Wife," or that his slashed arm reminds us of the Indian husband with the slashed foot in "Indian Camp," resting in the bunk above his Indian wife as Nick's physician father performs upon her a jackknife Caesarean without anaesthetics: it is rather the whole pattern of blindness, obtuseness, and denial where human suffering is concerned, the role of parents or adults in propagating such patterns upon each other and above all upon their children, and the function in each case of the American Indian in providing a "sentimental" standard. Mrs. Adams's blindness to her husband's humiliation by the half-breed Dick Boulton, Dr. Adams's obtuseness to the sufferings of the silent husband and his screaming wife and of the son too soon exposed to such violent and disastrous feelings—this is the "sentimental" education that Hemingway's "little savage" shares with Marryat's Frank Henniker, an education which, as we shall see, affects later Hemingway heroes like the Flaubertian Frederic Henry in *A Farewell to Arms,* and which ultimately leads David Bourne, in *The Garden of Eden,* to swear as a boy that he will "never tell anyone anything again" about his deepest feelings, not in the face of his father's deliberate slaughter of the majestic elephant who rouses them.[8]

Marryat's precedent for this "sentimental education" is also oddly relevant to Hemingway's early years. Once Frank Henniker becomes master of his blind adult companion, for instance, he is determined to force him to answer all the questions he has hitherto ignored. Beginning with the fateful story of Jackson's relations with his parents, he quickly shifts and broadens his interest when Jackson identifies two items from the ship wrecked on the island as a Bible and a prayer book. From the latter Jackson is able to identify where the Morning Service begins, and to teach Frank the letters of the alphabet from his own recollection of the words of the prayer that follows. Thus, Henniker learns to read from Bible and prayer book, and soon moves on to another text from the cabin shelf, "Mavor's Natural History" of beasts and birds, with plates representing each and descriptions annexed—upon which Jackson is also forced to elaborate. Such religious and naturalist works were of course staples of the Hemingway household. His parents' muscular Christianity, the avid interest in natural history shared by his father and his paternal grandmother, were ingrained aspects of his boyhood education; and if he leaned even then more toward the latter than the former, his religious feelings were never wholly quiescent. Indeed, his mother's six months' blindness from scarlet fever in childhood, and her miraculous recovery, may have prepared for his own sense of miraculous delivery from death in World War I. He would have responded easily to Jackson's sense of providential punishment for the sins committed against Frank Henniker's parents, and to their eventual revelation as the dying man, having fallen from a cliff in his blind gropings, finally confesses his sins to Henniker and asks his forgiveness. The unusual emphasis in this tale, then, on "parental" blind-ness, its religious, punitive, and retributive colorations, may well relate to Hemingway's knowledge of his mother's childhood blindness, to his strong animus against her pieties, disapprovals, and denials of things unpleasant, and to his creation therefrom of Mrs. Adams in "The Doctor and the Doctor's Wife," resting in her darkened room, blinded by Christian Science to her husband's humiliation, calling symbolically for Nick's company at her bedside—the company, that is, of a reader of books like herself, books which she, like the inimical Jackson, must have first made available to him.

After Jackson's death young Henniker lives for a number of years alone on his guano island, and that too relates to Hemingway's boyhood—to his dreams of isolation, of runaway freedom from his family, and of on-the-road adventures in backwoods regions, which he would eventually embody through Nick Adams. Thus, young Henniker provides a distant model of "the wild child enisled," left alone like Robinson Crusoe when Jackson dies, and forced to fend for himself, which he proceeds to do with great resource-fulness. First he begins to create new life around him, bringing back flowers from the other side of the island to replant around his cottage—following Jackson's remembered advice on the care and improvement of the English gardens pictured in *Mavor's Natural History*. Next he collects a few young birds as pets and ties them by the leg with fishing lines on the platform outside his cabin. He feeds fish to them daily, gives them names from his

Natural History to which they learn to respond, and reads, sings, or talks to them as friends. Later, he clips the wings of the female birds but leaves the males free to bring back fish for them when they are pregnant, and so enlarges his own food supply.

One day he discovers and is frightened by his own echo in the hills. On another day he discovers seals on rocks on the other side of the island, reads up on them in his *Natural History,* and decides to capture a young one for a pet, and to kill and skin others for bedding. Soon he teaches the seal to dive for fish, to be his companion and playmate by day and bedfellow at night—a relation Hemingway may have forgotten by the time he wrote briefly about seals in *The Garden of Eden* and attributed his hero's knowledge (wrongly) to Kipling's *Naulahka*. But certainly something of Henniker's companionship with animals—along with that of Kipling's Mowgli—went into the writing of the elephant tale in *The Garden of Eden,* "a very young boy's story."⁹

Henniker is fourteen when his blind mentor Jackson dies. Some three years later a boat comes safely over the rocks into his calm bathing pool on shore, and by a series of deceptions and betrayals Frank acquires a surrogate mother. For these newly shipwrecked sailors have with them a missionary's wife whom they wish to leave behind; and after Frank helps them to restock their supplies of food and water, and to renerve themselves with the rum he has preserved from the previous wreck, they slip off while Frank and the missionary's wife are back at the cabin preparing to join them. Left alone together on the island, this newly paired mother and son begin to help each other to survive. When she tells him the story of her marriage, and of how she and her husband first joined in the imperial task of spreading Christian light among the savages, she defines not only the nature of British colonialism but also her function as the proper maternal source for the Christian education he has hitherto imperfectly received. And so the "little savage" becomes civilized, or prepared for his return to imperial civilization. Meanwhile, he provides food for his new companion and helps her to improve their primitive surroundings.

One incident from this period in Henniker's island life suggests how deeply Hemingway's reading of Marryat, whether in boyhood or early manhood or even in later years, would affect his fictions. Since the sailors have run off with their food stores and a storm has removed their stock of live fish from the bathing pool, Frank's new mother, Mrs. Reichardt, herself proves resourceful at this time by manufacturing deep-sea fishing lines which Frank lets down from a shelf of rock into a sheltered nook of deep water. One day, while Frank is imagining how he might himself relive the story of his new mother's courtship with some "imaginary benefactress," some parish clerk's daughter who helps her poor German lad toward his new religious vocation, he is "rudely disturbed out of this day-dream" by finding himself pulled off the shelf by the tugging line of a large hooked fish. Nearly drowned at first in the deep water below, he struggles back to the surface, loosens the line, and holds on with both hands while the powerful fish pulls him through the water:

> At first, by main force I was drawn through the water; then, when I found the strain slacken, I drew in the line. This manoeuvre was repeated several times, till I succeeded in obtaining a view of what I had caught; or, more properly speaking, of what had caught me—it was merely a glimpse, for the fish . . . made some desperate plunges, and again darted off, dragging me along with him, sometimes under the water, and sometimes on the surface.
>
> His body was nearly round, and about . . . eight feet long—rather a formidable antagonist for close quarters; nevertheless I was most eager to get at him, the more so when I ascertained that his resistance was evidently decreasing. I continued to approach, and at last got near enough to plunge my knife up to the haft in his head, which at once put an end to the struggle.
>
> But now another difficulty presented itself. In the ardour of the chase I had been drawn nearly a mile from the island, and I found it impossible to carry back the produce of my sport, exhausted as I was by the efforts I had made in capturing him. I knew I could not swim with such a burthen for the most inconsiderable portion of the distance. My fish therefore must be abandoned. Here was a bountiful supply of food, as soon as placed within reach, rendered totally unavailable. (158–59)

The action prefigures modestly the capture and loss of the great fish in *The Old Man and the Sea,* during the writing of which—not incidentally— Ernest's mother had died, making him recall how beautiful she had been before the family troubles started and "how happy they had all been as children."[10] Such comforting thoughts are certainly part of Frank's experience now as he returns to Mrs. Reichardt. Indeed, he thinks "of her steadfast reliance upon Providence, and what valuable lessons of piety and wisdom she would read me, if she found me depressed by my disappointment," as he disconnects his tackle from the dead fish and strikes out manfully for shore, without (at this point) observing "any sharks." And she does attribute his

15. Ernest as Huck Finn with a fishing pole

safe return, and her own continued support and protection from him, as "Divine interposition" in their common favor. The effect upon him is again strikingly suggestive:

> I promised that for the future I would run no such risks, and added many professions of regard for her safety. They had the desired effect; I pretended to think no more of my disappointment, nevertheless, I found myself constantly dwelling on the size of my lost fish, and lamenting my being obliged to abandon him to his more voracious brethren of the deep. These thoughts so filled my mind that at night I continued to dream over again the whole incident, beginning with my patient angling from the rock, and concluding with my disconsolate swim to shore—and pursued my scaly antagonist quite as determinedly in my sleep as I had done in the deep waters. (161)

The abandonment of the large fish to its "voracious brethren" recalls once more the destruction of Santiago's catch by sharks in *The Old Man and the Sea;* and the continued dreams at night of patient angling and pursuit suggest Nick Adams's waking dreams, in "Now I Lay Me" (1927), of fishing rivers he has known or made up to ease his insomnia after shellshock:

I had different ways of occupying myself while I lay awake. I would think of a trout stream I had fished along when I was a boy and fish its whole length very carefully in my mind; fishing very carefully under all the logs, all the turns of the bank, the deep holes and the clear shallow stretches, sometimes catching trout and sometimes losing them. I would stop fishing at noon to eat my lunch; sometimes on a log over the stream; sometimes on a high bank under a tree, and I always ate my lunch very slowly and watched the stream below me while I ate. . . . Sometimes I would fish four or five different streams in the night; starting as near as I could get to their source and fishing them down stream. When I had finished too quickly and the time did not go, I would fish the stream over again, starting where it emptied into the lake and fishing back up stream, trying for all the trout I had missed coming down. Some nights too I made up streams, and some of them were very exciting, and it was like being awake and dreaming. Some of those streams I still remember and think that I have fished in them, and they are all confused with streams I really know. I gave them all names and went to them on the train and sometimes walked for miles to get to them.[11]

The last lines recall Nick's actual trip by train to the Big Two-Hearted River, after the war, and the dreamlike quality of his therapeutic actions there which many critics have noted. Indeed, these two stories are often correlated in Hemingway criticism to demonstrate how much his surface descriptions of such events are states of mind, patrollings of imaginative frontiers where, as Saul Bellow once remarked, "an economy of imagination" prevails as the fisherman, hunter, boxer, or bullfighter sets the terms of his projected actions and then lives up to them.[12] What now seems clear, from my further correlation of "The Little Savage" with these tales, is that the moral and imaginative frontier is also an imperial and a childhood territory, a deliberately chosen wilderness in which a lone adolescent works out the terms for his return to adult civilization.

MOWGLI

Much of Frank Henniker's fondness for this territory is invested in his pet seal, Nero, his playmate by day and bedfellow by night. At one point during his years alone the seal fails to return from his daily ocean swim, and Frank, feeling deserted, bursts into his first flood of tears: "For the first time in my life . . . I felt truly miserable—my whole heart and affections were set upon this animal, the companion and friend of my solitude, and I felt as if existence were a burden without him." Frank had pelted Nero with pieces of rock that morning for disturbing his own attempts to fish in the bathing pool; he reasons now that Nero would not have left him "for that." But when the seal fails to return by nightfall, he again bursts into tears, declares that his was the greater love, since "I would not have left him in that way," then explains that his grief was not inordinate, since the affectionate animal had been his "only companion and friend, the only object that I loved or cared about." And so he cries himself to sleep until, early the next morning, the returning seal nudges his hand: "Need I say that I was overjoyed, that I hugged him as if he had been a human being, that I wept over him, and that in a few minutes afterwards we were asleep together in the same bed-place? Such was the fact, and never was there in my after-life so great a transition from grief to joy" (96).

Later, when Mrs. Reichardt comes to the island, Frank is distressed that he will have to leave the seal behind when they join the departing (and ultimately deceptive) sailors. Still later, the seal proves his love by giving his life for his friend, and again the circumstances touch upon *The Old Man and the Sea*. Thus, when Frank builds a small rowboat with Mrs. Reichardt's assistance and takes Nero and his pet gannets with him for a trial run around the island, he suddenly finds himself in the midst of a shoal of sharks who become excited by the frail boat's presence. They dive, rush to and fro, and jostle each other, but keep a respectful distance while rising on all sides of the craft. The gannets become restless and fly off, Nero begins to growl as the sharks grow bolder and more violent; then, as Frank struggles to keep the boat going, a tremendous blow from beneath makes it rise in the air, "scattering Nero and myself, and the oars, in different directions" (178). Frank swims for the rocky shore with a large shark pursuing; he is about to be devoured when Nero interposes and attacks the shark fiercely, thereby losing his life but allowing Frank to gain a precarious hold on a rocky ledge. As the sharks regather below Frank, Mrs. Reichardt diverts them with a rock thrown from the cliff above, and he climbs to safety.

Hemingway would not write a story like this, about a boy's love for an animal, until the late 1950s. Instead, his attitude toward nature remained steadily knowledgeable, respectful, and—in a detached way—engaged. He chose imagined frontier arenas—bullrings, boxing rings, fishing and hunting grounds—for the token conflict between man and nature that serves in his fiction as a kind of private alternative to public life even when society embraces it. And within such arenas his imagination might extend to "how the lion feels" when it is wounded, as in "The Short Happy Life of Francis

Macomber," and he might even make such interesting connections crucial to successful hunting, fishing, or bullfighting; but more characteristically he simply described the behavior of nature's creatures. Then, in the early 1950s, his boyhood romanticism began to reemerge. It was then, for instance, that he wrote his only animal fables, "The Good Lion" and "The Faithful Bull," to please the children of Venetian friends. In those lyric moments in *The Old Man and the Sea*, moreover, when the old fisherman describes the flying fish as his "principal friends on the ocean," expresses his sympathy for the delicate terns when the ocean becomes cruel, and his love for the sea "as feminine and as something that gave or withheld great favors, and if she did wild or wicked things it was because she could not help them"—in such lyric moments his boyhood feelings and imaginings would return, his affections would extend even to the great fish the old man loves and respects like a friend yet paradoxically wants to kill.[13] Or not so paradoxically if the creature's function is to insure his superior strength, his emotional command of the things he loves but cannot otherwise control.

Similarly in "The Last Good Country," an unfinished novella written at this time, Nick and his sister feel religious awe as they walk through one of the last hemlock forests with overarching branches that recall old cathedrals. Such tracings of the original romantic recovery of nature in the early nineteenth century take an even deeper impress in *The Garden of Eden* (ca. 1958), as Hemingway imagines the admiring love of the young David Bourne, raised in Africa, for the majestic bull elephant his father and the native hunter Juma kill on the day after the elephant visits the grave of the "friend" they have slain the previous year, and the boy looks on his murderous elders as "friend-killers." This paradoxical expression of regret for a life devoted to killing animals (who, like the great fish in *The Old Man and the Sea*, are considered nobler if not more intelligent than humans) reads like a long-buried confession of deeply troubled ambivalence about such "friend-killing." Had hunting and fishing become, one wonders, a lifelong refuge from adult relations, so difficult to control, so often disastrous in outcome? The boyhood alliance with animals as "lesser" creatures, often cruelly subject to adult control, finally implodes, in any case, as Hemingway writes his own version of a Kipling tale for grown-up children, "a very young boy's story."[14]

Mowgli, a Kipling character we have met before, is our next "little savage." We have already seen the imperial direction Kipling gave to his legend of this wild boy raised by wolves: the arrangement of the Jungle as a mini-Empire whose laws involve predatory and territorial rights, struggles for dominance or survival; the placement of Mowgli himself as the superior human intelligence among nobler animal brothers; his alliance with these brothers against the Man-Pack, the adult Indian world outside the Jungle, and the destruction of the native compound through that alliance—all in preparation for Mowgli's eventual role as a forest guard (aided by his animal friends) for the Department of Woods and Forests which tends teak and rubber trees and gallnuts for the Empire. We have also seen how Hemingway twice quotes from "The Outsong" of Mowgli's animal friends as he leaves the Jungle to rejoin his nominal native mother, Messua (or in Hemingway's boyhood misremembering, "when he leaves the jungle to get married")—first in a letter of July 13, 1914, to his classmate Emily Goetsmann, then forty years later in a letter of July 1, 1954, to his friend Bill Lowe—causing the animals to lament that he will then "lie / Prisoned from our Mother-sky / Hearing us, thy loves, go by; / . . . Heartsick for the Jungle's sake."[15] Mowgli's preparation to reenter the world of adulthood, fused in Hemingway's mind in 1914 with Huck Finn's attempt to escape that world and with his Indian friend Billy Gilbert's domestication by a squaw who dislikes the woods, would become a paradigm for his own marital fate, as recorded in Nick Adams tales like "The Three-Day Blow" and "Cross-Country Snow" or in novels like A Farewell to Arms, where the choice between marital or romantic responsibilities and male bonding on imaginative frontiers is a painful one.

There are two counts on which The Jungle Book deserves some further comment. The first is the extent to which friendships between wild boys and animals become politicized (or perhaps "Rousseauisticized" might be the better term) as part of the conflict between children and adults; the second is the extent to which maternal sufferings become pivotal to such conflicts. And here Kipling's story is again more exemplary than Marryat's. Thus, Mowgli's friendships with Akela the wolf, Bagheera the black panther, Baloo the bear, and Kaa the rock python are useful not only in resolving territorial battles with red-dog packs, tigers, and monkeys, as well as conflicts within the wolf pack; they are also crucial to his differences with the villagers, particularly as he extends his alliances to include Hathi the elephant and Hathi's three stalwart sons: for these are the friends by whom Mowgli, as Master of the Jungle, "lets in" the Jungle on the village. They organize, as it were, the process of destruction by tramplings, croppings, and vegetative creepings, simply by striding away in four directions with rumors of better food and water in another valley. Pigs, deer, nilghai, and buffaloes come cropping, with Eaters of Flesh close behind; then the returning elephants finish things off by breaking down walls and plucking off thatched roofs. The rains and the Jungle vegetation complete the takeover as the summer wears on and the villagers leave for safer lands. In *The Garden of Eden* (1986) Hemingway would work the other side of Kipling's coin, as white and black hunter join to bring down mammoth elephants, jungle kings admired by the small boy who betrays one mourning elephant on his way to the other's grave. The triumph of the adults over the children and their stronger animal brethren—whose muscles, snouts, trunks, claws, and teeth have been enlisted for the generational struggle—is Hemingway's modern twist on Kipling's several models.

Meanwhile he works, early and late, under Kipling's shadow. Thus Mowgli's grudge against the villagers, like Nick's against his father in the first of the Adams stories, "Indian Camp," is founded on maternal suffering—indeed, upon a mother's blood. That vaguely menstrual association becomes evident, in "Letting in the Jungle," when Mowgli returns to the village to free the woman named Messua, who together with her husband has been accused of witchcraft for sheltering him as some devilish version of their lost son Nathoo, stolen by tigers. These foster parents, now threatened with death by fire, have been bound so tightly by thongs that their wounds bleed openly when Mowgli steals into their hut to cut them free; but though both parents bleed, "it was at *her* wounds that Mowgli looked," gritting his teeth "when he saw the blood," and vowing "There is a price to pay" (157). Later, when he has hit upon the price—the destruction of the entire village—we learn that it is the *smell* and not the sight of the mother's blood that most disturbs him:

> Mowgli had never seen human blood in his life before till he had seen, and—what meant much more to him—smelled Messua's blood on the thongs that bound her. And Messua had been kind to him, and, so far as he knew anything about love, he loved Messua as completely as he hated the rest of mankind. But deeply as he loathed them, their talk, their cruelty, and their cowardice, not for anything the Jungle had to offer could he bring himself to take a human life, and have that terrible scent of blood back again in his nostrils. His plan was simpler, but much more thorough. (170)

The taboo seems to be against shedding the blood of his own kind, yet it is Messua's blood that moves him, and that further moves the "long-lived" elephant Hathi when Mowgli persuades him to enact his "simpler" plan. Thus, when Mowgli reminds Hathi of "the Sack of the Fields of Bhurtpore" by Hathi and his three sons, their destruction of five villages in revenge for a wound from a trapfall onto a sharpened pit stake, the wise old elephant is reluctant to repeat that action without some quarrel of his own. It needs "the red rage of great pain" to justify such destruction, he argues, for he too would avoid further killing and the smell of human blood—until Mowgli defines his own "red rage":

> "I have seen and smelled the blood of the woman that gave me food—the woman whom they would have killed but for me. Only the smell of the new grass on their door-steps can take away that smell. It burns in my mouth. Let in the Jungle, Hathi!"
>
> "Ah!" said Hathi. "So did the scar of the stake burn on my hide till we watched the villages die under in the spring growth. Now I see. Thy war shall be our war. We will let in the Jungle!" (174–75)

Even Mother Wolf is troubled by Mowgli's new interest in his own kind. Following the one she loves best, her own "Little Frog," she asks to "see that woman who gave thee milk," and on looking into her hut before Mowgli frees her, reminds him that she too has given him milk: "but Man goes to Man at the last." So Mowgli does, but to British rather than Indian man, after bloodless revenge for the sufferings of his bleeding Indian mother.

NICK ADAMS

A noisier kind of female suffering occurs in Hemingway's first Nick Adams story, "Indian Camp," where the screaming of an American Indian wife as Dr. Adams performs a Caesarean delivery upon her has disastrous consequences. "Oh, Daddy, can't you give her something to make her stop screaming?" asks an unsettled young Nick Adams of his father. "No. I haven't any anaesthetic," Dr. Adams replies. "But her screams are not important. I don't hear them because they are not important"; and indeed he has just explained to his son that the screams are a natural part of the birth process, a necessary and even helpful reaction ("All her muscles are trying to get the baby born. That is what is happening when she screams"), and therefore not to be understood as horrific suffering. But the Indian men of the village have "moved off up the road," out of earshot, so as to avoid those unimportant screams; and the husband, who has remained behind, trapped in his upper bunk by an ax wound to his foot, has now rolled over against the wall. His pipe smoke meanwhile fills the room, and there is no sound to fix the moment when he can no longer bear that pain with which he apparently indentifies or experiences vicariously from his helpless perch, or for which he takes responsibility and feels unbearable guilt. Whatever the case, his empathetic reaction is so overwhelming that he slits his throat.

Young Nick has meanwhile had his fill of jack-knife operations performed without anaesthetic, of bloody afterbirths, and of bellies sewn back up "with nine-foot, tapered gut leaders." Forced to serve as his father's little intern, he has been looking away, trying not to see what is happening, all through the operation. He gets a good look at the upper bunk, however, when his father decides to check upon "the proud father" resting there and makes his little joke: "they're usually the worst sufferers in these little affairs." On the way back up the road to the lake where boats lie to take them back to their fishing camp, a deflated Dr. Adams apologizes to Nick for bringing him along, acknowledging now that "It was an awful mess to put you through." And indeed he has left Nick with many hard questions to ask, and no easy answers:

"Do ladies always have such a hard time having babies?" . . .
"No, that was very exceptional."
"Why did he kill himself, Daddy?"
"I don't know, Nick. He couldn't stand things, I guess."
"Do many men kill themselves, Daddy?"
"Not very many, Nick."
"Do many women?"
"Hardly ever."
"Don't they ever?"
"Oh, yes. They do sometimes." . . .
"Is dying hard, Daddy?"
"No, I think it's pretty easy, Nick. It all depends."[16]

Considering the family suicides that would follow—his father's in 1928, Ernest's in 1961, his sister Ursula's in 1966, his brother Leicester's in 1982—this passage reads tragically enough today on real as well as imagined grounds. But on cultural grounds, back in 1924 when it was written, the passage reads like a modern twist on the Victorian device of testing out sensitive issues—a woman's suffering, a man's responsibility for it—under wilderness conditions. Messua's blood in "Letting in the Jungle," Mrs. Reichardt's safety in *The Little Savage,* and the offstage death of Henniker's mother under Jackson's guilty care are Victorian precedents for the Indian wife's suffering in Caesarean childbirth and for the suicide of that supposedly stoical natural standard—the adult American male Indian—for the pains a man can bear. Why does Hemingway's work begin with such an odd testing-out of such old-fashioned sensitivities?

One answer is that the standard of the suffering Indian mother and her sensitive spouse offered him a way of dealing with his own deeply ambivalent feelings toward his own mother's sufferings, in childbirth or out, and his own contribution to them. Another is his use of the same standard against his father's obtuseness in exposing him, early and late, to medical attitudes toward suffering that he found difficult to adopt. The young doctor's son who sometimes thought of following in his father's footsteps took an ax to one foot, in this light, and changed direction. His sister Marcelline would report on his queasiness in watching his father operate in a Chicago medical ampitheatre;[17] and the story itself—though fictional and imagined—tells us about similar queasiness in the too-young Nick Adams, unable to ignore screams, unable to watch Caesarean deliveries, and dazed by the personal implications for himself of the Indian husband's solution to a woman's suffering. Indeed, in the discarded first section of the tale, called "Three Shots" and now published in *The Nick Adams Stories,* Nick had been so frightened by the thought of his own inevitable death, generated a few weeks before by a church hymn, that he had fired three emergency shots to bring his father and uncle George back to the tent from their night fishing expedition. Plainly his closing thought in "Indian Camp"—"he felt quite sure that he would never die"—is wishful and self-protective. He has just been given an all too real agenda for his imagined fear of dying.[18]

That the woman in Hemingway's tale is an Indian rather than a Victorian was also Kipling's way of dealing with the problem, using the screams of wolf mother and eastern Indian mother to cover his own ambivalence about the mother who sent him off to the mistreatments of a foster home in England, creating a wolf-child who must leave behind animals and Indians alike in order to live at the edges of the British empire as its faithful forest servant. More straightforward in his oedipal dramatics, Marryat would place his little savage between a dead white mother and her Christian replacement, using the American Indian as a verbal standard only for the learned cruelty and inhumanity of a second son whose father gave him shorter shrift than he cared for, and who like Jackson went to sea and failed to get his just rewards for battles fought there. Significantly, of these three creators of little savages, Marryat had the least trouble in loving his mother, at least in his old age. It was his father's missing love he always longed for.

Hemingway, of course, had the most trouble with his mother. He knew his father loved him, and for some things loved him back, but had good reasons to disrespect him and resent him. But it was his mother's sufferings in childbirth that had disturbed him most deeply: thus, the memory of her sentimental versions of bearing four children after him, one before, and himself, above all, would reduce another version of the imagined self from *In Our Time,* Soldier Krebs, to infantile obedience:

"I'm your mother," she said. "I held you next to my heart when you were a tiny baby."

Krebs felt sick and vaguely nauseated.

"I know, Mummy," he said. "I'll try and be a good boy for you."

"Would you kneel and pray with me, Harold?" his mother asked.[19]

Similarly Hemingway would describe the inevitable outcome of his parents' quarrels—his father's abject defeat—in just such empathetic terms:

Then the inevitable making up, loser received by victor with some magnanimity, everything that had been told the children cancelled. The home full of love, and mother carried you, darling, over her heart all those months and her heart ah yes and what about his heart and where did it beat and who beats it now and what a hollow sound it makes.[20]

This lament for his father, sounding curiously like a lament for himself, repeats the Victorian refrain of the burden of a mother's childbearing love and how men and boys should feel about it. If we compare the treatment of that refrain in "Soldier's Home"—a home located in Oklahoma, and the only approximation in Hemingway's early fiction of his life in Oak Park before and after the war—if we compare that other prayer and pregnancy story from *In Our Time* (indeed, one of several) with the disastrous consequences of "Indian Camp" and their hidden connections with church and home, we may begin to understand the virtues of fictional displacements to the wilderness of home-front problems that elude direct treatment. Young Nick's fear of dying has much to do, then, with troubling Victorian attitudes about childbearing and male responsibilities for it. As will Lieutenant Henry's feelings about Catherine Barkley's death in childbirth in *A Farewell to Arms*. These male characters are so deeply into maternal sufferings as to define their lives by them—and quite possibly their deaths.

TOKEN FRONTIERS

In his review of *The Garden of Eden* E. L. Doctorow speaks of the hero's "consummate self-assurance in handling the waiters, maids and hoteliers who, in this book as in Hemingway's others, come forward to supply the food and drink, the corkscrew and ice cubes and beds and fishing rods his young American colonists require."[21] Here Doctorow is mocking Hemingway for acting as a kind of travel guide for provincial Americans back home, for whom his characters are advance colonists, new imperial settlers in the old world, American innocents abroad for whom tourism is a form of invasion and appropriation. That kind of sophisticated colonization is preceded, in the early Nick Adams stories, by a coarser version of wilderness settlement in the American pioneer tradition; and it is here especially that Hemingway begins to imagine his young hero as a kind of permanent settler in northern Michigan, a backwoodsman with access to "the last good country," rather than a mere "summer person." In only one of the early Adams tales, "The Three-Day Blow," does Nick speak (retrospectively) of going "down home" and getting a job, so as to marry his girlfriend Marjorie, with whom he has broken up in the previous story, "The End of Something"; but where "down home" is we never know. The suspension of Nick's early life in northern Michigan (in "The Killers" he reaches a Chicago suburb; in the war he reaches Italy) is a curiously devised convention, as many critics have noted, given the writer's actual "down home" boyhood for nine months of each year in Oak Park, Illinois—unless we attribute to him the imagination of a token version of the wilderness first set forth by Defoe and Marryat and more recently by Kipling. Certainly it is no accident that Nick is trying to read *Robinson Crusoe* at the outset of "Three Shots," so as to calm his childish fears of the dark forest and the remembered threat of dying. Survival in northern Michigan, as on Crusoe's island, or the little savage's, or in Mowgli's Jungle, is a serious and many-sided matter. The last frontier is a state of mind (witness "Big Two-Hearted River") we have long accepted without question, but which now seems like a historically derivative, readerly state of mind indeed. Hemingway's texts, his boyhood reading in Kipling and Marryat especially, help to explain why there is no Oak Park to go to, no life "down home" to worry about: only the northern woods, the small towns and backwoods stations, the lake cottages and sawmills, the Indian villages and the fishing camps, of an all-too dwindled frontier.

Chapter 8

Three Wounded Warriors

In late September 1929, when Ernest Hemingway first met Allen Tate in Sylvia Beach's Paris bookshop, there was more on his mind than Tate's indirect discovery, through Defoe, of Marryat's strong influence on his work; he was, in fact, far more deeply troubled by Tate's discovery, in his review of *The Sun Also Rises*, of his penchant for sentimentalizing his own weaknesses through fictional personas like Jake Barnes. Thus, in a letter to Carlos Baker dated April 2, 1963, Tate recalls not only how Hemingway had accosted him "without preliminary" about wrongly attributed influences, but had also accosted him about the Barnes-like impotence of their mutual friend, Ford Madox Ford:

> We walked up the street to the Place de l'Odeon and had an aperitif at the old Cafe Voltaire. . . . The next subject he introduced I can repeat almost in his words; "Ford's a friend of yours. You know he's impotent, don't you?" . . . I listened, but finally said that his impotence didn't concern me, even if it were true that he was impotent, since I was not a woman. I learned soon in the local gossip of the *petit cercle Americain* that Ford had been one of the first persons to help Ernest, and as you know Ernest couldn't bear being grateful to anybody.[1]

Tate may be making another indirect discovery here, for not only had Ford befriended Ernest and made him subeditor of his literary journal, the *transatlantic review;* he had also written a "tale of passion," *The Good Soldier* (1915), which like *The Sun Also Rises* is narrated by an "impotent" man and may well have served as another hidden source of influence! At any rate, Tate's response to Ernest—that he was not a woman, and so untroubled by

197

Ford's presumed impotence—was exactly right, and seems to have sealed the fast friendship which from then on held between them. It was the assurance Ernest needed of a common toughness of outlook, a common stake in that hard-boiled modern sensibility that each of them—as novelist and critic—was now serving, and (not least among these assurances) a common witty maleness.

Actually Tate had challenged such assurances in his harsh review of *The Sun Also Rises*. As we have seen, in his two previous reviews of Hemingway's work for *The Nation*, he had welcomed him for the seriousness and integrity of his prose in *In Our Time*—"the most completely realized naturalistic fiction of the age"—and had praised his "indirect irony" and satiric bent in *The Torrents of Spring*, deeming the book itself "a small masterpiece of American fiction."[2] But in reviewing *The Sun Also Rises* he had sharply registered his disappointment at Hemingway's lapse from the achievement of *In Our Time:*

> The present novel by the author of "In Our Time" supports the recent prophecy that he will be the "big man in American letters." At the time the prophecy was delivered it was meaningless because it was equivocal. Many of the possible interpretations now being eliminated, we fear it has turned out to mean something which we shall all regret. Mr. Hemingway has written a book that will be talked about, praised, perhaps imitated. . . . [He] has produced a successful novel, but not without returning some violence upon the integrity achieved in his first book. He decided for reasons of his own to write a popular novel, or he wrote the only novel which he could write. . . . One infers moreover that although sentimentality appears explicitly for the first time in his prose, it must have always been there.[3]

There we have it. Hemingway, betraying his artistic integrity, pandering to the public, had revealed the hidden sentimental basis of his early prose:

> The method used in "In Our Time" was *pointilliste*, and the sentimentality was submerged. With great skill he reversed the usual and most general formula of prose fiction: instead of selecting the details of physical background and of human behavior for the intensification of a dramatic situation, he employed the minimum of drama for the greatest possible intensification of the observed object. . . . The exception, important as such, in Mr. Hemingway's work is the story of Mr. and Mrs. Elliott. Here the definite dramatic conflict inherent in a sexual relation emerged as fantasy, and significantly; presumably he could not handle it otherwise without giving himself away. (43)

Here Tate all but accuses the author of projecting his own impotence upon one of his characters, the poet Elliott, whose marriage to an older Southern woman is barren and whose penchant for long poems becomes an obvious substitution for his failed relations with his wife, now happily sharing her bed with an old girlfriend. Thus, when Hemingway turns his attention from intensified objects to intensified dramatic situations, home truths will out. In *The Sun Also Rises,* a full-length novel, his characters are not only puppets and caricatures, unable to stand by themselves; they are also products of a sentimental failure founded in impotence:

> It is not that Hemingway is, in the term which he uses in the contempt for the big word, hard-boiled; it is that he is not hard-boiled enough, in the artistic sense. . . . And he actually betrays the interior machinery of his hard-boiled attitude: "It is awfully easy to be hard-boiled about everything in the daytime, but at night it is another thing," says Jake, the sexually impotent, musing on the futile accessibility of Brett. The history of his sentimentality is thus complete. (43)

Understandably enough, Hemingway was stung by this treatment from a previously strong admirer. In a letter to Maxwell Perkins written on December 21, 1926, a week after the appearance of Tate's review in *The Nation,* he begins with news of Edmund Wilson's enthusiasm for the novel ("best . . . by any one of my generation"), then praises the editor of *Scribner's Magazine* for proposing to run together three complementary stories that "would make a fine group. And perhaps cheer up Dos, Allen Tate, and the other boys who fear I'm on the toboggan." Then, in a long postscript, he begins with his friend Dos Passos's criticism of the Pamplona scenes in the novel, and ends, significantly, with Tate's several criticisms of his characters and, above all, his toughness:

> Critics, this is still Mr. Tate—have a habit of hanging attributes on you themselves—and then when they find you're not that way accusing you of sailing under false colours—Mr. Tate feels so badly that I'm not as hard-boiled as he had publicly announced. As a matter of fact I have not been at all hard-boiled since July 8, 1918—on the night of which I discovered that that also was Vanity.[4]

The title of Tate's review for *The Nation* had been "Hard-Boiled." July 8, 1918, was, of course, the night on which Hemingway was wounded by shell fire and machine-gun fire while serving canteen supplies in the Italian trenches at Fossalta. It would not be the last time he would use the authority of being wounded as an answer to unwounded critics. But the interesting point, in view of the later public hardening of his personal attitudes, is his insistence on his own vulnerability, his own stake in his character's nightly fears. Indeed, he shares in the kind of self-pity to which Tate objects in his fiction, as to a sentimental indulgence unworthy of true art, a disclosure of personal impotence.

JAKE AND BRETT

What are we to make, then, of Jake Barnes's sexual wound? Hemingway was certainly not an impotent man when he created that curious condition—a lost portion of the penis—for his first-person narrator. His own wounds had been to the legs and scrotum, the latter a mere infection suggesting perhaps that worse had been barely avoided. In a late letter (December 9, 1951) he explained to a Rinehart editor, as an example of the complications of a writer's involvement in his own fictions, "the whole genesis of The Sun Also Rises":

> It came from a personal experience in that when I had been wounded at one time there had been an infection from pieces of wool cloth being driven into the scrotum. Because of this I got to know other kids who had genito urinary wounds and I wondered what a man's life would have been like after that if his penis had been lost and his testicles and spermatic cord remained intact. I had known a boy that had happened to. So I took him and made him into a foreign correspondent in Paris, and, inventing, tried to find out what his problems would be when he was in love with someone who was in love with him and there was nothing that they could do about it. . . . But I was not Jake Barnes. My own wound had healed rapidly and well and I was quit for a short session with the catheter.[5]

The last point is interesting in that there is nothing in the novel to indicate if or when Jake was quit with the catheter, or how he urinates now. But more interesting still is the choice of war wounds for an unmarried foreign correspondent in Paris otherwise much like himself. We know that Hemingway's close relations with his friend Duff Twysden, the ostensible model for Jake's beloved Brett Ashley, had much to do with the choice. As Scott Fitzgerald (who knew something about that relation) opined, Jake seems more like a man trapped in a "moral chastity belt" than a sexually wounded warrior: and indeed, it was Hemingway's marital fidelity to Hadley that apparently kept him from having an affair with Duff; so too, Fitzgerald implies, Jake Barnes with Brett, though there is no Hadley in the novel.[6]

There may, however, be an Agnes Von Kurowsky. Barnes and Lady

Ashley had met each other in a British hospital where Brett worked as a nurse's aide, just as Ernest had met Agnes at a Milan hospital where she worked as an American Red Cross nurse. This prefiguring of the plot of *A Farewell to Arms* is no more than a background notation in *The Sun Also Rises;* but it does remind us of the emotional damage Ernest had sustained from his rejection after the war by Agnes Von Kurowsky and his complicity in that rejection. If Jake's sexual wound can be read as an instance of the way in which war undermines the possibilities of "true love," then we begin to understand to some extent why Hemingway chose that curious condition as an index to the postwar malaise, the barrenness of waste-land relations among the expatriates he knew in Paris—and brought with him to Pamplona. It was in a way a self-inflicted wound he was dealing with which had the war's connivance.

Lawrence's Clifford Chatterley, paralyzed from the waist down by a war wound, is a good example of such projected impotence since he functions obviously enough as the bearer of Lawrence's condition while he was writing the novel, the victim by that point in his life of tubercular dysfunction. But Hemingway was there before him with Jake Barnes, as of course Joyce had been there before Hemingway with Leopold Bloom, his imagined Jewish alter ego in *Ulysses,* and Henry James with Strether in *The Ambassadors,* and Ford Madox Ford with Dowell in *The Good Soldier;* and much farther back, Laurence Sterne with *Tristram Shandy.* The tradition of impotent narration or of impotent heroes, whether comic, serious, or tragic, is an old and honorable one; and our only question is what went into Hemingway's decision to employ it.

Our most recent clue comes from the posthumously published edition of *The Garden of Eden* (1986), the hero of which engages in androgynous forms of lovemaking with his adventurous young wife in the south of postwar France, and at one point in the original manuscript imagines himself as one of the lesbian lovers in a mysterious statue by Rodin, called variously *Ovid's Metamorphoses, Daphnis and Chloe,* and *Volupté,* and deriving from a group called *The Damned Women* from *The Gates of Hell.*[7] Since the hero also changes sex roles at night with his beloved, we have one interesting explanation for Hemingway's postwar choice of a symbol for his own unmanning by war wounds and the American nurses who tend them: for if Jake remains "capable of all normal feelings as a *man* but incapable of consummating them," as Hemingway told George Plimpton in a famous interview, his physical wound suggests also the female genitals as men erroneously imagine them, at least according to Freud.[8] The exact nature of the wound, moreover, is literally nowhere spelled out or explained in the novel; we have only Hemingway's word for the intended condition. It becomes clear nonetheless from the type of mannish heroine he imagines, after Lady Duff Twysden's British example, that an exchange of sexual roles has indeed occurred, prefiguring that of *The Garden of Eden*, and that it is Jake and not Brett who wears that traditionally female protection, the chastity belt.

What are we to make, then, of Brett Ashley's British mannishness? Her Britishness, as we have seen, goes back to that quasi-British establishment, the Hemingway household in Oak Park presided over by Abba Ernest Hall, a British emigrant in mid-nineteenth century, and his talented daughter Grace, with his wife's brother Tyley Hancock, another mid-century emigrant, as a frequent visitor. These American Fauntleroys, tourers of the British Isles, one of whom almost sang before the queen, others of whom wore mutton chop whiskers and walked tiny dogs, set the at times bantering, smoking, and tippling, at times religiously serious, tones of the household; and the talented Grace's music lessons and concerts helped to further differentiate that home from those of surrounding neighbors like the Hemingways, from whom Grace's husband Clarence, the young doctor whom she met when he tended her dying mother, had gravitated. In Grace and Clarence's favorite Victorian novel, *John Halifax, Gentleman*, one of Dinah Mulock Craik's most striking figures was the Catholic Lady Caroline Brithwood, who came to no good end, and whom we may take as the first fictional harbinger of Lady Ashley in young Ernest's boyhood reading.

Lady Caroline's appeal, in this staunchly moral novel, stems from the mixture in her portraiture of Catholic leniency with European license. In *The Sun Also Rises*, of course, it is Jake Barnes who is the lenient Catholic, Brett Ashley the licensed European; but the combination is striking, especially if we consider Jake for a moment as an aspect of his beloved British lady, or her lesbian lover:

> Brett was damned good-looking. She wore a slipover jersey sweater and a tweed skirt, and her hair was brushed back like a boy's. She started all that. She was built with curves like the hull of a racing yacht, and you missed none of it with that wool jersey. . . .

> I told the driver to go to the Parc Monsouris, and got in, and slammed the door. Brett was leaning back in the corner, her eyes closed. I got in and sat beside her. The cab started with a jerk. "Oh darling, I've been so miserable," Brett said. . . .

> The taxi went up the hill. . . . We were sitting apart and we jolted close together going down the old street. Brett's hat was off. Her head

was back. I saw her face in the lights from the open shops, then it was dark . . . and I kissed her. Our lips were tight together and then she turned away. . . .

"Don't touch me" she said, "please don't touch me." . . .

"Don't you love me?"

"Love you? I simply turn all to jelly when you touch me."

"Isn't there anything we can do about it?. . .

"I don't know," she said. "I don't want to go through that hell again." . . .

On the Boulevard Raspail . . . Brett said: "Would you mind very much if I asked you to do something?

"Don't be silly."

"Kiss me just once more before we get there."

When the taxi stopped I got out and paid. Brett came out putting on her hat. She gave me her hand as she stepped down. Her hand was shaky. "I say, do I look too much of a mess?" She pulled her man's felt hat down and started in for the bar. . . .

"Hello, you chaps," Brett said. "I'm going to have a drink."[9]

The cab ride is a setup for the ending, when Jake and Brett are in another such cab in Madrid, pressed together as the cab slows down, with Brett saying, "Oh, Jake. . . . We could have had such a damned good time together," and Jake replying: "Yes. Isn't it pretty to think so." A hard-boiled ending, but those early kisses tell us otherwise. For through them Jake's vulnerability to pain through the essential feminization of his power to love has been established; like a woman, he cannot penetrate his beloved but can only rouse and be roused by her through fervent kisses; nor is he ready, at this early stage of the sexual revolution, for those oral-genital solutions which recent critics have been willing to impose upon him. His maleness then is like Brett's, who with her boy's haircut and man's felt hat may be said to remind us of the more active lesbian lover in the Rodin statue, named playfully Daphnis in one version to an obvious Chloe. Which again makes us wonder if Jake is not in some sense an aspect of his beloved—not really her chivalric admirer, like Robert Cohn, but rather her masculine girlfriend, her admiring Catherine from the novel years ahead who similarly stops her car on the return from Nice to kiss her lesbian lover, then tells her androgynous husband about it and makes him kiss her too—or, in Jake's more abject moments, her selfless Catherine from the novel next in line.

True enough, we see Jake enduring a form of love about which nothing can be done, working out what could be called a peculiarly male predicament, a sad form of a common wartime joke, in accord with Hemingway's stated plan; and in his struggles against his own self-pity we see a standard of male conduct against which we are asked to measure Robert Cohn's more abject slavishness to his beloved lady, and Mike Campbell's, and even (more to its favor) young Pedro Romero's manly devotion. And truer still, we are asked to judge Brett's liberation as a displacement of male privilege and power in matters of the heart and loins, a sterile wasteland consequence of postwar change. But what if the secret agenda is to admire and emulate Brett Ashley? What if Brett is the woman Jake would in some sense like to be?

"She started all that," he tells us admiringly, and perhaps even predictively. Brett's style-setting creativity becomes, in *The Garden of Eden,* the leading characteristic of Catherine Bourne, whose smart boyish haircuts, blond hairdyes and matching fisherman's shirts and pants—all shared with her androgynous husband David—are plainly expressions of the new postwar mannishness, the new rivalry with men for attention and power, for a larger stake in the socio-sexual pie: new sexual freedoms and privileges, then, new license. They are also forms of artistry, like Catherine's unexpected talent for talk; and if Brett's talent is less for talk than for putting chaps through hell, she is oddly also the same risk-taking character, the same sexual adventurer we ultimately meet in Catherine Bourne, though strictly heterosexual in her conquests—except perhaps with Jacob Barnes. "I suppose she only wanted what she couldn't have," muses the latter, not seeing as yet how well those words describe himself (31).

I do not mean to imply here that Jacob, a soulful wrestler with his own physical condition, would also like to make it with bullfighters and other males—that seems to me misleading—but rather that—in accord with the oddly common attraction for men of lesbian lovemaking, the imagining into it that exercises suppressed femininity, and indeed the need for such imagining, such identification with the original nurturing sources of love—he wants Brett in a womanly way. Hemingway's childhood twinning with his older sister Marcelline may have made him more sensitive to such desires and more strongly liable first to suppress and then ultimately to express them; but he was in fact expressing something common, difficult, and quite possibly crucial to coming of age as a man in this century's white bourgeois circles. His admiration for the liberated ladies of the 1920s was widely shared, and his ultimate enslavement by their androgynous powers may tell us more about ourselves and our times than we care to know.

Certainly Jake is enslaved by Brett as are Robert Cohn and Mike Campbell and even Pedro Romero, who escapes her only through her charitable withdrawal of her devastating love. That is the Ulyssean predicament, the

Circean circle. But there are worshipful precedents for it in childhood that make it seem less ironic and pitiful (in a novel struggling to get beyond those judgments) than inevitable and rather touching. One thinks of Guy Halifax's boyhood crush on Lady Caroline, in *John Halifax, Gentleman,* as a possible source in this regard of Circe's awful power. Lady Caroline, whom I earlier described as "a handsome charming hedonist hellbent on adultery," was also "the magic centre of any society wherein she chose to move," an irresistible charmer, like Brett, floating easily "upon and among the pleasantnesses of life," above the ravages of pain. Ultimately, like Brett, she is ravaged by pain, and has done her share of ravaging; but when we first meet her at Longfield, the Halifax estate after which Grace Hemingway would name her farm and music sanctuary across the lake in northern Michigan, the wicked lady receives a curious certification as the preferred romantic mother of little Guy Halifax. This "little gentleman from his cradle" is the first to announce her arrival; he boldly asks her, "Isn't this a pretty view?" as they approach the house, and having touched her green gown (as opposed to his mother's gray), he proceeds to install himself as "her admiring knight attendant everywhere."[10] Later, as a young adult in Paris, he will even strike her seducer and abandoner, Sir Gerard Vermilye, just as Robert Cohn will strike Lady Ashley's rival admirers in Pamplona. Meanwhile in childhood he gathers for her that magnificent arum lily which would eventually appear on the Hemingway family shield, and at bedtime lifts up his face to her to be kissed as by a new and more romantic mother. The kiss is thwarted since Lady Caroline, as we earlier saw, is unable to return it because of sudden distress at her own sinful condition—an earlier version, perhaps, of Lady Ashley's "Don't touch me." At any rate, this confessed adulteress, who resembles Brett in that she defends her sin vigorously on the grounds of her husband's brutality and her lover's kindness and devotion, but who is nonetheless so far gone that she finds the pastoral domestic love of the Halifaxes impossible for herself, even as Brett can't live "quietly in the country . . . with [her] own true love" (55)—this wicked woman is Guy Halifax's "pretty lady," and quite possibly Ernest Hemingway's earliest source of attraction to Brett's prototype, Duff Twysden, his first preferred alternative to real and fictional mothers like Ursula Halifax and Grace Hemingway—the romantic lady, then, of his boyhood reading dreams.

Still another "romantic lady" would figure in the making of Brett Ashley. Critics have long noted the influence of Michael Arlen's heroine Iris March, in *The Green Hat,* possibly because of the fetish made of Brett's man's hat but also because of the modern twist on an old tradition. As Allen Tate observed in criticizing Hemingway for sparing certain characters in *The Sun*

Also Rises from equitable judgment, Brett "becomes the attractive wayward lady of Sir Arthur Pinero and Michael Arlen"; whereas "Petronius's Circe, the archetype of all the Bretts, was neither appealing nor deformed" (44). Such observations are useful in that Brett is indeed given special treatment, early on, as "one of us"—that is to say, "one of us" stoical and perhaps Conradian survivors—and is granted a certain nobility at the end for her refusal to destroy the worthy Pedro, to say nothing of her repeated returns to Jake Barnes for support and reassurance, as to the novel's touchstone for stoic endurance. Similarly Arlen's attractively wayward heroine in *The Green Hat* is given more than the usual share of male honor as she protects her suicidal first husband's good name at the expense of her own, assuming to herself the "impurity" (i.e., syphilis) that killed him, and then, in another grand gesture of self-denial, sending her true love back to his wife before roaring off in her yellow Hispano-Suiza to a fiery and quite melodramatic death; and Iris too is characterized as "one of us" and is said to "meet men on their own ground always."[11] Even so, Brett is probably based on still another Arlen heroine in more important ways. Thus, as Carlos Baker reports, Scott Fitzgerald had passed the time on a motor trip with Hemingway in May 1925 "by providing detailed summaries of the plots of the novels of Michael Arlen," one of which—a tale called "The Romantic Lady"—seems to have moved him (though he denied it) to go and do likewise.[12]

"The Romantic Lady" is a Men's Club story told to the narrator by his good friend Noel Anson, whom the narrator has not seen for six years and who has been divorced just six months before, he at once explains, by "a perfect woman." Much later in the evening Anson reserves for his friend the title story, proceeding in a manner our narrator likens to Marlow's as he leads his transfixed hearer "inexorably through the labyrinth of Lord Jim's career, and through many another such intricacy of Conradian imagination."[13] Anson calls it an "ageless tale of the inevitable lady sitting alone in an inevitable [theatre] box" (4)—a story, that is, of a genteel pickup, the twist being that the picker here is in fact himself picked by the lady though he proceeds at first otherwise. Thus, while sitting alone in a stall one night at the old Imperial, Anson suddenly sees in the upper boxes "a marvellous lady in white, amazing and alone and unashamed" (4–5). He at once works out a note inviting this instance of "real, exquisite life" to dinner, receives a reply to call at her box after the revue—and is taken home by her to a table already set for dinner. In other words, he is her guest; she, not he, is the host for dinner, and she actually laughs at him for imagining he has "picked [her] up":

"'Don't you know that it was decided this morning that you should come to supper with me, decided quite, quite early? Or some one like you, perhaps not so charming—but then I have been so lucky—. . . . Are you very angry with me?'"

"She was very close to me, smiling, intimate. Pure coquetry of course, —but what perfect *technique!* You knew that she was playing, but that did not prevent the blood rushing to your head; and she was so clean, so much 'one of us'! . . .

"'Anger isn't exactly one of my emotions at the moment,' I said, stupidly enough. 'But will you please be very gentle with me, because never, never have I met any one like you?'" (12–13)

The Conradian phrase is out; the lady is the right sort, she is "one of us": she is calling the shots, moreover, in what must be candidly recognized as a 1920s Mayfair version of "the zipless fuck," as Erica Jong would later call it—indeed, an anticipation of the new female terms for it as Jong would work them out ("will you please be very gentle with me . . . ?") through her own sexually adventurous ladies.[14]

Our more immediate problem, however, is Hemingway's similar terms for Brett's conquest, and the curious way they bear on modern marriage. For Arlen's lady is not only married; there is a portrait of her husband on the wall, "a very distinguished looking person . . . in the toy uniform of some foreign cavalry, gorgeously decorated," and with "a thin hawk-like face, which with its perfectly poised mixture of ferocity and courtesy would have carried its fortunate owner as easily into the heart of any schoolboy as into the boudoir of the most unattainable "lady" (15). One thinks of Count Mippipopolous, the Greek escort, replete with chauffeur, who drives Lady Brett around Paris in his limousine, brings Jake flowers, exhibits his arrow wounds, values food, wine, and love, and is also characterized by Brett as "one of us." Arlen's romantic lady's husband may have sat for that portrait too, since he turns up later in the story as the coachman who not only takes Anson home, but on being recognized by him, explains the lady's game. Thus he too had first met his wife at the theatre, had himself been picked by her for an evening's romance, and had been told by her upon parting—as Anson has just been told—to forget the address, to settle for one perfect night of love. Instead he had gone back the next day, she had been delighted by his return, had married him—and then tired of him, as she had grown tired of her previous husband to whom he too had then been introduced as his predecessor in the endless game of beautiful one-night stands. Indeed, marriage had been his punishment for insisting upon seeing her again:

"... and I had to acquiesce in her mere affection for me—that affection with which all splendid women enshroud their dead loves. And how much in oneself dies with their dead love! Why, there dies the ritual of love, the sacrament of sex! For sex can be exalted to a sacrament only once in a lifetime, for the rest it's just a game, an indoor sport. . . ."

"You see, such women as she make their own laws. It is not her fault, nor her arrogance, it is ours, who are so consistently susceptible. Physically she belongs to the universe, not to one single man. She never belonged to me, I was just an expression of the world to her. She has never belonged to any one, she never will—for she is in quest of the ideal which even she will never find. And so she will go on, testing our—our quality and breaking our hearts." (34–35)

One thinks of Brett surrounded by wreathed dancers when the fiesta at Pamplona explodes (155); or "coming through the crowd in the square, walking, her head up, as though the fiesta were being staged in her honor" (206); or of the book's epigraph from Ecclesiastes—"the earth abideth forever"—and Hemingway's odd assertion that "the abiding earth" is the novel's hero.[15] If Arlen's romantic lady is any evidence, "abiding heroine" might be more to the point—"earthy" ladies who make their own laws, confine sex to adventurous one-night stands which, in Hemingway's more cynical world, do not mean anything, but which are in fact cynical enough in Arlen's formulation—his Marlovian narrator having been divorced six months before, he now reminds us, for having himself gone back for the punishment of marriage. "Be very gentle with me" indeed: those oddly passive, now androgynous remarks remind us all too tellingly that it was Pauline who pursued and won Ernest away from Hadley in 1926, the year in which *The Sun Also Rises* was first published.

FREDERIC AND CATHERINE

In the same letter in which he recalls for Carlos Baker his first meeting with Hemingway, Allen Tate recalls also the hospital-like conditions under which he first read and—as it were—reviewed *A Farewell to Arms:*

I remember distinctly the time he brought me one of the first copies received from NY of *A Farewell to Arms.* I was in bed with flu at the Hotel de l'Odeon. He came to the door of our room, and asked Caroline to hand me the book so that he would not be exposed to the germs. He asked me how soon I could read it. I answered, at once. I began it as soon as he had left, and didn't put it aside until I had finished it. He came back the next morning to ask how I liked it; I said it was a masterpiece. (I still think it is.) He was very childlike: he wanted me to admire his latest book to counteract my rough handling of (I think) *The Torrents of Spring*.

It was of course *The Sun Also Rises* that Tate had roughly handled; *The Torrents of Spring* he had called "a small masterpiece"; but one can understand why, more than thirty years later, he would want to reverse that judgment, and he himself pleads in his opening statement: "What I remember goes back thirty years, and I may not remember it accurately; but some things stand out." At the moment what stands out, remarkably, is the association in Hemingway's mind of Tate's harsh judgment of Jake Barnes as a sentimental figure and Tate's reversal of that judgment where Frederic Henry was concerned. Yet Frederic is as much the passive victim of wounds and circumstances as Jake Barnes, and constitutes a kind of replay of Jake's wartime predicament, that which preceded the action of *The Sun Also Rises* now revisited, but this time with a female rather than a male victim of those damaging times, a woman who dies in childbirth rather than the Indian brave with the slashed foot in the bunk above her; indeed, the Indian brave survives to tell the tale.

What are we to make, then, of Frederic's suffering, which Tate from his convalescent's bed in 1929 (and still in 1962) finds unsentimental; whereas other critics have often thought quite otherwise about the degree of sentimentality in these two novels and in the portraits of their heroes? Perhaps a look at Robert Cohn, in *The Sun Also Rises,* will help us on our way.

I am referring now to the satire of Cohn's postwar role as the chivalric lover, the romantic fool who has not learned the war's painful lesson about the death of love, the dissolution of romance into one-night stands and brief affairs, the impossiblity therefore of romantic marriage. When women like Brett become laws unto themselves, when men like Jake are unmanned—the knights devitalized even as the ladies acquire new knightly powers—there can be no chivalric romance, and only a fool like Cohn would continue to think so. One irony of the text, of course, is that Jake Barnes secretly continues to think so until the final revelation that Brett could not make a go of it with Pedro Romero, that she would destroy him by her liberated (or single standard) love, and that Jake's loss of a penis would in fact make no difference were it miraculously restored by some priestess of Isis, some Lawrencean goddess devoted to male ithyphallic powers—for as we see in the next novel, *A Farewell to Arms,* those types have also been victimized by the war, and only the Bretts and Irises and Daisies have survived it, and they can't be quiet in the country, not even with their own true Jakes, Napiers, and Gatsbys, their own unmanned or wounded or romantic postwar warriors.

Hemingway's direct confrontation, then, of Cohn's romantic folly, Cohn's sentimental view of the postwar possibilities of romantic love, and Hemingway's artful recognition of Jake's and his own complicity in that view, even as Jake serves as a stoic standard against it, had been missed by Tate, much to Ernest's disappointment and chagrin; he felt misunderstood by Tate's hard-boiled judgment of Jake himself as sentimental, for Hemingway too understood Jake's weakness. As for Cohn, whose Jewishness had troubled Tate in his review of *The Sun Also Rises* ("Robert Cohn is not only a bounder, he is a Jewish bounder. The other bounders, like Mike, Mr. Hemingway for some reason spares"), was not Hemingway himself also Hemingstein in his youth, a self-mocking (hence Jewish) outsider with intellectual pretensions, a would-be novelist and pugilist?[16] Such unarticulated feelings must have determined Hemingway's strong reaction to Tate's disapproval of his first real novel. What he missed in Tate's judgment, what we are now indeed able to see better for ourselves, was the connection Tate was making between Jake's self-pity as the "impotent" pursuer of an inaccessible woman, and the special treatment, the sparing, given to Brett as to Mike and other "tough" characters in the postwar waste land. As the husband of a professional woman, Caroline Gordon, Tate may have known something about equity in the treatment of women characters that Hemingway did not and perhaps never would know: namely, that "Petronius's Circe, the archetype of all the Bretts, was neither appealing nor deformed."[17]

But then why shouldn't Brett be appealing? As the free-floating hedonist of the postwar era, the style-setter, the mannish woman with whose sexual adventurousness shy or passive or frustrated men may identify, she may well be the woman we vulnerable males, we antiheroes of the modern age, would all like to be, even as Catherine Barkley in the next novel is the healing woman whose ministrations we might all like to command. Hemingway's stake in creating new versions of old archetypes has to be given its literary and perhaps cultural due. The war's devastations, and those of the culture that made the war, had indeed made it difficult for men and women alike to avoid the consequences of change: shifting power relations, new displacements of confidence and possibility, bewildering breakdowns of old values, old lines of support and reassurance. Elsewhere Tate would recall that "it was enormously difficult to live then, and not entirely pleasant"; the nineteenth century was at an end, a "vast change, the result of the first World

War," had occurred; people were shocked out of their complacency; sensiblity itself was altered; there were "external difficulties that everybody faced in that time," and at least "some of [Hemingway's] excellence was largely due" to them or to the way he faced them: with "a mind of great subtlety," with "enormous powers of selective observation," and with "a first-rate intelligence." Indeed, "he's one of the most intelligent men I've ever known and one of the best-read," Tate had concluded, thus giving Hemingway, at last, the critic's finest kudos.[18]

What then was the well-read Hemingway doing with this amalgamation of Cohn and Barnes, this wounded wartime lover who learns the hard way that to be hard-boiled is also Vanity, who loves and loses arms romantic and military, and so undergoes firsthand the chivalric disillusionment of the First World War? We know that Hemingway was of two minds as to how to approach him: as a very foolish and excited young man like himself named Emmett Hancock, in his first attempt to write the novel; and as a somewhat jaded, somewhat older man named Frederic Henry in the novel at hand. "Emmett" obviously comes from Emmett County, Michigan, where Hemingway summered as a boy: and "Hancock" decidedly comes from the revolutionary Hancock side of Grace's family; it is her mother's maiden name. Frederic, on the other hand, comes from Frederic Moreau, the disillusioned hero of Flaubert's *L'Education Sentimentale* (one of the novel's possible titles) so that the choice of "Frederic" over "Emmett" reveals a shift from Hemingway's youthful enthusiasm for the war—still evident in the early Hancock fragment—to weary disaffection in the novel, even as the choice of "Henry" over "Hancock" suggests an ironic play on Patrick Henry, a patriot who, unlike Frederic, was willing to die nobly for his country. As for the addled nurse, Catherine Barkley, whom war-weary Lieutenant Henry meets on the Italian front, her most obvious literary prototype is Emily Brontë's addled heroine, Catherine Earnshaw Linton, who also identifies with a radically disaffected lover, dies in childbirth, and haunts him after death. She owes something more, however, to such live prototypes as Agnes Von Kurowsky, Pauline Pfeiffer, and Hadley Richardson; and especially perhaps to the sheltered Hadley, who at twenty-nine was ready to break the world's jail with a younger Ernest, escape to the freer life in Paris, and so make amends for past confinements.[19]

Having lost a sweetheart in the war to whom she failed to yield herself, Catherine is ready to make similar breaks and amends with Frederic. Her compensatory love will prove selfless, nonetheless, and will involve a lesson in caring—or, as some critics call it, *caritas*—which might better be called a lesson in androgyny. Consideration for others—which Grace Hemingway expected of Ernest and taught him to show his sisters—is a Fauntleroy ideal endorsed by Christian gentlemen. For Ernest it was a feminine version of manly character, which helps to explain why Catherine is the exemplary "source of instruction" for Frederic in this novel. Their selfless love is formed in one hospital, moreover, and dissolved in another, in keeping with the author's childhood familiarity with his father's medical world, where male and female caring intermix, and with his own experience as a caring Red Cross corpsman who recovered from war wounds in a Milan hospital.

The first version of the novel begins, in fact, with Emmett Hancock's arrival at the Milan hospital; and in Book Two of the final version, Frederic Henry's love for Catherine Barkley begins there too. Until this point, Henry has taken Catherine as a windfall, a welcome change from the prostitutes he has known at the front and on leave. Unlike the younger Hancock, who had known no prostitutes and had never been naked before a woman outside his family but who had decidedly wanted a nurse "to fall in love with," the older Henry has "not wanted to fall in love with anyone."[20] But now, flat on his back in the hospital, he immediately falls in love with Catherine. Perhaps Hancock's eager expectation explains Henry's sudden reversal.

In the hospital, the wounded hero in both versions is in masterful command. Neither the porters nor the stretcher-bearers nor the elderly nurse they rouse know where to put him. He demands to be put in a room, dispenses tips to the porters and stretcher-bearers, tells the befuddled nurse she can leave him there to rest. As E. L. Doctorow observes of a similarly passive character, David Bourne in *The Garden of Eden*, he seems rather like an arriving American colonizer of foreign fields.[21] Indeed, he is nowhere more authoritative than when flat on his back and served by gentle attendants and adoring nurses; in previous chapters of the novel he has been relatively restrained with peers and subordinates. Plainly, his wounds, which certify his manliness and relieve him for a time from further heroism, are one source of his new-found authority. His position as the first and only male patient in a hospital overstaffed to serve him is another; and the author's early authority when surrounded by admiring sisters, both before and after his return from the war, is not irrelevant to it. In Henry's certified passivity, then, lies his greatest power; he has license to reign from his bed as Grace Hemingway had reigned when served breakfast there by her husband Clarence—or as Joyce's Molly had reigned when served by Leopold Bloom. In effect, he has finally arrived at something like a woman's passive power.

His feminization takes still other interesting forms. He is tenderized by love, made to care like the caring Catherine, in whom his selfhood is immediately invested. In a discarded passage, he feels that he goes out of the room whenever she leaves.[22] More crucially, he is like a woman in the lovemaking that takes place in his hospital room at night. As no one has yet puzzled out, he would have to lie on his back to perform properly, given the nature of his leg wounds, and Catherine would have to lie on top of him. This long-hidden and well-kept secret of the text is one Mary Welsh Hemingway implies about married love with Ernest and even quotes him on in *How It Was,* one Ernest seems to imply about himself and Hadley in *A Moveable Feast* and makes fictionally explicit, at the least, in his portrait of characters like himself and Hadley (the painters Nick and Barbara Sheldon) in *The Garden of Eden.*[23] That—James-like—Hemingway could not articulate that secret in *A Farewell to Arms* indicates the force not merely of censorship in the 1920s, but of chauvinist taboos against it. The interesting thing is that Hemingway—for whom the idea of female dominance was so threatening—could so plainly imply the female dominant without being understood or held to his oblique confession. Of course, the straddling Catherine in the superior position was more than he was willing, much less able, then to specify; but for anyone interested in "how it was"—and we have long since become interested to excess—that iceberg conclusion was there for the drawing, or the thawing. Happily we now have books and movies that sanction female mountings of receptive males. But that Hemingway could overcome his own and everyone else's fear of female dominance—could give it tacit public expression—seems to me remarkable. Compare explicit sexual writers of the day like Joyce, who could imagine an abjectly transvestite Bloom but not a masterfully supine one; or Lawrence, for whom supineness was an unthinkable abandonment of ithyphallic powers! So perhaps Hemingway might also be supposed to have felt, but apparently did not; perhaps because, like the supine Frederic, the wounded hero, he already felt masterful enough to enjoy it; perhaps because he saw good androgynous women like Catherine as unthreatening to his essential maleness, in the initial stages of love, and to that side of the male ego—male identity—the bitch woman seemed so immediately to jeopardize.

In *The Garden of Eden,* where the exchange of sex roles is an explicit and troubling issue, his heroes would feel greater qualms. But in this novel the hero's power is never greater than in the hospital love scenes. Not only does he impregnate Catherine from his supine position; he is also delivered of his own shell fragments by the romantically named Dr. Valentini, who in turn offers to deliver Catherine's baby free. As the analogy between his operation and her Caesarean suggests, Catherine—lacking Valentini's assistance—cannot emulate Frederic's successful parturition. He undergoes and survives an ordeal by suffering to which Catherine in her comparable situation will succumb.

Meanwhile, their hospital-based love enters a mystic phase. Before the operation she effaces herself, says she'll do, say, and want anything he wants. "There isn't any me any more," she concludes, "Just what you want" (106). Afterwards, in discussing why they needn't marry, she repeats her point: "There isn't any me any more. I'm you. Don't make up a separate me" (115). Her declaration, like Catherine Earnshaw's famous pronouncement—"I am Heathcliff"—is a time-honored Christian Romantic version of the union of two souls. The friendly priest at the front has predicted and blessed their union for the lesson in selfless caring it entails. But Catherine and (more ambivalently) Frederic are Romantics whose Christianity has lapsed: "You're my religion," she tells him now (116), and so invokes a Romantic heresy, the religion of love, going back to the eleventh century (as the Catholic Hemingway, then married to Pauline, well understood). Lacking any connection with God or immortality, this atheistic faith will eventually fail them, leaving the ambivalent Frederic alone and bereft with the memories here recalled. But for a time they are fused in mystic selflessness.

The androgynous nature of their fusion is further developed when they flee to Switzerland and Frederic's turn as the caring, selfless partner begins. This idyllic phase has been anticipated by Frederic's loving (indeed colonizing) description of the priest's home in Abruzzi, which he has failed to visit, but which he then imagines as a "place where . . . it was clear cold and dry and the snow was dry and powdery and hare-tracks in the snow and the peasants took off their hats and called you Lord and there was good hunting" (13). Switzerland is like that, except for the hunting, which Frederic selflessly eschews. He has abandoned sports and war for a world circumscribed by love, and now reads about them somewhat wistfully in newspapers. The escaped lovers reside, moreover, in the chalet near Montreux where Hemingway and Hadley once lived and which Ernest prized for its "ideal blend of wilderness and civilization."[24] In that idyllic region, the lovers read, play cards, stroll together in the powdered snow, stop at country inns, or visit the nearby village where Frederic watches with excitement while Catherine has her hair done at the hairdresser's—the kind of scene that becomes a leitmotif in *The Garden of Eden*, some twenty years ahead. Later the lovers decide that Frederic must grow a beard, or better still, let his hair grow long while she has hers cut short to match it: then they will be alike, one person, as they are now one person at night (298–300)—and this too will become a leitmotif in *Eden*. They settle now, however, for the beard, which grows splendidly through the winter, like a gradually reemerging form of male identity. In the spring the rains come, washing away the powdered snow; they move to Lausanne so Catherine can have her baby at the hospital; and Frederic takes up boxing at the local gym.

Their edenic love dissolves when Catherine dies from her Caesarean operation and their child is stillborn (a fate which Pauline and her first Caesarean child had just avoided).[25] Supposedly Catherine has been caught in that "biological trap" which, in its absurdity and futility, is the female equivalent for death on the modern battlefield; and certainly her death has been carefully foreshadowed in just these cosmic terms. You may enjoy edenic and androgynous bliss in this world, Hemingway surmises, but in the end "they" will take it from you. The punishment for stolen happiness is death. But since the same punishment is meted out to honest misery, and since death in childbirth has been unusual in white bourgeois circles since the end of the nineteenth century, the novel's tragic resolution seems arbitrary to many readers, and again suggests the displacement of an essentially Victorian dread onto alien grounds. It may be too that Catherine's small hips—that androgynous feature—have determined her fate in more ways than one. The love she offers so absorbs male identity that she is as threatening to it, finally, as any bitch heroine; and though she dies bravely, like a true Hemingway hero, it may be that she is sacrificed to male survival—so that this time the Indian in the upper bunk lives on!

Whatever the case, Hemingway bids farewell to androgynous love in this novel and turns for the next ten years to the problem of shoring up his own male identity. The legend of the hard-boiled "tough guy" writer, already predicted by Tate's asperities, may be said to have begun with the sentimental dodge of Catherine's death. It was not of course the world but those stronger women—Agnes, Grace, and Pauline—who brought to an end the androgynous idylls in Milan, Michigan, and Paris; and in Pauline's case especially we begin to see why this is so.

ERNEST AND PAULINE

When Emmett Hancock first enters the Milan hospital, in the original beginning of *A Farewell to Arms,* he loses control of his urinary and sphincter muscles several times in succession, is cleaned up by nurses, has his sheets changed, and feels embarrassed at being "looked after like a baby."[26] We see no such embarrassing regression when his older counterpart, Frederic Henry, enters the same hospital; and yet at least two recent critics have remarked upon the "infantilism" of his ensuing love affair with Catherine Barkley. Thus, in approaching this novel as "Personal Metaphor," Millicent Bell finds the lovers' raptures "curiously suspect":

> Frederic has only delusively attached himself to an otherness. Far
> from the war's inordinate demand upon his responses, he has been

converted to feeling in the isolation of his hospital bed, where, like a baby in its bassinet, he is totally passive, tended and comforted by female caretakers, the nurses, and particularly by this one. The image is regressive, and the ministering of Catherine, who looks after all his needs, including sexual, while he lies passive, is more maternal than connubial. The relation that now becomes the center of the novel is, indeed, peculiar enough to make us question it as a representation of adult love. More often noted than Frederic's passivity is the passivity of Catherine in this love affair, a passivity which has irritated readers (particularly female readers) because it seems to be a projection of male fantasies of the ideally submissive partner. It results from her desire to please. She is a sort of inflated rubber woman available at will to the onanistic dreamer. There is, in fact, a masturbatory quality to the love of each. The union of these two is a flight from outer reality and eventually from selfhood, which depends upon a recognition of the other; . . . of . . . the alien in the beloved and therefore the independent in itself. The otherness that Frederic and Catherine provide for one another is not enough to preserve their integral selves, and while the sounds of exteriority become more and more muffled in the novel, their personalities melt into one another.[27]

In her essay "Hemingway and the Secret Language of Hate," Faith Pullin similarly argues that Frederic and Catherine are ciphers rather than existing human beings and that Hemingway's talent is less for creating characters than for reporting the experience of extreme sensations and emotions; and she too raises the charge of infantilism:

War naturally simplifies the relationship between the sexes, by removing surfaces and revealing the basic power situation. Catherine confuses the Italians because they don't want nurses at the front, only whores; on the other hand, to be a nurse is in itself to be de-sexed, or rather, to be cast in the role of mother. Catherine's mistake is that she is to be a mother to a real child, thereby removing herself from a position of total subservience to the infantile demands of Frederic. To Catherine, sex seems to be something extraneous to herself, an abstract possession which can be used to please Frederic, but not, apparently, herself.[28]

Such well-taken charges are not, of course, new. In 1941 Edmund Wilson had noted Hemingway's increasing antagonism to women; he had also found Catherine and Frederic "not very convincing as personalities" and had called their love a "youthful erotic dream." In 1949 Gershon Legman had similarly remarked on Hemingway's extreme hatred of women; and Isaac Rosenfeld in 1951 and Richard Hovey in 1968 had made similar charges about mother love and narcissism.[29] But the new chorus of feminist critiques is nonetheless refreshing, and often newly perceptive, in taking over a protest that belongs to it. The only question I want to raise at this point is whether infantilism and self-repression altogether explain these relations, or whether feminization, or better still androgyny, might further explain them, especially if it serves now as the experiential "wound" against which Hemingway raises his artistic "bow." The kind of wound that Jake Barnes sustains in the previous novel; the fact (which Bell fails to note in this one) that Frederic is curiously masterful in his passivity; the interesting possiblity, entertained by neither Bell nor Pullin, that Catherine is the active and superior partner in the hospital trysts (indeed, Judith Fetterley even speaks of her striking "aggressiveness . . . in the service of Frederic's passivity" and of the "inner space" created when she lets her hair fall over him "like a tent")[30]—all of this suggests a hidden agenda in these fictions, a secret and ambivalent language about androgynous impulses, a form of self-hatred and self-love of the female within the male that begins to define itself at this time as the secret wound in modern romantic relations as Hemingway saw them, against which he disciplined his masculine art.

If we suppose for a moment that Catherine is a vital part of Frederic, and not simply an inflatable rubber object of his fantasies, then we may well be witnessing a historic flight from tenderness, or from tender aspects of male humanity, with cultural as well as personal implications. Certainly the initial loss of Agnes Von Kurowsky's love, the ensuing loss of Grace Hemingway's regard and approval, the frustrations with Duff Twysden, the loss of Hadley's love through separation and divorce, and the aggressive appropriations of Pauline, all point to a propensity in Hemingway for self-wounding which, while extremely painful for his life, yet proved to be extremely fruitful for his art; and if as Edmund Wilson surmises, his art was also then a gauge of public morale, then perhaps we are dealing also with a propensity of early modern times. Two observations by Millicent Bell may help to clarify these points.

In her insistence that Frederic and Catherine lack sufficient otherness, that selfhood itself "depends upon a recognition of the other," or of "the alien in the other and therefore the independent in itself," she is not simply complaining as others do that Hemingway fails to define characters, or that he defines emotions better than characters; she is tracing that phenomenon to a type of romantic love which the author here endorses: selfless fusion or

interfusion by which these "personalities melt into each other." Hemingway's borrowed romantic ideal, the adolescent fusion so defiantly pro-
claimed in Brontë's *Wuthering Heights* (and so brilliantly presented there as a
shared state of mind), is seen as a key to his creation of this "pitiful pair."
More seriously, it is a variant of that "affective failure" Bell finds at work
throughout the novel, that stylistic tension between realism and the seemingly irrelevant by which the war becomes "an objective correlative" of the
narrator's state of mind, the lyrical projection of "an inner condition." And
finally it is her attempt to define that condition which strikes me as most
helpful:

> In fact, an unvarying mood, established by the narrative voice, domi-
> nates everything it relates, bathes uniformly all the images and levels
> events which are seen always in one way only. That the principal
> descriptive elements—river, mountains, dust or mud, and above all,
> rain—are all present in the opening paragraphs suggests not so much
> that later scenes are being predicted as that the subsequent pages will
> disclose nothing that is not already evident in the consciousness that
> has begun its self-exhibition.[31]

Here and later, then, Bell suggests that it is not the events or the characters that make this novel compelling: it is the numbly elegiac style, the
registration of loss and betrayal, the capturing of a state of mind that now
becomes both public and personal as that "gauge of morale" that Wilson first
defined: so that the failure to transcend that numbed impression which the
tenderness between the hospital-based lovers should achieve becomes instead an unwitting sign of its pervasiveness. And here perhaps a few small
objections should be registered, to the effect that Frederic's selfishness is not
simply a revelation of the author's growing hatred of women, as these new
critics hold, but in great part an intended exposure; and that the idyllic
waiting time in Switzerland is not simply a failed attempt to show how
Frederic overcomes his egotism, but in great part how he tries to, how he
imagines himself into Catherine's states of mind in the clear cold mountain
air (compare *Wuthering Heights*) which partakes of the selflessness of the
priest's idyllic world, the Abruzzi, which Frederic has earlier failed to visit,
though at least one critic (Judith Fetterley) reduces such strivings to securely
selfish "inner space" in a work characterized by sexual nausea and murderous
intent; and finally that Frederic's entry into Catherine's death struggles, as
opposed to Hemingway's, is at least another stretching of male imagination
(like that of the Indian in the upper bunk in "Indian Camp") into a woman's
suffering—even if, as Fetterley justly holds, the only good woman in this
novel is a dead one.[32] But let us stop a moment to sort things out.

Elsewhere I have remarked on how the love mode of *The Sun Also Rises* differs markedly from that of *A Farewell to Arms:* how the stress is on male independence from the threat of absorption and destruction which the bitch heroine seems to represent; how the ideal of men without women becomes embodied through the survival of the young bullfighter, Pedro Romero, as a necessary option in postwar wasteland times.[33] Thus, whatever the sentimental hazards of Jake Barnes's self-pity, this novel seems in retrospect tougher and tauter than its successor, just as Brett Ashley seems tougher and tauter, or at least more carefully defined, than Catherine Barkley. The ideal not simply of stoic endurance, but of independent survival, whether for men or women, has been worked through with some effectiveness. To be a woman like Brett is finally more attractive, for men as well as women, than to be a woman like Catherine Barkley. But that may be precisely because with Catherine something in Frederic, and by the same token something in his creator Ernest, is lapsing or dying—namely, his capacity for nurturing tenderness, his sympathetic sameness, his identification with women in their selfless suffering rather than in their bitchy independence. As we shall see, that identification will return in other guises; but for the time being, the ideal of selfless romantic fusion, the *Wuthering Heights* mystique, seems to be lapsing out through that very aggressive passivity in Catherine on which feminist critics have in one way or another focussed. The androgynous secret behind this kind of fusion, the androgynous threat to male identity, is finally more threateningly absorbing than abject service to the bitch goddess Brett Ashley, which at least drives men back upon themselves. So the extremely female Catherine dies that Frederic/Ernest may regain his maleness.

What, then, does it mean, at this point, if the "wound" is androgyny and not, as Philip Young so early established, the actual physical wounds that Hemingway himself sustained at Fossalta? For one thing, as we saw earlier, those physical wounds help to certify Frederic's manliness and so free him for a time from future heroism; for another, the obverse condition also obtains, in that Frederic can enjoy being weak, frail, "female," without being ashamed of his condition: the inevitable fear of being cowardly, unmanly, exposed to pain and death, is now transposed into a pleasurable condition since he has survived his wounds and can enjoy his obvious vulnerability. To be wounded, then, is both the badge of manhood and the secret entry into womanhood: it is not so much infantilism that now besets him as that vulnerability we attribute to both women and children but deny to men— hence his masterful response to being wounded and his immediate love for Catherine Barkley as for an aspect of himself, his extreme vulnerablity, that he is for a time free to accept.

Interestingly, it is Catherine rather than Frederic who will now face death bravely; and therein lies another meaningfully psychosocial implication. As we have seen, a number of recent critics have questioned the reality of Catherine's existence as a character, and some have presented her as a projection of male fantasies, with good cause. But there is a case to be made for her all-too-painful reality as an addled heroine, a woman so obsessed with culturally imposed guilt at her lover's virginal death as to want not simply to give herself sexually to some fantasized replacement for him—a game she half-knowingly plays with Frederic Henry—but also to die for him, to enter the biological trap so as replace him with a child or join him in literal death. We can attribute all this, of course, to Hemingway's neurotic maneuverings of his heroine and to his chauvinistic emphasis on her madly "careless love"; but whatever her reckless ways, there is something bitterly true about her sacrificial selflessness as a cultural trap into which many women fall "in our time." Hemingway's case for Catherine, as for Frederic, is that she transcends her obsessions, is genuinely selfless and caring in her half-mad love, and therefore loves and dies well, even as Frederic loves better than he might otherwise have done. That seems to me a fairer statement of the book's or rather the author's intentions than we psychosocial critics generally grant him. What I am saying, then, is that Catherine is believable, as well as the object of male fantasies, since she is also the subject of female fantasies that we know to be "true," that do exist, however embarrassing we may find her enactment of them. Thus, if she annoys women readers today, it is precisely because she continues to deny herself in all-too-believable ways well lost and to protect Frederic thereby from confronting his own inveterate selfishness: a great many women do these terrible things for selfish men, all the time; and some men like Frederic try to respond in kind, and fail, since the kind is deadly for both, but deadlier for those like Catherine who try harder—which (as Pauline's letters to Ernest well attest) is also surely believable. Indeed, war openly, as well as peace insidiously, does place this premium on male primacy and survival—which is another reason why Catherine's supposedly analogous death seems so unconvincing: it is Frederic she dies for, if not for her previous lover, in what seems to be an interesting inversion of that genteel tradition, women and children first, but also a true inversion for fortunate male survivors.

Certainly these public meanings of the text are in keeping with its tired, elegiac tone, its war-weary rehearsal of inevitable loss and failure and of circumstantial betrayal. We know that Hemingway himself felt no such jaded emotions in World War I. Frederic Henry, the novel's hero, is older than Hemingway was then and considerably more experienced. He has been on the Italian front for a much longer time than Ernest, who spent only a few weeks there before being wounded; and he undergoes the disastrous retreat from Caporetto, which occurred a year before Hemingway even reached Italy.[34] His war-weariness, out of which the early chapters especially are narrated, and perhaps the entire book, was a state of mind Ernest never felt; and Frederic's decision to make a separate peace, to say farewell to arms military, was one Ernest never made. As we know from several sources, the wounded Ernest was an enthusiastic patriot, eager to return to the front—so eager that he returned too soon, came down with yellow jaundice, and had to be carted back to the hospital in Milan.[35] Thus, where Frederic Henry's disillusionment with the war occurs in the retreat from Caporetto, Ernest's was a postwar acquisition—much of it inspired by literary sources. He had absorbed his antiwar sentiments from postwar readings of poets like Owen and Sassoon and novelists and friends like Ford and Dos Passos. What he had read squared, however, with the military histories which then absorbed him and with what he had personally heard and seen at and behind the front; and it squared also with the disillusionment of his postwar return to Oak Park, where his own war stories had gradually palled and gone out of fashion, as he partly records in "Soldier's Home" (1924). In his long recuperation, during which he continued to wear his British cape and Red Cross uniform and his high military boots, he had even become a figure of fun to his neighbors.[36]

It was then, of course, that he also suffered the sequential blows of rejection by Agnes Von Kurowsky and his mother and for a time had to bid farewell to arms romantic. But if Bell is right, it was his farewell to Hadley and his ensuing marriage to Pauline Pfeiffer that truly determined the novel's tone of loss and failure. His father's suicide came too late in the order of composition to affect the initial setting of narrative tone and consciousness by which Frederic may be identified as a "sufferer from blunted affect," or from "affective failure," as from "an emotional apparatus already in retreat from the responsibilites of response." Bell speaks further of his remarriage as creating "a keen sense of guilt . . . along with the recognition [of] compulsive forces he was powerless to restrain"; and also of stories related to the novel ("In Another Country" and "Now I Lay Me") which "suggest a fear associated with marriage—either one will somehow kill it oneself, as he had done with his own first marriage, or it will kill you, or at least emasculate you, as his mother had emasculated his father"; in either case "death and destruction arrive in the end."[37] His pessimistic feelings, then, about his own romantic sensibility and where it had led him had been crystallized by the marriage to Pauline, which in confirming one love had betrayed another. In this sense the dying Catherine is the dying love for Hadley, as for Agnes and Grace before her, whereas the brave Catherine who risks such a death might well be Pauline, as well as Hadley and Grace before her, by whom the guilt of sexuality itself, and its potentially tragic consequences, had severally been stirred. Certainly it was Pauline who had served him so aggressively, in his passivity, as to lead him to betray himself. Thus, with Pauline especially, the wounds of war and peace had crystallized as the wound of androgyny, the wound that is of identification with women and with the female within oneself, felt now as an almost intolerable vulnerabilty, a hidden emasculation, a secret loss of male identity, a self-betrayal—as that delayed time-bomb, *The Garden of Eden,* would eventually, in its own personally metaphoric ways, reveal.

Chapter 9

Tough Mamas and Safari Wives

THE OLD LADY

Hemingway's dedications of his books offer a rich field for speculation. *The Sun Also Rises,* in which he predicts the end of his first marriage, was dedicated to Hadley. *A Farewell to Arms,* in which he mourns the loss of Hadley, was dedicated, not to his second wife, Pauline, but to her rich uncle Gus. The book he would dedicate to Pauline was *Death in the Afternoon,* a study in the ritual proving of manhood. Certainly his life with Pauline was given over to such ritual provings—hunting in Africa, fishing off Key West and Bimini, boxing on shore with all contenders—and was characterized also by insulating affluence. Not surprisingly, the African stories of this period reflect these personal themes. They are about cowardly or corrupted men who must achieve modes of integrity that insure their independence from rich or beautiful women; and they inquire into the failure of love and marriage between bought husbands and wives. The relations between such men and women are brutally damaging; there is no room for the tenderness and consideration of the selfless love mode in *A Farewell to Arms.* Indeed, the numbing of affect, the secret hostilities and self-hatreds of that novel seem to be confirmed, as if the writer himself had discovered and embraced them. In the two long nonfiction studies that precede the African stories—*Death in the Afternoon* (1932) and *Green Hills of Africa* (1935)—we can observe that brutalization process at work, as if by autobiographical transmission.

Death in the Afternoon may be characterized as a guide to the tragic art of bullfighting or as a natural history of an exotic spectacle; it is in either case a defense of what the author himself calls "one of his greatest minor passions" and likens to a taste for fine wines.[1] For both his admirers and detractors, the problem in this book, together with *Green Hills of Africa*, has been to justify or explain the channelization of great talents into narrow fields (i.e. big-game hunting and bullfighting) with obvious affinities as ritualized forms of killing. In the first book Hemingway observes as well as comments on his minor passion; in the second he acts as well as narrates. In either book his defensiveness about what he is doing is, to say the least, overdetermined. His strong artistic talents are decidedly at work: he tells stories, describes scenes or landscapes, delineates characters, introduces dialogues, and in the grand nineteenth-century manner comments wisely on his materials and sets his own norms. But he remains defensive about his aims, and in varying degrees his readers also have been uncomfortable with them. The preoccupation with death, with killing, is in some sense being used as a substitute for his more meaningful concern with life and death, and with the crossovers between them, in his fiction; and we are all, himself included, aware of the substitution. How then to explain it?

The author himself begins with a defense of taking brutal and cruel actions in stride for their aesthetic value. On going to his first bullfight he had "expected to be horrified and perhaps sickened" by the goring and killing of the picadors' horses (1); but in fact he did not mind these actions. In his excitement over "the tragedy of the bullfight," its well-ordered complications and ritual provings, "the minor comic-tragedy of the horse" seemed incidental (8). His own now-famous intention had been to learn how to write, "commencing with the simplest things," one of which was "violent death." It was "one of the subjects that a man may write of," and since the war was over he meant to study it in the bullring. There he might transcribe "the real thing, the sequence of motion and fact which made the emotion and which would be as valid in a year or ten years or, with luck and if you stated it purely enough, always" (2). This aesthetic justification for a book on his minor passion is introduced, then, as a defense of goring and killing horses to readers who may find such actions morally indefensible, along with the spectacle of which those horses are a part. Such a defense requires him to be "altogether frank" and to confess to "those who read this . . . with disgust" as being written "by some one who lacks their . . . fineness of feeling," that "this may be true": but such a judgment will depend on whether or not the readers have been to bullfights (1).

This test of experience, which many will fail to pass, is another defensive ploy. The author includes himself, however, among the uninitiated by recounting an anecdote about himself and Gertrude Stein in which, after witnessing the breaking of the legs of baggage animals when the Greeks abandoned Smyrna in the Balkan wars of the 1920s, he told that aficionado

224

that he "did not like the bullfights [which he had not yet seen] because of the poor horses" (1–2). Next, after insisting that there is "no standard of civilization or experience" by which to separate those who are affected by the killings from those who are not, he goes on to suggest one: those who identify themselves with animals versus those who identify themselves with human beings, the former being "capable of greater cruelty to human beings than those who do not identify themselves readily with animals" (4–5). He means, of course, that sentimental people like animal lovers are crueller than hard-boiled ones like himself, for whom animals are only individually loveable through some special quality. In later pages we see him identify, in this specious light, with "truly brave" bulls as stoic heroes, true bravery being the special quality he loves them for (124). In an appendix he further illustrates the incalculable nature of reactions to horse-killings without bothering with sentimental or hard-boiled identifications; but by then the hard-boiled norm has done its work.

Twice in the opening chapters he indicates one personal source for his own hardened feelings: "the death of his father" (3) and "suicides" (20), both subjects of much interest to him—as indeed they might be, given his father's death five years before by his own handgun. Once he mentions war and journalism as experiences that might have made him callous (8). It is only midway through the book, at the end of chapter 11, that he mentions the passing of love as making a deadness for its survivors, and so invokes that "numbing of affect" which, as we have seen, characterizes the narrator's consciousness in *A Farewell to Arms*. The occasion is a conversation with that interrupting *"Old lady"* whom he has borrowed from another "cock and bull story," Laurence Sterne's *Tristram Shandy*, told by another playful (if impotent) narrator who frequently addresses a "fair reader" called "Madam"; and the passage itself follows, in fact, hard upon a question from "Madame" about the polygamous "love life" of seed bulls, who, as we soon learn, "weaken and end in impotence" if assigned more than fifty cows, but are sometimes oddly monogamous:

> Sometimes a bull on the range will come to so care for one of the fifty cows that he is with that he will make no case of all the others and will only have to do with her and she will refuse to leave his side on the range. When this occurs they take the cow from the herd and if the bull does not then return to polygamy he is sent with the other bulls that are for the ring.
>
> I find that a sad story, sir.
>
> Madame, all stories, if continued far enough, end in death, and he

is no true-story teller who would keep that from you. Especially do all stories of monogamy end in death, and your man who is monogamous while he often lives most happily dies in the most lonely fashion. There is no lonelier man in death, except the suicide, than that man who has lived many years with a good wife and then outlived her. If two people love each other there can be no happy end to it.

Sir, I do not know what you mean by love. It does not sound well as you say it.

Madame, it is an old word and each one takes it new and wears it out himself. It is a word that fills with meaning as a bladder with air and the meaning goes out of it as quickly. It may be punctured as a bladder is punctured and patched and blown up again and if you have not had it it does not exist for you. All people talk of it, but those who have had it are all marked by it and I would not wish to speak of it further since of all things it is the most ridiculous to talk of and only fools go through it many times. I would sooner have the pox than to fall in love with another woman loving the one I have.

What has this to do with the bulls, sir?

Nothing, Madame, nothing at all, it is only conversation to give you your money's worth.

I find the subject interesting. What way are people marked who have had this thing or is that only a way of speaking?

All those who have really experienced it are marked, after it is gone, by a quality of deadness. I say this as a naturalist, not to be romantic. (121–22)

If not Madame, then certainly we readers have been given our money's worth. The story is like that of the major in "In Another Country" whose wife has just died and who therefore argues that a man must never marry, since he is then in a position to lose everything. But this story is obviously a screen for still another, that of the foolish author, who has loved one woman and left her for another, and would now sooner have the pox than the deadness that possesses him. What all this has to do with bulls is, of course, everything, if the deadness that follows lost love may be said to explain this callously playful immersion in a world of tragic and comi-tragic killings of men, bulls, and horses. All that steady preoccupation with brave or cowardly animals and men, all those playful asides for the sake of the feisty *Old lady* for whom the narrator also tells those playful stories, including "A Natural History of the Dead," may well be ways of coping with a personal deadness, a numbing of affect, a movement down the stoic spectrum from the intensities of tough-minded fictions with tender implications to hardened feelings about bullfighting, big-game hunting, and dying men and marriages. The emergence at this time of Papa Hemingway, old before his time, the complete naturalist, now thoroughly hard-boiled in his art, or at least in certain masculinist poses, seems evident in these narrow ventures into ritual provings and killings in the name of minor passions.

Why then the *Old Lady* for a comic foil, in this book, and Poor Old Mama in the other? When the former first interrupts to say she likes it when the bulls hit the horses because it seems "sort of homey," we get our first important clue, that of a truth-telling mama interested in how it really was or is, willing to entertain such cocky matters as the narrator's discourses upon syphilis, which boxers, bullfighters, and soldiers contract out of their characteristic "disregard of consequences"; or upon promiscuity and monogamy in bulls and bullfighters; or, with recurrent insistence, upon homosexuality, as in the passing mention of Villalta's high voice, or in the story of the writer Raymond Radiguet, whom Jean Cocteau regarded as decadent because he loved women, or in the even more interesting story of the sobbing young man who had threatened to kill himself rather than rejoin his rich benefactor but when last seen had made peace with him and like androgynous David Bourne in *The Garden of Eden* "had had his hair hennaed" (182).

We will meet other tough old ladies who take an interest in sexual deviance and hennaed hair and who recognize the connection between gorings and things homey—all tougher mamas, apparently, than the genteel, pollyannish mama Ernest came from, but with whom he would keep up in this manner a lifelong dialogue, a kind of ongoing debate. In *Death in the Afternoon* the *Old lady* is finally abandoned, after expressing some genteel distaste for the author's character, but is soon replaced by Aldous Huxley, whose similar distaste for the author's feigned stupidity had caught him out in a hardened pose, an inherent weakness in his hard-boiled strategy which I. A. Richards would have been quick to identify as a sign of reverse sentimentality.[2] Ignoring that exposure, Hemingway had countered that he always knew more than he revealed, that his strength as a writer depended on just such withholdings, even as the dignity of movement of the iceberg depended on "only one-eighth of it being above water" (192). Then, characteristically, rather than let the matter drop, he went on to "please Mr. Huxley" by showing off some withheld knowledge, picking his quarrel this time with a German art critic, Julius Meier-Graefe, who had made the mistake of preferring El Greco to Goya and Velasquez on the basis of their painting of the crucifixion. That position was stupid, Hemingway argued, because you can judge a painter only "by the way he paints the things he believes in and cares for," and of the three Spanish painters, only Greco had cared for crucifixions:

> Greco liked to paint religious pictures because he was very evidently religious and because his incomparable art was not then limited to accurate reproducing of the faces of the noblemen who were his sitters for portraits and he could go as far into his other world as he wanted and, consciously or unconsciously, paint saints, apostles, Christs, and Virgins with the androgynous faces and forms that filled his imagination. (204)

Then comes the story of the woman in Paris who was writing a fictionalized life of El Greco of whom Hemingway had asked, "Do you make him a maricón?" and, when she betrayed her ignorance of such matters, of whom he had further asked, had she ever seen more classic examples of "queers" than in his paintings, and did she think it was an accident that all his saints were made to look that way? He then closes by invoking—quite lyrically—the different things that Velasquez, Goya, and El Greco believed in, commending Goya in passing for his belief "in his own cojones" and El Greco for his contrary belief "in fairies"—apparently because of its religious and aesthetic affinities and its redeeming function:

> El Greco believed in the city of Toledo, in its location and construction, in some of the people who lived in it, in blues, grays, greens and yellows, in reds, in the holy ghost, in the communion and fellowship of saints, in painting, in life after death and death after life and in fairies. If he was one he should redeem, for the tribe, the prissy, exhibitionistic, aunt-like, withered old maid moral arrogance of a Gide; the lazy, conceited debauchery of a Wilde who betrayed a generation; the nasty, sentimental pawing of humanity of a Whitman and all the mincing gentry. Viva El Greco El Rey de los Maricónes. (205)

These are lines by a well-read man who has thought with venomous precision about homosexual writers, but who much admires El Greco for going beyond them in his art. The venomous adjectives, "prissy," "lazy," "sentimental," and "mincing," help to place these rival writers as unmanly and undisciplined poseurs, betrayers of their trade: but wonder of wonders, the lyric admiration of the androgynous El Greco disrupts such hard-boiled counter-posing like an iceberg revelation from hidden depths.

There are no such androgynous uplifts in *Green Hills of Africa*, but there are homophobic moments of great import, and there is another tough old lady, P.O.M., meaning Poor Old Mama, meaning Pauline, spouse to Poor Old Papa, the irascibly rivalrous hunter. And there is Hadley, always, waiting in the background where memory rouses dying fires.

POOR OLD MAMA

Green Hills of Africa begins with a deliberate juxtaposition of safari life, seen as "the good life," with the falsifications of literary life. The narrator tells us that he is "altogether happy" after a day of hunting kudus, even though his chances of shooting one have been spoiled by a passing truck.[3] Returning to camp that night he comes upon the stalled truck and engages in literary conversation with the spoiler, a German traveller named Kandinsky, who at once recognizes him as the poet whom he has read in the *Querschnitt,* for which Hemingway had written what he now calls "some rather obscene poems" and a long story, "years before [he] could sell anything in America" (7). Kandinsky then quizzes Hemingway on his likes and dislikes among contemporary German writers (Ringelnatz, Heinrich Mann, Rilke), questions his desire to shoot kudu as if discussing a brutish habit, and leaves for tomorrow the question of what Joyce is like. Hemingway departs, marvelling about having met in mid-Africa "a caricature of Benchley in Tyrolean costume" who knows him as a *Querschnitt* poet, admires Joachim Ringelnatz, and wants to talk about Rilke (9–10). On the very next day, as if roused by the encounter, he makes the first of many comparisons between hunting and writing, finding it unpleasant to have a time limit set on either activity:

> It is not the way hunting should be. It is too much like those boys who used to be sent to Paris with two years in which to make good as writers or painters after which, if they had not made good, they could go home and into their fathers' business. The way to hunt is for as long as you live against as long as there is such and such an animal; just as the way to paint is as long as there is you and colors and canvas, and to write as long as you can live and there is pencil and paper or ink or any machine to do it with, or anything you care to write about, and you feel a fool, and you are a fool, to do it any other way. (12)

One might note in passing that Hemingway himself had spent two years in Paris without making good and had been forced by Hadley's pregnancy to return home and take up his old job on the *Toronto Star.* He knew something firsthand, then, about time limits set on writing as on hunting. Now, within the context of his nervousness about those limits, he returns to base camp and again meets the Tyrolean Kandinsky. "Hello girl," he says to Poor Old Mama, a wife located somewhere between these odd locutions, who subtly leads Kandinsky into further self-exposures about the literary crowds he aspires to, and who loyally touts Ernest to him as "the greatest writer in America" (12, 18–19). The best part of life, Kandinsky now argues excitedly, is the life of the mind, not the killing of kudus; Ernest then obliges him with a sample of his own thinking on American literary history, including a disparagement of "writers of rhetoric" but sparing those who "find a little, in a chronicle of another man and from voyaging, of how things, actual things, can be." "Do not pretend to be stupid," responds Kandinsky, following Huxley's line, and so evokes further disparagement of those exiled colonials who wished to be gentlemen. Then, citing fellow naturalist Thoreau, whom he has not been able to read, Hemingway begins to defend his own kind of lonely writing since the break with Hadley:

> Writers should work alone. They should see each other only after their work is done, and not too often then. Otherwise they become like writers in New York. All angleworms in a bottle, trying to derive knowledge and nourishment from their own contact and from the bottle. Sometimes the bottle is shaped art, sometimes economics, sometimes economics-religion. But once they are in the bottle they stay there. They are lonesome outside of the bottle. . . . They are afraid to be alone in their beliefs and no woman would love any of them enough so that they could kill their lonesomeness in that woman, or pool it with hers, or make something with her that makes the rest unimportant. (21–22)

The attack on New York as a writing center is an evasion, of course, of the Paris life that nourished his own early writing; and the definition of a woman's love that kills lonesomeness, or allows its pooling, or some private bonding, is an allusion to his present life with Poor Old Mama. Her toughness on safari is touched on in chapter 3, where she is called a "little terrier" in her endurance and courage and canine admiration for the guide Pop, alias Mr. J.P., to whom among others this book is dedicated; and it is she who delivers the crucial lines when the real point of Ernest's anti-literary talk is finally exposed:

> "Let's talk about Mr. J.P. . . . Don't you think he's wonderful?"
> "Yes, and he doesn't have to read books written by some female he's tried to help get published saying how he's yellow."
> "She's just jealous and malicious. You never should have helped her. Some people never forgive that."

"It's a damned shame, though, with all that talent gone to malice and nonsense and self-praise. It's a god-damned shame, really. It's a shame you never knew her before she went to pot. You know a funny thing; she never could write dialogue. It was terrible. She learned how to do it from my stuff and used it in that book. She had never written like that before. She never could forgive learning that and she was afraid people would notice it, where she'd learned it, so she had to attack me. It's a funny racket, really. But I swear she was damned nice before she got ambitious. You would have liked her then, really."

"Maybe, but I don't think so," said P.O.M. "We have fun though, don't we? Without all those people."

"God damn it if we don't. I've had a better time every year since I can remember." (65–66)

Who needs Paris, then, and that tough androgynous literary mother Gertrude Stein, who stole his stuff and called him yellow? The projection upon her of his own malice and resentment for past favors is perhaps too obvious for comment, but the evidence of betrayed love is not, and together with those Catherine Barkley lines—"We have fun though, don't we? Without all those people"—makes us ponder. Having Pauline, having money enough for African safaris—the rich wife and the rich life that competes with writing—will be the self-searching theme of "The Snows of Kilimanjaro"; but here it seems for a moment preferable to that shoestring Paris life with Hadley, when the associations with Joyce, Ford, Stein, Fitzgerald, Pound, and others had nurtured his growing talents, as he would repeatedly and with great nostalgia acknowledge elsewhere, and to which he turns in fact within the next few pages, while reading Tolstoy's *Sevastapol* with his back against a tree, praising war as a subject for writing and recalling that postwar literary ambience:

Then Sevastapol made me think of the Boulevard Sevastapol in Paris, about riding a bicycle down it in the rain on the way home from Strassburg and the slipperiness of the rails of the tram cars and the feeling of riding on greasy, slippery asphalt and cobble stones in traffic in the rain, and how we had nearly lived on the Boulevard du Temple that time, and I remembered the look of that apartment, how it was arranged, and the wall paper, and instead we had taken the upstairs of the pavilion in Notre Dame des Champs in the courtyard with the sawmill (*and the sudden whine of the saw, the smell of sawdust and the chestnut tree over the roof with a mad woman downstairs*) and the year worrying about money (*all of the stories back in the mail that came in through a slit in the sawmill door, with notes of rejection that would never call them stories, but always anecdotes, sketches, contes, etc. They did not want them, and we lived on poireaux and drank cahors and water)* and how fine the fountains were at the Place de L'Observatoire *(water sheen rippling on the bronze of horses' manes, bronze breasts and shoulders, green under thin-flowing water)* and when they put up the bust of Flaubert in the Luxembourg on the short cut through the gardens on the way to the rue Soufflot *(one that we believed in, loved without criticism, heavy now in stone as an idol should be)*. . . . And that last night, drunk, with Joyce and the thing he kept quoting from Edgar Quinet, "Fraiche et rose comme au jour de la bataille." I didn't have it right I knew. And when you saw him he would take up a conversation interrupted three years before. It was nice to see a great writer in our time. (70–71)

"What I had to do was work," adds Hemingway, warming up for the part of Harry in "The Snows of Kilimanjaro," which this passage plainly anticipates, the "we" being Ernest and Hadley, then Pound and Joyce and the others, the time that of happy working poverty in Paris, the early making of his style. Not surprisingly then, it is Hadley whom he has replaced with Africa:

All I wanted to do now was get back to Africa. We had not left it, yet, but when I would wake in the night I would lie, listening, homesick for it already. . . . I loved the country so that I was happy as you are after you have been with a woman that you really love, when, empty, you feel it welling up again and there it is and you can never have it all and yet what there is, now, you can have, and you want more and more, to have, and be, and live in, to possess now again for always, for that long, sudden-ended always; making time stand still, sometimes so very still that afterwards you wait to hear it move, and it is slow in starting. But you are not alone, because if you have ever really loved her happy and untragic, she loves you always; no matter whom she loves nor where she goes she loves you more. So if you have loved some woman and some country you are very fortunate and, if you die afterwards it makes no difference. (72–73)

This orgasmic equation of Africa with Hadley, a place for which he is homesick while supposedly there, a woman who will love him more and always and is therefore never lost, seems doubly resonant; it reminds us on the one hand of Kipling's Mowgli, heartsick for the Jungle he has lost through a dubious marriage, and anticipates on the other the sleeping bag in

For Whom the Bells Tolls and the magical repossession there of all lost and timeless loves and countries. But more immediately it poses for us the embarrassing question of what to make of Poor Old Mama, her name and current function as the provider, through Uncle Gus, of the funds for this safari. As the woman who kills loneliness, who stands with him against a literary world supposedly well lost, offering fun for two along with a fishing boat named with her early nickname, *Pilar,* plus African safaris, Spanish bullfights, and the money for writing books about them, she is in a peculiar way a well-loved wife against whom a bill of particulars is being filed.

It is not surprising therefore that in this book she is given false credit in chapter 2 for shooting a lion that Ernest actually felled, or that she quizzically states in chapter 1 (29), "So that's what you do," when Ernest defines the women who harm American writers as "the ones you get involved with when you're drunk," or that she forces him to give their Florida friend Karl the better chance for kudu horns at the salt lick in chapter 8, or that they elsewhere quarrel about her sore feet from inappropriate boots, or that he mildly resents her admiration for Mr. J.P., alias Pop, with whom, of necessity, she spends much time alone. These minor irritations blend in, however, with the running critique of his own rivalrous and irascible nature on which the narrative largely focuses. Pauline is good-natured, as he is not; she calms him when he seethes, encourages him when he sags, prays for his success when he vies with Karl. That he is at times "Poor Old Papa" to her "Poor Old Mama" further clarifies her supportive role and helps to explain her merely bemused response to the women he goes to when drunk. She serves him as Catherine Barkley serves Lieutenant Henry. She exhibits that "desire to please" which Millicent Bell attributes solely to "male fantasies of the ideal submissive partner."[4]

As her letters to Ernest from 1926 onward amply attest, Pauline was that ideal partner, or strove to be through fourteen years of marriage, unfailingly praising and supporting him, and with increasing poignance expressing her heartfelt frustration at their long and frequent separations.[5] "Poor Old Mama" is not only the loyal wife he leaves behind with the handsome guide: she is the wife he has *always* left behind, to go off on fishing trips by himself in Cuba or Bimini, to hole up alone for spells of writing, to conduct thereby his affair with Jane Mason and his drunken sprees, and ultimately, to go off to war again with mistress Martha. Indeed, when Hadley forced Ernest and Pauline to stay apart for one hundred days, back in 1926, so as to test the sincerity of their passion, she unwittingly gave Ernest the clue to his authority in his second marriage. He would keep Pauline waiting and longing for him for the next fourteen years, beginning with that trip to Italy with his friend Guy Hickok in March 1927 by which he postponed their marriage until May, and ending with his final trips to Spain with Martha, the Kiplingesque "daughter" from "The Story of the Gadsbys," who would in fact as in fiction replace P.D.M., for Poor Dear Mama, and would ironically leave Ernest behind—sore and lonely and resentful—throughout their brief marriage, by going off alone on her own writing assignments.

Meanwhile, in *Green Hills of Africa*, "Poor Old Mama" is a locution for a *woman* always left behind, always waiting, serving, longing, keeping busy, living for reunions on bought safaris, gamely holding on like "a little terrier," gamely repeating the magic formula that won Ernest's heart—"We have fun though, don't we? Without all those people."—but for which he never forgave her. That he loved and learned from her seems evident in his newly hardened cynicism about himself and women, and paradoxically enough, from his new openness to the sufferings of women at the hands of men like himself. We shall see something of both lessons in the African stories ahead and in the social novels that follow.

MARGOT AND HELEN

Toward the end of *Green Hills* Hemingway speaks of Africa as the "good country" that America once had been, a younger continent not yet spoiled by foreign intruders who exploit it with machines and fail to renew the soil with the residue of man and beast. In this unspoiled continent he feels at home as he had once felt at home in northern Michigan; indeed, he likens these places to old and new frontiers:

> Our people went to America because that was the place to go then. It had been a good country and we had made a bloody mess of it and I would go, now, somewhere else as we had always had the right to go somewhere else and as we had always gone. . . . Let the others come to America who did not know that they had come too late. Our people had seen it at its best and fought for it when it was well worth fighting for. Now I would go somewhere else. We always went in the old days and there were still good places to go. (285)

By "we" and "our people" Ernest means his pioneer ancestors, whom he will now emulate by finding a new frontier, a place where he can "really live," by which he seems to mean hunt and fish: "Here there was game, plenty of birds, and I liked the natives. Here I could shoot and fish. That, and writing, and reading, and seeing pictures was all I cared about doing. And I could remember all the pictures" (285).

His view of the new frontier is, of course, distinctly colonial. Unlike Kandinsky, who early asks the pointed question, "Why are you not more interested in the natives?" (14), and who goes on to recommend their dance festivals and to expose himself as a recruiter of natives for an Indian sisal plantation, Ernest cares for them as individual gunbearers, or as beautiful wives and warriors, or as noble brothers in the hunt: so again we have the distinction between the sentimentalist (Kandinsky) who loves "the poor animals" Ernest and his friends would outwit (17) but who exploits the natives, and Ernest who really likes the natives—excepting those like the theatrical Garrick, whom he would "shoot in the ass" as a cure for pomposity (187). But then for Ernest, "the country was always better than the people," about whom he "could only care . . . a very few at a time" (73). His apolitical stance, his inability to distinguish between his kind of safari imperialism and Kandinsky's recruitment is reinforced by mocking banter on revolutions in chapter 10 (191–93) and by his interesting confession, in the final chapter, when the natives balk against his hunting plan: "If there had been no law I would have shot Garrick and they would all have hunted or cleared out" (264)—in the light of which his own qualms of conscience about gut-shooting animals lose much point.

Whatever the brutalities of the hunt, Africa emerges in this book as an imaginative frontier like those he will reconstruct in his two famous stories "The Short Happy Life of Francis Macomber" and "The Snows of Kiliman-jaro."[6] These fictional reworkings of his African experiences are among his finest tales; they reflect the hardening of his sexual attitudes and his con-scious awareness and judgment of that hardening. Further, they extend his use of imaginative frontiers as private testing grounds for manly courage, as in "The Undefeated" and "Big Two-Hearted River," to more social con-cerns, his conscious expansion of frontier arenas to include and assess marital conflict as well as manly provings.

In the Macomber story the new masculinist hardening can be seen in his portrait of the guide Wilson, which seems to me largely favorable. Our first clue to the author's intention comes at the end of *Green Hills of Africa* as Karl, Ernest, and Poor Old Mama are sitting by the Sea of Galilee in Palestine:

"You know," P.O.M. said. "I can't remember it. I can't remember Mr. J.P.'s face. And he's beautiful. I think about him and think about him and I can't see him. It's terrible. He isn't the way he looks in a photograph. In a little while I won't be able to remember him at all. Already I can't see him."

"You must remember him," Karl said to her.

"I can remember him," I said. "I'll write you a piece some time and put him in." (295)

The "piece" became—not *Green Hills of Africa*, where the guide Pop is never described—but "The Short Happy Life of Francis Macomber" in which the guide Wilson is largely modelled on Mr. J.P., alias Jackson Phillips or Pop in the book, but Philip Percival in life, one of the book's three dedicatees. We know from Carlos Baker's biography that Hemingway admired and befriended Percival, drew on his campfire tales of courage and cowardice and double-sized cots for his story, and borrowed his laconic speech and ruddy features as well as his "enviable combination of courage and judgment" for his portrait of the British guide.[7] The question of whether Hemingway subscribed to Wilson's judgment has been raised, however, by other critics and is still much debated. What is certain is the new hardening of outlook which the guide's focal presence quite literally involves, as we see from his first description: "He was about middle height with sandy hair, a stubbly mustache, a very red face and extremely cold blue eyes with faint white wrinkles at the corners that grooved merrily when he smiled" (4). A few pages later he looks at Macomber quizzically "with his flat blue machine-gunner's eyes" (8), and at the end of the story he looks unfavorably at Mrs. Macomber "with his flat blue eyes" (37). Those judgmental eyes—cold, flat, deadly—can be read as cruel and inhuman or as impersonal and extremely accurate, among other possibilities; their hardness is in any case evident, and what they see in Mrs. Macomber is even harder:

[American women] are, he thought, the hardest in the world; the hardest, the cruelest, the most predatory and the most attractive and their men have softened or gone to pieces nervously as they have hardened. Or is it that they pick men they can handle? They can't know that much at the age they marry, he thought. He was grateful that he had gone through his education on American women before now because this was a very attractive one. (8)

When she left, Wilson was thinking, when she went off to cry, she seemed a hell of a fine woman. She seemed . . . to be hurt for him and for herself and to know how things really stood. She is away for twenty minutes and now she is back simply enamelled in that American female cruelty. They are the damnedest women. Really the damnedest. (9)

So, Robert Wilson thought to himself, she *is* giving him a ride, isn't she? Or do you suppose that's her idea of putting up a good show?

How should a woman act when she discovers her husband is a bloody coward? She's damn cruel but they're all cruel. They govern, of course, and to govern one has to be cruel sometimes. Still, I've seen enough of their damn terrorism. (10)

So Wilson seesaws, trying to place Margot within the context of his strong prejudice against American women. Does Hemingway share in that prejudice? In *Green Hills of Africa* Mr. J.P. is similarly caustic about American women, as when P.O.M. reports on Kandinsky's view that American women are terrible, and Pop responds: "Very sound fellow" (184).[8] But Pop is partial to P.O.M. and treats her respectfully, perhaps because she wants so obviously to serve and support rather than govern. The issue of governance in marriage is certainly crucial to the story, and on that score we know where Hemingway stands at this juncture, that is to say, with the guide, if a little to one side on his prejudice. This useful outsider allows him to present the Macombers with a stiff upper lip, with clipped speech and a hardened yet pliant outlook, reserving for himself those further qualifications needed for our final judgments of characters and events.

Through a hardened observer, then, and through his own narration, and through occasional extended sorties into the points of view of Macomber and the wounded lion, but never of Mrs. Macomber, Hemingway presents the following events:

Francis Macomber, the rich, cowardly, and dependent protagonist, has bolted from a lion while on a hunting trip in Africa. His wife then cuckolds him with their stoic British guide. In his angry reaction to such open shaming, Macomber proves his manhood while hunting buffalo. But when a wounded buffalo suddenly charges and seems about to gore him, his wife shoots at the buffalo from the safety of a nearby car, using a 6.5 Mannlicher gun, and kills her husband instead of the buffalo. Since she has openly resented Macomber's newfound courage, the guide attributes the accident to her unconscious desire to murder him: "He *would* have left you too," he tells her (36), indicating that the husband's independent manhood—his happy life—had been assured before he died. Earlier the guide had mused upon this transformation: "Probably meant the end of cuckoldry too. . . . Be a damn fire eater now. . . . More of a change than any loss of virginity. Fear gone like an operation. Something else grew in its place. Main thing a man had. Made him into a man. Women knew it too. No bloody fear" (33).

The principle of renewable and transferrable manhood is clear; but so too is the principle of female recalcitrance. If Macomber now has the personal integrity, as the guide sees him, to stand up to his wife and if necessary to leave her, she has meanwhile grown accustomed to her dominance, has hardened into it, and now acts unconsciously to preserve it. Her conscious impulse to save him has given way to her deeper impulse to destroy him.

This ambiguous ending, which both affirms transferrable manhood but denies its utility, is our clue to a problem Hemingway never solved. A man may leave a bitch-woman like Brett Ashley or Margot Macomber for a good androgynous woman like Catherine Barkley—one willing to die for his survival; but he cannot live with a bitch—a bad androgynous woman—without being killed himself. And yet a strong wife is the only kind worth having.

Hemingway's attraction to strong women seems undeniable. His animus is not against Mrs. Macomber's strength, ostensibly, but against her destructive use of it: her apparently enameled cruelty, and her ultimate refusal, however unconscious, to accept her husband's transformation. And even these judgments are ambivalently delivered. Thus, the guide admires not only Mrs. Macomber's beauty but her brains; he knows that she is neither stupid (8) nor insensitive. When she goes off to cry over Macomber's cowardice, she seems to him "a hell of a fine woman," one who is "hurt for him and herself" and knows how things stand (9). If he dislikes the hardened cruelty that follows, he knows that it began with male default (8) and, further, that she responds with innocent freshness to his own virile love (27). And Hemingway himself writes of the marriage: "She had done the best she could for many years back and the way they were together now was no one person's fault" (34).

Some critics take this statement as a clue to Mrs. Macomber's "shorter happy life" when she tries to save her husband and shoots at the buffalo. But as the ironic framing of her shot confirms—from the safety of the car, with a "manly" or "man-licking" gun—the statement merely distributes blame over time. As the story's opening action reveals, by frontier analogue, it was Macomber's initial cowardice and dependence in the marriage that insured his cuckoldry and his wife's dominance. As the story's closing action reveals, she now likes to dominate and—like Brett Ashley before her—is no longer able to change. True to its period, the story is not about mutual honoring and the tragic loss of selfless love, as some critics hold, but about independent manhood—which even cowardly "boy-men" may achieve—as a defense against ingrown bitchery or, if that fails, unhappy death.

There is however another story, that of the guide's relations to his clients, that undermines these conclusions and indicates their unresolved or conflictual nature. It is the guide, after all, who makes renewing love to Mrs. Macomber and who later forces her to say please, as if extending the authority of her dead husband's newfound courage; and it is the guide who recognizes the change in Macomber and who initiates him into the brotherhood of courageous men with those Shakespearean lines, "A man can die but once. . . ." What does it mean, then, when he says "their standards were his standards as long as they were hiring him," to explain his willingness to accept night visitors to his bed like Mrs. Macomber, but then claims, "They were his standards in all but the shooting"? He seems willing to hire himself out, as it were, as my lady's fucker and to restore thereby her refreshing innocence, as opposed to her professional beauty as an endorser of products she never uses; and yet his own professional standards in the hunt are removed from such unbrotherly betrayals, such "windfalls" from women seeking their "money's worth . . . with the white hunter" (26). If the guide is a used product himself, a sort of passive male hooker, what happens to the principle of transferrable manhood—integrity in cot and wold?

In *The Sun Also Rises* the bullfighter Pedro Romero performs for himself as well as for his beloved, whether in bed or bullring: yet there is no question that he would be destroyed if his deadly beloved chose to stay with him. In the Macomber story the choice for the husband is similarly to *leave* his wife should she refuse to relinquish governance, not to stay with her and confront her deadly power. This at least is how the guide sees their situation, or how he judges it from her apparent desire to destroy what she can no longer govern. But as his forcing her to say please suggests, it is she who must acknowledge and respect her husband's belated strength—not he who must acknowledge hers. And why, after all, is hers so deadly? Why does the guide believe, with Hemingway somewhere behind him (as I try to show in Appendix A), that women are ultimately vengeful killers, that they will not allow men to live as men, only as little boys, unless forced to yield to governance themselves? Why are men powerless before this deadly vengeance, always facing the wrong way, shooting at buffaloes instead of disarming the wives behind them who would rob them of their newfound happiness? Or is Margot Macomber's vengefulness projected upon her by a frightened author? or by a frightened author hiding behind a punitive guide? or—as kinder critics feel—by a jumpy and biased guide who at one point thinks that Macomber might shoot *him* in the back of the head in vengeful anger (25)?

Whatever the case, the story proceeds on false or contradictory premises established by the guide, which Hemingway here and elsewhere underwrites, but which break down under close examination. From the guide's point of view, for instance, wouldn't it take more courage to live with Margot, given her deadliness, than to face charging lions or buffaloes? Isn't there a domestic lioness here before whom brave men smartly flee? Isn't that why the guide is a bachelor (unlike Philip Percival) and a hired stud who confines himself to minor putdowns and who pointedly believes that "women *are* a nuisance on safaris" (25)? If so, finally, isn't it a fallacy to suggest, as Wilson does, that courage acquired on safaris—the courage to dominate and destroy—has any bearing at all on the constructive courage required in homes, in domestic relations, wherein grown men often prove evasive, one might well say cowardly, whatever their frontier performances? Facing up to the lioness requires a different kind of courage, does it not— the courage to live with and let live—than merely facing her down (i.e., putting her down) and / or leaving? Only through such constructive courage will that balance of power, that mutual honoring and respect that kinder critics attribute to this story, occur. Its vengeful direction, after the example of Captain Marryat in *Snarleyyow* and *Percival Keene* (from which Heming- way derived his opening and closing actions, the coward's flight and the hunting "accident," as I show in Appendix A), tends to blot out the essen- tially false premises on which *any* reading of this tale proceeds, as to the correlation between frontier and domestic courage: for if Francis Macom- ber, like Pedro Romero before him, has only learned how to dominate and destroy, not how to live with and let live; and if Margot Macomber, like Brett Ashley before her, can't live with a man without destroying him, or without yielding her equal need for strength and authority, then all domi- nant males are killer-bastards, even as all dominant females are killer-bitches, and there can be no mutual governance between them.

Certainly the protagonist in "The Snows of Kilimanjaro" is a killer- bastard. "If you have to go away," his much-maligned wife asks of him, "is it absolutely necessary to kill off everything you leave behind? I mean do you have to take away everything? Do you have to kill your horse, and burn your wife and burn your saddle and your armour?" (57–58). Through this image of military immolation she captures her bought husband's legitimate desire to go down fighting, as he dies of a gangrenous infection while on African safari, and, conversely, his perverse desire to keep alive by killing the life around him (58), by destroying, as it were, the sources of his self-corruption in the life they've had together. We know, at any rate, that he has traded his writing talents for the comforts his rich wife provides, that he has settled for a marriage of convenience, and that his infection seems appropriate to his moral sloth. Conversely, we also know that he wants to work the fat off his soul, to recuperate his integrity by writing stories in his mind—the only way left to him—and thus make a last-ditch struggle against demeaning death.

There is no question in this story, then, of overcoming bitchery; the question, rather, is whether to die creatively or destructively, and on that issue the wife plays little part. As his original name—Henry Walden—suggests, the writer Harry is a loner in this marriage; his conflict is essentially with himself. True enough, he calls his wife "this rich bitch, this kindly caretaker and destroyer of his talent" (60); he curses her "damned money" (58), tells her that he doesn't love her, and tells himself that he has always made love better when lying about it for his bread and butter (55, 61). But he also acknowledges to himself that it wasn't his wife's fault, that he had himself destroyed his talent "by not using it, by betrayals of himself and what he believed in, by drinking so much that he blunted his perceptions, by laziness, by sloth" (60). He admits, moreover, that each woman he has fallen in love with has been oddly richer than the last, that he has made his living with his penis rather than his pen (60).

Hemingway's harsh critique of this selfish writer and his loveless marriage seems frankly self-directed. He too wants to work the fat off his soul, wants to leave Pauline behind by writing his lonely way toward death. As Carlos Baker surmises, he too was afraid he might die before he wrote "the things he had saved to write until he knew enough to write them well" (54); he too wondered if he had put them off because he couldn't write them.

In the tale itself, of course, he doesn't leave Pauline behind; she is there in the portrait of Helen, the "rich bitch" who prides herself on serving Harry well ("I left everything and I went wherever you wanted to go and I've done what you wanted to do," 55), who protects him even now by telling him not to drink, who shoots well and loves excitement and is always thoughtful about his needs and pleasures, and who loves the "good destruction" they share in bed. But she exists a little to one side in this story, a wife discarded in fiction if not yet in fact, and serves chiefly as a foil for Harry's irritability, for his bastardly selfishness even in death, and for his finer desire to face that demeaning prospect head-on. Thus, Harry describes her, rather dismissively, as this "damned nice woman" who "was very pleasant and appreciative and . . . never made scenes" (62); and he decides that "if this is how [life] ended . . . he must not turn like some snake biting itself because its back was broken" (60).

The self-consuming snake is an interesting image, encompassing as it does Harry's lacerating quarrels with himself and with his wife. One obvious source for this incongruous image is the hyena, as seen in chapter 2 of *Green Hills of Africa* by the native gunbearer M'Cola:

It was funny to M'Cola to see a hyena shot at close range. There was the comic slap of the bullet and the hyena's agitated surprise to find death inside him. It was funnier to see a hyena shot at a great distance, in the heat shimmer of the plain, to see him go over backwards, to see him start that frantic circle, to see that electric speed that meant that he was racing the little nickelled death inside him. But the great joke of all, the thing M'Cola waved his hands across his face about and turned away and shook his head and laughed, ashamed even of the hyena; the pinnacle of hyenic humor, was the hyena, the classic hyena, that hit too far back while running, would circle madly, snapping and tearing at himself until he pulled his own intestines out, and then stood there jerking them out and eating them with relish.

"*Fisi,*" M'Cola would say and shake his head in delighted sorrow at there being such an awful beast. Fisi, the hyena, hermaphroditic, self-eating devourer of the dead, trailer of calving cows, ham-stringer, potential biter-off of your face at night while you slept, sad yowler, camp-follower, stinking, foul, with jaws that crack the bones the lion leaves, belly dragging, loping away on the brown plain, looking back, mongrel dog-smart in the face; whack from the little Mannlicher and then the horrid circle starting. "*Fisi,*" M'Cola laughed, ashamed of him, shaking his bald black head. "*Fisi.* Eats himself. *Fisi.*"

The hyena was a dirty joke. (37–38)

As a hermaphroditic self-eater the hyena becomes an obscene image of deadly androgyny, chasing its tail when hit by the Mannlicher bullet, feeding off itself as off the dead, a stinking full-belly-dragging filthy animal joke. In "The Snows of Kilimanjaro" this suggestive image is split between the backbiting snake that mirrors self- and marital lacerations and the hyena who, along with vultures and bicycle riders, prefigures Harry's death, crossing the open every night, coming with "a rush . . . of a sudden evil-smelling emptiness" on the edge of which it slips "lightly along" (63–64), resting its head on the foot of Harry's cot until he can smell its breath, crouching its full weight on his chest (74–75), making "a strange human, almost crying sound" when he dies (76). But in the transfer from *Green Hills* the hermaphroditic joke is lost or buried beneath the hardened surface toughness; indeed, there is little to remind us of androgyny in this hard-mannered tale, beyond the pompons and white ballet skirts worn by the Turkish corpses Harry recalls from the Balkan wars (65–66) in one of those oddly autobiographical passages that Hemingway uses to show off, in effect, his own unused wares, the things that he, like Harry, might have written but never did.

These writer's memories, arranged in five italicized passages of varying length and interspersed between roman passages on Harry's present siege with hyenic death, are about war blunders and peacetime follies Harry has witnessed in snowy alpine settings, the life in Paris where his writing career began in blessed poverty, the squelching of an old romance he hoped to revive, an innocent western killing by a half-wit, his own mercy killing of a dying friend. They are conveyed in rapid nonstop prose designed to challenge the stream-of-consciousness techniques of Hemingway's competitors, Faulkner, Woolf, and Joyce, in psychological resonance. This they fail to do. As autobiographical wares they are even open to charges of self-pity and self-aggrandizement, and therefore of reverse sentimentality, that extreme hazard of the tough-minded manner. But they are suitable to Harry's spiritual and moral efforts to go down fighting, that is to say, writing; and they apparently earn him an imagined plane ride—in roman prose to indicate its essential reality—over Mount Kilimanjaro.

Harry's imagined pilot is, appropriately, a bluff Kiplingesque Britisher, like the guide in the Macomber story, and one can fantasize the male chauvinist heaven these manly comrades approach as a series of bullrings, fishing and hunting grounds, boxing arenas, and baseball diamonds just beyond the mountain's snowy crest. Hemingway himself had imagined heaven in just such terms toward the end of his marriage to Hadley. On July 1, 1925, in a boisterous letter to Scott Fitzgerald, he had defined its essential features: a bullring where Ernest holds tickets for the best seats; a trout stream outside it that only he can fish in; two lovely houses in town, one (where his wife and children live) for monogamous true love, the other for his nine beautiful mistresses; and a fine Spanish church to confess in as he goes from one house to the other. By the 1930s, however, the mortgage on one such heavenly home had been foreclosed. The rich bitch who accompanies Harry shoots well, and makes love well, and serves him well, like Pauline, and she may even qualify as a hunting companion atop Kilimanjaro at some future date; but there is no longer any question of monogamous—or androgynous—true love.

MARIE MORGAN

Except, that is, among the tougher denizens of the lower classes. In *To Have and Have Not* (1937) Hemingway creates the only middle-aged love affair in his fiction—perhaps in all modern American fiction—between the smuggler Harry Morgan and his wife Marie. Described as "a big woman, long-legged, big handed, big hipped, still handsome," an old man's felt hat "pulled down over her bleached blonde hair," Marie at forty-five enjoys her forty-three-year-old one-armed husband's lovemaking, cries at the Tartar beauty of his "goddamn face," loves to watch him move "like some kind of expensive animal," admires him as he sleeps, cares for him rather than their three daughters, and genuinely mourns his inevitably bloody death.[9] But Marie is as tough as her tough-guy husband; the bond between them is earthy and erotic, and her Molly-Bloom-like soliloquies are charged with frank appreciations of his *cojones*. Her domestic functions and Harry's piratical tasks, his risky means of supporting his wife and children, are the forms that selfless consideration takes in this novel, and these roles are sharply separated. Harry is very much a loner in his work, moreover; so much so that his dying insight—"a man alone ain't got no bloody fucking chance" (225)—is the novel's proletarian moral.

Plainly Hemingway admires this rough-and-ready man, this rum-running Teddy Roosevelt, this heartless Humphrey Bogart with a heart of gold, who kills brutally when he has to, which is often; smacks men who insult his wife; insults the rich when they deserve it; and loves monogamously. And in a novel notable for its sympathy for women with integrity, he admires Marie too. Harry and Marie are the only quasi-Lawrencean lovers in Hemingway's fiction; they make a go of it while the rich people around them squabble viciously, betray each other, perform badly in bed, masturbate themselves to sleep, or commit suicide. And perhaps because of their earthy independence, Harry and Marie are the only successfully androgynous lovers in Hemingway's fiction. She admires and emulates his masculine toughness; he admires and almost covets her bleached blonde hair. In the novel's closing soliloquy, she describes that bleaching and their common excited response to it as the defining episode in their marriage (258–60). Harry's death is founded, then, in social rather than marital causes—perhaps because he spends so little time at home.

Hemingway's portrait of Marie is a kind of proletarian tribute to his own "old woman," his second wife, Pauline, who had once bleached her hair for him with similarly exciting results, and who had early taken to praising and identifying with his masculine beauty.[10] He attributes to Marie also something of his own dead feelings after the breakup of his first marriage with Hadley, as when she asks herself after learning of Harry's death, "How do you get through nights if you can't sleep?" and answers readily, "You just go dead inside and everything is easy. You just get dead like most people are most of the time" (261). More interesting still, he projects his own infidelity to Pauline with Jane Mason, and Pauline's Catholic view of such betrayals, onto the fatuous writer Richard Gordon and his angry wife Helen. Thus, Helen's famous diatribe against her straying husband is a distinctly Catholic indictment of the sterility of modern secular marriage:

"You wouldn't marry me in the church and it broke my poor mother's heart as you well know. I was so sentimental about you I'd break any one's heart for you. My, I was a damned fool. I broke my own heart, too. It's broken and gone. Everything I believed in and everything I cared about I left for you because you were so wonderful and you loved me so much that love was all that mattered. Love was the greatest thing, wasn't it? Love was what we had that no one else had or could ever have? And you were a genius and I was your whole life. I was your partner and your little black flower. Slop. Love is just another dirty lie. Love is ergoapiol pills to make me come around because you were afraid to have a baby. Love is quinine and quinine and quinine until I'm deaf with it. Love is that dirty aborting horror that you took me to. Love is my insides all messed up. It's half catheters and half whirling douches. I know about love. Love always hangs up behind the bathroom door. It smells like lysol. To hell with love. Love is you making me happy and then going off to sleep with your mouth open while I lie awake all night afraid to say my prayers even because I know I have no right to any more. Love is all the dirty little tricks you taught me that you probably got out of some book. All right. I'm through with you and I'm through with love. Your kind of picknose love. You writer." (185–86)

Still another writer, Harry in "The Snows of Kilimanjaro," seems to agree with that religious assessment, as when he says to his own Helen: "Love is a dunghill, . . . And I'm the cock that gets on it to crow" (57). Apparently life with Pauline had roused Ernest to an awareness not only of his own hypocrisies, but also of those sufferings that Pauline had either endured herself, or had taught him to see among the Key West types around them. Even his portrait of the masturbating mistress and Hollywood wife, Dorothy, with her assorted vanities and superficialities, includes the telling lines:

> The better you treat a man and the more you show him you love him the quicker he gets tired of you. I suppose the good ones are made to have a lot of wives but it's awfully wearing trying to be a lot wives yourself, and then some one simple takes him when he's tired of that. I suppose we all end up as bitches but who's [sic] fault is it? The bitches have the most fun but you have to be awfully stupid . . . and well-intentioned and really selfish to be a good one. (245)

What is evident, in these first stylistic attempts to think his way into the minds and hearts of women, is that Hemingway had already begun that "study of women" that Robert Jordan proposes to make after the war, in

Hemingway's next novel, beginning with the Spanish guerrilla leader Pilar.[11]

PILAR AND MARIA

If Marie Morgan is a proletarian version of Hemingway's second wife, Pauline, Pilar in *For Whom the Bell Tolls* (1940) is the Spanish gypsy version. "Pilar" was the secret nickname Pauline chose for herself when she first went after Ernest; it was the name also for the fishing boat, *The Pilar,* which he bought in 1934 and christened in her honor; and in both cases the name derived from the shrine at Zaragoza in Spain, Nuestra Senora del Pilar (Our Lady of the Pillar), and from the fair for "Pilar" each October. The shrine consists of an image of the Blessed Virgin on a pillar of porphyry. The image suggests why the young girl Maria is the middle-aged Pilar's protégé in the novel: the victimized virgin who depends on the strong woman's support. Since the novel is dedicated to Hemingway's third wife, Martha Gellhorn, it suggests also that Hemingway felt that Martha—a St. Louis girl like his first two wives—was in some sense an extension of Pauline's beneficence (an idea that he would develop, over the next two decades, through the *ménage à trois* in *The Garden of Eden*).[12] But the ambitious Martha contributes only physical features to Maria; that "little rabbit" in her selfless caring for the novel's hero, Robert Jordan, is more like Hadley or the younger Pauline in Spanish guise. Having been raped and cropped by Spanish fascists, she is also more like Hemingway's "twin" sister Marcelline, whose hair was cropped by his mother to resemble his, one childhood summer, and who suffered for it, as we have seen, for some time after. So Maria is Grace's gift as well as Pauline's, in the novel's psychogenesis, and that strong woman Pilar may owe as much to Grace as she does to Pauline. She is the tough, outspoken gypsy mother Ernest would have preferred, apparently, to the one he got, whom in many ways she nonetheless resembles.

Pilar's husband Pablo, for instance, has become a coward whose lapse from leadership forces her to take control of their guerrilla band. Ernest's father Clarence was a coward, in Ernest's view, who was dominated by his wife—along with the rest of the family—and who committed suicide in 1928 to escape his many problems. Ernest had touched on that tragedy in "Fathers and Sons" (1933) but felt that he could not write about it directly. In *For Whom the Bell Tolls,* he found a somewhat specious way to deal with it. Thus, Robert Jordan too has a cowardly father who committed suicide, and though Jordan can eventually forgive and understand him, he cannot forgive his failure to stand up to his bullying wife. We have, then, still another version of female governance in the face of male default, as in the Macomber story. But instead of confronting that problem, Hemingway shunts it off to the subplot, where the generous Pilar—with the profound wisdom of an older woman from an older culture—yields power to her husband Pablo once he resumes his manly ways near the end of the novel. Thus there is no question as to whether the doomed Robert will stand up to his docile Maria at some future time. Instead the novel turns, dramatically, on the question of whether Jordan will take his own life, like his cowardly father, when facing fascists rather than females, or whether he will die bravely as his grandfather the Indian-fighter would have wished. At one point Jordan even wonders whether his grandfather's bravery has passed down to him intact through his father, or whether the bully in his mother has passed down to him to make up for what his father lacked (338–39). Like a Faulkner hero, he wants his grandfather with him, to talk to; and in the end, injured and alone, a man no longer with his supporting women, he does talk to his grandfather (469) and decides to die bravely rather than shoot himself (470) as he waits for the approaching fascist troops.

Meanwhile he shares most of his problems with the bully Pilar, an older woman he openly cares for and whose leadership role he comfortably accepts (92). Though she has read death in his palm, she gives him Maria to love and protect, rewards him as they work together for a hopeless political cause. Apparently she believes, as the lovers do, that a whole lifetime together may be concentrated into a few idyllic days. The setting is pastoral—the Spanish mountains covered with pine-needled forests—and the romance is a Spanish family romance. At one point Maria refers to the guerrilla band as a family, and Jordan concurs (139). The assembled cast—or "this sentimental menagerie," as Pilar calls it (140)—is about the size of a Hemingway family picnic in the Michigan woods. The old man Anselmo, who later dies at the bridge, is the surrogate grandfather; the boy Joaquin is the youngest brother; Jordan is the favored son; and Maria is his sisterly companion, his close-cropped twin in selfless androgynous love. "You could be brother and sister by the look," Pilar says of this pair. ". . . it is fortunate that you are not" (67). At the end, Jordan will make much of their fortunate fusion: "If thou goest then I go, too. . . . Whichever one is there, is both. . . . You are me now" (463). Meanwhile, "the earth moves" when they make love, and Pilar expounds that mystery for them (114–15), among many others. Indeed, it is her version of manly character—the Fauntleroy ideal of transmuted virility—that defines their relation and channels sexuality into something spiritually profound.

But it is not very profound. The fusion with nature, the Lawrencean part of the ideal, depends on the separate existence of integral beings, and again, as in *A Farewell to Arms,* the lovers' selfless union dissolves that vital independence. The lyric descriptions of the lovemaking are accordingly somewhat insipid in their breathless running participles. And the love itself is suspiciously wishful. At one point, Jordan even compares it with "the dreams you have had when someone you have seen in the cinema comes to your bed at night and is so kind and lovely" (137). Maria is Jordan's film fantasy come true, and only the detailed violence and earthiness of guerrilla life keeps the wishful element subdued. But she is not an incredible character. Though less vividly realized than Marie Morgan, or even Catherine Barkley, she is a credible type of unformed innocence. It is the love itself that seems incredible. It lacks what Marie Morgan in her strong personal integrity brings to her love for Harry; it lacks what Pilar provides as she blends with Maria in their common family romance. Pilar even tells Jordan that she could have taken him away from Maria when she was young (156)—as Pauline took Ernest away from Hadley; and in fact the novel and the love it champions would have been more credible if Pilar were Jordan's lover at any age—as the more balanced love in *To Have and Have Not* confirms. But that love was only briefly delineated, and Hemingway here separates what he could not for long unite—considerate androgynous love between partners of equal strength.

Interestingly, he introduces a deviant component into his dubious Spanish blend that anticipates his next epic manuscript, *The Garden of Eden* (1946–58). Pilar's attraction to Maria is stronger than her attraction to Jordan; she is more jealous of Jordan than Maria, and though she explains this aspect of her fondness for Maria as something always present in human relations and therefore only incidental (154–55), she reminds us for a moment of another tough old woman in Hemingway's life, Gertrude Stein—whose writing he mocks in a later passage (289). But finally, she is jealous of Maria's youth, and that tip-off of things to come is our last clue to the dilution here of the androgynous ideal. Hemingway has begun to look to much younger women for sisterly admiration, for adoring, selfless ministration to his shaky male identity. In *Across the River and Into the Trees* (1950) he will push that middle-aged fantasy to its absurdly immature conclusion. Meanwhile, in *For Whom the Bell Tolls,* his admiration for Pilar keeps his three-day dream-float on the ground. As Pilar says to Maria, "You will not be nineteen always" (157).

Chapter 10

Daughters and Sons

PILAR AND MARIA REVISITED

In many ways Pilar is the great puzzle of *For Whom the Bell Tolls*. Hemingway had created her with an oddly more generous sense of female wisdom and strength than he had shown in previous fictions or would ever show again. His attraction to strong older women is the surprising revelation. His early devotion to his literary mother, Gertrude Stein, is often subsumed by his later animus against her, the lament for betrayed love in *Green Hills of Africa*, the parody of her style in this novel, the savage attack on her in *A Moveable Feast*. We see a similar pattern in his ambivalent relations with his older wife Pauline, the devoted yet tough-minded "little terrier" who called herself Pilar during their surreptitious courtship; and behind Pauline there is the paradigm of his early love for and later savage rejection of his strong-minded mother, Grace Hall Hemingway. If, as already suggested, we take the group in the cave in this novel as Jordan's guerrilla family, then Pilar functions as the dominant mother whom Jordan frankly admires, who supports him in his soldierly tasks, and who even supplies him with the inestimable comfort of a wartime lover and three-day wife. What seems to emerge, then, is the positive side of Hemingway's ambivalent feelings about his mother's strength and independence, as opposed to the negative side we see through Jordan's mother, a bully whom his father lacked the courage to confront and who even drove him to suicide—as the joke in chapter 6, that he shot himself to avoid being tortured, broadly implies. Pilar is thus a kind of ideal mother for Hemingway, tough-talking and profane—even though her profanity comes through so blandly (e.g., "What are you doing now, you lazy drunken obscene unsayable son of an unnameable unmarried gypsy obscenity?" 30) as to offend not even Grace Hall's genteel pieties. Pilar is also frank and wise about sexual matters and the mysteries of love, which Hemingway's pious parents never discussed. But setting these rather adolescent forms of rebellion aside, a number of odd similarities come through, not the least of which is that Hemingway's mother was herself a tall, broad-beamed, athletic woman, a distinctly muscular Christian who could kick as high as the ceiling, who wanted her daughters to be tomboys as well as musicians, but who most of all admired her firstborn son's manly little body and stoic fortitude, favored him over his four adoring sisters once he emerged from androgynous infancy, and taught him then to protect and care for them in traditional ways. The tangled web of childhood feelings so engendered helps to explain the family resemblance Pilar finds in Maria and Roberto, and the ease and rapidity with which they fall in love—a Hollywood fantasy, as we have seen, that draws sustenance from Hemingway's early twinning with his older sister Marcelline and from his easy access thereafter to supportive younger sisters. The good mother Pilar in Spain, like the good mother Grace in Oak Park, has handed Maria over to Jordan for curative and protective love; and perhaps in compensation for the death she reads in his palm, she has provided him also with a three-day lifetime in the fifth dimension where true love dwells. The urgency of wartime love must also be cited, with death's imminence as the great mother of romantic beauty; and in all fairness one should mention that Hemingway did meet a Spanish nurse named Maria during the civil war who had been raped by Spanish fascists but who was now quiet, devoted, and the soul of serenity.[1] My point is merely that he had met her counterparts a great many years before and had in androgynous fact been brought up with them.

Whatever the source of these strange arrangements, it is Pilar's controlling role that helps to make them plausible. Indeed, she lends considerable credibility to what might otherwise seem like a rather puerile love affair. When she speaks openly of being jealous of the lovers, for instance, and of being able to take either away from the other if she chose, she makes the interesting point that Jordan as well as Maria is an emotional pushover. As Edmund Wilson argues, Jordan's first-sight response to Maria, the throat clearings and other signs of sexual discomfort, are adolescent yearnings in the Hollywood-dream tradition, without any enrichment of emotional give and take;[2] nor is there admiration for solid strengths in the beloved person, including independent-mindedness—which Pilar has in some abundance, but which Maria eschews in her eager desire to serve her man in self-effacing ways. While not altogether a cipher, as dream girls go, she needs Pilar's certification before she acquires much reality; and in fact it is only when we

16. Ernest, Marcelline, and Ursula playing with a gun and horn at Windemere
Cottage

assume that Jordan loves Pilar-Maria that we get any balanced sense of a fully
credible and possible love. Similarly, Pilar's sense of herself as a complicated
person with lesbian yearnings, though not an actual lesbian, helps to remind
us that Hemingway knows (or hasn't forgotten) that love is never as simple
as he is about to wishfully make it. Perhaps this is why he later has Maria
express an odd desire to make love to Roberto while holding onto the
machine gun's legs as it fires—one of the few complications of her psyche in
the novel. Nevertheless this motherly-sisterly-androgynous love is bound to
fail, as earlier argued, because there is no balance of independent strength in
the partners. These pushover lovers are nothing without Pilar's strength, on
one side, and the good death ahead on the other, whereby Jordan's manliness will be affirmed in the only way his creator can affirm it. Thus, when
Jordan ponders wartime love—"Maybe that is what I am to get now from
life. Maybe that is my life and instead of it being threescore and ten it is . . .
threescore hours and ten or twelve rather" (166)—these speculations seem
like a rationalized attempt to drive up the excitement of such love into
mystical apotheosis, whereby the earth may move once or twice before the
good death takes place.

Still, to frame these three days by androgynous love and the good death is at least to isolate them as the best Hemingway could come up with in the way of heterosexual union and selfless sharing. The repeated assertion by the lovers as to being the other person through mystic exchange—"I am thee and thou art me"—may also be seen, I think, as Hemingway's attempt to affirm and express his feminine feelings, his androgynous yearnings from infancy onward, his experience of twinship with Marcelline as an early edenic phase in life; and perhaps it is only when we speculate that Jordan does want to become Maria, to survive as a beautiful young girl, and not simply through one, that the lurking poignancy of this dream arrangement can be spelled out and acknowledged. Perhaps this is what Jordan means when he later says (381) that Maria is the sister and the daughter as well as the wife he never had. As he grew older, Papa Hemingway badly wanted a daughter through whom he might express those feminine feelings, and for this reason I think he addressed all women as Daughter—which suggests, not incidentally, that he might never have committed suicide if he had had one.

As a heterosexual pair, at any rate, this fictional couple wouldn't last six months back in the academic circles at the University of Montana, and Jordan has trouble even now in imagining Maria with him there, or even at Gaylord's in Madrid, in the inner sanctum of wartime communist society. But as the continuation of the suppressed feminine side of his personality and perhaps under Pilar's continuing care, Maria is a credible figure. There is some poignancy, then, in the acting out of her manly creator's androgynous fantasy of love and war. I think a case can be made that it works, that he pulls it off in spite of all the obvious showing through of his own wishful investments, and in spite of all its obvious difficulties as an ethic to which we might assent. It seems rather an ingenious and often effective synthesis of real stratas of human feelings which the author can bring together only in this way, only in this small-scale epic context, and without really knowing what he's up to.

ROBERT JORDAN REVISITED

One of the things he was up to, more knowingly, was the extension of interiority through objective means. The epic scale of the novel is, as just suggested, rather deceptive: the main action is a minor one, the destruction of a bridge to prevent reinforcements from reaching a battlefront; and the cast of characters is also limited to guerrilla bands and their assailants; but the scope of action and character is extended, often quite effectively, through the memories and musings of a few key characters. Pilar is one of them. We learn as much about her through two stories that she tells as we do from direct depiction. The first story is of wartime and serves to demonstrate how war converts everyone, including the people we side with, to its brutalizing ways. Thus, Pilar's husband, Pablo, enjoys the systematic brutalities he arranges for twenty fascist leaders, all forced to run the town gauntlet before being thrown off a cliff at the end. But Pilar, as the independent-minded teller, records the horror and inhumanity of that arrangement in the sealed-off square. As often noted, the event resembles the bull runs in Spanish villages and may partake of their endemic cruelty. The easy conversion of that primitive sport into a wartime atrocity seems to be the lesson, though aficionados like Jordan and Joaquin try to keep alive its peacetime legitimacy—and that of the Spanish people who enjoy it. Still, Pilar's second tale—about her bullfighter lover's courage in the ring and fear outside of it—suggests that Hemingway himself has become critical of the sporting tragedy he once endorsed so confidently in *Death in the Afternoon;* or, at the least, that he wants to demonstrate once more the greater complexity and many-sidedness of his artistic outlook. Though Chaucer and Fielding before him had chosen spirited women to tell such intervening stories, whether for comic or pathetic ends, the choice of Pilar to convey *this* kind of Spanish tragedy was oddly personal, as if only an ingested female persona—the tough mama inside a tough Papa—could speak to the inhumanity that men without the softening influence of women sometimes relish, or to the terrors that accompany their manly provings. That Pilar is a teller, or talker, is also instructive, given the importance of talking for Catherine Bourne in *The Garden of Eden,* Hemingway's next epic-scale manuscript, as a form of feminine artistry in a novel dominated by her outspoken presence.

Robert Jordan is, by contrast, a ruminating artist. For long stretches of the novel we are inside his mind, musing about love and the good life in relation to war, about political intrigue at Gaylord's in Madrid, or about bravery versus cowardice in facing the death that awaits him. From such ruminations we learn that Jordan is an anti-fascist rather than a Communist, that he accepts Communist discipline for the duration of the war because "they were the only party whose program and whose discipline he could respect," and that he limits his own stake in the war to that of a man who loved the country where it started and believed in the Republic. This last statement has always seemed insufficient to skeptical critics as a compelling reason for Jordan's commitment, perhaps because the real source of his excitement is delayed until the eighteenth chapter, where he distinguishes between the corrupting atmosphere at Gaylord's and the religious atmosphere at the headquarters of the International Brigade, and of the Lincoln

Brigade that was later absorbed into it. Thus Jordan speaks of these volunteer groups from many countries as "a religious order":

> At either of those places you felt that you were taking part in a crusade. . . . You felt . . . something that was like the feeling you expected to have . . . [at] your first communion. It was a feeling of consecration to a duty toward all of the oppressed of the world which would be as difficult and embarrassing to speak about as religious experience and yet it was authentic as the feeling you had when you heard Bach, or stood in Chartres Cathedral . . . [or] saw Mantegna and Greco . . . in the Prado. It gave you a part in something that you could believe in wholly and completely and in which you felt an absolute brotherhood with the others who were engaged in it. It was something that you had never known before but that you had experienced now and you gave such importance to it and the reasons for it that your own death seemed of complete unimportance; only a thing to be avoided because it would interfere with the performance of your duty. But the best thing was that there was something you could do about this feeling and this necessity too. You could fight. (235)

This passage comparing the dedication of such fighters to religious and aesthetic experience, this heralded brotherhood with a group of noble, self-sacrificing soldiers fighting for the world's oppressed, is like the French Foreign Legion in reverse: not a group of cynical outcasts but of dedicated idealists willing to fight in accord with a Marxist credo for which Jordan doesn't even have to be responsible. These are new frontiersmen he can admire because they have no political power or function and can simply fight and die, as it were, for unexamined ideals. Jordan has joined them for the free spiritual ride, the purity which music, architecture, and painting can attain, a kind of military version of the bullring to which Hemingway also gave this quasi-religious quality in *Death in the Afternoon*. To be against oppression, to give one's life to remove it, is decidedly more noble than fighting bulls; but the question of who is oppressing whom, or where and why and how, is not really answered in the novel, except as war makes oppressors of us all. Still, this moment of boyish reference to crusades and first communions makes one thing clear: the war has provided Jordan, and Hemingway too, with an outlet for all that suppressed boyhood idealism that Hemingway had learned to hunker down behind his tough-guy facade for some twenty years; it has provided a good cause worth dying for, and therefore an occasion for the good life and the good death that justify the good soldier's happy call to duty. The trouble is, as Hemingway the honest writer also knew, that everything else going on in Spain contradicts this pure idealism and largely undercuts it.

But not altogether. Through Jordan's memories of General Golz and journalist Karkov, two cynical secret idealists like himself, Hemingway gives some support—as with El Sordo—to the idea of men who fight on in spite of their awareness of the failures occasioned by bureaucracy and braggadoccio and betrayal. And this kind of suppressed idealism—suppressed to the point of stoic courage from which Hemingway derived his own early strength as a writer in the postwar wasteland—is finally more reliable than the state of grace Jordan and the other members of the volunteer brigades had been able to maintain for the first six months of the war and no longer, against the inroads of harsh realities.

Through Jordan, then, Hemingway offers a fairly complex state of mind about the war and how to take it. The mind in question is interesting, knowing, aware of political and military maneuvers in an informative way, and even able to place its own boyish idealism in perspective. As a reporter Hemingway had been a fairly good judge of international affairs, if not a pundit on the issues behind them. But when we realize that these musing sections in which he conveys what he knows about love and war are the equivalent for the stream-of-consciousness novels by which Joyce, Faulkner, and Woolf had gained artistic fame in the 1920s, and that this is the kind of interiority he offers in his obvious attempt to compete with them, then we are—or at least I am—given pause. This is a mind that systematically dodges complex ideas, on the one hand, and emotional depths on the other—a mind that prefers to externalize scenes and actions rather than probe inner feelings or express them freely.

Fortunately it is also an honest mind, and we do get spaced revelations from it, as when Jordan ponders Pilar's troubled behavior on the way back from El Sordo's camp and decides that she "took a beating" from Pablo because of her generous attempt to give the lovers more time together. "She is a damned sight more civilized than you are and she knows what time is all about," he thinks (168); and by the end of the chapter he will say, "When you get through this war you might take up the study of women. . . . You could start with Pilar" (176). He has been thinking about Pilar's age and ugliness with some sympathy, as if Hemingway had put himself in Pauline's place in viewing his current liaison with Martha Gellhorn. There is a study of women going on, then, in Jordan's mind, as he ponders this imagined fusion of Pauline and Grace and their best possibilities and sufferings, including the price of their imagined generosities.

We also glimpse the machismo side of Jordan's mind when he admits to being indifferent about the killing, or even liking it, "as all who are soldiers by choice have enjoyed it at some time" (287); or when he accepts the necessity of executing those who panic in battle, or the Russian practice of shooting cowardly generals and other traitors that he hears about at Gaylord's, where he admits also that he likes the soft, corrupting life. Such attitudes are tested by the events of the third day, as Jordan wakes to the sound of a horse's hooves and shoots his first fascist this time out, and is then overcome by guilt when he finds while dutifully reading the dead man's letters that his sister loved him supportively.

Meanwhile Jordan has been putting up a good front as a man indifferent to his own death; but as the third day progresses we see that he secretly worries about his courage when death comes—the death Pilar has read in his hand and which he seems to accept as the fated outcome of his ill-starred mission. News of the fascist beheadings of Sordo's band has impressed him with this possibility, has reminded him of how Indians scalped their victims as he turns now to the example of his grandfather for support and makes the comparison we have seen between his grandfather's bravery and his suicidal father's cowardice, his final evasion of his strong wife's bullying. One conclusion to be drawn from these musings is that women warriors like Pilar who put down their cowardly husbands do what is necessary; they are like good soldiers and are therefore admirable; whereas women who put down husbands on the domestic front, where Hemingway himself had always proved rather cowardly, are bullies. It was his own inability to stand up to the strong women he admired that plagued him, then, and that he attributes here through Jordan to his father, whose suicide was in fact based on a neglected illness—diabetes leading to a gangrenous leg—and upon the loss of family money he had managed in the Florida land bust of 1928, money largely from Grace's patrimony and her musical earnings.

Such projective thinking about his father seems even more evident when the bridge-blowing expedition begins and Jordan, feeling uneasy and unreal, is reminded of his father's tearful farewell at the train station when he was about to depart for college—an exact replica of the situation when Hemingway left home for his reporting job in Kansas City.[3] Jordan has just had a heartfelt handshake from Pablo, a kind of sealing of friendship between the now courageous Spanish father and his surrogate American son. But what Jordan recalls is his embarrassment at his own father's tears and at "the damp religious sound" of his father's prayer: "May the Lord watch between thee and me while we are absent one from the other." This prayer was actually more often on his mother's lips, and in her many letters to Ernest; and the feminine association seems to be what Hemingway through Jordan cannot

17. Ernest as Huck Finn with shotgun and bird, ca. 1914

stand. Pablo's tears on the night he loses command of the guerrilla band to his wife are thus signs of masculine default; but now he has redeemed himself by returning with five men and five horses for the attack and the escape (he will later shoot the men and keep the horses), and his manly goodbye, "*Suerte,* Inglés," is supposed to contrast with Jordan's father's tearful prayer, whereby Jordan, though feeling awfully young and afraid to go to school a moment before, now feels superior to and older than his father.

257

Ironically enough, tears and prayers for men raised in the genteel tradition of muscular Christianity used to be called manly tears, until Hemingway and others broke with that tradition and turned them into abject feminine behavior. Still more ironically, Hemingway's father had initiated that switch, for in his own yearnings to be an Indian fighter like his father—Jordan's grandfather in this novel—he had raised his son to become the frontier scout he had always wanted to be himself, had taught him how to load, cock, and shoot a pistol in target practice at the manly age of two years and eleven months, had taught him also gun safety rules from that age onward, which is why Jordan speaks earlier of his father's "misuse" of the grandfather's pistol in committing suicide, a strange locution indeed. But that is where it all began, this new version, misreading rather, of the old frontier code whereby pistol-packing scouts don't cry but concern themselves with the good death ahead, and so carry within them throughout their lives this too early responsibility for life and death, this projective contempt for manly tears and the fathers who indulge them.

FATHER AND DAUGHTER

If, in her wisdom about time, Pilar had concluded that it waits for no woman, not even the nineteen-year-old Maria, she may not have spoken wisely about men. Indeed, for middle-aged male fantasts in a patriarchal world, there is always a new crop of nineteen-year-olds; and their own emotional age may be said to be fixed—as Hemingway's apparently was—at about nineteen. That was the year of his war wound in Italy and of his hospital romance with Agnes Von Kurowsky, and to that year he returns emotionally, in *Across the River and Into the Trees* (1950),[4] with the accumulated wishfulness of three more decades. In this nostalgic novel—dedicated nominally to his fourth wife, Mary Welsh, but implicitly to his nineteen-year-old Italian muse Adriana Ivancich—the aging Colonel Cantwell, who at fifty is likely to die at any moment from heart failure, takes the daughterly love of nineteen-year-old Countess Renata as a tribute to his continuing virility. She makes him work at being the good, gentle, and considerate man he can be, in the tradition of Fauntleroy and John Halifax; makes him temper his brutal rage at the military blunders of all the commanders he has known in World War II; and listens with fascinated admiration to all aspects of his manly life. But the mechanical oscillation between her lesson in redemptive gentleness and his in military wrath parodies rather than reconciles these opposing views of manly character, reduces them to middle-aged folly and bluster, on the one hand, and small-boy obedience on the other.

258

The coarsening of Hemingway's sensibility in World War II to that of a war-lover whose boyhood enthusiasm has soured into grizzled rant is every-where evident, as is the coarsening of his youthful androgynous charm with peers and elders into dutiful middle-aged gallantry toward a teenage fan. The novel is thus doubly insulated from the realities of postwar nostalgia it tries to recreate. Neither World War II nor the kinds of love that survived it are remotely touched by the Venetian tryst between the aging warrior and his precocious ward. It does not even help that Cantwell calls himself a "good boy" (165, 173) when he tries to be gentle; or that he sees in an old motorboat like himself "the gallantry of the aging machine" (52); or that, like Catherine Barkley, Renata wants to be him (156) or one of his soldiers (231) or his selfless server (143); or that they "play" at exchanging identities (261); or that their lovemaking is confined—since she is menstruating—to magical manipulations beneath a gondola blanket with his maimed but mysteriously potent hand ("I dreamed it was the hand of Our Lord," says Renata on p. 84), and is thus chastely religious; or, finally, that this caring sparing Colonel, like Harry Morgan and Robert Jordan before him, goes off to die well alone. The attempt to deal lightly or wondrously or delicately with these androgynous gestures only heightens their tiredness and misap-plication.

Hemingway's intentions are nonetheless serious and self-critical. In Colonel Richard Cantwell he attempts a military portrait—much like that of the writer Harry in "The Snows of Kilimanjaro"—of an irritable, con-temptuous, paranoid, selfishly impatient man trying to die tenderly and gallantly. As the novel opens, the Colonel thinks of his recalcitrant boatman as a "surly jerk," a now dated wartime epithet he bestows liberally thereafter on all who cross him. Like Hemingway himself, he sits in bars with his back to a corner wall, spends much time defining "tough" and avoiding being "rough," yet spoils for fights with younger men. At one point he decks two sailors who have whistled at the Contessa; yet at the same time he regrets having killed off most of his regiment three times in three bad battles; and he obviously regrets what he euphemistically calls his "wild-boar truculence" (71): "Why am I always a bastard and why can I not suspend this trade of arms, and be a kind and good man as I would have wished to be. I try always to be just, but I am brusque and I am brutal, and it is not that I have erected the defense against brown-nosing my superiors and brown-nosing the world. I should be a better man with less wild boar blood in the small time which remains" (65).

In Hemingway's own life at this time such truculence came perilously close to paranoid hysteria. He understood that propensity in himself, however, and tried bravely, in this novel, to cope with it. At the same time he was probing deeper into its origins, in *The Garden of Eden* manuscript, which runs concurrently with this one, and which is echoed in its safer pages. Thus, Colonel Cantwell asks his daughterly girlfriend Renata if the four ladies sitting at the next table at Harry's Bar are lesbians:

> "I do not know," she said. "They are all very nice people."
>
> "I should say they are lesbians. But maybe they are just good friends. Maybe they are both. It means nothing to me and it was not a criticism."
>
> "You are nice when you are gentle."
>
> "Do you suppose the word gentleman derives from a man who is gentle?"
>
> "I do not know," the girl said, and she ran her fingers very lightly over the scarred hand. "But I love you when you are gentle." (86)

Plainly the lessons of Dinah Mulock Craik's *John Halifax, Gentleman,* the Hemingway family bible, were not lost on Ernest, who recalls them now at fifty in his own effort to be gentle, to act in accord with his mother's teachings through this fictional version of himself (and of his friend Chink Dorman-Smith) as a dying colonel. But the lesbian question, in relation to a nineteen-year-old Italian girl, reminds us also of Marita in *The Garden of Eden,* another version of Adriana Ivancich as the switch lover in a *ménage à trois,* moving out of her early lesbianism into heterosexuality as she shifts her affections from Catherine to David Bourne. Indeed, it is Marita's impress upon David that helps him to accept their own androgynous lovemaking as a normal variation rather than a perversion—which may explain this safer approach to deviant sexuality, and to the humanity of lesbians as "nice people," as troubling conditions endured by the scarred hand that Renata reassures with her loving touch.

The question of incest is similarly broached as the bar chapter continues. Renata has just asked the colonel where he will hang the portrait of herself she will give him, and whether others will see it and speak badly of her:

> "No, they damn well will not. Also I'll tell them it is a portrait of my daughter."
>
> "Did you ever have a daughter?"
>
> "No. I always wanted one."
>
> "I can be your daughter as well as everything else."
>
> "That would be incest."
>
> "I don't think that would be so terrible in a city as old as this and that has seen what this city has seen."

"Listen, Daughter."

"Good," she said. "That was fine. I liked it."

"All right," the Colonel said and his voice was thickened a little. "I liked it, too." (98)

The intentional *frisson* created by the mention of incest is a mild version of the androgynous thickenings of male response in *The Garden of Eden*. Two chapters later the intensity steps up with further references from that steamier source: "The Colonel whispered; holding her tight, and with his heart broken, honestly and fairly, in his whisper that was as barely audible as a silent dog whistle heard close to the ear, 'I love you, devil. And you're my Daughter, too. And I don't care about our losses because the moon is our mother and our father. And now let's go down to dinner'" (114).

In *The Garden of Eden*, meals and carefully described menus will also frame David Bourne's troubled relations with his devilish wife Catherine; and the spell upon them both of the Rodin statue of two lesbians making love may be compared to this safer image of the moon as androgynous parent of incestuously innocent lovers, father and daughter, gentle man and devil child, in a text which merely ruffles such relations.

FATHERS AND SONS

The bad critical reception of *Across the River and Into the Trees* so angered Hemingway that, like Macomber after the lion, he decided to prove himself again with a giant fish. His mother had died in 1951, and though he refused to go to her funeral, he recalled in a letter to Carlos Baker "how beautiful Grace had been when she was young before 'everything went to hell in the family,' and also how happy they all had been as children before it all broke up."[5] Two years earlier she had sent him his baby books, which he read and responded to with real gratitude. His hostile feelings toward her were softening, apparently, and in the prize-winning novella *The Old Man and the Sea* (1952), he seems to have broken through to something like his old childhood tenderness. The old man of the tale is genuinely rather than dutifully gentle, and his responses to the sea and its inhabitants have the lyric grace of a childhood fable. Indeed, the blend of gentleness and toughness in his makeup is designedly exemplary; his lonely pursuit of the giant fish begins and ends with the boy on shore who once accompanied him, but whose parents forbade it when the old man proved unlucky. Now he is proving himself lucky again for the boy's sake, teaching him the value of lonely stoic patience and loving regard for their common world, teaching him to withstand pain and privation, teaching him the dignity, finally, of significant defeat.

From his twenties onward Hemingway had been calling himself Papa, in emulation of that Christian gentleman, his maternal grandfather and namesake, "Abba" Ernest Hall.[6] He had written stories of parents and children from the child's point of view and one—called "Fathers and Sons" after Turgenev's example—from his own paternal point of view; and he had always been a kind of fatherly travel guide to his readers, their paternal instructor in the empirical hows of sporting or expatriate or military life, the lay of landscapes, towns, cities, and the stoic wisdom needed for survival in such climes and times. In *Across the River and Into the Trees* he had even allowed Papa Cantwell to exchange lessons in valor and tenderness with daughterly Renata. But *The Old Man and the Sea* was his first and best attempt to concentrate on a Papa figure who is himself an example of gentle manliness.

For the first time, moreover, the world itself is conceived as feminine and in loving rather than threatening terms. "They" are no longer out there to break or kill impartially the good and the brave and the gentle, as in *A Farewell to Arms*. If there are harsh realities to confront, they take their place within a benignly feminine context. Thus, where younger fishermen call the sea *el mar* and see it "as a contestant or a place or even an enemy," the old man fondly calls it *la mar* and sees it always "as feminine and as something that gave or withheld great favors, and if she did wild or wicked things it was because she could not help them. The moon affects her as it does a woman, he thought."[7]

This may be the only place in Hemingway's fiction where he takes feminine behavior as a benign explanation of the world's arbitrariness and allows for menstruation as its biocosmic source. Certainly it is the only place where he acknowledges the true sex of his chief rival and, from the token struggle with nature which so often absorbs him, draws an implied parallel between Mother Nature and Mother Grace—and draws it, moreover, with renewed tenderness.

But *The Old Man and the Sea* is a fable for gentle men and boys. There is no brutality in it and there are no women to complicate the lesson in how men must live. In *Islands in the Stream* (1970), the posthumously published manuscript from which *The Old Man* was extracted, bachelor father Thomas Hudson would give more direct lessons in manhood to his three visiting sons from within a similar male preserve; but in this realistic novel, there is plenty of male brutality within that preserve and not a little sexual bravado; and though Hudson himself refrains from both and is implicitly loving with his boys, his conduct elsewhere in the book—especially with women—is scarcely exemplary (though at one point toward the end, when he dreams that his first wife returns to him and, in an exchange of identities, makes love to him as the active and superior partner, it is certainly androgynous in *The Garden of Eden* manner).[8]

Essentially, however, Hudson raises his visiting sons as Clarence Hemingway had raised Ernest and Leicester: as empirical novices in a simplistic world of externals, a world of physical adventures from which complicated questions about human relations are excluded or unasked. Ideally, the moral lessons from this physical world should be transferrable to human relations; but since Hudson himself has failed to make that transfer, except with a servant, his anthropomorphized cats, and a few bar companions, we see quite otherwise. Hudson's attempt to play papa in this novel is thus painfully shallow and unconvincing, as is his stoic grief after the convenient deaths of all three sons. But at least he makes the attempt, and the novel's closing revelation—that he never understands anybody that loves him—is at least touching in its honesty. Meanwhile, what stands out like a signature is his supine relation with the cats who sleep upon his chest and with whom he seems more intimate than with people, as if the kitten games of the author's childhood, the forlorn cats in the early rains of marriage, and the many Cats and Catherines in his fictions and affections had somehow crystallized or essentialized into lonely, anthropomorphic love. Such love may be appropriate, however, for a novel in which the author has imagined himself as someone he never was, a bachelor father who has finally learned how to live without women—"how not to get married" (8).

In "The Last Good Country" the love is less lonely. The cat named Littless in *Islands in the Stream,* after the cat with the same name at Hemingway's Cuban home, becomes Nick Adams's sister Littless in this late, unfinished novella, the very type of adoring sisterly affection and androgynous emulation, the very essence of childhood tenderness. The surprising presence of this sister in Nick's male world comes as a late revelation of early feminine support, of that "softening feminine influence" from which in fact Hemingway was never free and which at this formative stage at least he seems to have cherished. The Hansel and Gretel story, as here reimagined, provides a corrective counterpoint to those early tales of Nick alone on the road, toughing it out with whores and hobos, the last of the lone frontiersmen—who takes his sister along for company when he runs away from home! And decidedly needs her. Indeed, without her comforting, restraining, and sustaining presence, how else could he pursue "original sin"? how else could he even *live* for long in "the last good country"?

Half Western melodrama, half childhood fable, "The Last Good Country" takes as its difficult task the definition of childhood affections within that wilderness home away from home, that forest world where fleeing children set up sibling households, which Hemingway had first discovered while reading Captain Marryat's *Children of the New Forest.* In Marryat's exemplary adventure tale of seventeenth-century England, four Cavalier siblings—two brothers and two sisters—take refuge in a royal forest during the bloody Civil War, set up their own household, raise crops, poach deer and other game, and elude and foil villainous keepers from the Roundhead ranks. It was, in short, a fiction close to the farm and forest life that Hemingway knew in northern Michigan; and along with other poaching and forest tales by Marryat—such as *Jacob Faithful, The Poacher,* and *The Settlers in Canada*—it gave him plenty of leeway and precedent in composing his own version of the blue heron episode, when he too had fled from game wardens through the wilderness, reaching safety for the time being with the Dilworths at Horton Bay and with Uncle George in Ironton. An outlaw at last, like the several heroes of his boyhood reading, he had saved this episode for fictional exploitation late in life and could now develop it after the heart's desire. He had begun writing it late in 1951, while corresponding with troublesome biographers and critics like Charles Fenton, Philip Young, and Arthur Mizener, who threatened in their several ways to rob him of such treasures. He was on his good behavior that year, trying to avoid rancorous quarrels with these scavengers (as he saw them), pulling away from them with some success into the creative possibilities of his fiction, not the least of which was the secret source of his tender regard for wives and "daughters" who had always wanted to be boys, and for the adoring fictional heroines who feel the same way but whose credibility is sometimes undermined by the dreamlike situations that underlie their realistic portraits.

In "The Last Good Country" the controlling dreamlike fantasy beneath the surface realism is too obvious to undermine the heroine's credibility; but what it expresses—or enables Hemingway to express—is not so obvious. On April 24, 1952, Hemingway had written to Adriana Ivancich, the daughterly model for Renata in *Across the River and Into the Trees,* that he had begun a story "about Michigan long ago" that was inwardly complex but outwardly "very simple."[9] Among its inward complexities was a curious notion of original sin. The notion is first broached by Mr. Packard in a flashback conversation with Nick Adams:

Mr. John liked Nick Adams because he said he had original sin. Nick did not understand this but he was proud.

"You're going to have things to repent, boy," Mr. John had told Nick. "That's one of the best things there is. You can always decide whether to repent them or not. But the thing is to have them."

"I don't want to do anything bad," Nick had said.

"I don't want you to," Mr. John had said. "But you're alive and you're going to do things. Don't you lie and don't you steal. Everybody has to lie. But you pick out somebody you never lie to."

"I'll pick out you."[10]

Mr. Packard returns the compliment, gives Nick some explicit sexual advice that Scribner's editors have excised on the grounds of taste but which helps nonetheless to establish Packard as a more useful sexual authority than Nick's father (who in "Fathers and Sons" dismisses all such matters as "heinous crimes"), then questions Nick closely on a girlfriend he has lost. Nick says he feels bad about losing her, but proves an apt pupil when he admits that "none of it was her fault. She's just built that way. If I ran into her again I guess I'd get mixed up with her again." Whether the lost girlfriend is Trudy, the Indian girl mentioned earlier in the story, or a girl like Marjorie, with whom Nick hopes to get "mixed up" again in "The Three-Day Blow," is unclear.[11] But the connection between original sin, lost girlfriends, and repentable things worth doing has been firmly made.

On April 22, 1953, about a year after he began to develop "The Last Good Country," Hemingway wrote to Bernard Berenson about his long-dead paternal grandmother, Adelaide Hemingway, an Oberlin graduate who sprang from western pioneer stock and taught botany and astronomy to all her children and grandchildren. In the letter he describes her as a beautiful woman who wrote excuses for him for school whenever he wanted to box instead and who told him that the only things she regretted in life were those she had not done.[12] The truthfulness between them, her willingness to cover his truant behavior, and her life prescription as to doing rather than regretting are very much the substance of Mr. Packard's relations with and prescriptions for Nick Adams.

Packard's western experience may also owe something to Hemingway's family heritage. Though his prototype, Jim Dilworth, was a blacksmith, and though the Dilworths were old settlers at Horton Bay, Hemingway's biographers say nothing about their western background. Hemingway's forebears on both sides had lived in the West, however, as guides and early settlers; and his indulgent paternal grandfather, who gave him his first gun when he was ten, had often told him stories about coming west to Chicago in a covered wagon. Hemingway's special fondness for Anson and Adelaide Hemingway, his implicit preference for them over his own parents, may explain his similar preference for the indulgent Dilworths and their backwoods ethos. In his late unfinished novella the Packards represent that "ideal blend of wilderness and civilization" that his grandparents and the Dilworths first afforded; they are the "good frontier parents" who assist Nick and his sister in escaping the game wardens to "the last good country."

If "original sin" means doing things you will regret not having done, and getting into trouble for doing them, then Nick's several violations of the game laws must also come under this heading. As his sister reminds him, he is guilty of at least three such violations: shooting a moose out of season, selling rainbow trout to the Packards, and killing the unmentionable thing the game wardens took from his boat—unmentionable because "that was the [only] proof they had" of his sinful doings (60). Later, when the wardens identify their proof as a buck deer shot out of season, the hired girl tells Mr. Packard that the local warden's boy must have found the meat where Nick "had it hung up in the old springhouse" (89). As that interesting discrepancy suggests, and as the original manuscripts confirm, Hemingway had begun with a more likely cargo for Nick's boat—the blue heron from whose slaying this albatross tale derives—and had then changed to the buck deer in the springhouse midway through, creating thereby a second version of the opening events that Scribner's editors have failed to splice well with the first.[13] But whether for bird, beast, or fish, found in boat or springhouse, one thing is certain: the local warden has been after Nick for the last four years because of such misdemeanors and now means to make an example of him by sending him to reform school.

For Hemingway as for Nick, the prospect of being tried for all such crimes at once had seemed frighteningly real. He had been raised in a home, moreover, where the list of punishable offenses, major and minor, was legion; and his exaggerated sense of guilt and punishment at this time may reflect that woodshed outlook. His invention of a western past for the "down-state" warden, as for Mr. Packard, was decidedly juvenile; but here again his outlook was familial, albeit in a different and more complicated way. If, as Philip Young argues, the escape to "the last good country" is an American dream as in Huck Finn's flight to the "territory," it was a dream which all of Hemingway's forebears had realized; and if, as Young also notes, the escape with one's sister is a universal fantasy, as in *Hansel and Gretel*,[14] it was a fantasy which again linked Hemingway with his forebears, especially as it called for adventurous spirits among his sisters, frontier throwbacks like himself, "original sinners" for whom the family circle had proved unusually confining.

In this sense all the Hemingways were their grandparents' rather than their parents' children; all wanted to escape from the family's present circumstances to something like its frontier past. Having been taught to shoot, fish, boat, and swim at Walloon Lake, having been raised on tales of the family's frontier adventures, they felt out of place and ill at ease in the strict environs of their Oak Park home. They felt different from their neighbors, too, and at different stages of conformity or rebellion, they felt different from each other.

Thus, as "The Last Good Country" begins, Hemingway tells us that Nick and his sister Littless "loved each other and . . . did not love the others" (56–57); and later, when they reach their forest refuge, Littless tells Nick that "crime comes easy for you and me. . . . We're different from the others" (99). From such imagined difference with each of his four sisters, and from the blue heron episode itself, Hemingway had fashioned Nick's escape with Littless to "the last good country"—a detailed action covering two nights and three days of sibling closeness. More than that he could not imagine without violating the law of failed relations that governs all his fiction; but the wonder is that he could imagine even that much unabashed tenderness. His basic motive for inventing that escape now seems clear: it was something he had always wanted to do in fact and was now able to do in fiction; something he had thought of many times in childhood and regretted never doing; something which, late in life, he wanted to understand better and to affirm, especially as it clarified his lifelong difficulties with affectionate love and challenged his ability to convey such tender feelings. He needed Littless, then, because she gave him access to "repentable" emotions he had for a long time deliberately underplayed.

His introduction of Littless in the first line of the story indicates her crucial importance to it. Though he had originally begun the story with a brief paragraph written in the first person—"I was watching the bottom of the spring where the sand rose in little spurts with the bubbling water. . . . Behind us was a cedar swamp"[15]—he had quickly shifted to the third person and had lifted Littless from that subordinate "us" into special prominence:

> "Nickie," his sister said to him. "Listen to me, Nickie."
> "I don't want to hear it."
> He was watching the bottom of the spring where the sand rose in small spurts with the bubbling water. . . . His back was against a big cedar tree and behind him there was a thick cedar swamp. His sister was sitting on the moss beside him and she had her arm around his shoulders.
> "They're waiting for you to come home to supper," his sister said.

"There's two of them. They came in a buggy and they asked where you were." (56)

As the expanded paragraph makes clear, Littless supports her reluctant brother even as she warns him of a crisis he doesn't want to face. She reminds him now that leaving her behind will be difficult, since he will be lonely without her. When the game wardens pass by in their buggy, and the children slide back out of sight, Nick tells her that he wants to kill those "sons of bitches." But Littless opposes killing: she will go along to prevent it, she is old enough to go; she has already helped him and will help him more. When he argues that the wardens will look harder for two, that "a boy and a girl will show up more," she tells him that she will cut her hair and "go like a boy," having "always wanted to be [one] anyway" (57). Nick agrees to take her with him, though "only for a couple of days." The clear spring water into which he initially gazes, the cedar swamp behind it, are tangible signs of his dilemma. When he and Littless reach their forest refuge, they will camp beside another clear spring with a cedar swamp behind it. As in his famous early tale "Big Two-Hearted River," Hemingway again chooses to external-ize the simplicities of the "good life" and the complications which threaten it; and as always in his fiction, he tries to make us feel the outward shape and texture of inward complexities. Thus, as the story opens, the wellspring of childhood affection flows fresh and clear. Nick will abide by it as he escapes from threatening complications, if only to stave off loneliness.

On the surface, Nick's decision to bring Littless with him seems like a tactical error. If she will ease loneliness and prevent killings, she will also require considerable care and protection and might well limit the time needed for lying low till the wardens tire of waiting. In a variant version of the opening such considerations weigh so heavily that Littless is forced to trick Nick into taking her against his will. But whether tricked or persuaded, Nick consciously defies still another source of censure: "I shouldn't take you," he says in the published version. "But then I shouldn't have done any of it" (58). The first "shouldn't" refers to family rather than legal restric-tions. To flee with Littless is a repentable crime against them, another form of "original sin." Though Littless will leave a note under her mother's door that night, announcing that she has joined Nick to keep him out of trouble (this is her trick on him in the variant version), Nick recognizes his respon-sibility, as her older brother, for pitting the two of them against his mother's displeasure. If the game wardens overtly threaten his freedom, his mother and the "others" are from the first the essential threat from which, along with Littless, he wishfully flees.

As noted earlier, Hemingway reverses family history at this point. In fiction Mrs. Adams retreats with a sick headache when the wardens encamp in her cottage and leaves the details of flight to her children; in fact, Mrs. Hemingway had driven the wardens off with a shotgun and had instructed Ernest on his escape. His fictive rearrangements, then, were designed to put down his mother, now safely dead, and perhaps more importantly, to bolster his image of himself as a responsible son and brother. The occasion which moved him here was not the blue heron episode but his banishment from the cottage at Windemere shortly after his twenty-first birthday. That edict had followed the "innocent" midnight picnic at Ryan's Point on the lake to which his sisters Ursula and Sunny had invited him and his friend Ted Brumback, along with four young neighbors (two of them girls of thirteen). Their absence was soon detected, and by the time of their return at 4 A.M. they faced a grim reception by Grace Hemingway and the irate mother of one of the young girls, who wanted to know what those grown men, Ernest and Ted, were doing out there with such little girls. The Hemingway girls were then forbidden late dates for the rest of the summer; and Ernest and Ted, judged old enough to know better, were banished to Horton Bay to work for their room and board at the Dilworths' hotel. Some thirty-two years later, still smarting from such reprimands, Ernest would ironically create a protective and responsible Nick Adams, very much concerned with Littless's health, safety, and feelings, and in that sense very much Grace Hemingway's loving son, even as he carries out his repentable flight to the woods with Littless, an action apparently better done than regretted.

Still another form of family disapproval emerges on the eleventh of the original thirteen-page start for the tale as Littless asks a pointed question:

"It isn't dirty for a brother and sister to love each other, is it?"
"Who said it was?
"Somebody in the family."
"I can guess."

"Don't guess," says Littless, and then indicates that it isn't who he thinks it is. Whether the offending member of the family is a jealous sister or some older relative is never shown. But the question of whether a brother and sister can love each other is one which children often ponder; and here, as elsewhere in the tale, Hemingway works to distinguish between the innocence of such affections and the cultural fear of incest which may attend them. When on an early variant page Littless tells Nick, "We've done wrong already," and Nick denies it, Littless quickly insists: "I don't mean that kind of wrong like you and Trudy. I mean I've stolen for you and I keep your secrets and now I'm warning you about [the game wardens]." But Nick has taken her cultural point, and when she asks if she can run off with him, he tells her that "people wouldn't understand." In the published text this issue is limited to Nick's musing, in the forest: "He loved his sister very much and she loved him too much. But, he thought, I guess those things straighten out. At least I hope so" (101).

What he means by too-muchness is then illustrated by Littless's innocent prattle about becoming his common-law wife and having children by him while still a minor so that he'll have to marry her under "the Unwritten Law" (104). As the text makes us see, this open testing of half-understood limits is scarcely a neurotic revelation. The issue is easily and playfully aired; the love in question is basic to emotional growth; the affections are, as we say, healthy, and without them we would not be able to love one another tenderly as adults. As in "Soldier's Home," where the returned veteran Harold's "best sister" Helen similarly wants him to be her beau and love her always, the affections are open, uncomplicated, and crucial to any future tenderness Harold may feel for adult women. If he now prefers the easy sexuality he knew with German and French women to the complications of American courtship, he also prefers his sister's easy affection to his mother's demanding and demeaning pieties, even as Nick prefers Littless to the "others."

Reviewers have not been exactly quick to see this affirmation. Their comments on "The Last Good Country"—"barely sublimated incest," "slightly soppy narrative," "a mawkish shard of an abandoned novel," "too much . . . sentimental talk," "the verge of incest," "right out of James Barrie, even to the sexual undercurrents"—suggest how unthinkingly we still operate under the post-Victorian, that is to say, Freudian, dispensation.[16] We are so embarrassed, apparently, by any genuine expression of affection, or any playful testing of limits, that we can only assign it to sentimentality or neurosis. Hemingway himself has contributed to this contemporary attitude, perhaps more than any modern writer, through the widespread influence of his deadpan style and through popular legends about his stoic toughness; so it is not surprising that reviewers influenced by both have missed the persistent defense of vulnerable feelings in his work, or the constant demand for emotional support in his life, and are now at a loss to account for a direct display of family closeness and its modest ambivalences. It is not the "verge of incest" that Hemingway treads in this decidedly revealing story; it is the frontier of childhood affections, rather, which the completely open issue of incest helps to outline. Philip Young almost sees this when he speaks of "hints of physical love" which "highlight the innocence of actual relationships" in such stories, and of "overtones," without which "we would never think to realize how immaculate is the conception."[17] Never, at any rate, in our slightly addled time, when we are unable to distinguish between the sensual closeness of friends and relations and the sexual closeness of lovers.

In "The Last Good Country" Hemingway himself seems to understand this distinction. Nick's tender regard for his sister is carefully played off against his sexual connection with the Indian girl Trudy, who though pregnant by him is not even "second best" in his affections. The editors of Scribner's have done the fragmented tale a large disservice by cutting out the dialogue pertaining to Trudy; for, surprisingly, the girl who "did first what no one has ever done better" in "Fathers and Sons" (243) is here edged out by Nick's concern for his sister—or not so surprisingly, perhaps, if we recall how Nick is determined to kill the Indian boy Eddy Gilby if he tries to sleep with his sister Dorothy in that earlier tale, though it is all right for Nick to "make plenty baby" with Eddie's half-sister Trudy (239–41). Now, with Trudy literally pregnant and Nick himself an outcast, Nick feels he ought to rejoin Trudy until Littless persuades him to run off with her instead. Though she is plainly jealous of Trudy's sexual hold on Nick, she is willing to help him find Trudy so long as her own innocent hold on his affections is stronger—as it proves to be, once she tricks him into taking her along on his escape. In other words, she saves him from the consequences of his sexual as well as his legal "crimes," and it is this double or—considering his family's disapproval—this triple jeopardy which the editors of Scribner's forfeit by their cuts. The whole force and point of the later argument about Trudy, and of Nick's decisive exclamation, "The hell with Trudy," is also lost (70–71); but more to the point, the innocent nature of love between brother and sister is needlessly obscured throughout the text—so much so that a recent reader, Kenneth Lynn, even supplies Nick with a wholly conjectural erection when Littless sits on his lap.[18]

The unlikeliness of that savvy twist becomes evident early in the tale, when Littless marvels at the idea of knockout drops like those which whores use in rolling lumberjacks and thinks they "ought to have some for in emergencies," at which point Nick wants to kiss her "just for in emergency" (64). It is here, in the original manuscript, that the missing dialogue about Trudy begins. Among its several lost beauties is Littless's reason for withholding until now her knowledge of Trudy's whereabouts: "I thought we'd go away together and I'd take care of you and you'd take care of me and we'd hunt and fish and eat and read and sleep together and not worry and love each other and be kind and good." The juxtaposition of this ingenuous option with Nick's baby-making life with Trudy is what the tale is chiefly about; it is an enactment of Littless's dream, which Nick seems to share, or which he at least seems to prefer to life with Trudy, for when he is now reminded of the "sweet-grass" smell he associates with making love to her in "Fathers and Sons" (244), he frankly says: "I'm sorry Littless. . . . I'm not a good brother, and I'm not a good man and I'm not a good friend even," and then acknowledges that he prefers Littless and that finding Trudy is not even his "second best hope."

The discounting here of loveless sex is like the discounting of Lieutenant Frederic Henry's whoring in *A Farewell to Arms:* his love for Catherine Barkley is a different thing entirely—at least in Hemingway's ingenuous imagination. So too is Nick's love for Littless different from his "sweet-grass" love for Trudy, which seems to undergo a radical change with pregnancy at stake. Hemingway is up to something new, apparently, in this story, something he could not altogether work out, but something nonetheless intriguing as far as it goes. Among its more fascinating aspects is the attempt to affirm the innocent closeness between brother and sister as the historic basis for responsible adult love. When Nick and Littless sleep together in the forest and Nick wakes in the cold night to "spread his Mackinaw over his sister," he rolls closer to her for warmth; and feeling "the warmth of his sister's body against his back," he thinks; "I must take good care of her and keep her happy and get her back safely"—and falls asleep again. When he wakes once more in the early light he watches his sister, still asleep, and, admiring her "high cheekbones and brown freckled skin light rose under the brown" and "the beautiful line of her head," he wants to draw her or, at the least, to describe her resemblance to "a small wild animal" and "the carved look" of her sleeping face (101).

This same configuration will recur in *The Garden of Eden* as David Bourne gazes on his sleeping wife Catherine in a moment of aesthetically mindful innocent love. We know that it reverses Hemingway's memory of his sister Ursula's caring watchfulness, when on his return from World War I, she bedded with him to ease his insomnia, and that he views such watchful care as benignly innocent. But even without such reminders it seems a real failure of critical apprehension to speak of "barely sublimated incest" in this passage or of sexual undertones or overtones. The too-muchness of Nick's sister's love for him, on which he now remarks, might lead that way if it were intense, obsessive, or cloying; but since it is none of these, it leads instead to Nick's protective and nurturing regard, his parental concern to see her through; and if Nick is borrowing or emulating a real sister's love, or acting as Grace Hemingway's caring if originally sinful son, he seems to have learned early nonetheless what Lieutenant Henry may have learned late or not at all: that selfless consideration for another is the crux of love; and it may be that like Hemingway himself, or as he now likes to see himself, he has learned this from a position of early strength, as an only brother surrounded by adoring sisters.

What he did not learn—how many of us do?—was how to love another from a position of equality. Meanwhile, his greater strength—his protective and nurturing love—is at least appropriate to its subject. Nick will always have a parental or big brotherly edge on his younger sister, and there is no point in denying its validity as a human bond or doubting its persuasively innocent expression. The real problem that Nick's creator could not solve was how to deal with love between adult men and women of equal strength or status. And here, if anywhere, the question of neurosis and its sentimental expression may be legitimately raised.

In at least three of the major novels, for instance, Hemingway seems unable to connect affection with sexual love without making the Victorian payment for that connection. In Victorian fiction, where incest is often a hidden force, the punishment for sexual love is death. In Hemingway's fiction the same punishment seems to be administered, always by external and physical agencies, to affectionate lovers, as with Catherine's death by childbirth in *A Farewell to Arms,* Robert Jordan's by the approaching enemy in *For Whom the Bell Tolls,* and Colonel Cantwell's by heart failure in *Across the River and Into the Trees.* The selfless heroines of these novels—Catherine, Maria, Renata—are subservient partners like Littless, devoted admirers of their military beaus, willing to do all they can to please them. But they are, alas, unequal admirers; they receive less than they give, and the love they give and receive is in each case overvalued as an adult norm. Its mystification as a mutually selfless exchange—a mixing together of two as one—is accordingly suspect, and we may well want to call it sentimental and, considering its rigged and punitive outcome, neurotic.

"The Last Good Country" provides still other clues to this sentimental overweighting of adult romances. Thus, Catherine and Maria share with Littless the wearing or intended wearing of short-cropped hair, a leitmotif used differently in different stories. In "The Last Good Country" Littless crops her hair at the forest camp so she will look like a boy and be less detectable to pursuing game wardens. But the action has other meanings: "I should have asked you," she tells her brother, "but I knew it was something we had to do" (96). Since it is also something she wanted to do anyway, so as to become her brother's companion on a more permanent basis, it may also be something he wanted too. "I like it," he now tells her. "To hell with everything. I like it very much." Huck Finn's break with social expectations is couched in similar terms when he decides to "go to hell" and rescue Nigger Jim. Philip Young cites forbidden but innocent love as the common denominator in these frontier tales of sibling and brotherly relations;[19] it is only in adulthood, apparently, that the forbidden will cease to be innocent, as in the presumed marriage between Ad Francis and his sister in that early story "The Battler," or in the shared cropping and bleaching of David and Catherine Bourne in the late *Garden of Eden* manuscript, where the incestuous hazards of androgynous mergings become evident once they are extended to mature relations.

Meanwhile Littless is like Catherine Barkley, if not like Catherine Bourne, in other ways. When she refers to having fun, as she often does, or to having "a lovely time" (71), she even sounds like her. The forest dialogues are especially resonant with such accents. When Littless sits on Nick's lap, rubs her cropped head against his cheek, and amuses him with imagined stories about getting knockout drops for their trip from the Queen of Whores in Sheboygan, and with her fear of being ruined morally by the taste of stolen liquor, she is Catherine Barkley writ small, the "good girl" we remember from the novel who wants to do "something really sinful" (152– 53), like catching gonorrhea because her lover caught it, or staying with his many bad girls so she can make fun of them to him afterwards (299). The innocent woman mocking and envying the women her initiated lover has known is common enough in double-standard times; and her dilemma is part of what Hemingway caught in tonal focus in *A Farewell to Arms;* but what he also caught, as "The Last Good Country" reveals, was the appeal for him of uninitiated "good girls" playing with the terms of male privilege— indeed, questioning those dubious freedoms—while at the same time offering redemptive love. As Nick puts it in the excised passage about Trudy, "I'm not a good brother, and I'm not a good man and I'm not a good friend even." But with Littless he becomes all these things, and when Frederic Henry is all these things and more with Catherine Barkley, they have "a lovely time."

As indeed they do. The love and the lovely time may be limited, but they seem to me genuine in all such cases; and the women in question— Catherine, Maria, Renata—seem to me credibly portrayed. It is the over-weighting and mystification of such romances, the inequality of the exchanges, and the convenient deaths that follow, which seem to me suspect. Only in *The Garden of Eden* manuscript, where the heroines are aggressive women with lesbian tendencies and the selfless love is dangerously androgynous, is there anything like a fair assessment of these sentimental and neurotic hazards.

PARANOIA

In "The Last Good Country," then, Hemingway looks for reassurance in the place where all such loves began, the Michigan woods he often tramped in boyhood with some currently favored sister. When Nick worries about whether Littless is eating or sleeping well, or performing her daily ablutions, or when he performs his own carefully detailed outdoor tasks—fishing, hunting, cooking—the author's pride in the survival skills of his frontier children informs his loving prose. Their pastoral home away from home is a testament to the idyllic summers Hemingway spent in Michigan; and their imagined escape from wardens, family restrictions, and sexual consequences is a revealing instance of the author's many imagined escapes to lost frontiers. The many parallels with *A Farewell to Arms* are accordingly instructive: two loving fugitives who have committed "crimes" feel different from the "others"; their several "crimes" and their escape to "the last good country" are sanctioned by redeeming love; their repentable action may have serious consequences but is better done than regretted; once beyond the social pale they talk of common-law marriage; they care for each other selflessly and bravely; the "good girl" amuses her protector with imagined tales of being bad; she crops her hair to be more like him; and their pastoral retreat, where they will read romantic books and talk often about writing, is an "ideal blend of wilderness and civilization" like the Swiss chalet in the mountains near Montreux where Ernest stayed with Hadley in 1922 and where Frederic stays with Catherine in 1918. Indeed, as the long fragment ends, Nick is about to read aloud to Littless from *Wuthering Heights,* a romantic novel about another British heroine named Catherine who enjoys both moor and mansion, goes mad and dies in childbirth, and so identifies with the boy with whom she was raised ("I am Heathcliff") as to remind us of Catherine Barkley's selfless love for Frederic Henry—who (like Heathcliff) mourns her loss long after she is dead.

There is, of course, no death in childbirth in "The Last Good Country"; but Prudence Boulton, the model for pregnant Trudy, was said by some Petoskey natives to have died in childbirth, and Ernest was rumored to be the father of her child. We now know that the rumor was misleading, that Prudence died pregnant in a suicide pact with another young man, as Hemingway probably learned on his return to Petoskey in 1919–20.[20] From which circumstances he seems to have imagined Nick as Trudy's luckless lover and impregnator. If he further imagined her death in childbirth in pages never written, one "criminal" consequence would be conveniently resolved. That hypothetical resolution would also reinforce the separation Hemingway now makes between sex and affection. What he had joined together so tragically in *A Farewell to Arms* he now deliberately sunders. It seems almost as if he returns to the childhood source of his adult affections for selfless and adoring women so as to affirm his own investment in redeeming love. Or perhaps, by again separating it from loveless sex, he hopes to clarify its puzzling dissolution in adulthood. But as we have seen, he cannot face his even greater stake in inequality. He can only create a legitimately protective love; and there the affection plot breaks off.

What he did create, in opposition to redeeming childhood love, was an almost unredeemable form of childhood anger. If Mr. Packard has for the time being stymied the game wardens, Nick still must deal with the relentless tracking of the local warden's son; and in the fragment's final page his forest idyll is disturbed by reminders of that approaching nemesis. Nick feels sick and uncertain as he tries to think out what might happen if the boy should find them, a predicament which moves him to the curious pronouncement: "I have to think about things now the rest of my life" (110). That seems to be the price for original sin, or for doing repentable things worth doing, and though Nick seems ready to pay it, he is almost overwhelmed by the desire to kill the boy who forces that moral fate upon him. He knows that Littless can feel that desire "because she is your sister and you love each other" (113); but he tries nonetheless to enlist her in the fiction that nobody ever talked or thought about killing. He knows that he "can't do it while she's along" (111); but that only means that without her restraining presence, he is helpless before his own murderous impulses. It seems evident at this point that the game warden's boy, like those academic biographers whom Hemingway detested, is a symptom of deep-seated hostility against punitive pursuers, censor-figures, shamers, blamers, disapprovers: a symptom then of paranoia. Against it we may range such gentling images as Nick's stroking of his sister's head when she crawls through a fence on their journey and he asks if she is tired; his fondness for her in the morning light; and the coldness and freshness of the water they drink from the forest spring. But the force of Nick's anger, and its origins in family strictness and disapproval, are left unexplored. All we have—in considerable strength—is the countervailing force of family affection, the wellspring of childhood love.

The importance of that force in Hemingway's romantic fictions was also considerable. In 1925 or 1926, two or three years before Ernest took his sister Sunny along with him to Florida to help with the typing of *A Farewell to Arms,* she had written him about an experience which must have reminded him of his wartime romance with the American nurse Agnes Von Kurowsky, from which the novel largely sprang.[21] After graduating from high school in 1924, Sunny had gone into nurse's training at West Suburban Hospital in

Oak Park, had fallen in love with one of her patients—a newspaperman like her brother—and had written Ernest for advice. As she tells it in her memoir, the story takes on unintended resonance:

> After two years' training, I thought I was in love with a patient named Robert St. John. I enjoyed our secret meetings and note-passing when I was off duty. Bob influenced me to stop nurse's training and try college.
>
> I remember writing Ernie at the time for his opinion of this man. He answered promptly, honored that I had consulted him, and allowed as how any guy who could work as a rewrite man on that particular Chicago newspaper must be a good guy and just might be worthy of his kid sister.
>
> But Bob and I fell out of love as easily as we had fallen in.[22]

This story about secret meetings and note-passing between an off-duty nurse and a patient who must measure up to her may have been a catalyst for Hemingway's famous novel about wartime love. Though Hemingway drew on his romance with Agnes Von Kurowsky for the central situation in that novel, Agnes seems to have been a much more confident and flirtatious woman than Catherine Barkley. She was also older and more experienced than Ernest, his superior in age and practical wisdom, and her nature and her eventual rejection of him seem to have been reworked in the novel into a type and situation closer to the heart's desire. As we have seen, Catherine's admiration for Lieutenant Henry, her desire to please him and be like him, are like the admiration and fondness that Sunny and her sisters had for brother Ernie; and it seems to me something like a tribute to them all that he created such qualities in adult heroines like Catherine—whose social defiance and whose bravery in the face of death may also owe something to their postpioneer courage. Of course, Hemingway had also found such qualities in his first and second wives, Hadley and Pauline, who served as more obvious models for Catherine Barkley; but by the 1950s he was drawing consciously on their forerunners, Sunny and her sisters, for those healthy family affections which he had often betrayed or discounted or suppressed but which had nonetheless sustained him as that good androgynous man—friend, brother, husband, son, lover—he was always capable of being.

Interestingly, the last date on his unfinished manuscript for "The Last Good Country" is July 20, 1958, which means that it was broken off so he could revise and complete his long manuscript about androgynous couples, *The Garden of Eden*. The troubled nature of those androgynous relations in adulthood now reabsorbed him; and it may be that he moved toward a more hopeful resolution of such problems with a renewed sense of his own best possibilities for achieving it. That he could not really do so seems less important than his struggle to revive his innocent childhood affections as he fictively approached their adult conflictions in his several marriages. Meanwhile, he has left us with a tomboyish sister who may be little-or-less than Catherine Barkley or Catherine Bourne, in their bolder adventures into the wilds of androgyny, but who seems far more likely to survive them; and a nurturing and protective older brother who already knows the feminine secret that Frederick Henry "was always able to forget," and—perhaps more importantly—who still retains the feminine sources of creative strength that writer David Bourne and his creator will ultimately deny.

Chapter 11

Papa's Barbershop Quintet

At the end of Scott Fitzgerald's *Tender Is the Night* Dick Diver and his wife, Nicole, have gone to the barber's together, as is their custom, to "have haircuts and shampoos in adjoining rooms." As they reach the Carleton Hotel in Cannes, Nicole's lover, Tommy Barban, sights them from a passing car and follows them to the barber shop for a dramatic showdown. Though Dick is half-shaved and Nicole half-shorn when Tommy enters, they agree to talk things out at a nearby cafe. There Tommy holds that the Divers' marriage "has run its course" and demands a divorce for Nicole so the lovers can marry. After a few parries Dick accedes, cuts off further discussion, and, leaving the lovers behind, returns to the barber shop to finish his shave.

Their talk at the cafe has been twice interrupted, first by an American newspaper vender heralding the Tour de France with a cartoon clipping of "millions of Americans pouring from liners with bags of gold," next by the commotion of the Tour itself as the cyclists swarm by, all but the confident leader expressionless, indifferent, weary, "endlessly tired." As Fitzgerald's all-too-evident ironies suggest, Dick Diver, the man who loved to be loved, the inventive host for the first American summer guests on Riviera beaches, the indulgent doctor who married his mad client to effect her cure, has finished among the losers with some style.

In the previous chapter Dick has characteristically gone to the rescue of an old friend, Mary North, who seems to have been engaged in a protolesbian escapade with Lady Caroline Sibley-Biers. Mary and Lady Caroline have disguised themselves on a "lark" as sailors on leave and have picked up "two silly girls" who have in turn "got the wind up and made a rotten scene in a lodging house." The police have arrested the larkers, who have then appealed to Dick to bail and bribe them out of jail. His response when he arrives and hears their tale is instructive:

> Dick nodded gravely, looking at the stone floor, like a priest in the confessional—he was torn between a tendency to ironic laughter and another tendency to order fifty stripes of the cat and a fortnight of bread and water. The lack, in Lady Caroline's face, of any sense of evil, except the evil wrought by cowardly Provençal girls and stupid police, confounded him; yet he had long concluded that certain classes of English people lived upon a concentrated essence of the anti-social that, in comparison, reduced the gorgings of New York to something like a child contracting indigestion from ice cream.[1]

The "evils" of lesbianism, about which our priestly inquisitor begins to muse, are diffused here by cryptic oral metaphors and countersnobberies: Lady Caroline's antisocial view of "cowardly Provençal girls and stupid police" is matched by Diver's long-held view of "certain classes of English people" whose refined enormities, seen as daily fare, reduce urban American "gorgings" to ice cream indigestion by comparison; Fitzgerald's oddly chauvinistic pride in those innocent gorgings serves, moreover, to screen out or displace still another kind of chauvinism—his strong "distaste" for and punitive response to lesbian practices; and yet the strength of his homophobic response comes through and seems to have moved at least one emulative reader to exploit its hidden connections with the barbershop drama that follows.

SCOTT AND ERNEST

In 1946, when Ernest Hemingway began writing *The Garden of Eden,* Scott Fitzgerald had been dead for nine years, Rudyard Kipling for ten. Both writers were much on Hemingway's mind as he fashioned what now seems to be his most experimental and easily his most ambitious novel. Fitzgerald's life and work, particularly *Tender Is the Night,* would offer precedents for the troubled triangles in Paris and on the Riviera which dominate the main narrative; Kipling's *Jungle Books* would inspire the African tale of an elephant hunt, the composition of which becomes a dynamic counterpoint to that narrative. Hemingway would measure himself, as always, against expired and admired competitors and try to beat them at their own games; but it would be his game, as always, that mattered.

As early as May 28, 1934, Hemingway had written Fitzgerald a predictive letter, complaining about Fitzgerald's tragic stance in *Tender Is the*

Night, his failure in that novel to use rather than abuse his personal dilemma in caring for his mad wife Zelda:

> Forget your personal tragedy. We are all bitched from the start and you especially have to be hurt like hell before you can write seriously. But when you get the damned hurt use it—don't cheat with it. . . . You see, Bo, you're not a tragic character. Neither am I. All we are is writers and what we should do is write. Of all people on earth you needed discipline in your work and instead you marry someone who is jealous of your work, wants to compete with you and ruin you. It's not as simple as that and I thought Zelda was crazy the first time I met her and you complicated it even more by being in love with her and, of course, you're a rummy. But you're no more of a rummy than Joyce is and most good writers are. . . . All you need to do is write truly and not care about what the fate of it is.[2]

By 1946 the Fitzgerald dilemma, as Hemingway saw it, became the basis for his own novel about artists with mad wives who must learn to stick to their jobs in the face of "tragic" circumstances. But it was the curious late sequence from *Tender Is the Night*—the "lesbian lark" and the "barbershop showdown"—that seems to have set him off.

There were, of course, still other and much more private urgencies. According to Jeffrey Meyers, Hemingway's second wife, Pauline Pfeiffer, had become disillusioned with men in the years following their divorce in 1940, and "about 1946 [had] turned to her own sex" for love.[3] By this time Hemingway had been divorced by his third wife, Martha Gellhorn, for whom he had left Pauline, and had just married his fourth wife, Mary Welsh. His sympathies with Pauline had been reawakened by his rueful experience with the fiercely independent Martha, and perhaps also by his new marriage to a better caretaker, a petite, devoted, and rather boyish woman like Pauline. By 1947 Pauline herself was in Cuba, helping him to cure their ailing son Patrick in Mary's absence, and was on such good terms with Mary when Mary returned as to become her nurse and host in Florida, later that same year, while Mary was recuperating from the flu. The good relations between these wives, as colored by Pauline's emergent lesbianism, and perhaps also by the resumption of androgynous sexual practices with Mary that recalled Pauline, seem to have confirmed and perhaps even shaped Hemingway's decision to create fictional versions of his first and second marriages with Hadley Richardson and Pauline: for in those marriages, too, good relations with lesbian shadings had seemed to obtain between paired wives, and the hair fetishisms from childhood (which Pauline especially had exploited) had similarly led to or been bound up with androgynous experiments.

His first awareness of such connections seems evident in the fiction written during the early years with Pauline. Thus, late in *A Farewell to Arms* (1929), ex-Lieutenant Henry describes in oddly suggestive terms his visit to the hairdresser's in Switzerland where his common-law wife Catherine is having her hair waved:

> It was exciting to watch and Catherine smiled and talked to me and my voice was a little thick from being excited. The tongs made a pleasant clicking sound and I could see Catherine in three mirrors and it was pleasant and warm in the booth. Then the woman put up Catherine's hair, and Catherine looked in the mirror and changed it a little, taking out and putting in pins; then stood up. "I'm sorry to have taken such a long time."
>
> "Monsieur was very interested. Were you not, monsieur?" the woman smiled.
>
> "Yes," I said.
>
> We went out and up the street. It was cold and wintry and the wind was blowing. "Oh darling, I love you so," I said.[4]

The sexual excitement recorded here seems to have been based on Pauline's early efforts to distinguish herself from Ernest's first wife, Hadley, through tonsorial stylings and seductions. She had apparently sensed a similar excitement in Ernest, a kind of secret identification with her own three-mirrored stylings that she might appropriate for herself, even as Catherine appropriates it, a few pages later in the novel, when she asks Henry to let his hair grow longer while she shortens hers:

> "Then we'd both be alike. Oh, darling, I want you so much I want to be you too."
>
> "You are. We're the same one."
>
> "I know it. At night we are."
>
> "The nights are grand."
>
> "I want us to be all mixed up." (299–300)

The androgynous direction of these early romantic scenes—even their latent threat of male unmanning and female manning—now seems clear. What Hemingway had brought to Fitzgerald's novel, what he had pieced together for himself over the years with Pauline and Martha and in the new life with Mary, was his own understanding of why Fitzgerald had put lesbian and tonsorial fiascos in zany sequence and what he himself might make of such conjunctions out of his own long-nurtured hunches.

RODIN

Among Fitzgerald scholars the connection between his homosexual anxieties and his writing problems has become a critical commonplace. In a recent contribution to this view Angus Collins speculates that certain homosexual sequences in "The World's Fair," an early version of *Tender Is the Night*, are "projections of vocational insecurity." Fitzgerald's paralyzing fear of "vocational emasculation" had become identified in his mind with gay and lesbian sexuality; he had in effect chosen a homosexual vocation whereby his notoriously "insecure masculinity" had become "related to matters of craft"; and only when he "had mastered any suspicion of himself as emasculate artist" could he make significant progress on *Tender Is the Night:*

> Homosexuality therefore defines the circle of his creative difficulties in that he is homosexual both in his moral and artistic commitment *and* in his proneness to moral collapse: homosexuality can convey to him both his own much greater emasculation (the attenuations of art) and his own capacities for self-abandonment (the perils of self-indulgence). The novel is completed only when the sense of apostasy begins to predominate, when Fitzgerald learns that his choice of career is far less reprehensible than his failure to follow it.[5]

Here Collins argues that in writing *Tender Is the Night* (1934) Fitzgerald would break the homosexual circle, resolve his creative difficulties, and so exercise the very discipline that Hemingway had denied him. But as Arthur Mizener notes in *The Far Side of Paradise*, Hemingway would soon modify his original harsh judgment and in 1935 would tell Maxwell Perkins of how strange it was that "in retrospect" the novel "gets better and better."[6] Meanwhile he had correctly identified Fitzgerald's "dangerous self-indulgence," his importation of "feelings about his own decline" into the character of Dick Diver, as a problem Hemingway would himself have to face in his own version of the writer's struggle with "tragic" circumstances. Thus, David Bourne, his chief persona in *The Garden of Eden*, would make of the act of writing a stoic buffer against such circumstances and would stubbornly resist their debilitating power. He would confront the hazards of androgyny that Fitzgerald had only dimly understood (though he had oddly caught their form) and would overcome them through courageous masculine artistry.

The interesting point in this standoff with Fitzgerald is that Hemingway sensed how lesbianism connects with soldier Tommy *Barban*'s barbarian triumph over the Divers' barbershop androgyny—their oddly tonsured harmony, their symbiotic alliance as Riviera prima donnas. He would give

Barban's healthy claims a far less cynical twist in his own view of masculine artistry and would exploit the Divers' civilized shavings far more deviously than Fitzgerald had imagined. Whether he understood that Abe and Mary North were based upon his boyhood hero, Ring Lardner, and his wife Ellis, or that Fitzgerald's barbershop scene was surely influenced by Lardner's "Haircut" (that famous early narrative model for his own juvenile style), or that Abe and Mary together offer fictional analogues for the Divers' decline and fall—whether or not he understood all this, he decidedly sensed that Mary North's emergent lesbianism after her husband's death was like Pauline's after her divorce, that it reflected upon Nicole Diver's man-hating propensities, and Pauline's too, and upon Nicole's previous madness, and Zelda's too, and that of his mistress Jane Mason during the troubled years with Pauline: for this would be the pith and point of his own adventures into barbershop disharmonies in *The Garden of Eden* with the fictional likes of Pauline, Zelda, Hadley, Jane, even of later loves and wives like Adriana and Miss Mary, perhaps Miss Martha too. More interesting still, he seems to have understood that in all this biographical scramble androgyny, and not homosexuality per se, was Fitzgerald's underlying problem as well as his own, many critics of both writers and much patriarchal and even feminist sentiment to the contrary notwithstanding.

All of which helps to explain why *The Garden of Eden*, in its roughly completed manuscript form, is chiefly a novel about haircuts—or about haircuts and the narratives and counternarratives they inspire. Ring Lardner's talkative barber has in this respect little or nothing on Hemingway's talkative heroines and their emotional investments in hairstyles. Indeed, the first chapter of the 1,500-page manuscript swings upon newlywed Catherine Bourne's account of her "dangerous" surprise for her husband David, her trip to the barbershop for a boy's haircut like his—an account excised, like so much else, from the 247 pages of the printed version of the novel issued by Scribner's in May 1986.[7]

One can understand the excision. The account is not on the surface the "dangerous" adventure that Catherine makes of it as she tells of her fright when the barber holds "everything out to one side" and goes "snip-snip-snip," then does the back and the other side, and explains that she felt confident nonetheless about going on because she had seen him cut David's hair the week before and had now told him "to cut mine just the same as yours" (Ms. 1/1/insert 18). But the excision of this "little drama" is in fact a violation of the novel's manuscript style, its attempt to get at unsuspected depths through selective descriptions of supposedly insignificant (even silly) actions, its claustrophobic concentration upon the surface details of eating,

THE METAMORPHOSES OF OVID. BRONZE. BEFORE 1886.   OVIDISCHE METAMORPHOSE

18. Rodin, *The Metamorphoses of Ovid,* bronze sculpture of lesbian lovers, from
the *Gates of Hell*

drinking, swimming, diving, tanning, barbering, bantering, bickering, but above all talking, and below all, writing and making love—a violation, then, of the novel's narrative status as an expansive account of an inner journey, a "sea change" as seen from inside the iceberg, and therefore not an ordinary novel at all, like his own early icebergs, or his recent war epic, *For Whom the Bell Tolls,* or for that matter, Fitzgerald's *Tender Is the Night,* with its solidly realized social context and wide cast of characters—as Hemingway's persona almost explains ("It's not a novel. . . . It's an account. Travels and Voyages." Ms. 3/16/27) in one of many excised implications of the author's conscious intent.

One of the nicer signposts of that inner journey, the Rodin statue from "The Gates of Hell," based on Ovid's *Metamorphoses* and Baudelaire's *Les Fleurs du Mal,* has also been removed from the opening chapter, quite possibly because it ties in directly with the Paris couple Nick and Barbara Sheldon, whom Scribner's editor, Tom Jenks, decided he must remove along with the subplot they enliven starting with book 2 in the manuscript. Thus, on the evening after her barbershop story, when the newly shorn Catherine asks David to make love to her as she is, she also asks him in an

19. Rodin, *The Metamorphoses of Ovid*, plaster, from side

20. Rodin, *The Metamorphoses of Ovid*, plaster, from rear

excised passage if he remembers "the sculpture in the Rodin museum," and with that in mind, if he will now "try and be good and not think—only feel." A moment later she asks, "Are you changing like in the sculpture? . . . Are you trying to?" Then, as his resistance slackens until they cannot tell "who is who," she becomes even more insistent:

> "Now will you please be that way now? . . . Will you change and be my girl and let me take you? Will you be like you were in the statue? Will you change?"
>
> He knew now and it was like the statue. The one there are no photographs of and of which no reproductions are sold. (Ms. 1/1/170)

The statue in question, from a group sometimes called "The Damned Women," consists of two lesbians making love, the more active of whom looks (in the bronze version in the museum) like a naked man with a woman's breast plainly visible on his chest as he enfolds a naked woman, but who proves on closer inspection to be a naked woman with a short haircut like Catherine's. About the lack of photographs and reproductions in the 1920s David may be right; but in 1939 and again in 1953, while Hemingway was writing the novel, a reproduction did appear in a German edition of Rodin's work, and others have since become available.[8] Still, whatever its accessibility, the important point is that Hemingway chose not to describe it, even as he chose not to describe with any exactness the lovemaking between his sexual seekers after dangerous knowledge. For them as for us, it is the edenic invitation to forbidden mysteries and disturbing sexual ambiguities that matters. As Catherine tells David, she has thought about the statue "ever since . . . that day in the Rodin," and though she doesn't understand why "it works," she knows that it does; and David too not only feels its metamorphic powers but admits them to himself while struggling with his conscience: "You know the statue moved you and why shouldn't it? Did it not move Rodin? You're damned right it did and why be so holy and so puritanical? You're lucky to have a wife that is a wild animal instead of a domestic animal and what is a sin what you feel bad after and you don't feel bad" (Ms. 1/1/23–24).

In book 2, which consists solely of the excised Paris chapter, we learn more about this "moving" statue, this public inspiration for troubling private changes. Indeed, the book opens with a clumsy overview of its effect on both couples:

> With the other two it had started at the end of February. It had really started long before that but there had been no actual date, as there was for the day in May that Catherine had ridden up to Aigues Mortes and back to Le Grau de Roi [sic], until this night and the following morning at the end of February in Paris. None of them remembered the actual dates of commitment and none of them remembered the dates on which they had first turned in off the rue de Varennes to the Hotel Biron with the beautiful gardens and gone into the museum where the changings had started. One girl had forgotten that it had started there and, for her perhaps, it had not but she too had seen the bronze long before.
>
> "Let's think of something fun to do that we've never done that will be secret and wicked," the girl had said. (1)

Hemingway's revision here of the biblical Garden of Eden plot seems plain enough: two couples pass through the beautiful gardens at the Hotel Biron, enter the Rodin museum, and are so moved by the statue there of metamorphic love that they begin their own androgynous experiments; and in each case the "girl" is the active agent, the Eve-like tempter. The editorial loss of this magic matter seems sad enough; but the loss too of the Paris plot with its lively change of pace and its range of useful meanings, is perhaps sadder. We soon learn, for instance, that Nick and Barbara Sheldon are poor but happy artists and therefore healthy foils to the rich, unhappy Riviera Bournes. Indeed, they have experienced androgynous love without previous qualms, and as the chapter opens they experience it again, in their cold and barren Paris flat, with Barbara pressing down lightly but firmly upon her supinely cooperative spouse. Thus, it is not androgynous love per se that causes trouble ("We've always done that when you wanted to," says Nick on page 2 in response to his wife's enticement), so much as its public expression through statues, hairstyles, and conversations—especially as they convey controlling female power. And even then, a thoughtful, cooperative, and sympathetic spouse like Nick can let his hair grow long over a five-month period as a surprise present for his wife, without her discovering it, in true O. Henry fashion. We witness a second excised barber scene, at any rate, as—after their simple breakfast of brioche, ham, and eggs—Barbara shapes Nick's hair to resemble hers, then shares the excitement of his gift by making more androgynous love:

> "It ruins work," she said, "but it's so exciting. Why should something so simple be so exciting?"
> "I'm not sure it's so simple."
> "It's so much fun it must be very wicked."
> "I'm pretty sure it's wicked."
> "But Nickie how did you get it so long?"
> "It took five months."
> "It must have. But how did you do it?"
> "Don't you remember when you asked me to?"
> "I always asked you to."
> "Well anyway this time I told the barber I wanted to let it grow because you liked it. The same barber that cuts yours. The Spanish one. He said how long? I said like yours." (12–13)

How Nickie did it is indeed a mystery (and perhaps cause in itself for Jenks's editorial clippings), but presumably he combed it back and up rather than out and down, and so hid the change from Barbara. What counts is the liveliness of the telling, the cheerfulness of these loving American babes in foreign woods who "go to sleep like good children" after another crazy day (19, 23), who seem at ease with androgynous changes ("It's just like all the Indian kids were," says Nick on page 15 as if recalling his namesake's life in northern Michigan), and whose inner life seems only mildly troubled with thoughtful moments at night and ebullient stream-of-conscious wonderment.

In book 3 of the manuscript, however, when the Sheldons meet the Bournes, and Barbara and Catherine respond to each other with erotic intensity, the latent danger of "possession" by androgyny is openly acknowledged. Thus, in a confessional passage, Barbara tells David of her troubled feelings about herself:

"I know I'm strange. But I'm not a queer or I never was. Crazy if you like and with special things or one thing that I wanted and got it or have it or had it. It was just a simple delight or ecstasy. It was private but I made it public. That's the danger, the necessary danger. And I didn't know things took possession of you. There's where you've gone wrong of course." (Ms. 3/4/8 bis 1)

The "necessary danger" of making things private public—that's where, according to Barbara, they've all "gone wrong." Their experiments with androgynous coiffures—long for the Sheldons, short for the Bournes—are public expressions, then, of private love modes which now possess them and which ultimately lead to sexual betrayals and beckoning disasters—madness for Catherine, suicide for Barbara, accidental death for Nick, expulsion from Eden for David and his new "girl" Marita. From such impending consequences, moreover, the explicit barbershop scenes acquire their curious resonance.

Where David and Catherine are concerned the Scribner edition does some justice to this fateful dimension. For them it may be enough that we hear Catherine's account of her Eton haircut in chapter 5 and witness the coiffeur's artistry in chapter 9 as he bevels and blonds the couple's hair to make them look alike. Catherine's hysteric fear of death, and the meeting with their common mistress Marita, follow hard upon these public expressions of androgynous "possession," and after they dye their hair again in another elided scene in chapter 22 they both feel appropriately "damned." Still, the riskiness of art itself—the coiffeur's, David's, Catherine's—is lost by the disconnection of such scenes from the Rodin statue's fatality and from Marita's recognition too (another sad excision) of how well Catherine's artistry in talking matches David's in writing. And again the editor shears too close in chapter 29, where Marita loses her African haircut and the novel ends without the fateful implications of *her* impending possession by androgyny.

She has by this time shown extraordinary sympathy for David's work, and has thereby won his love, and Catherine herself has numbed his loyalty by burning his African stories so as to leave unrivalled his narrative account of their "journey" into androgynous wilds. Marita has become the good wife, then, the one who admires all his writing and shares with him its mystery (another excised dimension). Further, he has rescued her from her purely lesbian past (also excised) and converted her to heterosexual love of the missionary as well as the androgynous order, as if to counteract his own conversion to androgyny and his wife's to lesbian love. All the more "dangerous," then, when Marita tells David, at the end, that she wants her hair cut to resemble that of his first girlfriend during his African boyhood. If she in turn has converted him from a sick sense of severe "perversion" to a healthy sense of "variety," the signs of her own Catherine-like obsession with androgyny burgeon in the late chapters—largely excised, alas, along with the complexities of her nature and her alarming African haircut which, as it turns out, makes her look more like a street Arab than a tribal princess.

CORRUPTION

We are all bitched from the start and you especially have to be hurt like hell before you can write seriously.

Was that "All-American bitch" Grace Hall Hemingway on Ernest's mind when he admonished Scott Fitzgerald with such a grim view of childhood and its painful aftermath? Certainly his mother had twinned him from the start with his older sister Marcelline, dressing them alike in infant smocks and frocks, arranging their hair in matching Dutch-length cuts, holding Marcelline back a year so they might start school together, and when Ernest received his first boy's haircut that preschool summer, giving Marcelline a boy's haircut too. Was Ernest in that sense *paired* with a bitch from the start, or paired with one bitch by another, as he later saw it? Or was that triangulated pairing in fact edenic at first and only gradually too grim and painful to acknowledge?

It is at any rate to Marcelline and Ernest, their mother's twin Dutch dollies in infancy, at seven and six her grade-school gamins, that we must turn for childhood models of the long-haired Sheldons and short-haired Bournes—even for the painful aftermath of such dangerous stylings. As we have earlier seen, Marcelline's hair grew out unevenly that fateful summer, after her first boy's haircut, and was further botched in the fall by a helpful scissors-wielding playmate. As punishment her mother sent her to school in sister Sunny's baby bonnet until a wise teacher intervened, some two weeks later, and persuaded Grace to remove the bonnet and let Marcelline escape to the second grade, where she belonged.[9] No wonder then that hairstyles became the observant Ernest's lifelong measure of female manipulations, androgynous twinnings, arrangements of the heart and breasts and loins; no wonder that the Bournes in *The Garden of Eden* see themselves as brother and sister as well as brothers with matching hair styles, or that Pilar sees the cropped Maria and Roberto as brother and sister in *For Whom the Bell Tolls,* or that Littless cuts her hair short to become Nick's forest brother in "The

21. The young Ernest Hemingway, 1900

Last Good Country," or that Catherine Barkley proposes matching hair-styles to Lieutenant Frederic Henry in *A Farewell to Arms,* or that Marie Morgan dyes her hair blonde to excite her pirate husband Harry in *To Have and Have Not*—even as Pauline surprised Ernest by dyeing her hair blonde on her thirty-fourth birthday in July 1929, or indeed, even as Ernest first urged his fourth wife Mary to bleach her hair blonde, then doused his own hair copper bright, during the composition of *The Garden,* claiming that he had mistaken the bottle for his ex-wife Martha's "old shampoo."[10] As his frequent chapter notations—"Hair," "Hair Cutting," "Hair Symbol"—attest, hair was for Hemingway the public expression of his own private obsession with androgyny; his easy, imaginative access to a woman's manip-ulative, talkative, stylistically inventive powers; his secret envy of her breasts and womb; his unconfessed desire to rest confident in her supine passivity; and his honest awareness of her oppression by men much like himself. Beyond that he obviously liked women, liked having them around as ador-ing wives or "daughters": indeed, he desperately needed their attentive presence, and in *The Garden of Eden* he finally attested to that terrible dependency, as when the betrayed David tells his returning wife Catherine and future mistress Marita, after their first lesbian experiment, "I missed you both" (Ms. 3/21/31).

Vulnerability and dependency, then, were the blissful conditions which "hurt like hell" after four serial marriages, and which moved Ernest to write about "the happiness of the Garden that a man must lose."[11] His ambivalent feelings about androgyny had become the very subject of his novelistic search, his three-mirrored account of inner voyages, his condensation of successive marital and extramarital entrapments, with only his African pen-

22. Ernest and Marcelline in twin dresses with baby Ursula on the Oak Park boardwalk

nings to pull him through his own Ulyssean weakness for long- and short-haired sirens, his own Samsonian blindness and loss of hairy strength (cf. Ms. 3/25/29). As we shall see, these inner weaknesses are intimately bound up with the hero's writing skills and with the novel's curious construction as an account that could only have been written by David Bourne, whom we constantly observe either in the act of writing something like it or of living what he writes. This is Hemingway's most self-reflexive novel about the art of and need for writing his own kind of "found" and "invented" fictions; and that art is intimately bound up with his life and work during all his marriages, but especially his first and second as measured by and through his fourth.

One biographical question this novel speaks to, for instance, is what kind of husband and lover was Ernest Hemingway? The complicated answer—since Ernest plays all the main male roles, assigning aspects of himself or stages of his life to Nick Sheldon (Paris), David Bourne (the Riviera), Andrew Murray (Spain), and David's unnamed father (Africa)—can be put into simple if painful terms: he was an extremely dependent man in all these roles. As chapter 7 in the Scribner edition opens, for instance, the editor excises a long passage from book 3, chapter 13, of the manuscript in which

David muses over the word "Innocence," on which the previous chapter ends. There, David's friend Andy Murray—a square character who refuses to change his hairstyle and whose initials point in this respect to Archibald MacLeish and to Hadley's second husband, Paul Mowrer—has held that the Bournes bring more saving innocence to the time they're in than he does. Certainly David's musings over their life together are at this point innocent enough—that is to say, honest and to the heartfelt point—as he makes "a head for a coin" (6) out of his sleeping wife's face, imagining lines and angles like a sculptor, then acknowledging that "she's the sculptor with her lovely head. I see why she likes to do it" (7). Then, having emulated her close-cropped artistry with loving and imaginative care, he reviews his own emotional progress, his new freedom from remorse, his lessened anxiety about where they're heading and about his continuing failure to write, his concern all the same with the danger of such heady freedom and with the lack of helpful "signals from the pits" to "tell you where you stand" ("or maybe there are and you can't read them," 9); then he thinks of their latest experiments:

> The only signal was she asked you this time and you said yes. And do you still say yes? I said yes and I neither apologize nor explain. You know the danger? All right what would be the danger of No? You don't think it would be greater? How do I know? I didn't say no. You don't think that you will have to learn to say it? Very possibly. (9)

The danger of saying no, then, as reviewed by a man who obviously can't say no, or who says it rather so that it always means yes—as both his wife and his mistress understand. Thus when David calls Catherine "an intriguing corrupter" after she provides them with a common mistress, she tells him "an old secret": "You aren't very hard to corrupt and you're an awful lot of fun to corrupt" (*GE* 150). And when she persuades him to dye his hair once more to resemble hers, she says, "I love to make you do things you really and truly don't want to and then you like them when we do them"—at which point David begins to realize "what a stupid thing he had permitted" (*GE* 178). And again, as her illness increases and David becomes "sick of crazy things," she repeats what he also knows: "You always do everything I want because you really want to do it too" (*GE* 196). Even his mistress Marita tells him playfully and definitively, late in the novel, that she loves to hear him say no: "It's such a non-definite word the way you say it. It's better than anybody's yes" (Ms. 3/45/5); and then, being a better and more protective caretaker than Catherine, she reassures him that she loves his weaknesses as much as his strengths, for "they're what makes the strengths."

That seems to be the second self-revelation from Hemingway: that his emotional dependency on his wives and mistresses, his androgynous complicity with their several obsessions with hair, skin, dress, gender, and lesbian attachments, is what makes for his strength as a creative writer. That crucial argument occurs again and again in the actual manuscript, as when in book 3, chapter 23, David ponders the division between his life with Catherine and Marita, whom he sorely misses though he knows it is wrong "to want them both," and his creative work:

> If you live by the senses you will die by them and if you live by your invention and your head you will die by that too. All that is left entire in you is your ability to write and that gets better. You would think it would be destroyed. By everything you have been taught it should. But so far as you corrupt or change, that grows and strengthens. It should not but it has. Is it possible that the only creation that is a moral act is pro-creation and that is why all other kinds are suspect? It could be but it seems too simple and too much like a justifying. All you know is that you have written better, clearer and *plus net,* he used the French phrase in thinking, as you have deteriorated morally. But that could be temporary or it could be a building up and strengthening by what good there is trying to build against the destruction. That could be. Don't apportion blame for the destruction now. It will all be apportioned in due time and not by you. (9)

Scribner's editor elides this passage, and all others like it, and appropriates only the ending as it applies to David's newly triangulated love (*GE* 132); but in the actual manuscript it is the entanglement of the *ménage à trois* with the writing process that matters, the complicity in "corruption" that increases creative strength. Thus in book 3, chapter 27, of the manuscript, when Marita tells David that he writes now in his own defense "and under impossible conditions," David thinks that maybe the impossible conditions make it possible for him to write (12); and again in book 3, chapter 29, of the manuscript, as he thinks about another African story, he speculates on the probable androgynous sources—whether disastrous or enabling—of his new effectiveness:

> It is going to be rough to do but so far they have gone well and maybe you can thank Catherine and her disasters for them. Not her disasters, her disaster that embraces everything. You can thank the other girl who loves you and handles and canalizes you like an engineer or tries to when you don't impede her. You probably would have blown up with Catherine here alone. . . . But would any of it have happened if

you'd been alone? Of course it would. It had built steadily to happen. Don't go into that now. That is as useless to go into as to think what would have happened if you and Kibo had not learned to hunt at night with the full moon. How wrong that was to do. If life was only conducted for survival . . . how much you would have missed. What happened with Catherine goes in the narrative. Don't confuse things. (10–11)

The extension of the fateful principle to his African boyhood, and the imagination of his own passivity in the hands of the two women he loves, are instructively alike. He understands his complicity in the events of the "found" narrative we read—the one Catherine has asked him to write about their life together—and in the boyhood events of the counternarrative, the African tales he "invents" for himself. That it is David's mirrored narrative we read in either case becomes strikingly evident in book 3, chapter 3, of the original manuscript, in which David and Catherine run into the Sheldons at Hendaye and David starts to write about events in their lives that we have already witnessed in book 2, the Paris chapter:

He had started to write about the Sheldons, taking it up when he had seen them in the bistrot [sic] together at dinner on a cold night in Paris at the end of last February and how excited and happy they had looked and how absorbed they had been in each other. He put down how Barbara had smiled at him as though he were a co-conspirator and he remembered being in the coiffeur's when they had come in together. It had gone simply and easily. So easily that it was probably deceptive and that, having seen them only the day before, he saw them so vividly himself that he might not be making them come alive to some one else. But as he read it over it seemed to be what he had tried to get in its complex simplicity and he thought that perhaps he was writing so easily because, not having tried to force any writing before, he was coming fresh to it now. If it is worthless, he thought, it will be good five finger exercises to get started with. God knows I do not have to write about them nor the length at which they choose to wear their hair while living in the Vth arrondisement [sic] in Paris. That's banal enough. Certainly I am not limited to that as a subject and what importance has it? He is a painter and a damned good painter and what difference does it make, any of it. (p.1)

The effect of this passage is startlingly reflexive, perhaps because it is more detailed than the similar moments when David indicates how he writes about himself and Catherine, but more probably because it involves other characters whose lives he must invent from the few events he has witnessed—and that five-finger exercise in complex simplicity, as he calls it, is not a bad description of the Paris chapter and its lively change of pace, its bed and brioche harmonies. But the point is that David fuses at such moments with his own creator, Ernest Hemingway; he becomes an aspect of his creator's life and work in the way Stephen Dedalus figures as the young artist who will eventually write *Ulysses* and *Portrait of the Artist,* only now our portrait is of the artist as a young newlywed on a disastrously overextended honeymoon, and that too is not a bad description of Hemingway's life with Pauline, or with his later wives, once the purifying poverty and cultural richness of the Paris years with Hadley were over. As with Joyce, at any rate, the invitation to read the novel, or the account of inner journeys, biographically is a built-in aspect of the text. And in that light the connection between androgynous "corruptions" with wives and mistresses and the author's writing strengths becomes a matter of critical speculation and concern.

Whether in the printed or manuscript version, that connection is conveyed by the two kinds of narrative David writes: the main narrative on which Catherine wants him to concentrate and for which she tries to find illustrators like Picasso, Marie Laurencin, and Nick Sheldon, and the African tales that she resents so much she ultimately burns them. One can see, from the tension between these narrative impulses, why the Sheldon subplot remains unfinished in the manuscript, only sketchily continued in four later fragments called "Andy's Story," and why Scribner's editor decided to scrap it: for how could David continue to speak for the Sheldons, in his ongoing account of his own triangulated troubles, without altogether becoming Ernest Hemingway? It was a problem in point-of-view narration that Hemingway himself could not altogether solve, as his decision to let Andy Murray solve it suggests. What Andy tells us about Nick's accidental death while Barbara and Andy make love, and about Barbara's eventual suicide while under Andy's care, David could not have witnessed, and therefore could not reinvent as a plausibly imagined part of the main narrative, an integrated part of his own ongoing quarrel with androgyny. And the alternative device of a story within the story—the old Fielding strategy—must have seemed a bit too tired to pursue. So the later Sheldon story was left in fragments and could not be salvaged by Scribner's editor without connecting links of his own invention. Nor could he answer for himself the questions David initially raises about the subplot: "what importance has it? . . . and what difference does it make, any of it?"

A great deal, of course, for Hemingway scholars, or for any biographical critic with half an eye for literary dynamics. For plainly the Sheldon subplot was Hemingway's substitute for the missing link in David and Catherine Bourne's life history: David's previous marriage to another woman, someone like Barbara Sheldon, whom he had betrayed at Catherine's urging in order to marry Catherine herself. David Bourne—whose very name suggests (among other things) that hidden burden[12]—was instead created "innocent," that is to say, previously unmarried and therefore free of Hemingway's guilt in leaving Hadley for Pauline, again at Pauline's manipulative urging ("You aren't very hard to corrupt"). And Catherine too was created free of Pauline's previous manipulations. The "innocent" Bournes, then, who just happen to begin their honeymoon year at Grau du Roi, as did Ernest and Pauline Hemingway in 1927, are juxtaposed with another happily married pair of "innocent" Americans, painters Nick and Barbara Sheldon, who just happen to live in Paris in the manner of Ernest and Hadley Hemingway, circa 1925. And these fictional versions of Hemingway's second and first marriages just happen to cross paths at Hendaye Plage, in the south of France, before going their separate ways!

Hemingway's pleasure in creating such conjunctions seems evident enough, as when Barbara Sheldon smiles at David Bourne in that Paris restaurant in February "as though he were a co-conspirator" (Ms. 3/3/1); or when Barbara and Catherine regard each other with mutual admiration and desire, upon meeting at Hendaye (Ms. 3/1/2–3), or wish each other well, upon parting, and Barbara says "Have . . . a lovely life, and take good care of David" (Ms. 3/8/4); or similarly, when Barbara advises David to get Catherine out of the Riviera ambiance if he loves her (Ms. 3/5/7). These moments are not surprising given Ernest's continuing use of Hadley, long after their divorce, as friendly adviser and admired first-married love, and given also her relieved and friendly transfer of Ernest into Pauline's hands, as those of a better, richer caretaker, back in 1926. But the insistence upon the mutual lesbian attraction between Barbara and Catherine, or Hadley and Pauline, is indeed surprising. We know from recent biographical diggings that Hadley left Bryn Mawr because of her mother's grim suspicions of her roommate's overly fond mother, Mrs. Rapallo, whom Hadley naively admired.[13] We know that Pauline's sister was a lesbian and that Pauline became one after her divorce from Ernest; and we know from the Hadley tapes preserved by her biographer that Pauline liked to crawl into bed with Ernest and Hadley in the mornings during her visits with them at Schruns and Juan-les-Pins.[14] We know also that Ernest was obsessed with lesbianism, that he considered his mother "androgynous"—probably because of the newly discovered incident in the summer of 1919 when his father banned from the house for unspecified reasons his mother's adopted protégée and "girlfriend," the young and pretty family helper Ruth Arnold, and because of Ruth's return in later years as his mother's paid companion.[15] And, finally, we know he was sexually drawn to Gertrude Stein as to a literary version of his "androgynous" mother during the Paris years with Hadley.[16] From all of which we may surmise, more broadly, that Ernest was drawn to women with lesbian and/or androgynous propensities, as with Hadley, Pauline, Gertrude, and Mary, and perhaps also Martha, Jane, and Adriana.

In this light, the lesbian link between Barbara and Catherine is itself the missing link in the Bourne's life history, the sanctioning of real betrayal by fictional admiration and desire—as if Ernest had simply acted out the desires of Pauline and Hadley in leaving one wife for another. "Do you have the faintest idea how beautiful you are and what you are doing to people?" asks Barbara/Hadley of Catherine/Pauline upon seeing her latest haircut (Ms. 3/7/3). What she has already done to David/Ernest is thus blessed, forgiven, exonerated, if not altogether explained. One possible explanation—that Ernest identified with supposedly lesbian lovers, or projected his own androgynous feelings upon them—must wait till we discuss the *ménage à trois* between Catherine, David, and Marita—whose very name compresses those hitherto missing wives, Martha and Mary, into verbal complicity with these strange arrangements.

KIPLING

Meanwhile, there is the counterimpulse to consider, the Kipling impulse, the writing of the African tales. Just before his honeymoon with Pauline, Ernest had put together a collection of stories called *Men Without Women* from which he said "'the softening feminine influence' was missing . . . whether as a result of 'training, discipline, death or other causes.'"[17] While at Grau du Roi with Pauline he had then completed two new stories for the collection, one about Nick Adams's boyhood called "Ten Indians," the other—called "Hills Like White Elephants"—about an insensitive man who tries to persuade his lover to have an abortion. The African tales that David Bourne composes on the Riviera are invented boyhood stories like those that Hemingway wrote about Nick Adams in northern Michigan, and David's disillusionment with his father in the crucial elephant tale is like Nick's disillusionment with Dr. Adams in tales like "Indian Camp," "The Doctor and the Doctor's Wife," "Ten Indians," and, much later, "Fathers and Sons." The lovely metaphor of "hills like white elephants," which the woman faced with abortion voices as the second story opens, suggests also the violation of the sacredness of life that young David witnesses in the

elephant hunt; but that mystery and that sacredness derive as well from
Kipling tales like "Toomai and the Elephants" and "The White Seal" from
The Second Jungle Book; "My Lord the Elephant" from *Many Inventions;* and
"Letting in the Jungle" and other Mowgli stories from *The Jungle Book*
itself.[18] Indeed, Hemingway's favorite poem from *The Jungle Book*—the
animals' lament when Mowgli leaves the jungle to get married—is a childhood paradigm of the tension in this late novel between the "marriage" story
on the Riviera and the boyhood tale of men without women in Africa; and
the writing of the latter tale is an act of manly resistance to the "corruptions"
of the androgynous married life which apparently make it possible. For
unlike Fitzgerald's Dick Diver, who accedes to his own corruption through
triangulated love, David Bourne resists his complicity in things feminine by
writing manly tales about African wars and hunting expeditions. His preoccupation with African stories is like Hemingway's preoccupation with such
stories in the 1930s, or with sporting tales about bullfighting, skiing, boxing, and fishing in the 1920s; and his oscillation between such stories and
the main narrative is like Hemingway's oscillation between novels of failed
sexual relations (*The Sun Also Rises, A Farewell to Arms*) and tales of stoic
male endurance. Indeed, it constitutes a curious paradigm, a defensive
rationale for the manly author's creative history and its apparent source in
reactive strength, in self-defining resistance to his own androgynous propensities, his own failed or failing marital and/or extramarital relations. The
long, unhappy, strenuous playboy life of Ernest Hemingway becomes more
devious and more valiant than we have supposed, given this resistive creative
strength and its frank location in his own androgynous weakness, his own
dependency and openness to the manipulations of many wives and mistresses whom he desperately needs, and with whom he secretly identifies.

E. L. Doctorow's puzzlement over the hero's curious passivity, in his
review of the published version of *The Garden of Eden,* is in this light relevant
to our understanding of the manuscript version and the life behind it.[19]
Doctorow locates "the ultimate deadness of the [published] piece" in
David's character: "His incapability in dealing with the crisis of his relationship does not mesh with his consummate self-assurance in handling the
waiters, maids and hoteliers who, in this book as in Hemingway's others,
come forward to supply the food and drink, the corkscrew and ice cubes and
beds and fishing rods his young American colonists require." Doctorow
goes on to mock this evidence of travel writing for provincial American
readers, the lack of any substantial disaster like war or postwar disorientation
to lend plausibility to the characters' suffering, the consequent "tone of
solemn self-attention" which rises to unjustified "portentousness" over

70,000 words of text. But then he also speculates about the missing 130,000 words, the excised subplot, and the clear evidence of Hemingway's attempt to transcend the limitations of his famous pared-down early style and to remake himself on a grand scale after recognizing the stylistic insufficiencies of his previous epic venture, *For Whom the Bell Tolls*. This seems to me exactly right, though Doctorow's further guesses about "a large cast and perhaps multiple points of view" in the actual manuscript lead us toward his kind of ambitious fiction rather than Hemingway's. But the exciting evidence of Hemingway's attempted new development as a writer is decidedly there; and Doctorow is again right to dismiss his failure in this regard, and the novel's failure also, as beside the point. What matters is "that he would have tried, which is the true bravery of a writer, requiring more courage than facing down an elephant charge with a .303 Mannlicher."[20]

That is indeed the point. *The Garden of Eden* is a novel about a writer's bravery—about Hemingway's bravery as he saw it in the daily struggle to transcend his own terrible dependencies and passivities. This is Hemingway's testament to the writer's trade as he practiced it, using his own hurts and weaknesses, his being five times bitched from the start, and then four and more times bitched again, by his own need to compete with women on honeymoon grounds, and to redefine himself therefrom by resistant actions and resistant writings, whether of found or invented fictions. The traveller's daily record of meals, bars, beaches, beds, and barbershops is there because that is how he chiefly lived, under "the softening feminine influence" of married love that he sorely needed to exist at all; and his bravery consists mainly of stripping away his daily portion of manly sports (save one marvellous fishing scene and much androgynous swimming) and of collapsing the essential isolation of his post-Hadley marriages into a single honeymoon year of touring, tanning, eating, drinking, and making androgynous love— as if to force the lonely essence of the writer's inner life into felt existence for us, while at the same time indicating, indeed demonstrating, the power, range, and varied richness of his writing.

The most direct demonstration comes from the tale of the elephant hunt, the writing and reconstruction of which (after Catherine burns the African tales) constitute the writer David's comeback, his triumph over those "tragic" circumstances to which Fitzgerald supposedly succumbs in *Tender Is the Night*—or at least Dick Diver does. Lacking the revelations about art and androgyny in the actual manuscript, Doctorow suggests that Hemingway might have succumbed in a different way: "David Bourne's passivity goes unexamined by the author, except as it may be a function of his profession. But the sad truth is that his writing, which we see in the elephant story, does not exonerate him: it is bad Hemingway, a threadbare working of the theme of a boy's initiation rites that suggests to its own great disadvantage Faulkner's story on the same theme, 'The Bear.'"[21]

Hemingway would have hated that last comparison, especially with regard to the one novel wherein he tries courageously to do new things, as Faulkner once said Hemingway never did; but there is a bit of "The Bear" in this initiation story, and some Sherwood Anderson too, and a great deal of Kipling, about whom Doctorow fails to speculate. Moreover, other reviewers—notably John Updike—found the elephant tale engaging.[22] Certainly it is a new kind of animal story for Hemingway, who prided himself on avoiding sentimental identifications with animals like those in the Mowgli stories, but who here unashamedly allows his young protagonist to find in the elephant a hero and brother, to resist and resent his killing (though he has himself enabled it by discovering the elephant at night while hunting with his African dog Kibo), and to react to the elephant's feelings as to human feelings.

At stake here is the alliance between children and animals that Kipling assumes in the Mowgli stories; the assumption of common ground as subhuman, prehuman, or demonic species; and the acquisition of animal power and mystery in the vengeful struggle against adult inequities, as when Mowgli directs the elephants to trample down the native village in "Letting in the Jungle" or when Toomai rides his musty elephant far into the jungle at night to watch the wild elephants dance and returns from the forbidden ground to tell his tale in triumph. Hemingway tries to temper and improve on such assumptions through his characteristic theme of disillusionment; and in fact, the alliance between the boy and the dying elephant does improve on Kipling, and on Faulkner too, in that it aligns the killing of such jungle monarchs not simply with the breakdown in trust between boy and man, father and son, but also between male friends. For the odd anthropomorphic point of the tale is that the old, tired, great-tusked elephant had been visiting the grave of a friend whom David's father and the native hunter Juma had killed the previous year, so that David thinks of the latter pair as "the god damned friend killers" (*GE* 198) and relishes the elephant's revenge when he throws Juma aside—as if recognizing his friend's killer—while charging off to his death, leaving David with "the beginning of the knowledge of loneliness" (*GE* 201) as he recalls the lapse of "dignity and majesty and . . . beauty" from the dying beast's sad eyes.

"It was a very young boy's story," thinks David as he finishes it (*GE* 201), thus underscoring the Kipling connection. Given its placement as the "hard story" David has wanted for a long time to write, it seems to me also a very

23. Male friendship at Oberlin, ca. 1890: Clarence Hemingway's college friends

self-critical story, in that David's father is more obviously based on Heming-way himself as a hardened big-game hunter and an insensitive father to three sons, than on his own father; and yet Hemingway's lifelong problem with male friendships does seem to be attributed here to his father's "friend-killing" role. Was the elephant's death, and the boy's reaction to it, a kind of breakthrough, then, of boyhood resentment against Dr. Clarence Heming-way for teaching his son how to kill rather than love, how to suppress rather than share his deepest feelings? If so, it provides some balance to the indictment here of Grace's androgynous ways, and indicates, perhaps for the first and only time, how much he felt his father—an obtusely sentimental if not a ruthless man—had failed to teach him how to be a friend. And perhaps also how much that hurtful failing had helped to shape his early stoic style. As David puts it in the tale, "I'm going to keep everything a secret always. . . . Never tell anyone anything again" (GE 181).

CATHERINE

Interestingly, it is Catherine rather than David Bourne who invests the Kipling connection with its largest meaning. Early in the manuscript Catherine and David meet Andy Murray in Spain and begin talking about things literary and artistic. Catherine has been reading Proust and James and visiting the Prado, trying to get outside herself by talking about her new interests, priding herself all the same on being "really sensational . . . in the practical not the scandalous meaning" in the world she has made up with David, when suddenly she poses an unusual question:

"Andy do you believe it about women for breeding, boys for pleasure, and melons for delight?"

"I only eat them."

"But isn't it a lovely proverb even if it isn't true?"

"It's an outspoken proverb."

"I always thought of it as everything Kipling left out," Catherine said. "Imagine how he would have been with all that in. Sometimes it's almost there but then it moves away. He knew it for a while and then he was ashamed of it. That's what I want David not to leave out."

"What if the proverb isn't true?"

"It must have been for someone. Or maybe it was a joke. But who it was true for ought to be in or who it was a true joke to. Anyway things you don't approve of you should understand. There's nothing worse than people that are for things they can't help than people that are against them. I hate professional fors and againsts."

"Let's eat the melon," David said.

"It's delicious," Catherine said. "Even better than [the one] we had for breakfast."

"It's sensational," Andy said. "In the finest sense. I'd like to have known Catherine when she was being sensational."

"It was only four weeks ago," Catherine said. "I think maybe I will be again."

"This afternoon?" David said.

"Yes. Why not?" (Ms. 3/9/14–15)

Why not indeed? From Catherine's point of view the improvement on Kipling is to include "sensational" things we need to understand, like the Greek credo whereby boys rather than women have priority on the pleasure scale. Her kind of amoral hedonism differs, however, from the Greek example (and from the "Greco-Roman household code" it epitomizes) in that women like herself, having bypassed breeding or sprung their biosocial bonds, now determine the priorities. It is Catherine, not David, who "makes all the surprises" (Ms. 3/13/6), invents all the "dangerous" games, determines all the androgynous risks. Her appeal for David and Andy, both delighted by her artful talk, seems evident enough as this chapter ends. Indeed, as E. L. Doctorow points out, *she* is the novel's great surprise, the improvement by Hemingway on Hemingway himself as he takes his daring new direction:

> The story is told from David Bourne's masculine point of view, in the intimate or pseudo-third person Hemingway preferred, but its major achievement is Catherine Bourne. There has not before been a female character who so dominates a Hemingway narrative. Catherine in fact may be the most impressive of any woman character in Hemingway's work, more substantive and dimensional than Pilar in "For Whom the Bell Tolls," or Brett Ashley in "The Sun Also Rises." Even though she is launched from the naive premise that sexual fantasizing is a form of madness, she takes on the stature of the self-tortured Faustian, and is portrayed as a brilliant woman trapped into a vicarious participation in someone else's creativity. She represents the most informed and delicate reading Hemingway has given to any woman. For Catherine Bourne alone this book will be read avidly.[23]

Catherine's dominant role, as Doctorow rightly defines it, recalls that of another dominant Catherine, in *Wuthering Heights,* who lent her name, her androgynous outlook, and her addled nature, first to Catherine Barkley in *A Farewell to Arms,* slightly dotty from the war's abrasions, and now to postwar Catherine Bourne. The latter's more demonic madness is not fairly defined, however, by sexual fantasizing, as Doctorow concludes from limited evidence, but rather, by the new freedom to pursue to excess, to be possessed or "spooked" by, forbidden pleasure in the Riviera atmosphere of changing styles and fashions and amoral upheaval; and the "evil" for these innocent Americans, these pioneers in new delights, is precisely this maddening and rather spectral possession. We see it in Barbara Sheldon as well as Catherine, both roused by the Rodin statue's mysterious appeal and by such other foreign stimulants as absinthe (which is supposedly "not good for girls" and makes them act strangely, Ms. 3/1/5), suggestive paintings by Marie Laurencin and others, and accessible partners like Marita and Andy Murray.

"And don't you try to tell me when pleasure good lovely pleasure turns into vice because I know," says Barbara Sheldon to David Bourne at Hendaye (Ms. 3/7/8 bis 2). The conversion of innocent pleasure into avid vice, and the definition of vice by its maddening avidity, are shared assumptions among these postwar characters, as when David lovingly calls Catherine his corrupting "Devil," or when each suffers a different form of remorse, he from androgynous practices, she from lesbian betrayal of their love. Yet, these suffering innocents also struggle to free forbidden practices from lingering taboos, and from time to time succeed, as when Catherine calls for understanding or when Marita later insists upon the difference between "variety" and "perversion." More skeptical than Fitzgerald about such innocence, Hemingway could also be more generous about its minimally effective presence and more precise in defining it. It was the line between evil and madness that he most often blurred, perhaps because it "spooked" him as much as it seems to have "spooked" his haunted characters.

But whatever the spectral mix of saving innocence and corrupting madness within her, Catherine is decidedly Hemingway's "most informed and delicate reading" of a woman character, as Doctorow holds. An amalgam of many women in Hemingway's life, she most obviously combines Pauline's possessive and controlling use of money, Mary's resentment of her own infertility and perhaps also of her gender, Zelda's artistic rivalry with Scott and her ultimately vengeful hostility, and Jane Mason's suicidal recklessness and emotional instability. Like Hadley, who once lost a suitcase containing her husband's early manuscripts, and who may have resented them, as Jeffrey Meyers asserts, for keeping her and Ernest apart, Catherine is jealous and resentful of David's African tales; and like Zelda, who once set fire to their bedroom while visiting Scott from the asylum, she rips in half and eventually burns the offending notebooks.[24] Pauline too may have had cause to resent such African stories, given the open portrait of Jane Mason in "The Short Happy Life of Francis Macomber" and of a rich wife like herself in "The Snows of Kilimanjaro"; but she was on most occasions, and by his own admission, Hemingway's best and most trusted literary adviser. In inventing Catherine he therefore seems to have wedded Pauline's wit, intelligence, and style with Zelda's open and Hadley's covert resentment of their husbands' writings, and to have drawn her madness out of his own entry, whether real or imagined, into lesbian triangles after the remorseful gardens of androgyny. In any case, Catherine is the androgynous lesbian muse within himself against whom her husband David reconstructs his boyhood world of "men without women," for whom he writes the main narrative, and through whom he goes beyond Kipling in either direction. (By functioning, moreover, as that angry, fiercely independent muse, that secret female version of himself against whom his masculine artistry has always been opposed, Catherine ironically completes and is completed by the masculinist hero. In these and other ways she strikingly anticipates the feminist Catherine of *Wuthering Heights* defined by Gilbert and Gubar in *The Madwoman in the Attic*. She also proves to be a richer and more ambivalent portrait of threatening androgyny than these critics allow for in their remarks on *The Garden of Eden* in *Sexchanges,* the second volume of their recent study of the modern climate for women's writing.)[25]

She is also, like Pauline, an extraordinary conversationalist. If, as Marita later argues, writing is David's "master" and therefore hers ("we are its servants," Ms. 3/33/28), so too with Catherine's speech: "She tells things in the same way you have to write them probably. Maybe that's her master. You know how well she can tell something" (Ms. 3/33/28). And indeed he does, or at least Hemingway does, as the Kipling/proverb passage briefly attests. There and elsewhere we see Hemingway's delight in capturing Pauline-Catherine's talent for talk and the good-natured repartee that apparently went with it. Such talk is everywhere evident in this dialogic manuscript, in which tag lines like "sensational" recur with grace and delicacy at breaks and chapter ends. Hemingway's chapter-head notations—which mention "Talk," "Conversation" (five times), "Good Conversation" (twice), and "Verbal Fights"—identify and confirm this aspect of the text, much of it ruthlessly expurgated by an editor who missed his expansive intention, or misconstrued it as uncontrolled verbiage which Hemingway himself would have lopped off in his prime, in keeping with his iceberg principle, as no doubt he would. But the experiment with expansive conversation was, more plausibly, a crucial part of his ambitious attempt to remake his style, or as Doctorow says, to remake himself, if only to accommodate the late emergence of the feminine in his makeup. Thus he tries to render for us the oscillating movement between "good conversation" and "verbal fights" as he had experienced it with four wives and several mistresses, but especially with Pauline, and to convey thereby that portrait of the "self-tortured Faustian," the "brilliant woman trapped into a vicarious participation in someone else's creativity," which Doctorow so nicely delineates.

But of course it is not only the self-tortured woman who concerns him: he wants also to portray his own complicity, his own domestication, his androgynous participation in dialogic delights and entrapments *against which* he too can reconstruct his manly writer's world. And beyond that, there is obviously a certain pride, as of a writer who has isolated himself from his kind, who has left the enriching Paris life with Gertrude Stein, Ford Madox Ford, Sylvia Beach, James Joyce, Scott Fitzgerald, Ezra Pound, and others for the honeymoon worlds of Cuba, Florida, Africa, Montana, even Spain, with only wives and sporting friends for company. One of the claustrophobic measures of this text, accordingly, is the smallness of its cast, the expansion of David and Catherine's world by one major character, Marita; and by limited contacts with only eight minor characters—Nick and Barbara Sheldon, Andy Murray, Colonel John Boyle, Madame Aurol (the hotelier's wife), Monsieur Jean the barber, Andre the waiter, and Marita's girlfriend Nina. Thus, conversations between David, Catherine, and Marita, together or in pairs, are the main substance of the text, abetted in the manuscript version by stream-of-consciousness passages for two women characters (Barbara and Marita) and for David Bourne, of which only David's survives in the printed version.

The elimination of Marita's as well as Barbara's soliloquies is understandable—they are poorly imagined, badly written versions of Molly Bloom's meanderings in Joyce's *Ulysses*—but the very attempt by David-Hemingway to think himself into women's inner worlds is cause for wonder. Hemingway's only previous attempt of this kind—Marie Morgan's painful musings in *To Have and Have Not* (1937) when her husband dies—again points to the influence of Pauline on his own understanding of what a woman is—or suffers.

Catherine's sufferings, as captured in dialogic form, are surely the triumph of this novel, as Doctorow argues. From the opening scene in which the whole village cheers as David catches a sea bass in the local canal, to the parting letter in which she likens the burning of the African stories to hitting a child with a car with "the crowd gathering to scream" ("The Frenchwoman screaming *ecrasseuse* even if it was the child's fault," GE 237), Catherine has been desperately competing with David, trying to assert some comparable form of creativity and self-importance through look-alike fashions (tanning, hairstyles, fisherman's shirts and shorts and pants); quarreling with him over publisher's clippings of reviews of his book which threaten her hegemony; insulting his childlike handwriting in the notebooks and his poor command of French; improving herself through Proust and the Prado and a Spanish grammar; setting him the task of writing about their life together and then (in a marvellously recreated scene, Ms. 3/38/2–5) seeking out Picasso to illustrate that private book; buying David's time and work thereby with her money; and above all, imposing her androgynous and lesbian needs upon him, as if taking over his creative male persona. Indeed, both David and Catherine consider her arrangement of their common affair with Marita, and of Marita's eventual succession as his wife, as her greatest "invention," her most substantial "surprise" or "plot." She manipulates their lives, in short, like a maternal novelist arranging close relations, though with no real sense of consequences; and thereby she commits her "maddest" and most maternal act, her enraged attempt to set David back on the right path—that of writing the main narrative which she dominates—by burning the African tales (as Nick Adams's mother burns his father's Indian relics, for instance, in "Now I Lay Me"). Interestingly, David has grumbled from time to time about not knowing how that main narrative will come out; but when the burning settles that question, he generously ascribes the outcome to Catherine's being rushed—too much in a hurry—as if, given time, she somehow might have plotted a better ending for all concerned.

Hemingway seems to have had similar fears about his own plotting. In May 1950, when he thought that "something might happen *before* book would be finished," he composed a tentative ending in which Catherine returns from the asylum for another Riviera summer with David (Ms. 2/1/1; 3/post 46/1). They again lie together in a beach cove, taking in the sun, talking over old times in Madrid; but instead of tanning naked, Catherine now has "a scarf across her breasts and a towel over her waist." "Weren't we strange children then?" she muses as the chapter opens; but when she adds "We were comic then. . . . We were a yell of laughter," David leaves her side, dives off a nearby rock into deep water, and "resists" breathing it in as he comes up for air. His suicidal intent prefigures hers and becomes the morbid theme of the brief chapter. Thus, Catherine, though she can no longer recall certain events (a second visit with Colonel Boyle, a trip to Africa), is gripped by a poignant sense of irreversible process:

> "Remember when I used to talk about anything and everything and we owned the world? All we had to do was see it and we owned it. And I was so proud and made everything in my image. I could change everything. Remember? Change me change you change us both. Change the seasons change everything for my delight.
>
> And then it speeded up and speeded up and then it went away and then I went away." (7–8)

"Then you came back," adds David; but Catherine says, "Not really," waves off the return of her sanity and their love as "comic," then asks for another surprise "like in the old days":

> "If it goes bad again so I'd have to go back to the place can I, may I, do it the way Barbara did? I don't mean in a dirty place like Venice."
>
> "I couldn't let you."
>
> "Would you do it with me."
>
> "Sure."
>
> "I knew you would," she said. "That's why I didn't like to ask."

"Probably it would never happen."

"Probably. Who knows? Now should we have the nice swim before lunch?" (10–11)

On that bittersweet note the provisional ending closes. Barbara has committed suicide in Venice as self-punishment for betraying Nick with Andy on the day of his biking death on the Hendaye road. Catherine wants to follow her example rather than go back to the Swiss asylum, and David, who always goes along with her surprises, seems half-inclined to join her. More importantly, perhaps, he stands loyally beside her in what seems to be a shared recognition of their common failure, and so avoids Dick Diver's aggrandized self-pity—or Fitzgerald's—at the end of *Tender Is the Night*.

By 1958, however, Hemingway seems to have decided upon a different ending. His extensive revisions in that year build upon the writer's life and wisdom and on Marita's crucial relation to that ongoing vitality. Her future marriage with David seems assured when, with her encouragement, David successfully writes the African stories, then reconstructs them from memory after Catherine burns their first inscription. Thus, whatever happens to Catherine, the transfer of David to the new and better caretaker has been made; and in the original manuscript at least, the terms of that transfer have been carefully defined. Marita is without effort the boy-girl whom David requires for his androgynous complicities. Already a lesbian who wants to please others, she is more nearly David's twin sister than Catherine, and her conversion to heterosexual love affirms his shaky maleness even as she keeps alive, as "variety" rather than "perversion," the androgynous option that his creative needs demand. Whether she too will become obsessed by androgyny remains to be seen. Meanwhile, we see her intuitive grasp of the writer's mystique, in the uncut manuscript, as she reassures him that he can't miss as a writer now since he's having a *belle époque,* that his gifts are like those of a great weight-carrying horse who must be cooled down and washed off after each morning's workout, that he participates in a *mystère* in which she too is an initiate, a kind of female trainer whose job is to keep him in good shape so as to serve their common master—and who even knows that he is his best self only when he writes. Scribner's editor, Tom Jenks, has eliminated from the published text this alter ego role, this bond in the mysteries of the writer's craft, as part of his rigorous paring down of Marita's character and of his surrogate distrust of Hemingway's ideas, and has reinforced thereby that embarrassingly easy transition from "the girl" Catherine to "the girl" Marita which makes them seem like interchangeable wives. But Marita is much shrewder about Catherine, David, and herself than Jenks's shears allow, and more interestingly knowledgeable about writing. Indeed, her several probing interviews of the writer David, who often seems closer to sixty than thirty in his gathered wisdom and experience, provide a compendium of Hemingway's late views on writers and writing which—along with his views on painters and painting, as elicited by mad Catherine—are among several good reasons why a complete scholar's edition of this unwieldly hybrid manuscript should be published.

One can almost forgive Jenks, however, for reducing to a few hints Marita's stream-of-consciousness desire at one point to give the sleeping David sweet erotic dreams of his first African sweetheart by oral stimulation—one of the odder indications of how well she understands her man and how far she will go to grant his deepest wishes. For the sad drift of this text is to reduce even more seriously "the girl," the replaceable androgynous-lesbian muse within and beside him, from the recalcitrant devil who strives for independent creativity at all costs, to the "good wife" who ministers to the creative mystery but has no creative life of her own, except as an adjunct of the great weight-carrying, narcissistic male she has married.

Of lesbianism and homosexuality per se David and Marita are meanwhile contemptuous and dismissive. As David puts it while discussing Marita's schoolgirl follies:

> "I'm glad you went through that nonsense and know it's worthless."
> "It's not for us. Anymore than queers would be for you."
> "I always tried to understand and to be fair," David said. "We've always had them and I'm never rude unless I have to be. But they give me the creeps." (Ms. 3/46/23)

So ends the inner journey into the wilds of androgyny. For the time being at least, all sexual dangers are diffused, all aberrations trivialized or safely "spooked." David has recuperated his manly strengths as a writer and a lover with Marita's help; Catherine's devilish struggle has been sympathetically portrayed; the enormity of her "crime" has been sharply rendered; and her replacement by the good androgynous wife Marita has been made to seem plausible and inevitable as "a grave and violent thing" (GE 238). Indeed, Marita herself seems plausible in preferring her new adjunct status over her early lesbian lostness: but neither David nor Hemingway seems to realize that the new arrangement also constitutes a travesty of female selfhood, a betrayal of truly androgynous love, as between creative equals, and a denial of the primacy of the female within the male for his own "independent" creativity. That kind of colossal self-deception was (to his credit) beyond Fitzgerald, and no real improvement on Kipling's dancing elephants.

BARBARA

In the four fragments called "Andy's Story" Hemingway returned to the Nick and Barbara Sheldon subplot for a dying fall. As a side note to the second fragment indicates, he planned to end the novel with Andy's account of his affair with Barbara and of her suicide following Nick's accidental death: "This comes in after David and Catherine's story stops in September. Rewrite for the part about their visit to Hendaye (*Very little*) (contributing to the crack-up)." The Fitzgerald term "crack-up" applies to Barbara, who goes into a severe depression after Nick's death and drowns herself in a Venetian canal.

An earlier entry, and the first of the four fragments, goes back to the Paris days that Hemingway presents in the main manuscript through David Bourne's imaginative recuperation. Apparently he had once thought of having Andy tell that story, or perhaps he meant him to retell it now from his different point of view. In any case, as the fragment opens, Andy responds to questions about the Sheldons from an unnamed girl:

"And what happened to them finally?" the girl asked. "It's a very strange story. How did you ever know it?"

"She told me. And I made up what she didn't tell. But she told me more than I used."

"You did very well about the girl I thought," she said. "But it isn't like a girl now. Nobody would believe it now because everything is changed. Just technically. Things aren't done that way anymore. It's all so primitive."

"Things were primitive then. You don't know." (Fr. 1 / 1)

Here Andy seems to be assigned a role like David Bourne's, to recreate the Sheldons imaginatively from life, and with the iceberg depth suggested by material not used. And yet he only embroiders now on a story at least partly and perhaps wholly told. The Sheldons were "wonderful looking," he adds, and "didn't know there was anyone in the world except themselves." She was "heartbreak beautiful" and never worked at it. He had "a dark sort of go to hell look and women were crazy about him." He was a better painter than Winslow Homer and was working well then, "painting very fine and very strange snow landscapes." The Sheldons were "very beautiful together and very happy and minded their own business." They were both workers. "You only saw them after work." That winter he wore his hair "as long as hers and cut the same way": "Right after the war lots of young men in Italy wore their hair that way. Italo Balbo was one. It just looked like the old days when that was how people had their hair cut. Nick was a painter and a

damned good one and whose business was it? He looked quite handsome."
(Fr. 1/4)

As Andy's defensiveness suggests, the hair question is unsettling. A moment later we learn that Nick felt that way too:

> "Can I ask you something Andy?"
> "What Nick?"
> "Do you think I look like a bloody sodomite?"
> "No. Of course not. Who thinks you look like a bloody sodomite?"
> "I do."
> "You don't," I said. "You look like a condottiere out of work." He did and he always looked like some sort of dangerous big cat and he moved that way.
> "Don't ever start anything you can't finish," he said. (Fr. 1/5)

That Nick is afraid of being taken for a homosexual is the obvious point; that he shares in Barbara's obsession is the subtler one. Thus, when Barbara goes off to cancel their appointment at the barbershop, he runs after her; and when Andy says he can always cut his hair, that he doesn't hold Barbara by a haircut, Nick says that he does it to please her "and the hell of it is now I like it too." Then as if to emphasize his entrapment, he tears off his Austrian hunter's cap, letting his long hair tumble down, and again asks Andy to tell it to him straight, "Do I look like some bloody sodomite?" (Fr. 1/5–6).

In the next fragment (pp. 7–19) Andy sees the Sheldons at a cafe table near the beach at Hendaye. They are wearing Basque fishermen's shirts and shorts and espadrilles; they are tanned dark as Indians, and their hair is cut the same, coming down to their shoulders black and red gold. "We're a scandal," Barbara calls out to him. "We went to St. Jean de Luz . . . and they wouldn't serve us." "Everybody thinks we're queer," Nick later adds. "But who cares. . . . All I give a damn about is Barbara and working. She's happy and she has what pleases her and I'm working well." But Barbara is in fact quite restless, both she and Nick seem to need others now, and there is much talk about being "spooked," first by haircuts (Nick likens his to Col. William T. Cody's in the Wild West shows that he—like Hemingway—saw as a kid), then by sand castles, then by imagined seascapes of Barbara painting Nick painting on a surreal beach with red balloons, green rubber fish, and yellow and green alligators. At this point Nick moves off up the beach, leaving Barbara and Andy standing together "looking out at the sea coming in over the sand in the almost darkness," and Barbara puts her hand in Andy's pocket "very naturally as though it were her own pocket." With this almost magical event their affair begins. Indeed, Hemingway's headnote for the chapter reads "Hendaye/Hair/Barbara's Hand in Andy's pocket."

What are we to make of this imagined infidelity? Presumably it comes as a consequence of Barbara's sexual adventurousness, her initial androgynous obsession with Nick over matching hairstyles and exchanged identities and sexual roles. As Barbara tells Andy in the next fragment,

"I only have you and Nicky. . . . I nearly had something else but I gave that up. I've thought it all out and I'm not going to tease you. There's two of me and there are two of you. You and Nicky. Nicky makes three because I made him two. . . . At first I thought it would be nicer if you could be two like Nicky. But now I know better."

The poor poor lost bastard, I thought.

"I understand," I said. "Sure. I understand."

"I knew you would," she said.

"I'm no good at being two," I said. (Fr. 3/6–7)

As the conversation develops, we learn that Catherine Bourne was the "something else" that Barbara gave up and that Barbara considers her "destructive." But it is Barbara's destructiveness we now see at work. Though Nick later says that Barbara is "worth a thousand girls like that Catherine," he also implies that he senses the lesbian attraction between them; and at the end of the previous fragment he has even told Andy that all of Barbara's bad luck "is her own bad luck." It is Barbara, then, who divides herself and Nick into split identities, loves him androgynously, and then further splits her love between Nick and Andy. Whether she harms Nick thereby, as well as herself, is left in question. When she asks Andy if he thinks she is harmful to Nick, he says "No. I don't think anything can hurt him." Nick remains strong in his "big cat" artistry, that is, whatever his lostness, whatever his split identity and homophobic fears; he must die accidentally in order to bring home to Barbara the full extent of her betrayal of their love.

That Barbara is based almost wholly on Hadley Richardson, Hemingway's first wife, seems obvious; and that Hadley remained faithful to Ernest, though he sometimes feared otherwise, seems likely. It was Ernest who betrayed Hadley with Pauline, and perhaps with others before Pauline, and who now apparently projects his own infidelities upon her, and in a curious way, his own forthcoming suicide, as a kind of fictional shifting of blame, in the first instance, but ultimately as a fictional expression of his own propensities. Through Barbara, that is, he reenacts and rejects his own behavior, blames and exonerates himself by becoming that aspect of himself he most wants to expunge: the unfaithful suicidal androgyne.

The account of Barbara's suicide in the final fragment is thus instructive. She has already felt remorse about her second fling with Andy while Nick is away painting; indeed, they drink absinthe together afterwards "to try to get her in shape for when Nick would be back." Then comes the news of his accidental death while biking on the road to St. Jean de Luz. Barbara goes into shock and must be placed in a nursing home while Andy attends to funeral arrangements and legalities: "Probably I should have taken her to Switzerland. . . . But she would not go. . . . The strangest thing was that no matter how bad things were I could write. Try to figure that out. But it was true. I do not think I ever wrote better." (Fr.4/24)

What Andy finds strange is not simply another version of the wound and the bow, as with David Bourne; it is also a recapitulation of how Hemingway reacted when his father committed suicide while he was writing *A Farewell to Arms;*[26] and the connection with his father's suicide and his own are what gives this passage from Nick's death to Barbara's reactive suicide its grim resonance. Thus, as Barbara recovers in the nursing home, she begins to talk more: "I've been thinking about what's the most intelligent and loving thing I can do for you," she tells Andy. "I've been so damned selfish and so stupid. I'm thinking about the present I'm going to make you." That she chooses Venice as the place to deliver that present, even though she prefers clean water, reminds us also of Hemingway's Venetian muse Adriana Ivancich and his own guilty reasons for choosing those polluted waters for Barbara's death. "But I'll pretend it is our old absinthe," she explains to Andy in her suicide note. "It's just about the same colour and I never minded how it tasted. I didn't like the taste of it though." Then she adds that she has saved her "legal sleep things for a month so it's truly legal" and signs the letter "Catherine," adding in a postscript "Your best friend Barbara. Thank you so very much Andy for everything" (Fr.4/27).

All through the fragments Hemingway has used Catherine's name for Barbara's, then crossed it out. His confusion at this point as to which of his wifely doubles he is writing for seems understandable; and there was Pauline's sudden death, back in 1951, after his abrasive phone call blaming her for their son Gregory's latest cross-dressing incident, as one probable cause for his own fictional cross-dressings, his own crossed expiations.[27]

What he pondered in 1958 connects in these and other ways with his "present" to Mary in 1961: a vestibule suicide that seems neither loving nor intelligent, but which must have been fostered by his reduction in his own mind by depression and paranoia, injury and illness, alcoholism and impotence, electric shock treatments and hospital confinements, to a self-effacing self-destructive androgyne. Perhaps that explains why, on the night before his death, he joined his fourth wife Mary in singing from an adjacent bathroom the last lines of a gay Italian song, *"Tutti Mi Chiamono Bionda"*— "They all call me blond."[28]

Appendix A

A Source for the Macomber "Accident":

Marryat's *Percival Keene*

Late in 1925 Hemingway's lifelong admiration for the popular Victorian novelist Captain Frederick Marryat began to surface in letters to his friends. On December 20, 1925, he informed Archibald MacLeish that his winter reading included "two Capt. Marryat's" and that "Capt. Marryat, Turgenieff, and the late Judge Fielding" were his "favorite authors." A few days later, on December 24, 1925, he wrote Scott Fitzerald that he was reading Marryat's *Peter Simple*, a "great book" which he hadn't read since boyhood, and then listed as Marryat's "four great books" *Frank Mildmay, Midshipman Easy, Peter Simple*, and *Snarleyyow*. "If you want to read about war," he concluded, "read any of those first three." As Sylvia Beach also testifies, Hemingway had spent his mornings in a corner of her Paris bookshop, as early as 1922, "reading magazines and Captain Marryat and other books." His Key West inventories for 1940 and 1955 list three Marryat titles, *Jacob Faithful, Masterman Ready,* and *Midshipman Easy*. As James Brasch and Joseph Sigman show in their more accurate listing, two copies of the last-named novel appear, each bound in a volume with Marryat's fictionalized biography of a French acquaintance, *The Travels and Adventures of Monsieur Violet in California, Sonora, and Western Texas*. After his move to Cuba in 1940, Hemingway also purchased Christopher Lloyd's *Captain Marryat and the Old Navy* (1939) and a complete set of Marryat's works in twenty-four volumes (1896–98). In 1935, moreover, he began his *Esquire* list of novels which aspiring writers should read with two by Tolstoy and three by Marryat (*Mildmay, Simple, Easy*). Again in 1958, in his *Paris Review* interview with George Plimpton, he listed Marryat among those who had influenced his "life and work."[1]

Thus, from boyhood onward Hemingway's enthusiasm for this martial man turned novelist remained constant. Though his earliest favorites were Kipling, Lardner, and O'Henry, by the 1920s Marryat (along with Turgenev and Fielding) had supplanted them. The adult Hemingway would draw upon Marryat's life and work in a variety of unsuspected ways, but most obviously he was influenced by Marryat's novels of naval warfare, smuggling, and privateering—all written in the 1830s and '40s—which would affect his own novels about smuggling, deep-sea fishing, and antisubmarine patrols. Less obviously, but no less intriguingly, Marryat's novels and tales of wilderness survival would anticipate his own tales of backwoods life in upper Michigan and big-game hunting in Africa.

As early as 1929 Hemingway had accused Allen Tate of suggesting in his reviews "that Defoe and Marryat had influenced his work" in this regard.[2] Actually Tate had suggested only Defoe as an influence and had cited his *Captain Singleton* for its Hemingwayesque account of an African trek by mutinous pirates; he had not cited Marryat, but the confused Hemingway—who disliked having his sources exposed by others—had himself given the case away by making the connection between Defoe's realistic depictions of wilderness survival, as in *Robinson Crusoe* and *Captain Singleton,* and such Marryat tales of privateering, shipwreck, outcast, or frontier life as *The Privateer's Man, Masterman Ready, The Children of the New Forest, The Settlers in Canada, Scenes in Africa, The Little Savage,* and *The Travels of Monsieur Violet.* In most of these works a familiar Hemingway pattern appears as older men teach boys how to cope with wilderness conditions. In *Masterman Ready, Scenes in Africa,* and *The Privateer's Man,* moreover, there are African treks and subplots that might be said to evolve from Defoe's example in *Captain Singleton;* and in *Masterman Ready* there is even a familiar Hemingway sequence involving fear of and flight from roaring lions.

Significantly, all but one of these wilderness tales appear among the fourteen Marryat volumes owned by the Oak Park Library by 1904, which suggests among other things that Hemingway was first exposed to wilderness themes, and to their African offshoots, by reading Captain Marryat.[3]

But there is another novel on that library list, *Percival Keene,* which bears even more importantly upon Hemingway's African imaginings and which he may also have read in childhood. As Michael Reynolds informs me,[4] Hemingway had used his family's library cards during the school year in boyhood. Every summer, moreover, he and his family would check out thirty to forty books for the two months they spent at Walloon Lake in northern Michigan. Between the ages of eight and seventeen, then, Hemingway had access to some three or four hundred library books during the summer months alone. Given his habit from boyhood onward of reading in depth the authors he liked, we can assume that he read a fair number of the library's Marryat holdings. But internal evidence alone suggests that he had read *Percival Keene* by the 1930s, when he wrote "The Short Happy Life of Francis Macomber."

Readers of that African tale will remember how the British guide Wilson quotes Shakespeare, at a crucial point, so as to share with his newly courageous client "this thing he had lived by": "By my troth, I care not; a man can die but once; we owe God a death and let it go which way it will he that dies this year is quit for the next."

These famous lines have been repeated, of course, in a great many literary works over the past four centuries. But variations on them occur no less than three times in *Percival Keene*. Early in the novel, for instance, a black pirate captain responds to the charge that his profession "seldom ends well" by saying, "And what matter does that make? We can die but once—I care not how soon." The second occurrence comes late in the novel as the hero's ship threatens to run aground when caught by a gale during combat: "Not a soul will be saved, sir," cries the shuddering master; "we all owe Heaven a death," replies the plucky Keene. A few chapters later, when Keene and his friend Cross are captured on land by enemy forces and threatened with execution, his friend similarly responds, "We all owe Heaven a death."[5]

But Shakespearean parallels are one thing, deadly accidents another. What matters here is that the first two parallels have been preceded by suggestive accidents. Thus, the black pirate captain who quotes Shakespeare commands a crew of escaped slaves and vengefully executes all white prisoners. But, impressed by the bravery and cleverness in the face of death of one such prisoner, young Percival Keene, he spares his life, makes him his white cabin boy, and—when Keene artfully blackens his face and body to please him—takes him into his confidence as his first and only friend. When the pirate ship puts in to a hidden Cuban bay for repairs—in what may have been the young Hemingway's literary introduction to life on that island— Keene further cements this friendship by foregoing escape to save the captain's life. The captain then promises his eventual freedom; but when Keene later rushes to the defense of an old Dutch gentleman and his daughter and calls the captain a coward for condemning them to death, the enraged captain forgets his promises and snaps his pistol point-blank at his friend. The gun misfires; Keene negotiates the release of the white prisoners at the cost of his own freedom; but meanwhile his erstwhile friend is plunged into gloom and self-doubt. Keene finds him in his cabin "stretched upon the sofa, his face covered up with both his hands," angry at himself for having broken his oath in attempting the life of his only friend and for again denying him his freedom. Keene tries to reassure him by saying that he too had been "in a great rage" and would have fired at the captain if he had had a pistol in his hand, "so we may cry quits on that score"; but he nonetheless reaffirms his desire for freedom and wishes too that his friend would give up piracy. It is in this context that the captain justifies his professional fate—"a man can die but once"—on the grounds that vengeance against the enslaving white race is sweeter and more durable than love and friendship. But the puzzling questions of vengeful anger, and of his own motives for shooting at his friend in response to the charge of cowardice, continue to disturb him. As he admits to Keene, "Had I destroyed you in my passion, I should have been a miserable man. I know it; I feel it."

This murderous conflict between friends, one who seeks freedom from the other, seems to me richly, if obliquely, suggestive as a source for the Macomber story; but it is only prelude to the more important "accident" ahead. Before and after the pirate episode, Percival Keene serves on his father's ship and performs so bravely and so brilliantly as to win his father's secret regard. The regard is secret because Percival is the captain's illegitimate son, and Captain Delmar—a wealthy bachelor whose official title is Lord de Versely—wants to conceal his indiscretion while at the same time meeting his parental obligations. Though both father and son pretend ignorance of any kinship, their resemblance to each other is so strong as to confirm the suspicions of those around them. Thus, when Captain Delmar invites his unacknowledged offspring to the family estate, late in the novel, his cousin, Colonel Delmar, is troubled by the resemblance and by the hitch it raises in the family inheritance. Then, as the hunting season begins, a curious "accident" occurs:

> The next day . . . we had a large addition to our shooting party. I had not been out more than an hour, when, as I was standing near Lord de Versely, who was reloading his gun, a report, close to us, was heard, and I fell down close to his feet, apparently dead. A keeper, who was with us, ran to see who had discharged the gun, and found that it was Colonel Delmar, who now ran up to us, stating, in hurried terms, to Lord de Versely, that his gun had gone off accidentally as he was putting on a copper cap, and bitterly lamenting the circumstance. Lord de Versely was at the time kneeling down by my side (as I was afterwards informed), showing the greatest anxiety and grief. My hat had been taken off; it was full of blood, and the back of my head was much torn with the shot. I remained insensible, although breathing

heavily; a gate was taken off its hinges, and I was laid upon it, and carried to the Hall.

Before the surgeon had arrived, I had recovered my senses. On examination, I had had a very narrow escape; the better part of the charge of shot had entered the back part of my head, but fortunately not any had penetrated through the skull. After a tedious hour, employed in extracting this load, my head was bound up, and I was made comfortable in my bed. I must say that Lord de Versely and Colonel Delmar vied with each other in their attentions to me; the latter constantly accusing himself as the author of the mischief, and watching by my bed the major part of the day.[6]

The placing of the shot in the back of Keene's head, and the broad preparatory hints as to Colonel Delmar's hidden motives, suggests where Hemingway might have derived ideas for his own deadlier version of a hunting accident in the Macomber story. But as yet neither Percival Keene nor his friends have reason to doubt the solicitous colonel's version of the "accident." Evidence of the colonel's treachery becomes more apparent, however, when Keene recovers and the colonel—whose "kindness and attention" have meanwhile made them "very intimate"—accompanies him to Portsmouth, where Keene's ship is being prepared for its next voyage. There, the colonel soon introduces him to his friend, Major Stapleton, an "excellent fellow" who nonetheless picks a quarrel with Keene and by deliberate misunderstanding forces him to a duel. When Colonel Delmar first arranges that Keene will be standing with the setting sun in his eyes, and then when Keene objects, with a white-washed post behind him, Keene finally becomes suspicious and concludes that the colonel has been his enemy all along. He dispatches Major Stapleton and is himself wounded; but his suspicions are further confirmed when the colonel, who has sworn not to leave him, suddenly departs on learning that Stapleton is still alive and promises to recover. A few pages later Keene, in the face of the threatening gale, says, "We all owe Heaven a death."

That Hemingway should derive the ending of his African tale from this melodramatic sequence certainly confirms his greater artistry in handling similar action; but I have not yet indicated the full extent of his probable debt. Immediately before the shooting "accident" there is a comic sequence that feeds into it and ties in with the novel's revelatory conclusion.[7] While Keene is strolling through the family estate, he overhears the captain's wealthy aunt, Miss Delmar, discussing the possibility of his illegitimate kinship; lost in thought, he then vaults over a gate as he leaves the park, finds himself in a narrow, steep-banked lane from which proceeds "the low bellowing of an animal," and witnesses a "curious scene":

The parties who presented themselves were, first a cow with her tail turned towards me, evidently a wicked one, as she was pawing and bellowing in a low tone, and advancing towards two people who were the object of her attack. One was a very little man, dressed in black, the other a stout burly young fellow in a shooting jacket; but what amused me most was, that the stout young fellow, instead of being in the advance to defend one so much smaller than himself, not only kept behind the little man, but actually now and then held him by the shoulders before his own person, as a shield to ward off the expected attack of the vicious animal.

Keene, who has learned "how to manage unruly cattle" on shipboard, feels that he can handle the cow ("although with a bull it was not a very easy matter") and moves in close behind her as she begins to make her run:

The stout young man pushed the little man towards the cow, and then ran for it. The little one, in his attempt to recoil, fell on the turf and the cow made at him. I sprang forward, and catching the horn of the animal farthest from me in my right hand, at the same time put my left knee on the horn nearest me, threw all my weight upon it, so as to turn the animal's nose up in the air, and seizing it by the nostrils with the other hand, I held her head in that position, which of course rendered the animal harmless. In that position the cow went over the prostrate man without doing him any injury, plunging and capering, so as to extricate herself from my weight. I remained clinging to her for about ten yards further, when I perceived the stout fellow ahead, who hallooed out, "Hold her tight! hold her tight!" but that I would no longer do, as it was fatiguing work; so, as a punishment for his cowardice, I let go the animal, springing clear off, and behind it, the cow galloping away as fast as she could down the lane, and the fellow screaming and running before as fast as he could.

Setting aside the possible influence of this scene on the Spanish Hemingway, let us reconnoiter. In this chapter (35) a tall, stout, cowardly fellow runs screaming before a charging cow as the tall, well-built Macomber will run wildly, in panic, before a charging lion in Hemingway's African tale. In the next chapter (36) Percival Keene is shot in the back of the head in a hunting "accident" as Macomber will be shot there in a hunting "accident" in Hemingway's tale. Marryat's sequence is strikingly like Hemingway's and might well be called, in Jamesian terms, the germinal source for Hemingway's much more complicated and sophisticated story. One might even note that the "punishments" for cowardice in both works are followed by even more serious punishments for bravery, for Keene is present at his father's estate as a result of his attempts to win his approval, and to force him to acknowledge his birthright, through bravery at sea.

But we have not yet finished with the comic parallels. "Having thus rid [himself] of the cow and the coward," Keene turns back to the small man left on the ground, who thanks him, but speaks out against "that rascally clerk of mine, who wanted to shove me on the cow's horns to save himself." They exchange pleasantries at the expense of the fleeing clerk; they consider retreat if the cow returns head on; then the stranger asks if he is addressing Captain Keene:

> "That is my name," replied I; "but here is the cow coming back, and the sooner we get to the gate the better. I'm not ashamed to run for it, and I suppose you are not either." So saying, I took to my heels, followed by my new companion, and we very soon put the barred gate between us and our enemy.

The inimical cow and the inimical Colonel Delmar will together cement the bond of friendship between this fleeing pair. The stranger, a man named Warden, is Miss Delmar's lawyer. He is about to go to the Hall to make alterations in her will which will include Keene as his father's heir. His cowardly and deceitful clerk will in turn convey that information to Colonel Delmar, and Keene will observe but not overhear this dastardly exchange just before the shooting "accident." But let us suspend this melodrama and return to issues raised by the prudent retreat from the returning cow just witnessed.

Like Hemingway, Marryat was an adept at questions of bravery and cowardice and the slippery grounds between them. His novels abound with captains and sailors singled out for one trait or the other, and with situations which reveal those traits. Unlike Kipling or Conrad, he gives us no examples of cowards who become brave men—like Macomber—under further testing. But in one of his earliest novels, *The King's Own*, which is also on the Oak Park Library list for 1904, he does provide a long disquisition on the nature and scale of courage:

> There is, perhaps, no quality in man partaking of such variety, and so difficult to analyse, as courage, whether it be physical or mental, both of which are not only innate, but to be acquired. The former, and

the most universal, is most capriciously bestowed; sometimes, although rarely, Nature has denied it altogether. We have, therefore, in the latter instance, courage nil, as a zero, courage negative, half-way up, and courage positive, at the top, which may be considered as "blood heat," and upon this thermometrical scale the animal courage of every individual may be placed. Courage nil, or cowardice, needs no explanation. Courage negative, which is the most common, is that degree of firmness which will enable a person to do his duty when danger comes to him; he will not avoid danger, but he will not exactly seek it. Courage positive, when implanted in a man, will induce him to seek danger, and find opportunities of distinguishing himself where others can see none. Courage negative is a passive feeling, and requires to be roused. Courage positive is an active and restless feeling, always on the look-out.

. . . Paradoxical as it may appear, the most certain and most valuable description of courage is that which is acquired from the fear of shame. Further, there is no talent which returns more fold than courage, when constantly in exercise; for habit will soon raise the individual whose index is near to zero, to the degree in the scale opposite to courage negative; and the possessor of courage negative will rise up to that of courage positive; although, from desuetude, they will again sink to their former position.

It is generally understood that men are naturally brave; but as, without some incentive, there would be no courage, I doubt the position. I should rather say that we were naturally cowards. Without incitement, courage of every description would gradually descend to the zero of the scale; the necessity of some incentive to produce it, proves that it is "against nature." As the ferocity of brutes is occasioned by hunger, so is that of man by "hungering" after the coveted enjoyments of life, and in proportion as this appetite is appeased, so is his courage decreased. If you wish animals to fight, they must not be over-fed; and if a nation wishes to have good officers, it must swell their pride by decorations, and keep them poor. . . .

The strongest incitement to courage is withdrawn by the possession of wealth.

The disquisition concludes with a caution against marriage as a further detriment to courage, and with the observation that courage deserts us when we are ill and that even "a violent stomach-ache will turn a hero into a poltroon."[8] The impress of such sentiments on the young Hemingway is worth pondering. Assuming that he read this novel, Marryat had given him a recipe for attaining and maintaining active courage; and perhaps also he had given him an ingrained formula, early absorbed, for Macomber's passage from natural cowardice to active courage, involving fear of shame as an incitement and the security of riches, and perhaps also of marriage, as detriments. Certainly, the adult Hemingway came to the writing of Macomber's "short happy life" with some such complex of ideas well-ingrained, and it may well be that they stem from Marryat, among other possible sources. His own active and restless search for further tests of courage, and his similar reservations about wealth and marriage—even about illness—suggest as much.

Let us turn once more to *Percival Keene*. As the novel moves to its close, Captain Delmar has died, and Colonel Delmar, using one of Keene's indiscretions as a lever, has persuaded Miss Delmar to change her will in his favor. But Keene meanwhile has sent a letter to his friend Mr. Warden explaining that indiscretion. The lawyer takes the letter to the ailing Miss Delmar, who has not signed the second will and who postpones the signing until she can consult again with Colonel Delmar. But that villainous gentleman is now forced into a duel by his former accomplice, Major Stapleton, whom he had denounced—when he supposed him dead—as "the greatest scoundrel that ever disgraced his Majesty's uniform." Now Stapleton, who has learned of the slander, has his revenge. As Warden reports to Keene on the novel's final page,

> They fought at daylight, and both fell. The major, however, lived long enough to acknowledge that the duel with you had been an arranged thing between him and the colonel, that you might be put out of the way, after the information the colonel had received from my clerk, and that the colonel was to have rewarded him handsomely if he had sent you into the other world. *I suspect, after this, that the fowling-piece going off in the cover was not quite so accidental as was supposed.* (Italics mine)

This concluding revelation from the British lawyer Warden is, it seems to me, like the British guide Wilson's reading, at the end of the Macomber story, of Margot's unconscious motivation in "accidentally" shooting her husband. If so, it may help to settle a long-standing dispute about that ending, now in its third decade. For if Hemingway had been storing up since boyhood—or even since the 1920s—the possibility of writing his own version of a hunting "accident" grounded in hidden motives, the case for a purely benevolent view of Margot's motives (along with a lofty ironic view of life's mischances) might be put to its well-deserved rest.[9]

Knowing our disputatious nature as academics, I don't for a moment believe that will happen. But for those of us who still believe that Margot's aim, when she "shot at the buffalo . . . as it seemed about to gore Macomber," was deflected by deep-seated hostility toward him, the evidence of Marryat's probable influence on the action should at least provide some comfort. It looks very much as if Hemingway had stored up Marryat's piecemeal cowardice and "accident" sequence for some time, in order to put together his own well-ordered version of such events.

The signs of his superior artistry and more complicated aims are, of course, everywhere evident. If he derived from Marryat a formula for the necessary passage from natural cowardice to active courage, and perhaps also a few examples of natural cowardice, both comic (as in *Percival Keene*) and serious (as in *Masterman Ready*), he nonetheless imagined freshly an actual passage from one condition to the other and dramatized it with compelling power. And similarly, if he found in Marryat a suggestive hunting "accident" and a stage villain with hidden motives of the most obvious kind, he again imagined freshly his own hunting "accident" and worked for a complex of conflicting motives in his heroine which Marryat scarcely entertained—although the example of the black pirate captain's feelings, after misfiring at his only friend, might be cited here as a better precedent. For the black pirate not only dislikes being called a coward; he also dislikes white people as the enslaving race and, at the same time, dislikes losing an only friend who happens to be white, and who insists on freeing white prisoners, and therefore insists once more on his own eventual freedom. Perhaps the seeds of Margot Macomber's conflicting motives are there in Marryat's subplot, in the captain's desire to kill what he can't keep, and in his consequent self-doubt and confusion. Nonetheless, it was Hemingway's genius to use the more deadly action of the main plot—the hunting "accident"—to reveal his heroine's similar response to her husband's implied departure. As the enlightened advocates of an even "shorter happy life" for Margot Macomber insist, she does shoot at the buffalo because she wants consciously to save Macomber's life. But as her deflected aim suggests to the obtuse guide (as such critics see him) and to many similarly benighted readers, she has come to enjoy her power over Macomber, does not want to give it up, does not *like* his newfound confidence and the implicit threat of his now being able to leave her which the guide soon makes explicit ("That was a pretty thing to do. . . . He *would* have left you too"), and so compulsively denies him further "happiness." And perhaps also she wants in her brewing anger to pay him back for those painful years when his mental cowardice first initiated and then perpetuated the terrible conflict between them. The basis for genuine resentment is made evident in the following exchange:

"You've gotten awfully brave, awfully suddenly," his wife said contemptuously, but her contempt was not secure. She was very afraid of something.

Macomber laughed, a very natural hearty laugh. "You know I *have,*" he said. "I really have."

"Isn't it sort of late?" Margot said bitterly. Because she had done the best she could for many years back and the way they were together now was no one person's fault.

"Not for me," said Macomber.

Margot said nothing but sat back in the corner of the seat.[10]

Plainly, the power ratio in this deadly marriage has shifted: Francis is now confident; Margot, insecure. But Hemingway wants to show also that her bitterness is justified by those many years when her husband's unmanliness had defeated her efforts to make the marriage work. Indeed, the purpose of the story's opening action—the public exposure of Macomber's coward-ice—is an objective correlative for his particular contribution to "the way they were together now"; and as that revelation implies, Hemingway's great advance over the simplicities of his sources was to use his African safari to expose dramatically the weaknesses of this all-too-modern marriage. As the story begins, the exposed and shamed Macomber is goaded into manliness; as the story moves to its tragic close, the dethroned and hardened Margot—now insecure and resentful—will be goaded into manslaughter. If it is not too late for Macomber to benefit from his newfound courage, it may well be too late for her to cope with it: his callous rejoinder as to lateness, "Not for me," puts the question of his imminent departure on the line, and does little that I can see to justify the notion of renewed love in this fading and soon to be abandoned beauty, which the enlightened school assumes.

But let us credit that school for its unwitting enrichment of Margot's mixed motives. Though I would myself describe her conscious motive in shooting at the buffalo as a humane impulse—a tribute, that is, to her humanity—it is possible to construe it, with Warren Beck, as "that access of recognition and penitence and hope in which love can renew itself," or with Kenneth Johnson, as that valiant impulse by which Margot "risks all—marriage, money, reputation, freedom to save her husband, who has finally become the sort of man she has been desperately seeking all along."[11] But even granting these benign views, it is not possible to discard the powerful working within Margot of those hostile feelings that Hemingway has patiently built up in these closing pages—feelings that not only explain her implicitly deflected aim, but speak also to that mixture of motives within her that Hemingway was trying to dramatize through his objective correlative for them. To dismiss those feelings now—as presto! suddenly overcome—is to diminish the complexity and force of the conflict within Margot, to explain away as mere ironic chance her bullet's miscarriage, and to reduce the concluding sequence to a bungled satire on the guide's obtuseness and cruelty. Thus, if Beck and Johnson are right about the purity of Margot's motives, this is (as I have argued elsewhere) the worst conclusion Hemingway ever wrote. For not only is there no sign from Margot of her intentions, but the guide Wilson is given the last word on them. Indeed, he is given the only open exposition we have of Margot's motives, and the fact is that he speaks to both sides of the response—to its accidental or "innocent" outcome at the impulsive level, and to its hostile or compulsive depths. We may want to judge him as more cruel and more chauvinistic than the author as he forces Margot to say "Please" before he stops; but then Macomber is dead because of her intervention. The buffalo did not gore him; it merely supplied the occasion for her hostile feelings to displace her finer impulses and deflect her aim. Thus Wilson, who seems to understand that inner process and is "a little angry" now, takes up the power struggle just ended, speaks *in loco* Macomber, if not *in loco* Hemingway, and inflicts upon her the humiliation that Hemingway was in any case *loco* enough to want us to enjoy. Hence, for Wilson as for Margot—and, indeed, for Hemingway as for Marryat— vengeful passions might be said to predominate over tender ones in stressful moments. As the black pirate captain argues in *Percival Keene,* revenge is sweeter and more durable than love and friendship; it is the "one feeling that never clogs and never tires."[12] In the much-disputed ending of the Macomber story, Hemingway gives us a fresh and complex instance of that sad conviction.

Appendix B

A Retrospective Epilogue:

On the Importance

of Being Androgynous

My text for this retrospective epilogue is an item taken from the Sunday *New York Times* "Arts & Leisure" section for April 24, 1988, entitled "Reading Hemingway with One Eye Closed." It begins with a brief account of Hemingway's animadversions against biographers and selects from those unkind observations a summary remark: "Imagine what they can do with the soiled sheets of four legal beds by the same writer."[1] The remark is chosen by way of introducing still another object of animadversion, the recent television mini-series called "Hemingway," which "focuses on the women in Hemingway's life," his four wives and two of his many wished-for sweethearts. As the title of the article indicates, its author, James R. Mellow, himself a Hemingway biographer in the making, takes issue with the narrow focus on Hemingway's relations with women to the exclusion of his relations with men: "What one misses in this dramatized portrait," says Mellow, "is a real sense that there were men who were equally as important as the women in Hemingway's personal life and certainly more important to his literary career."[2]

Though Mellow's observation seems just and speaks to the Hemingway that many people—myself among them—admire, it may be that it speaks also to a kind of growing anxiety that such admirers are about to lose him. As indeed we are. The anxiety registered here, in the name of biographical inclusiveness and literary value, is actually being registered in the name of

This appendix is a modified version of a paper delivered at the Third International Hemingway Conference, Schruns, Austria, June 21, 1988.

that male camaraderie which the *Times* copyeditor highlights with a boldface insertion—**"The author's sense of male camaraderie gets little prominence in the mini-series"**—and which Mellow himself proceeds to apotheosize in no uncertain terms:

> At the age of 19, for instance, Hemingway, a wounded hero of the Italian Campaign in World War I, had attracted a small circle of male friends—significantly three to five years older than he—for whom he was the leader and the authority on subjects ranging from sports to sex. None of them objected to his role. It was Hemingway who made the plans for the summer fishing and camping expeditions on the Black and the Sturgeon rivers in Michigan, plotted the itineraries, fussed over the arrangements with a ritual insistence. It was more than the cultivation of a machismo image (though it was that, too). By then Hemingway had developed a sense of male camaraderie that verged almost on the mystical. It would haunt his fiction (most notably his Nick Adams stories) and his personal life.[3]

Never mind that Hemingway clobbered most of his male friends with surprising regularity, or that he was more wounded than heroic in the Italian campaign, or that he had little or no sexual authority at the age of 19, or that Nick Adams is more nearly a loner than a comrade in his stories, to the point where D. H. Lawrence might comfortably call him "the remains of the lone trapper and cowboy."[4] What matters here is the loving transcription of that mythical sense of mystical camaraderie that Hemingway has indeed created in his fiction and above all in his personal life. This is indeed the Hemingway who early wrote a group of tales called *Men Without Women*, the Hemingway who gave us male definitions of manhood to ponder, cherish, even perhaps to grow by. The machismo problem, so lightly touched on here, has everything to do, nonetheless, with those relations with women the perusal of which Mellow so anxiously calls "Reading Hemingway with One Eye Closed." For surely the point should be that critics have been reading Hemingway with one eye closed for years, that his peculiar world of men without women was in fact founded on relations with women that we are just now beginning to understand, and perhaps more importantly, on relations with himself, or on a sense of himself in relation to women, that we are also only recently and I think alarmingly just beginning to understand. It is this side of Hemingway, his secret and continuing dependence on women, now not so secret after all, and his own curiously androgynous makeup, that threaten to deprive his admirers—myself still among them—of that one-eyed myth of mystical camaraderie we have all more or less embraced.

There are changes in the offing, then, that might prove hard to take.

There is reason to be uneasy, if not to despair. It is not simply the new feminism that asks us to judge more carefully Hemingway's dubious (i.e.; abusive, triangulated, exploitive) relations with women, and with the more feminine aspects of himself, or the androgynous aspects that, like so many men, he found so hard to cope with. It is his own central role in the creation and perpetuation of cultural myths and codes that are now under scrutiny from many angles, chief among which is the myth of men without women.

He did not invent it. It began, rather, in imperial England when the code of the stiff upper lip first openly replaced the possibility of manly tears in schools for boys—schools for the instruction of future servants of the Empire; it received its first American impress after the Civil War in the fictions of Mark Twain and other celebrants of postpioneer nostalgia; and from imperial British celebrants like Marryat, Kipling, and Masefield, as well as from Twain himself, it passed into the life and fiction of Ernest Hemingway. It is his role as the receiver, transmuter, and perpetuater of such myths that requires us to judge him now in terms of his continuing cultural role as what Edmund Wilson once called our "gauge of morale."[5] And if the gauge seems singularly low in these days of professional cynicism and distrust, all the more reason to give it our serious attention.

Let us turn, then, to Hemingway's oft-quoted justification for the title of a new collection of his stories in a letter to his editor at Scribner's, Maxwell Perkins, dated February 14, 1927: "Want to call it Men Without Women [because] in all of these [stories], almost, the softening feminine influence through training, discipline, death or other causes [is] absent."[6] Hemingway was twenty-seven at the time and about to marry his second wife, Pauline Pfeiffer. His divorce from his first wife, Hadley Richardson, had become final only two weeks before, and he would delay the marriage with Pauline only a few months more so as join his friend Guy Hickok on a bachelor tour of fascist Italy, an excursion the disgruntled Pauline acidly called his "Italian tour for the promotion of masculine society."[7] Her remark seems apt enough. Masculine society was something Hemingway would always pursue from within the confines of marriage or near-marriage. From 1921 to his death in 1961 he was consecutively married to four wives without any significant pause between marriages. He literally never lived alone for as much as a year in his life. From the cradle to the grave he was himself never free of "the softening influence of women through training, discipline, death or other causes," though he certainly did his best to think and write otherwise, and with enormous success. Until recently, at least, none of his critics and admirers have made much of the fact that—like so many of us—he was extremely dependent on women.

In A Literature of Their Own Elaine Showalter offers a useful clue to

Hemingway's desire to free himself of that dependence by literary fiat. While discussing how British women novelists in the nineteenth century created model heroes as projections of how they might act and feel if they were men, or of how they felt men should act and feel, she compares these projections of wished-for power and authority with those of male novelists of the day like Thomas Hughes, author of *Tom Brown's School Days at Rugby*: "The love of sport and animals, the ability to withstand pain, the sublimation of sexuality into religious devotion, and the channeling of sexuality into mighty action are traits the model heroes share. In Hughes' novels, however, manliness is achieved through separation from women; in the women's novels, mothers, sisters, and wives are the sources of instruction on the manly character."[8]

It was the precedent of imperialist writers like Hughes, Marryat, Kipling, and Stevenson, then, whom he had read and admired in his childhood, that Hemingway was trying to extend when he wrote the tales that comprise *Men Without Women* and described them as free of those "softening influences"—those female "sources of instruction on the manly character"—that he too wished to avoid. Yet those influences would soon recur, as we can see in *A Farewell to Arms*, and would crop up periodically thereafter, as in *For Whom the Bell Tolls* and *Across the River and Into the Trees*, until their amazingly predominant resurgence in manuscripts of his final years like *The Garden of Eden* and "The Last Good Country," both now posthumously published in selective forms.

For Hemingway was never really free, as I have said, of those "softening influences." Their presence in his childhood and adolescence was in fact deeply formative. He was raised androgynously by parents peculiarly steeped in the conflicting codes of manhood that were vying for sway in the late nineteenth century and that would continue to press their rival claims upon him throughout his lifetime. His mother's early interest in feminism, her pursuit of a musical career with parental encouragement, her mother's admonition that she should stay out of the kitchen as much as possible, were matched by his father's early interest in Indian lore and his cultivation of the skills of camping, as in that famous expedition to the Smoky Mountains in his youth when he served proudly as camp cook. Her genteel feminism and his postpioneer nostalgia blended readily when it came to questions of rearing their six children, at least during the infant years and shortly after, when the children were schooled by their father in the outdoor skills of swimming, fishing, hunting, and cooking, and exposed by their mother to the arts of music, literature, and painting. It was no accident that the Hemingways' firstborn son at the age of two years and eleven months both loved to sew and to shoot his gun in target practice; or that he could hit the bull's-eye by four and still loved his mama kitty; or that he wore Dutch-length hair like his sister Marcelline's and was often dressed in similar smocks and frocks, or, alternately, in straw hat and Tom Sawyer rags while going barefoot.

The Fauntleroy craze that swept England and America in the 1890s helps in some ways to explain this peculiar blend of male and female definitions of manhood. For Frances Hodgson Burnett's controversial little hero was a kind of last-ditch representation of the claims of genteel feminism to "instruct the manly character" at an early age. His competitor on the best-seller lists of the mid-1880s was Huckleberry Finn, then entering the lists as America's contribution to the new imperial definitions of future manhood in England, its postpioneer equivalent of the new British belief that manliness is best achieved through separation from women. These vying codes could for a time blend in American households because they shared a common belief in the stoic virtues—courage under stress, the ability to withstand pain, the love of outdoor sports and animals—and differed only in their stress on consideration of women and of women's feelings about the nature of manliness. Hemingway was in fact raised by a blend of these then relatively compatible codes. The interesting point about his boyhood is his gradual separation of their hold upon him, his crossing over from one to another as he broke with his mother's and his older sister's influence, shifted his emotional allegiances to his younger sisters, and began to model himself upon the prevailing example in his turn-of-the-century culture of Teddy Roosevelt and Huckleberry Finn, the imperial and postpioneer representatives, respectively, of the new male codes.[9] The Fauntleroy impress would never, however, wholly leave him; and the androgynous impress of his early years would return to haunt him in his final years, even as it now begins to haunt us all.

From his peculiarly androgynous parents, then, Hemingway had received a mixed impress of blending and conflicting definitions of manhood. His father, Dr. Clarence Edmonds Hemingway, had tried to raise him as the frontier scout he had always wanted to be himself; yet he had also taught him the naturalistic lore that he had learned from his own college-educated mother, and had impressed upon him as well the importance of his own nurturing and healing profession, which Ernest would in effect follow when he joined the Red Cross ambulance corps in World War I and was wounded, not as a soldier in battle, but as a canteen worker at the front, serving food, cigarettes, candy, and postcards to men in the lines. His father was also a deeply religious man, a muscular Christian like his mother, and with a damp susceptibility to prayers and tears that his supposedly more toughminded son seems to have found embarrassing.[10] His mother, Grace Hall Hemingway, had named him Ernest Miller Hemingway after the two Christian businessmen she most admired, her father and uncle, Ernest and Miller Hall; and beyond the going androgynous fashions, she had curiously twinned him with his older sister Marcelline in his infant and boyhood years. In these ways she seems to have been projecting upon him her own fantasies of how she might act and feel if she were a man; for there is every evidence that her stake in his future was very much like that of nineteenth-century women novelists in their model male heroes. Indeed, one such novelist, Dinah Mulock Craik, had written a novel in the mid-nineteenth century called *John Halifax, Gentleman,* which served as the Hemingway family bible. It was about a heroic Christian businessman like Grace's father as well as her uncle, who had married an aristocrat named Ursula March after whom Hemingway's next younger sister Ursula was named, and who had brought his family to live on a country estate called Longfield, after which Grace would name the farm across from the Hemingway cottage on Lake Walloon in northern Michigan where she would eventually build herself a music studio. What Grace wanted for her son Ernest, then, was very much what she wanted for herself; and when she twinned him with his older sister, Marcelline, and began experimenting with their hairstyles, first Dutch-length in infancy, then close-cut when Ernest began school and received his first boy's haircut, she was telling her firstborn son something about the gender she favored in creating such twinships. For Marcelline too would receive her first boy's haircut at this time and would be punished when it grew out unevenly and seemed even more unsightly after a girlfriend tried to trim it. And on two occasions Marcelline would also be held back in school until Ernest caught up with her.

In such odd ways, apparently, Grace Hemingway would express her own need to find a place for her considerable talents in a culture which encouraged men to pursue careers and encouraged women to choose motherhood over careers, or to attempt somehow to combine them, as she had done shortly after her mother's untimely death. As with Clarence, indeed as with many parents, what she wanted for her children she wanted for herself. It does not seem surprising, then, that Ernest too might be influenced by such desires, or by their personal consequences, in his adult years. We have no hesitation in saying as much where his father was concerned. Now it is Grace's turn. She wanted and she got a distinctly androgynous son; but then so in his own way did her husband Clarence.

We have long known the places in Hemingway's fiction where mothers and sisters may be said to have provided "sources of instruction" for the hero's manly character. In *A Farewell to Arms* the message of selfless love which the priest first intimates and which Lieutenant Henry manages to forget is given its hospital workout when the wounded and supine and therefore interestingly feminine Henry finally falls in love with the crazy nurse, Catherine Barkley, with whom he had previously temporized, and is thus instructed in a love so selfless that the lovers become one another at night, even as an earlier fictional couple, mad Catherine Earnshaw and her foster brother Heathcliff, had identified with each other ("I *am* Heathcliff") as romantic lovers in a novel Hemingway had read and admired in adolescence and would emulate several times thereafter. One of those occasions, surely, is *For Whom the Bell Tolls,* where the motherly and sisterly sources of instruction, tough Pilar and close-cropped Maria, may be said to have worked the same selfless lesson on the hero, Robert Jordan, who not only resembles Maria like a brother but identifies with her in mystical succession as his female survivor. The model for *Across the River and Into the Trees* is more clearly Italian, that of Dante and Beatrice, and the source of instruction more daughterly than sisterly, as dying Colonel Cantwell is softened from his military ragings by his selfless love for young Countess Renata, a nineteen-year-old female replacement for the author's World War I persona, particularly in her desire to become well-versed in her own turn in military lore and tough battle attitudes. But let us turn from these easy examples, and the various hair-cropping or hair-lengthening scenes that may be said to go with them, and turn to another mad Catherine, or more precisely, to another sisterly *ménage à trois,* in *The Garden of Eden* manuscript and the novel selected from it and published in 1986, after which all things may be said (in Yeatsian terms) to have changed utterly.

What seems remarkable about this amazingly self-reflexive novel, this story about opposing kinds of stories, is its reenactment of the conflict between male and female definitions of the manly character in ways invidious to both, and its establishment thereby of a wound-and-the-bow approach to androgyny that speaks profoundly to Hemingway's struggle with himself, or with the opposing female muses within himself, one hostile, the other supportive, against both of whom he seems to establish the terms for his own distinctly masculine artistry. The ambitiousness, the risk-taking, in this unfinished, many-sided novel, this experiment in self-reflexive psychodrama which Faulkner at least might have recognized as a clear instance of going beyond safe limits,[11] will make it an object of study for some time to come; and not the least among its ponderable treasures will be the theory of androgynous creativity that emerges most clearly from its manuscript rather than its published pages. The decision of Scribner's editor, Tom Jenks, to remove from the published version visits by two American couples to the Rodin statue of two women making love, along with the subplot about the Paris couple, Nick and Barbara Sheldon, who are equally implicated in the statue's resonant meanings, diminishes that printed version considerably, and of itself turns us to the original manuscript for clues to the author's fascinating intentions—his decision, that is, to present the Garden of Eden theme as an androgynous love bond, a lesbian coupling, as it were, the peculiar happiness of which—in his own mournful words—"a man must lose." It looks very much as if Hemingway were trying toward the end of his life to come to terms with his own androgynous leanings, especially as they might help to define his lifelong quarrel with them in both external and internal ways, and with his ultimate sense that androgyny might after all be the wound against which he had always drawn his masculine bow.

Within the original manuscript, then, there are repeated assertions by Hemingway's chief male persona, the young writer David Bourne, that the worse his life becomes, the more his character deteriorates, the better he writes. "All that is left entire in you," he muses in book 3, chapter 23, "is your ability to write and that gets better. You would think it would be destroyed. . . . But so far as you corrupt or change that grows and strengthens. It should not but it has."[12] The corruption and change to which David refers involves his own absorption in the androgynous relations with his wife Catherine inspired by the Rodin statue. Thus, when making love at night, David accedes to Catherine's request, assumes her name, and imagines himself as the passive female partner in the statue; whereas Catherine assumes the active and dominant position and calls herself Peter. This role reversal is given a kind of public showing, moreover, when Catherine has her hair cut short to resemble his and persuades him to dye his hair blond like hers. The hair fetishism is the public expression, that is, of their private relations and of the new definition Catherine has given to David's male identity. For the first time in Hemingway's major fiction the female source of instruction on the manly character becomes, on romantic grounds, decidedly suspect.

To make matters worse, Catherine also encourages David to write a narrative account of their newlywed life on the French Riviera, much like that which Hemingway provides, so that the text itself becomes an expression of the author's stake in these suspect events. Thus David's narrative soon becomes a source of marital conflict. The jealously possessive Catherine prefers it to the tales of his African boyhood which David also attempts to write, as if trying to reclaim that world of men without women he once shared with his father. But the disillusionment with his father these tales record suggests that even exclusively male definitions of manhood are now suspect. The only way left for David to assert and reclaim his male identity is through the act of writing itself; it is there that he overcomes what seems to be the wound of androgyny. Thus, when Catherine destroys the African manuscripts, David is able to reassert that identity, and to overcome the corrupting effects of the androgynous wounding, by writing them again.

The parable that the novel offers on Hemingway's life is certainly instructive, and the novel virtually asks us to work it out, even as the supposedly impersonal Joyce asks us to extrapolate from Stephen Dedalus's experiences some implications about his own. The parallels with Scott and Zelda Fitzgerald are in this regard somewhat misleading. It is not so much Zelda's jealousy of Scott's writing that Catherine reenacts as that of Hemingway's several wives. One thinks of that suitcase full of manuscripts that Hadley left unguarded; or how impugned Pauline must have felt by "The Snows of Kilimanjaro" and the windfall approach to her rival, Jane Mason, in the Macomber story; or Martha's active rivalry as a novelist and foreign correspondent; or Mary's sacrifice of her own writing career to marriage. Similarly, one thinks of Pauline's refrain during the famous one hundred days of separation: "You and me are the same guy"; or of Mary's account of her androgynous relations with Ernest in *How It Was;* or of the sexual role reversals with the lost wife in *Islands in the Stream*. We have good reason to read this novel, then, as a revealing gloss on Hemingway's long adult quarrel with androgyny in his several marriages, and therefore as a revealing gloss on his own artistic struggles, his own self-definition as a writer with decidedly androgynous propensities.

That he presents David Bourne as the passive victim of those propensities is not surprising. Earlier male personas like Jake Barnes or the corrupt writer Harry in "The Snows of Kilimanjaro" are presented as passive victims of weaknesses or conditions which they nonetheless bear or struggle against with stoic courage. What is surprising here is David's strong attraction to androgyny, his fascination with the Rodin statue, and his attempt—like that of Hemingway himself—to do justice to Catherine in the main narrative, to create a sympathetic portrait of *her* painful struggles. It is the betrayal of those possibilities that makes this manuscript such a poignant record of Hemingway's ultimate failure to resolve his quarrel with androgyny—or better still, to continue it honestly rather than resolve it falsely. For if we take Catherine Bourne as she is ultimately meant to be taken—as an internalization of that fiercely independent creativity which Hemingway first recognized in his mother's prideful ways, including that twinning process which made him part of those ways from infancy onward and which he recognized again in the determination of his second wife, Pauline, to create an androgynous bond—perhaps a lesbian bond—between them, a bond at any rate with echoes and reflections in his other marriages—then the casting off of Catherine in favor of the supportive adjunct mate, Marita, whom like mother Grace with his younger sisters she thoughtfully provides for him, is like a casting out of his own creative strength, or of that secret muse within himself with whom he struggled to keep alive his own artistic pride, his own creative maleness as the author of wasteland narratives and assorted tales of boyhood disillusionments and of men without women. This, it seems to me, is the ultimate importance of Hemingway's lifelong quarrel with androgyny: that it was crucial to his creative strength throughout his life, and that he came remarkably, even heroically, close to affirming it before tragically betraying it as his life neared its grim conclusion.

Notes

INTRODUCTION: HEMINGWAY'S SECRET MUSES

1. Carlos Baker, *Ernest Hemingway: A Life Story,* 577–78, 583–84, 605, 684–85, 786; Aaron Lapham, "A Farewell to Machismo," *New York Times Magazine,* 16 October 1977, 51–55 and following.

2. Elaine Showalter, *A Literature of Their Own: British Women Novelists from Brontë to Lessing.* See esp. chap. 5, "Feminine Heroes: The Woman's Man," 133–52.

3. Peter Gay, *The Bourgeois Experience: Victoria to Freud,* vol. 1, *The Education of the Senses;* vol. 2, *The Tender Passion.*

4. Michael S. Reynolds, *The Young Hemingway,* 11, 37.

5. Peter Griffin, *Along with Youth: Hemingway, The Early Years,* 85. See also Griffin's doctoral dissertation, "Ernest Hemingway: In My Beginning Is My End" (Brown University, 1979).

6. Showalter, *A Literature of Their Own,* 136, 141, 338.

7. Patricia Meyer Spacks, "The Adolescent as Heroine," in *The Female Imagination,* 171–82.

8. Reynolds, *The Young Hemingway,* 11, 23–25, 27–30, 33–34, 51–52, 163, 230–33.

9. Baker, *Ernest Hemingway,* 234; Ernest Hemingway, *Selected Letters, 1917–1961,* ed. Carlos Baker, 245.

10. Hemingway Collection, John F. Kennedy Library, Boston, Mass.: Pauline to Ernest and Hadley, 16 January 1926; Pauline to Hadley, 14 February 1926; Pauline to Ernest, 25 September, 1926, 1 October 1926, 6 October 1926, 11 October 1926, and 13 December 1926; Ernest to Pauline, 12 November 1926. See also *Selected Letters,* 221.

11. Kenneth S. Lynn, *Hemingway,* 305–6.

12. E. L. Doctorow, "Braver Than We Thought," *New York Times Book Review,* 18 May 1986, 1, 44–45.

13. See especially my "Hemingway and Fauntleroy: An Androgynous Pursuit," in *American Novelists Revisited: Essays in Feminist Criticism,* ed. Fritz Fleischmann, 339–70, where I first stake out the argument of this book, indicate its line of progress, and provide minimal readings of novels and relevant tales; see also "Victorian Keys to the Early Hemingway: *John Halifax, Gentleman,*" *Journal of Modern Literature* 10 (March 1983): 125–50; "Victorian Keys to the Early Hemingway: *Fauntleroy* and *Finn,*" ibid. (June 1983), 289–310; "Victorian Keys to the Early Hemingway: Captain Marryat," *Novel: A Forum on Fiction* 17 (Winter 1984), 116–40; and "A Source for the Macomber 'Accident': Marryat's *Percival Keene,*" *Hemingway Review* 3 (Spring 1984), 29–37, which appear here with slight modifications as Chapters 1, 2, and 3 and Appendix A.

CHAPTER I: *JOHN HALIFAX, GENTLEMAN*

1. Marcelline Hemingway Sanford, *At the Hemingways: A Family Portrait,* 107.

2. Ibid., 134.

3. Gordon Home, Introduction to *John Halifax, Gentleman,* by Dinah Mulock Craik, vi–vii. Page references to this 1922 edition will appear hereafter in the text. See also Dent's 1983 reprint of its 1961 Everyman edition.

4. Showalter, *A Literature of Their Own,* 136. For other recent references to Craik, see Jenni Calder, *Women and Marriage in Victorian Fiction,* 33–34, 56; Vineta Colby, *Yesterday's Woman: Domestic Realism in the English Novel,* 186; and Sandra M. Gilbert and Susan Gubar, *The Madwoman in the Attic: The Woman Writer and Nineteenth-Century Imagination,* 169.

5. Showalter, *A Literature of Their Own,* 137.

6. Griffin, "Ernest Hemingway." See also Griffin's *Along with Youth.*

7. Sanford, *At the Hemingways,* 54.

8. Ibid., 58.

9. Constance Cappel Montgomery, *Hemingway in Michigan,* 81–82.

10. See, for example, Carlos Baker, *Ernest Hemingway,* 16; Peter Buckley, *Ernest,* 101–3 ff.; Scott Donaldson, *By Force of Will: The Life and Art of Ernest Hemingway,* 290–93; and Montgomery, *Hemingway in Michigan,* 71.

11. Sanford, *At the Hemingways,* 198.

12. Showalter, *A Literature of Their Own,* 61.

13. Dinah Mulock Craik, *Sermons Out of Church,* 27–28.

14. Showalter, *A Literature of Their Own,* 127.

15. Grace Hall Hemingway's memory book for Sunny, quoted in Madelaine Hemingway Miller, *Ernie: Hemingway's Sister "Sunny" Remembers,* 71.

16. Sanford, *At the Hemingways,* 87.

17. Ibid., 108.

18. Harold Loeb, *The Way It Was,* 228.

19. Colby, *Yesterday's Woman,* 161.

CHAPTER 2: *FAUNTLEROY AND FINN*

1. Hemingway, *Selected Letters*, 245.

2. Baker, *Ernest Hemingway*, 236.

3. Hemingway, *Selected Letters*, 260.

4. Virginia Woolf, "An Essay in Criticism," in *Ernest Hemingway: The Critical Reception*, ed. Robert O. Stephens, 54. See also p.47.

5. Hemingway, *Selected Letters*, 264–65.

6. Baker, *Ernest Hemingway*, 242–43.

7. Griffin, "Ernest Hemingway," 115.

8. Sanford, *At the Hemingways*, 111.

9. Showalter, *A Literature of Their Own*, 136–37.

10. Ibid., 137.

11. Frances Hodgson Burnett, *Little Lord Fauntleroy*, 130. Page references to this 1974 edition will appear hereafter in the text.

12. Baker, *Ernest Hemingway*, 232.

13. Sanford, *At the Hemingways*, 5, 15–16.

14. Ann Thwaite, *Waiting for the Party: The Life of Frances Hodgson Burnett*, 95. See also *Little Lord Fauntleroy*, 10.

15. Thwaite, *Waiting for the Party*, 77, 85, 183.

16. Ibid., 16, 151–52.

17. Ibid., 52.

18. Grace's memory book for Ernest, from which these and subsequent quotations are drawn, is in the Hemingway Collection, Kennedy Library, Boston, Mass.

19. Sanford, *At the Hemingways*, 21, 23–25.

20. Donaldson, *By Force of Will*, 290.

21. Ibid., 291.

22. Ibid., 294.

23. Jackson J. Benson, *Hemingway: The Writer's Art of Self-Defense*, 5.

24. Ibid., 9. For an antidote to Benson's views on the genteel tradition, see William Wasserstrom, *Heiress of All the Ages: Sex and Sentiment in the Genteel Tradition*.

25. Philip Young, *Ernest Hemingway: A Reconsideration*.

26. Sanford, *At the Hemingways*, 148.

27. See, for example, Fiedler's essay "Duplicitous Mark Twain," in *Mark Twain: A Profile*, ed. Justin Kaplan, 134–51.

28. Thwaite, Introduction to *Little Lord Fauntleroy*, 9. See also *Waiting for the Party*, 82, 92, 117–18.

29. Thwaite, *Little Lord Fauntleroy*, 9–10.

30. Ibid., 7, 10.

31. Baker, *Ernest Hemingway*, 583, 891.

CHAPTER 3: CAPTAIN MARRYAT

1. Hemingway, *Selected Letters*, 179. *Buddenbrooks* and another novel read at Schruns that winter, Turgenev's *Fathers and Children*, were borrowed from Sylvia

Beach's Paris bookshop on 10 December 1925. It seems likely that the books by Collins, Trollope, and Marryat mentioned above were bought or borrowed there at an earlier date, for which ledger entries have been lost. Thus, Sylvia Beach remembers Hemingway reading Marryat there as early as 1922. See Noel Fitch, "Ernest Hemingway—c/o Shakespeare and Company," *Fitzgerald/Hemingway Annual 1977*, 157–81; and Sylvia Beach, *Shakespeare and Company*, 77.

2. *Selected Letters*, 172–74. The letter is dated "Paris, 7 December 1925."

3. See his comments in *Selected Letters*, 624, 673, to William Faulkner and Charles Scribner.

4. Ibid., 624.

5. Ibid., 182. On 2 January 1926, in an unpublished letter from Schruns, Ernest also recommended *Peter Simple* in Dutton's Everyman Library to his friend Ernest Boyd.

6. See Michael S. Reynolds, *Hemingway's Reading, 1910–1940: An Inventory*, 155; and James D. Brasch and Joseph Sigman, *Hemingway's Library: A Composite Record*, 240. Brasch and Sigman also list a biography by Marryat, *The Travels and Adventures of Monsieur Violet*, as part of each of the two editions of *Midshipman Easy* that Hemingway owned. See also p.42 of the Oak Park Public Library "FICTION-AUTHOR LIST," published by the Directors in June 1904, for the fourteen volumes containing the following Marryat titles: *The Children of the New Forest, Frank Mildmay; or, The Naval Officer, Jacob Faithful, Japhet in Search of a Father, Joseph Rushbrooke; or, The Poacher, The King's Own, The Little Savage, Masterman Ready, The Mission; or, Scenes in Africa, Mr. Midshipman Easy, Newton Forster; or, The Merchant Service, Olla Podrida, The Pacha of Many Tales, Percival Keene, Peter Simple, The Pirate, The Phantom Ship, Poor Jack, The Privateer's-Man, Rattlin the Reefer* (attributed to but only edited by Marryat), *Snarleyyow; or, The Dog Fiend, The Three Cutters, The Travels and Adventures of Monsieur Violet in California, Sonora, and Western Texas,* and *Valerie*. I owe thanks for this information to William Jerousek of the library's Adult Services department.

7. *Selected Letters*, 176.

8. Reynolds, *Hemingway's Reading*, 16–17. Further references to Hemingway's Key West Book Inventories are to this volume.

9. See my two previous chapters. See also in this regard my ground-staking essay, "Hemingway and Fauntleroy: An Androgynous Pursuit," in *American Novelists Revisited: Essays in Feminist Criticism*, ed. Fritz Fleischmann, 339–70.

10. Thomas Hughes, *Tom Brown's School Days at Rugby*. See, in this Author's Edition of 1875, pp.73, 86, 97, 183, 238, 303–4, 323–24, 342, 368–70.

11. Ibid., 303–4. See also Hemingway's fable for children, "The Faithful Bull" (1951)—in which fighting is similarly exalted—in *The Complete Short Stories of Ernest Hemingway*, Finca Vigía Edition, 485–86.

12. Philip Collins, *From Manly Tears to Stiff Upper Lip: The Victorians and Pathos*, 16–17.

13. *Selected Letters*, 245.

14. As quoted by Oliver Warner in *Captain Marryat: A Rediscovery*, 13–14, from Conrad's *Notes on Life and Letters* (1921).

15. See Warner, *Captain Marryat: A Rediscovery*, 94–96.

16. Hemingway Collection, Kennedy Library, Boston, Mass.

17. Ibid.

18. Ibid. As Reynolds' inventory shows, Hemingway had written to Emily about Kipling's *Stalky & Co.* as well as *The Jungle Book*.

19. For my original brief discussions of these situations, see "Hemingway and Fauntleroy: An Androgynous Pursuit," in *American Novelists Revisited*, ed. Fritz Fleischmann, 339–70. I give a fuller discussion in Part 2, below. For a recent discussion of modern cross-dressing and of the "female sexual misrule" it implies for masculinist writers like Hemingway, see volume 2, *Sexchanges*, of Sandra Gilbert's and Susan Gubar's *No Man's Land*, 324–76.

20. Warner, *Captain Marryat*, 152.

21. Ibid.

22. The scene in question occurs in chapter 27 and includes a variety of quotations from other Shakespeare plays along with the lines from *Antony and Cleopatra* which Eliot alters at the beginning of part 2 of *The Waste Land*. In the next chapter Jacob takes the actor and his theatrical friends on a picnic party up the Thames to an island by Kew, starting from Whitehall, in the course of which the actors intone more Shakespearean lines, as well as a song about Love vs. Time, and address each other as Quince, Nick Bottom, Caliban, Titania, and Pyramus.

23. "Captain Marryat at Langham," *Cornhill Magazine* 16 (August 1867): 149–61. Oliver Warner suggests that the anonymous writer is probably Marryat's friend Capt. E.G.G.M. Howard, who earlier served as his assistant editor on *Metropolitan* and wrote *Rattlin the Reefer* under his editorial guidance. See Warner, *Captain Marryat*, 199, 92.

24. "Captain Marryat at Langham," 154. The *Cornhill* entries in Reynolds, *Hemingway's Reading*, occur on pp.47, 62, and 79. The *Cornhill* entry in the Cuban inventory of 1962 is numbered 665. Brasch and Sigman, who graciously provided me with this information, list it as 593 in their own inventory of the Cuban manuscript in *Hemingway's Library*. For other references to the reformed poacher Barnes, drawn from the *Cornhill* essay, see David Hannay, *Life of Frederick Marryat*, 141; and Florence Marryat Church Lean, *Life and Letters of Captain Marryat*, 2:137–38, 291. Mrs. Lean adds the interesting point that Marryat wished Barnes to be one of his pallbearers. In his recent biography, *Hemingway* (319, 321), Kenneth Lynn attributes Barnes's name to lesbian sources Djuna Barnes and Natalie Barney, residing respectively at the Hotel Jacob and on the Rue Jacob in Paris.

25. See Beach, *Shakespeare and Company*, 77; Ernest Hemingway, "Monologue to a Maestro: A High Seas Letter," *Esquire* 4 (October 1935): 21, 174A, 174B; Brasch and Sigman, *Hemingway's Library*, 221, 240; and George Plimpton, "An Interview with Ernest Hemingway," *Paris Review* 18 (Spring 1958): 60–89. The Marryat items acquired in Cuba were Christopher Lloyd's *Captain Marryat and the Old Navy* and

the Estes edition of *Capt. Marryat's Works,* 24 vols. As Carlos Baker notes in *Ernest Hemingway: A Life Story,* 263, Hemingway did upbraid Allen Tate in 1929 "for once having said that Defoe and Marryat had influenced [Hemingway's] work." But once his literary status was more secure, he proved more than willing to acknowledge "literary forebears" and favorites, as in *Green Hills of Africa,* his *Esquire* columns, and *A Moveable Feast.*

26. "Captain Marryat at Langham," 159.

27. Ibid., 154–55.

28. Warner, *Captain Marryat,* 186.

29. Baker, *Ernest Hemingway,* 476. By this time he had also probably read Lloyd's *Captain Marryat and the Old Navy,* which describes the duties of ship's boys in its early chapters and repeats the tale of little Willie's role in *The King's Own,* and of his early death, on pp.233–34. See also p.275, where Lloyd notes the death at sea of Marryat's oldest son Frederick while Marryat was himself ill at Langham.

30. Marryat's final testament first appears in his daughter Florence Lean's *Life and Letters of Captain Marryat,* 2:299–300. See also Warner's *Captain Marryat,* 191–92, and Virginia Woolf's "The Captain's Death Bed."

31. "Captain Marryat at Langham," 161.

32. Captain Frederick Marryat, *Japhet in Search of a Father,* 1:151. There are no chapter breaks in this novel.

33. For a fuller account of these parallels, see my essay, "A Source for the Macomber 'Accident': Marryat's *Percival Keene,*" *Hemingway Review* 3 (Spring 1984): 29–37, a modified version of which appears as Appendix A of this book.

CHAPTER 4: THE KIPLING IMPRESS

1. Mary Welsh Hemingway, *How It Was,* 399.

2. See, for instance, Carol Gilligan, *In a Different Voice: Psychological Theory and Women's Development,* 6–8 ff. Gilligan argues that masculine identity "is defined through separation [from mothers] while femininity is defined through attachment [to mothers]. . . . Thus males tend to have difficulty with relationships, while females tend to have problems with individuation" (8). She holds, however, that women's "failure to separate" is not "by definition a failure to develop," as Freud had concluded, but rather a different mode of development.

3. See Bernice Kert, *The Hemingway Women,* 42.

4. Marcelline Hemingway Sanford, *At the Hemingways,* 135.

5. As noted by Michael S. Reynolds in a private collection on view at the "In Their Time" exhibit at the University of Virginia in 1977.

6. This letter, cited in the previous chapter, is in the Hemingway Collection, Kennedy Library, Boston, Mass. See also Hemingway's letter of 1 July 1954 to his friend Bill Lowe, in which—almost forty years later—he cites the same lines from Kipling.

7. Roger Lancelyn Green, *Kipling and the Children,* 124–25.

8. Ibid., 122.

9. See Robert Moss, *Rudyard Kipling and the Fiction of Adolescence*, 34–35, 39–40, 42–43, 47–48, 51–52, 60, and esp. 79.

10. Rudyard Kipling, *The Jungle Book*, vol.7 of *The Writings in Prose and Verse of Rudyard Kipling*, 300.

11. Hemingway Collection, Kennedy Library. In *The Great American Adventure* (1984) Martin Green picks up on this "hunter-warrior" connection, as embraced by Hemingway and his father, and relates it to the code of the adventurer on imperial frontiers that Hemingway first found in Kipling's children's stories, notably *The Jungle Book* and *Stalky & Co.* See especially pp.172–74, 178.

12. *The First Forty-Nine Stories*, 114, 121; Hemingway, *The Garden of Eden*, 197–202. See also the exception to this rule: two animal fables for children, "The Good Lion" and "The Faithful Bull," in which Hemingway playfully personifies himself, in *The Complete Short Stories of Ernest Hemingway*, 482–86.

13. As cited in Reynolds, *Hemingway's Reading*, 145. Professor Reynolds informs me that his source for the citation was a Sotheby's sale catalog for which he has lost the date (either 29 March or 25 October 1977 or 12 April 1978). The relevant passage reads: "Your friend Masefield is certainly great. As soon as I received your letter I went to the library and got 'The Story of a Round House.' . . . Read all the ones you recommended and at the same time got another volume—Sea Ballads, or some such name. Hope you read Stalky and Co. You'll like it."

14. Rudyard Kipling, *Stalky & Co.*, vol.18 of *Writings*, 330. Page references to this edition will appear hereafter in the text.

15. Hemingway Collection, Kennedy Library. The reference to "Darland's police" is not altogether legible, and its meaning eludes me.

16. Rudyard Kipling, *The Light That Failed*, vol.9 of *Writings*, 197. Page references to this edition will appear hereafter in the text.

17. Ernest Hemingway, *A Farewell to Arms*, 154. Lieutenant Henry recites these lines to Catherine Barkley when a motor car honks in the street outside their hotel. In the original manuscript (Hemingway Collection, Kennedy Library, pp.302–3) he goes on—against Catherine's interjected protests—to quote additional lines: "Thy beauty shall no more be found. Nor in thy marble vault shall sound my echoing song" and "The grave's a fine and private place but none I think do there embrace."

18. The letter, dated 8 September 1914, reads: "May I *please* have some *long pants*. Every other Boy in our class has them." See Grace Hemingway, "A Record of Ernest Miller Hemingway's Baby Days," Book IV, Hemingway Collection.

19. Ibid., Book II.

20. *Rudyard Kipling's Verse, Inclusive Edition, 1885–1918*, 251–52, 403–4.

21. See, for instance, Kert, *The Hemingway Women*, esp. 42, 44, 152–53, 389, 414, 425, and 492.

22. Moss, *Rudyard Kipling*, 64. See also pp.43–44.

23. Ibid., 65–66.

24. Hemingway, *Selected Letters*, ed. Carlos Baker, 466.

25. Hemingway, *The Fifth Column,* in *The First Forty-Nine Stories,* 97–98; and Kipling, *The Light That Failed,* 115–18. See also *The Great American Adventure,* 182–83, where Martin Green finds even more extensive reworkings of *The Light Failed* in *The Sun Also Rises.*

26. Hemingway, *Selected Letters,* 721–25.

27. James Jones, *From Here to Eternity,* 574–76.

28. See Jones's letter to Perkins, 21 October 1946, and Perkins' reply, 19 November 1946, Scribner Archives, Princeton University Library, Princeton, N.J. I owe thanks to John Delaney, Manuscript Cataloguer, for this information.

29. Hemingway, *Selected Letters,* 722.

30. Rudyard Kipling, "Love O' Women," in *Many Inventions,* 322–25.

31. Hemingway, *Selected Letters,* 721.

32. Rudyard Kipling, "With the Main Guard," in *Soldiers Three and Other Stories,* vol. 2 of *The Collected Works of Rudyard Kipling,* 71. I owe thanks to my colleague Elmer Blistein for the Roshus/Roscius attribution which follows this quotation in my text, and for the correction thereby of my own "ferocious" misreading.

33. *The First Forty-Nine Stories,* 237.

34. Ibid., 243–44.

35. Ibid., 245–46.

36. Kipling, *Soldiers Three,* 66, 72.

37. See, for instance, Robert W. Lewis, Jr., *Hemingway on Love,* 158–60.

38. Rudyard Kipling, "On Greenhow Hill," in *Life's Handicap: Being Stories of Mine Own People,* vol. 4 of *Collected Works,* 72, 88.

39. Edmund Wilson, "Hemingway: Gauge of Morale," in *Eight Essays,* 111–12.

40. Elliott L. Gilbert, *The Good Kipling: Studies in the Short Story,* 41–42.

41. See Hadley's letters to Ernest in the Hemingway Collection, Kennedy Library, dated 8 April and 20 May 1921. On 12 April 1921, she also compared herself to "Mr. Gadsby" from *The Story of the Gadsbys,* so as to distinguish herself from "the femininity and adoring the fuss and feathers" of Mrs. Gadsby, "like to the fuss and feathers I'm gonna suffer" in the wedding ceremony ahead.

42. Kipling's "At the End of the Passage" appears in *Life's Handicap;* "The Strange Ride of Morrowbie Jukes" in *Under the Deodars.*

43. The metropolis in Thomson's "The City of Dreadful Night" is a necropolis of the living and despairing dead. The "River of the Suicides" runs through its center, and a bronze reproduction of Albrecht Dürer's "Melencolia" dominates its northern crest. It is from the final section of the poem (XXI) that Kipling draws (and misspells) the phrase "the Melancolia that transcends all wit" for Dick Heldar's version of Dürer's painting—to which Thomson also devotes an earlier poem. As Anne Ridler points out in her introduction to *Poems and Some Letters of James Thomson,* xliii, T. S. Eliot was early influenced by the "City" and seems to have drawn on it for his "unreal city" in *The Waste Land.* Kipling's sketch of a corpse-strewn city, using Thomson's title, appears in *Life's Handicap.* Hemingway would have been familiar with it by

1932, when he wrote "A Natural History of the Dead." A 1931 edition of *Life's Handicap* is listed as being in his Key West library.

CHAPTER 5: *WUTHERING HEIGHTS*

1. See Grace Hall Hemingway's "A Record of Ernest Miller Hemingway's Baby Days," Book V, Dec. 21, 1914–July 21, 1917, Hemingway Collection, Kennedy Library, Boston.

2. See Marcelline Hemingway Sanford, *At the Hemingways*, 100–102; Madelaine Hemingway Miller, *Ernie*, 51–53; Leicester Hemingway, *My Brother, Ernest Hemingway*, 35–37; and Mary Welsh Hemingway, *How It Was*, 287–88. See also Carlos Baker's summary account, in *Ernest Hemingway*, 31–33.

3. "The Last Good Country" has been published posthumously in Ernest Hemingway, *The Nick Adams Stories*, ed. Philip Young, 56–114. The text—which contains many discrepancies—was put together from two manuscript versions by the editors of Scribner's, who first published the above collection in 1972. Page references to the novella in my text are from the 1973 Bantam edition.

4. See Hemingway, *Selected Letters*, 675.

5. See ibid. for frequent references to his problems with Fenton and Young. See also Philip Young's foreword to the revised version of his book, *Ernest Hemingway: A Reconsideration*, 1–28, for his own account of such difficulties. Charles A. Fenton's *The Apprenticeship of Ernest Hemingway*, on Hemingway's reporting years in Kansas and Toronto, was published by Viking Press in 1958.

6. See Grace's letter to her husband, Clarence, describing the game wardens' visit, in Leicester Hemingway, *My Brother*, 35–37. In Madelaine "Sunny" Hemingway Miller's account (*Ernie*, 51–53), her mother says, "Sunny, go get the shotgun," when ordering the recalcitrant game wardens to leave her property.

7. See Baker, *Ernest Hemingway*, 19. For Grace's spirituality, and for the cover trip to New York to protect her ailing husband, see Reynolds, *The Young Hemingway*, 131–32, 83.

8. See Alice Hunt Sokoloff, *Hadley, The First Mrs. Hemingway*, 2, 6.

9. In a letter dated 24 June 1921, quoted in ibid., 1.

10. Sanford, *At the Hemingways*, 55, 57–58.

11. Leicester Hemingway, *My Brother*, 42.

12. Baker, *Ernest Hemingway*, 112.

13. Ernest Hemingway, *For Whom the Bell Tolls*, 235. Page references in the text are to the 1968 paperback edition.

14. In a letter dated 12 May 1927, Hemingway Collection, Kennedy Library. See also Miller, *Ernie*, 106–8.

15. See Montgomery, *Hemingway in Michigan*, 123.

16. Baker, *Ernest Hemingway*, 112, 169.

17. See Ms. p.84 of the second version, "The Last Good Country," Hemingway

Collection, Kennedy Library. The passage which Scribner's fastidious (or perhaps tasteful) editors have excised reads as follows (I include the framing lines from *The Nick Adams Stories*, 49, in italics):

> *"All right," Nick said, "I'll never lie to you."*
> "I don't mean I want you telling me everything," Mr. John said. "Like if you jerk off."
> "I don't jerk off," Nick told him. "I fuck."
> "I guess that's as simple a word for it as any," Mr. John said. "But don't do it any more than you have to."
> "I know. I started it too early I guess."
> "But don't do it when you're drunk and always make water afterwards and wash yourself good with soap and water."
> "Yes Sir," Nick had said. "I don't have much trouble with it lately."
> *"What became of your girl?"*

18. Leicester Hemingway, *My Brother*, 35–37.

19. R. D. Blackmore, *Lorna Doone*, 1:189.

20. Emily Brontë, *Wuthering Heights: An Authoritative Text with Essays in Criticism*, 2nd ed., ed. William M. Sale, Jr., p.39. Page references in the text are to this 1972 edition. For a metaphorical approach to Heathcliff's bastardy, see Gilbert and Gubar, *The Madwoman in the Attic*, 259, 294–98. Here the authors discuss Heathcliff's "illegitimacy," and his attack on "legitimate" society, by aligning him with Shakespeare's Edmund in *King Lear* ("Nature's bastard son") and with the femaleness of bastards, younger sons, devils, and orphans as rebels and outcasts from patriarchal society.

21. See Hadley's references to "The Brushwood Boy" as a shared interest in two letters to Ernest, 8 April and 28 May 1921, in the Hemingway Collection, Kennedy Library.

22. See Baker, *Ernest Hemingway*, 456. While visiting relations in Hawaii in 1941, Hemingway had spoken to several professors from the University of Hawaii, advising one of them not to let his students read *A Farewell to Arms*, which was "an immoral book," whereas *The Sun Also Rises* was "very moral." I owe thanks to a local Hemingway scholar, Robert Pilkington, for calling this passage to my attention.

23. In *Hemingway on Love*, Robert W. Lewis, Jr., argues that Hemingway readies himself for *agape* by rejecting the falsely selfless romantic love offered by Catherine Barkley in *A Farewell to Arms*, then moving on to Robert Jordan's purgation of egotism through his love for Maria in *For Whom the Bell Tolls*. See especially chapters 3 and 8.

24. See Gilbert and Gubar, *The Madwoman in the Attic*, 264.

25. See especially the early chapters of Frances Hodgson Burnett's *A Lady of Quality*.

26. See Gilbert and Gubar, *The Madwoman in the Attic*, 264–65.

27. D. H. Lawrence, *Selected Literary Criticism*, ed. Anthony Beal, 427.

28. See "The Last Good Country," Ms. pp. 11–13, second version, Hemingway Collection, Kennedy Library. The long excised passage falls between "'Let me kiss you,' her brother said, 'Just for an emergency,'" on p.64 of *The Nick Adams Stories,* and the next line in that text. At the end of the passage Nick apologizes to Littless for not having been a "good brother," a "good man," and a "good friend," and tells her that being with Trudy would not even be his "second best" hope.

29. See Madelaine Hemingway Miller's *Ernie,* 36.

30. Though he would later claim he always hated her, Ernest was especially close to Marcelline during the twinship experiments in his infancy. His comradeship with his tomboy sister Sunny, which began in the blue-heron period of adolescence, proved much more durable. On his return from the war in 1919, however, his second oldest sister Ursula proved especially comforting (*Selected Letters,* 697) and seems to have become his lifelong favorite. He called her his "best sister" in 1933 (*Selected Letters,* 398), and "the nicest and best" of all his sisters in 1948 (*How It Was,* 286). "When I was a kid we loved each other very much and we still do," he told Harvey Breit in 1956 (*Selected Letters,* 866). His baby sister Carol, with whom he shared birthday celebrations after her arrival in 1911, was another durable favorite, at least until her marriage against his wishes in 1933. Ernest considered her the "most beautiful of the family" and was "absolutely nuts about her," perhaps because "she looked as a girl exactly as he looked as a boy" (*How It Was,* 286).

31. Spacks, *The Female Imagination,* 171–82.

32. See ibid., 181: "The conviction that the old inevitably maim the young, not through desire but by emotional necessity, permeates *Wuthering Heights.*"

33. Charlotte Brontë, Preface to Emily Brontë, *Wuthering Heights: An Authoritative Text with Essays in Criticism,* 9–10.

34. Baker, *Ernest Hemingway,* 12.

35. Hemingway, *Selected Letters,* 99

36. Ibid., 697.

37. Ibid., 697–98.

38. See Montgomery, *Hemingway in Michigan,* 90; Mary Hemingway, *How It Was,* 286, 360; Baker, *Ernest Hemingway,* 32, 303, 306–7; and Hemingway, *Selected Letters,* 671.

CHAPTER 6: JOHN MASEFIELD

1. I owe thanks to Michael S. Reynolds for the letter quoted here, which he found in a Sotheby's catalog, ca.1977–78. I have been unable to locate the exact number.

2. In 1913 Macmillan published Masefield's *Salt-Water Ballads* and *The Story of a Round-House and Other Poems.* Page references to the latter will follow in the text.

3. See Reynolds, *Hemingway's Reading,* 155.

4. *The First Forty-nine Stories and the Play "The Fifth Column,"* 463–64.

5. Jeffrey Meyers, *Hemingway: A Biography,* 21. See also Baker, *Ernest Hemingway,* 15, 237, and Griffin, *Along With Youth,* 12.

6. See Constance Babington Smith, *John Masefield: A Life*, 9–30.

7. Ibid., 122–33, 158–59.

8. "Learns to Commune with Fairies, Now Wins the $40,000 Nobel Prize," *Toronto Star Weekly*, 24 November 1923, p.35, as cited by Robert O. Stephens, ed., in *Hemingway's Nonfiction: The Public Voice*, 131.

9. Reynolds, *Hemingway's Reading*, 156; Brasch and Sigman, *Hemingway's Library*, 243.

10. Smith, *John Masefield*, 4–14, 31–46, 51–55.

11. John Masefield, *Victorious Troy; or, The Hurrying Angel*, 193–94.

12. For Sunny and Ernie's nicknames and private language, see Miller, *Ernie*, 58, 89–91.

13. Smith, *John Masefield*, 101–5, 156–57, 159, 174, 182, 214, 224.

14. Baker, *Ernest Hemingway*, 55, 726; see also Grace's letter to Ernest, May 16, 1918, Hemingway Collection, Kennedy Library.

15. In *The First Forty-Nine Stories and the Play "The Fifth Column,"* 239–40. Page numbers that follow in the text are to this 1938 Modern Library edition.

16. Robert Scholes, "Decoding Papa: 'A Very Short Story' as Work and Text," in *Semiotics and Interpretation*, 110–26.

17. Alice Miller, *Prisoners of Childhood: The Drama of the Gifted Child and the Search for the True Self*, 12, 20. Miller also speaks, on p.67, "of the patient who was obsessively forced to make conquests with women, to seduce and then to abandon them, until he was at last able to experience in his analysis how he himself had repeatedly been abandoned by his mother."

18. See Peter Griffin's doctoral thesis, "Ernest Hemingway: In My Beginning Is My End," and his recent study of Hemingway's early years, *Along with Youth*.

19. Hemingway's sisters Marcelline, Ursula, and Carol had lifetime marriages with one person. Sunny was twice widowed. Hemingway's brother, Leicester, once divorced, had been the "last of the litter" and his mother's favorite once the other children had left home. He was also inclined to emulate his older brother, even to the point of suicide.

20. Max Westbrook, "Grace under Pressure: Hemingway and the Summer of 1920," in *Ernest Hemingway: The Writer in Context*, ed. James Nagel, 77–106. Neither Jeffrey Meyers nor Peter Griffin, in their recent biographies, have taken Westbrook's findings into account. Both accordingly perpetuate the mythic version of the clash.

21. Westbrook, "Grace under Pressure," 83.

22. Ibid., 91.

23. The "Bank Account" letter, dated 24 July 1920, is in the Hemingway Collection, Kennedy Library. See also Kenneth Lynn, *Hemingway*, 117–18, for a fairly full transcription of the letter—which Lynn characterizes as "a rejection slip with a vengeance."

24. Westbrook, "Grace under Pressure," 79–80, 83–86, 103.

25. Griffin, "In My Beginning Is My End," 133: "There is . . . good reason to

believe that the deficiencies which most of Hemingway's commentators are convinced Dr. Adams and Dr. Hemingway shared were actually projections of the inferiorities Ernest Hemingway feared were an ineradicable part of himself."

CHAPTER 7: THREE LITTLE SAVAGES

1. I quote here from a letter by Allen Tate to Carlos Baker, 2 April 1963, now on file at the Firestone Library at Princeton: "I first met Ernest in September in 1929 in Sylvia Beach's bookshop in Paris. I was talking to Sylvia and I was aware of a big dark fellow a few feet away; but I went out, only to be called back by Sylvia. She introduced me to Ernest Hemingway, who said without preliminary that I had been wrong in a review to attribute to him the influence of Marryat and Defoe. (Some weeks later John Bishop told me that when he first knew Ernest *Peter Simple* lay for weeks on his night-table.)" Tate himself shows no signs in this letter that he did not in fact mention Marryat in his reviews of Hemingway's work. This may not be surprising, since he later says that Hemingway "was very childlike: he wanted me to admire his latest book [*A Farewell to Arms*] to counteract my rough handling of (I think) *The Torrents of Spring*." Tate had actually called *The Torrents of Spring* "a small masterpiece of American fiction"; it was *The Sun Also Rises* he had handled roughly.

2. See Allen Tate, "Good Prose," *The Nation* 122 (10 February 1926): 160–62, and "The Spirituality of Roughnecks," *The Nation* 123 (28 July 1926): 89–90. The first is a review of *In Our Time*; the second of *The Torrents of Spring*. A third review, of *The Sun Also Rises*, appears in "Hard-Boiled," *The Nation* 123 (15 December 1926): 642–44. These are Tate's only recorded reviews of Hemingway's fiction; none of them mentions Captain Marryat. See Robert O. Stephens, ed. *Ernest Hemingway: The Critical Reception*, pp. 14, 25–27, 42–44, for transcripts of the review. The lines from *Captain Singleton*, which I cite below, are missing from the transcript of the first review.

3. Tate, "Good Prose," 162.

4. See p. 66 of the 1969 Oxford edition, ed. Shiv K. Kumar, *The Life, Adventures, and Pyracies of the Famous Captain Singleton*. Hemingway later owned a Dent Everyman edition (1922).

5. See Brasch and Sigman, *Hemingway's Library*, 96.

6. Lawrence, *Selected Literary Criticism*, 427.

7. Captain Frederick Marryat, *Peter Simple* and *The Little Savage*, Illustrated Sterling Edition, ed. W. L. Courtney, p. 1 of *The Little Savage*. Page references in the text are to this 1896 Estes edition.

8. Hemingway, *The Garden of Eden*, 181.

9. Ibid., 201.

10. Baker, *Ernest Hemingway*, 626.

11. Ernest Hemingway, *The First Forty-Nine Stories and the Play "The Fifth Column,"* 461–62.

12. Saul Bellow, "Hemingway and the Image of Man," *Partisan Review* 20 (May–June 1953): 340: "There is a repetition-compulsion in Hemingway, and he is the

poet of the crippled state in which men survive the heavy blows of fortune, the mutilations of war, the cruelties of women. Wounded and broken, they somehow mend; the hero establishes an economy of imagination that frees his muscles, his senses and his spirit to accomplish this recovery." See also Mark Spilka, "The Death of Love in *The Sun Also Rises*," in *Hemingway: A Collection of Critical Essays*, ed. Robert P. Weeks, 131–33.

13. For the origins of the animal fables, see Baker, *Ernest Hemingway*, 624, 904. The quotes from *The Old Man and the Sea* are from pp.20–21 of the 1952 Scribner edition.

14. Hemingway, *The Garden of Eden*, 198–201.

15. Letters in the Hemingway Collection, Kennedy Library, Boston. For "The Outsong," see Rudyard Kipling, *The Jungle Book*, in *Works*, 7:295. Page references in the text are to this 1898 New York edition.

16. Hemingway, *The First Forty-Nine Stories*, 193.

17. Sanford, *At the Hemingway's*, 134: "Daddy let Ernie help him in his office at times and watch while he dressed wounds, or when he treated the Ottawa Indians up at the lake. Once . . . Ernie helped while my father cleaned out a bad cut suffered by a young boy. . . . Later, Ernie watched an operation. Dressed in a white gown, he was permitted to stand at the top rear of the operating theater at the hospital where Daddy was on the staff as head of obstetrics. Ernie was interested, but he sat down when he felt faint and he did not go again."

18. Ernest Hemingway, "Three Shots," *The Nick Adams Stories*, 3–5; see also "Indian Camp," ibid., 10.

19. Hemingway, "Soldier's Home," *The First Forty-Nine Stories*, 250.

20. Item 383, Hemingway Collection, Kennedy Library, Boston.

21. Doctorow, "Braver Than We Thought," 45.

CHAPTER 8: THREE WOUNDED WARRIORS

1. Allen Tate to Carlos Baker, 2 April 1963, Firestone Library, Princeton.

2. Tate, "Good Prose" and "The Spirituality of Roughnecks," as quoted in Stephens, *Ernest Hemingway*, 14, 26.

3. Tate, "Hard-Boiled," as quoted in Stephens, 42–43.

4. Hemingway, *Selected Letters*, 239–40.

5. Ibid., 745.

6. See Fitzgerald's long letter to Hemingway on cutting the early chapters, in Frederic Joseph Svoboda's *Hemingway and "The Sun Also Rises": The Crafting of a Style*, 140: "He isn't *like an impotent man. He's like a man in a sort of moral chastity belt*" (italics mine). See also Baker, *Ernest Hemingway*, 203: "The situation between Barnes and Brett Ashley, as Ernest imagined it, could very well be a projection of his own inhibitions about sleeping with Duff."

7. *The Garden of Eden* manuscript, bk.1, chap.1, pp.17, 23–24, in Hemingway Collection, Kennedy Library, Boston, Mass. For reproductions of bronze and plaster

versions of the statues in question, see especially *The Sculptures of Auguste Rodin,* ed. John Tancock.

8. Plimpton, "Ernest Hemingway," in *Writers at Work.*

9. Ernest Hemingway, *The Sun Also Rises,* 22, 24–28. Page references in the text are to this 1954 edition.

10. Craik, *John Halifax, Gentleman,* 175, 249–53.

11. Michael Arlen, *The Green Hat,* 95, 229, 231.

12. Baker, *Ernest Hemingway,* 189. See also *Selected Letters,* 238. For Fitzgerald's acute observation that the original opening chapters are indeed written in the effusive style of Michael Arlen (to which Fitzgerald strongly objected), see Svoboda, *Hemingway,* 138: "You've done a lot of writing that *honestly* reminded me of Michael Arlen." See also chapter 14 of *The Torrents of Spring,* where Yogi Johnson tells a version of Arlen's "The Romantic Lady" in which a beautiful woman uses him for voyeuristic purposes (79–81). In *Along with Youth,* 65, Peter Griffin mistakes this obvious borrowing for autobiographical truth.

13. Michael Arlen, *The Romantic Lady,* 4. Page references in the text are to this 1921 New York edition.

14. See Erica Jong, *Fear of Flying,* and the novels that follow, especially *Fanny,* in which she more or less appropriates for her sex the previously male world of sexual adventure and conquest.

15. Hemingway to Maxwell Perkins, 19 November 1926, in *Selected Letters,* 229.

16. See Baker, *Ernest Hemingway,* 30, 41, for Hemingway's lifelong nickname "Hemingstein" and its high school origin in antisemitic games about pawnbrokers. His "Cohen and Stein" routine with his high school friend Ray Ohlsen is particularly relevant to Jake's affinities with Cohn in *The Sun Also Rises.*

17. Allen Tate, "Hard-Boiled," as quoted in Stephens, 44.

18. Tate, "Random Thoughts on the 1920s," *Minnesota Review* 1 (Fall 1970): 46–56.

19. For the Emmett Hancock chapters (Item 240, Hemingway Collection, Kennedy Library, Boston), see Bernard Oldsey, "The Original Beginning," in *Hemingway's Hidden Craft: The Writing of "A Farewell to Arms,"* 93–99. For Hadley's desire to break out of the world's jail with Ernest, see Sokoloff, *Hadley,* 1.

20. See Oldsey, "Original Beginning," 98, and Ernest Hemingway, *A Farewell to Arms,* 93. Page references in the text are to this 1957 edition.

21. Doctorow, "Braver Than We Thought," 45. Here Doctorow speaks of the hero's "consummate self-assurance in handling the waiters, maids and hoteliers of Europe who, in this book as in Hemingway's others, come forward to supply the food and drink, the corkscrews and ice-cubes and beds and fishing rods his young American colonists require."

22. *A Farewell to Arms* manuscript, variant p.206, Hemingway Collection, Kennedy Library: "And now that she was gone down the corridor, I felt as though all of me was gone away with her." See also Michael S. Reynolds, *Hemingway's First War: The Making of "A Farewell to Arms,"* 289.

23. For the most explicit confirmation, see Mary Welsh Hemingway, *How It Was,* 467, where she quotes from a diary insert written by Ernest on 12 December 1953: "She has always wanted to be a boy and thinks as a boy without ever losing any femininity. . . . She loves me to be her girls, which I love to be, not being absolutely stupid. . . . In return she makes me awards and at night we do every sort of thing which pleases her and which pleases me. . . . Since I have never cared for any man . . . I loved feeling the embrace of Mary which came to me as something quite new and outside all tribal law." For more implicit references, see pp.298–99 and 371. On p.466 sodomy is also clownishly implied as part of their sexual repertoire, again by Ernest. For androgynous precedents with Hadley, see Hemingway, *A Moveable Feast,* 20–21, where, after a discussion of homosexuality versus lesbianism with Gertrude Stein, Ernest returns home to share his "newly acquired knowledge" with Hadley: "In the night we were happy with our own knowledge we already had and other new knowledge we had acquired in the mountains." In *The Garden of Eden* manuscript at the Kennedy Library (where the phrase "outside all tribal law" frequently recurs), artists Nick and Barbara Sheldon make androgynous love as book 2, chapter 1, opens, with Barbara pressing down lightly but firmly on her supinely cooperative husband in a Paris flat like that which Ernest shared with Hadley, circa 1925. In book 3 Barbara's erotic attraction to Catherine Bourne (based largely on Pauline Pfeiffer) suggests also that the mountain knowledge referred to in *A Moveable Feast* may refer to androgynous activities inspired by Pauline Pfeiffer's visit to Schruns—at which time, according to reports on the Sokoloff tapes by Peter Griffin, she liked to crawl into bed with the Hemingways each morning.

24. Baker, *Ernest Hemingway,* 112.

25. Ibid., 250–51.

26. Oldsey, "Original Beginning," 98.

27. Millicent Bell, "*A Farewell to Arms:* Pseudoautobiography and Personal Metaphor," in *Ernest Hemingway: The Writer in Context,* ed. James Nagel, 114.

28. Faith Pullin, "Hemingway and the Secret Language of Hate," in *Ernest Hemingway: New Critical Essays,* ed. A. Robert Lee, 184–85.

29. See Wilson, "Hemingway: Gauge of Morale," in *Eight Essays;* Gershon Legman, *Love and Death,* 86–90; Isaac Rosenfeld, "A Farewell to Hemingway," *Kenyon Review* 13 (1951): 147–55; and Richard B. Hovey, *Hemingway: The Inward Terrain,* 75–76.

30. Judith Fetterley, "Hemingway's Resentful Cryptogram," in *The Resisting Reader: A Feminist Approach to American Fiction,* 59, 64.

31. Bell, "*A Farewell to Arms,*" 111.

32. Fetterley, "Hemingway's Resentful Cryptogram," 52, 64, 71.

33. Spilka, "Hemingway and Fauntleroy," 350–52.

34. For an account of these differences and of the novel's genesis, see Reynolds, *Hemingway's First War,* 3, 5.

35. See, for example, Henry Villard, "A Prize Specimen of Wounded Hero," *Yankee Magazine,* July 1979, 134–35; and Baker, *Ernest Hemingway,* 71–73.

36. Sanford, *At the Hemingways,* 190–92.

37. Bell, *"A Farewell to Arms,"* 112–13, 115–16, 120, 123–24.

CHAPTER 9: TOUGH MAMAS AND SAFARI WIVES

1. Ernest Hemingway, *Death in the Afternoon,* 11. Page references in the text are to this 1960 edition.

2. I. A. Richards, "Sentimentality and Inhibition," *Practical Criticism,* 253: "The man who, in reaction to the commoner naive forms of sentimentality, prides himself upon his hard-headedness and hard-heartedness, and his hard-boiledness generally, and seeks out or invents aspects with a bitter or squalid character, for no better reason than this, is only displaying a more sophisticated form of sentimentality."

3. Ernest Hemingway, *Green Hills of Africa,* 6. Page references in the text are to this 1963 edition. For a more positive reading of *Green Hills of Africa,* as a masculinist adventure story on the postcolonial frontier, featuring the "aristo-military caste" that Hemingway shares with Kipling, see Martin Green, *The Great American Adventure,* 167–83.

4. Bell, *"A Farewell to Arms,"* 114.

5. Hemingway Collection, Kennedy Library, Boston. E.g., the following: 13 December 1926: "Ernest is perfect, and very smart in the head, and in the suits, too, and a great classic beauty." 15 March 1927: "This is the late afternoon of the first day of the Italian tour for the promotion of masculine society—and it isn't too soon to say that I hope this tour will last you a long time, for I'm very sure your wife is going to be opposed to them." 6 August 1928: "When I get with you again I'm going to be a model of wifely arts and crafts. It's going to be *lovely, lovely, lovely* to be with you again, and Wyoming will be perfect." 12 November 1929: "This is certainly an empty house without you. . . . But I think it is really a good thing that you went away, because look how terrible I was about the suitcase (and how sweet you were) and now I just lie in bed and plan how to be a better wife." 13 May 1931: "I miss you all the time and I don't care about daily events and all I want is you." 11 August 1932: "It seems to me I'm very soon again a long way from you. Don't like this. Maybe when we get together again we will stay together for a long time." 23 April 1933: "Being a good girl, and certainly incidently having a dull time. Doing all the things I do when you're around—I mean the house, children, yard, etc. but oh the difference to me—no salt, no beans no coconut oil—if you know what I mean." 17 June 1934: "It will be lovely to have you and I will NEVER cross you in *anything.*" 29 September 1934: "My God it's lonesome with you gone, and if my hair were just a little better I'd be on the boat tomorrow." Undated 1935: "I thought maybe I'd disgusted you. Didn't really, but I had disgusted myself. And why the hell couldn't you make the exception anyway, without my acting like a fool. Who, I'd like to know, is the head of the house anyway. And your letter was so beautiful and has bound me to you with whoops [*sic*] of steel." 20 April 1937: "I love you and would like to see you sometime. Your loving and lonesome wife." 2 September 1938: "I miss you very much, but I feel surprising[ly]

serene about the fate of you and me—but I do hope you won't stay away from a loving wife too long."

6. *The Short Stories of Ernest Hemingway*. Page references in the text are to this 1966 edition.

7. Baker, *Ernest Hemingway*, 323, 363–64

8. See also *Green Hills of Africa*, 32, where Poor Old Mama reports that Kandinsky, an intelligent man, is "bitter about American women," and Pop responds, "So am I. . . . He's a good man."

9. Ernest Hemingway, *To Have and Have Not*, 116, 128, 258. Page references in the text are to this 1937 edition.

10. Baker, *Ernest Hemingway*, 786. See also Pauline's letters to Ernest: 25 September 1926: "And remember especially we're the same guy." 1 October 1926: "So we being the same guy . . ." 6 October 1926: "Oh you are so lovely. And a great classic beauty. And perfect." 29 October 1926: "I wouldn't be able to write this if we weren't the same guy."

11. Ernest Hemingway, *For Whom the Bell Tolls*, 176. Page references in the text are to this 1940 edition.

12. Baker, *Ernest Hemingway*, 332, 379–80. See also my concluding chapter.

CHAPTER 10: DAUGHTERS AND SONS

1. Baker, *Ernest Hemingway*, 417, 441.

2. Wilson, "Hemingway: Gauge of Morale," 111–12.

3. Hemingway, *For Whom the Bell Tolls*, 404–6; Baker, *Ernest Hemingway*, 45–46. See also p.410 of *For Whom the Bell Tolls*, where Jordan limits himself to a "dry" farewell with old Anselmo—who will soon die in the attack on the bridge.

4. Page references in the text are to the 1971 edition of *Across the River and Into the Trees*.

5. Baker, *Ernest Hemingway*, 626.

6. See Peter Griffin's *Along with Youth* for its ongoing account of the importance Grace Hemingway attached to her father as a model for the son who bore his name.

7. Ernest Hemingway, *The Old Man and the Sea*, 21.

8. See Ernest Hemingway, *Islands in the Stream*, 343–45. The page reference in the text is to this 1970 edition.

9. Baker, *Ernest Hemingway*, 634.

10. Ernest Hemingway, "The Last Good Country," in *The Nick Adams Stories*, 84. Page references in the text to this and other Nick Adams stories are to this 1973 edition.

In the original manuscript, in a passage excised from this exchange but quoted in full in note 17, Chapter 5, above, Packard advises Nick not to "fuck" any more than he has to, not to do it when he's drunk, "and always make water afterwards and wash yourself good with soap and water." We learn also that Nick doesn't "jerk off" when Packard says not to tell him everything, "Like if you jerk off." This earthy exchange—

while not without its own peculiarities—designedly contrasts with the avoidance of such matters by Nick's father in "Fathers and Sons."

11. As Constance Montgomery observes in *Hemingway in Michigan*, 133, Hemingway's girlfriend Marjorie Bump, the model for Marjorie in "The Three-Day Blow," had waited on tables at the Dilworths' hotel when Hemingway stayed there in 1919–20. This might explain Mr. Packard's awareness of Nick's lost girlfriend. But Nick is only sixteen in "The Last Good Country," and if his life follows Hemingway's, as Philip Young believes, he would not meet Marjorie until after the war. (See Young's case for the dating of the Marjorie stories in "'Big World Out There': *The Nick Adams Stories*," *Novel: A Forum on Fiction* 6 [Fall 1971]: 14.) Trudy therefore seems the likelier girlfriend. As Nick tells Mr. Packard, she is now "working up at the Soo"—that is to say, at Sault Ste. Marie at the Canadian border in Upper Michigan—where the wardens fear, with some justice, that Nick may flee. In an earlier excised passage, however, Littless tells Nick that Trudy is working at the "Indian Play," a spectacle usually performed north of Petoskey, between Petoskey and Harbor Springs.

12. Hemingway Collection, Kennedy Library, Boston, Mass.

13. Hemingway had begun the tale with a thirteen-page account of Nick's departure with Littless which does not develop their return to the summer cottage for supplies or their trip to the Packards' store to sell the illegal trout Nick has caught. Hemingway decided to include these episodes, along with other changes, and began writing a new version of the opening events which constitutes the bulk of the 102-page manuscript. The new version begins on a page numbered 3, which plainly indicates his intention to cut back into the original opening on that page. But Scribner's editors decided to include six of the original thirteen pages as the opening, thereby creating the discrepancy (which Hemingway would have avoided) of illegal game found in both boat and springhouse. Hemingway's decision to have Littless trick Nick into taking her rather than persuade him is also violated, with some damage to sense when Nick is upset by the letter Littless leaves for her mother (66), although Littless has already told him she would leave it (59). Littless's resourcefulness and astuteness, and her stake in the escape, are also diminished by these changes, as by the Trudy cuts in the second opening cited in my text.

14. Young, "'Big World Out There,'" 11–12.

15. The original opening paragraph appears on the same page with a roughed-out telegram to Philip Young dated 17 January 1952 (Hemingway Collection, Kennedy Library, Boston).

16. See the comments in Stephens, *Ernest Hemingway: The Critical Reception*, 483, 485, 487, 488, 493.

17. Young, "'Big World Out There,'" 12

18. Kenneth Lynn, *Hemingway*, 57: "The further the fugitives retreat from civilization, the more incestuous they become. Thus, the kisses they exchange at the outset of the story are merely warm-ups for the moment when Littless sits on Nick's lap and he gets an erection. The aggressive Littless also leads her passive brother into a whole

series of sexually suggestive conversations, about whores, menstrual periods, and above all, androgyny." The passage Lynn seems to have in mind here, in which Littless begins to talk imaginatively about getting knockout drops and assisting the Queen of the Whores in a Sheboygan saloon, is plainly humorous in tenor. Thus, instead of leading Nick into suggestive depths, the child spoofs adult sexuality and her own imagined part in it:

> "I'm the sister or the brother of a morbid writer and I'm delicately brought up. This makes me intensely desirable to the main whore and to all of her circle."
> "Did you get the knockout drops?"
> "Of course. She said, 'Hon, take these little old drops.' 'Thank you,' I said. 'Give my regards to your morbid brother and ask him to stop by the Emporium anytime he is at Sheboygan.'"
> "Get off my lap," Nick said.
> "That's just the way they talk in the Emporium," Littless said.
> "I have to get supper. Aren't you hungry?" (96–97)

The erection Lynn deduces here comes from the implications of the scene Littless imagines at the Emporium, which she may or may not understand but which puts a comic coat on Nick's practical demand that she get off his lap so that he can make supper. Whether that coat hides a real erection is anybody's guess; the essentially playful innocence of the scene—which wholly escapes Lynn—suggests otherwise.

19. Young, "'Big World Out There,'" 12.

20. See Paul Smith, "The Tenth Indian and the Thing Left Out," in *Ernest Hemingway: The Writer in Context*, ed. James Nagel, 67–68, 73–74.

21. The date of this letter is uncertain. Though Sunny speaks in her memoirs of meeting Robert St. John after two years of nurse's training, which would be in 1926, she mentions "Bob" in a letter to her brother in December 1925 as being jealous of another man with whom she had taken a recent trip. She passes off his jealously lightly ("I'm not a sort to worry. I have others—tra! la!"), which would seem to indicate that their romance was dissolving and that her letter asking Ernest for advice had been sent earlier in 1925. Its reception came, in any case, when Ernest was either in the midst of writing *The Sun Also Rises* or finished with it, and ripe for the seeds of a new novel.

22. Madelaine Hemingway Miller, *Ernie*, 105.

CHAPTER 11: PAPA'S BARBERSHOP QUINTET

1. F. Scott Fitzgerald, *Tender Is the Night*, in *The Portable F. Scott Fitzgerald*, ed. John O'Hara, 531–32. Though Hemingway bought and read the 1934 edition of the novel, he also bought the 1945 edition of "THE POTABLE FITZGERALD," as he called it, and probably reread the novel in that edition by 1946, when he began writing *The Garden of Eden*. Thus, in a retrospective letter to Fitzgerald's biographer,

Arthur Mizener, on 6 July 1949, he shrewdly diagnoses John O'Hara's introduction to the edition as being "wrapped in O'Hara's old coonskin coat that he never wore to Yale" (*Selected Letters* 657). Certainly O'Hara's closing nostalgic note—"And always, without fail, whether I'm going to the Plaza for a haircut or a drink . . . I am half-prepared to see Scott himself" (xix)—must have roused Hemingway's more critical memories of Scott's drinks and haircuts, or coincided, at the least, with ruminations about barbershops in his own and Fitzgerald's and perhaps even their common predecessor Ring Lardner's fictions.

2. *Selected Letters*, 408. A version of this passage also appears in Arthur Mizener's biography of Fitzgerald, *The Far Side of Paradise*, 238–39, which Hemingway received from Mizener in January 1951 and read with mixed feelings (*Letters*, 716–19).

3. Meyers, *Hemingway*, 346.

4. *A Farewell to Arms*, 292–93.

5. Angus P. Collins, "Homosexuality and the Genesis of *Tender Is the Night*," *Journal of Modern Literature* 13 (March 1986): 170–71.

6. Mizener, *The Far Side of Paradise*, 239. In this 1951 biography Mizener had reviewed Hemingway's relations with Fitzgerald, quoted from Hemingway's letters, and opened up slants on Fitzgerald's work and world that seem to have figured in Hemingway's ongoing work on *The Garden of Eden*. See, for example, the poem "Do you remember . . . That I hated to swim naked from the rocks / While you liked absolutely nothing better" (ibid., 235), which Hemingway would reverse for David and Catherine; or Zelda's "empty shell" letter (236), which becomes a model for Catherine's farewell letter (*The Garden of Eden*, 237). In his correspondence with Mizener Hemingway grudgingly admitted that "your book did tell me many things I did not know . . . I learned a lot and I was very grateful." *Letters*, 718.

7. *The Garden of Eden*, 247 pages, cited hereafter in the text as *GE* plus page numbers. References to the manuscript version of the novel are from the 1500-page copy in the Hemingway Collection at the Kennedy Library in Boston and are cited in the text as "Ms." plus book/chapter/and page numbers.

8. "The Metamorphoses of Ovid," *Rodin Skulpturen*, 1934 ed., plate 62; 1953 ed., plate 52; and in the white plaster version, *Rodin Sculptures*, ed. Jennifer Hawkins, plates 10–11; and *The Sculptures of Auguste Rodin*, ed. John Tancock, plates 36-1, 36-3. Interestingly, 36-3 is called "Daphnis and Chloe," as if the figures were male and female.

9. Sanford, *At the Hemingways*, 109–11.

10. Meyers, *Hemingway*, 435, 437.

11. Baker, *Ernest Hemingway*, 583, 891, from a letter to his friend Buck Lanham, 19 June 1948, on the novel's theme.

12. The name Bourne contains "born," "burn," "borne," and "bourn" as its obvious implied meanings, with "borne" suggesting either bearing burdens or being carried along passively. Hemingway himself plays with the second and fourth meanings late in the novel, as David and Marita find relief in verbal banter from the burning of the African tales: "Who burned the Bournes out? Crazy woman burned

out the Bournes," says David, and then decides "I'll write in the sand. . . . That's my new medium. I'm going to be a sand writer. The David Bournes, sand writers, announce their unsuccessful peak into that undiscovered country from whose bourne no traveller returns who hasn't been there. That's from a poem Shakespeare and I wrote together. He was extremely talented and Duff Cooper believes he was a sergeant. . . . It's a very convincing theory" (Ms. 3/44/24–25).

Interestingly, Hemingway seems to have drawn the name Bourne, along with such Shakespearean associations, from a story called "Her Privates We" that he included in 1942 in his anthology *Men at War* (775–83). The story begins with an epigraph from Shakespeare which Hemingway also used in the Macomber story— the famous "we owe God a death" passage—and concerns the trench experiences in World War I of a private named Bourne. I owe thanks to correspondent William Adair for drawing this derivation to my attention.

13. Griffin, *Along with Youth*, 142–43, 184–85; Meyers, *Hemingway*, 58, 346.

14. According to Peter Griffin, in private conversation, October 1986, on the tapes taken by Alice Sokoloff. See also Baker, *Ernest Hemingway*, 221–22.

15. Reynolds, *The Young Hemingway*, 78–81, 105.

16. Cf. Meyers, *Hemingway*, 76–77, and *Selected Letters*, 650: "I always wanted to fuck her and she knew it and it was a good healthy feeling and made more sense than some of the talk."

17. Baker, *Ernest Hemingway*, 234; *Selected Letters*, 245.

18. Hemingway read Kipling in boyhood and later owned all these works, but "The White Seal" reference requires some explanation. In book 3, chapter 44, of the manuscript, Marita and David see each other as seals in the water or on the beach (13–14). When Marita asks "Are seals nice?" David replies: "Did you read the Naulahka by Kipling? . . . That's all I know about them except in arctic and antarctic chronicles and circuses and zoos." Hemingway's mistake is interesting: there are no seals in *The Naulahka: A Story of East and West*, the action of which takes place in India and the American West; but its plot—the persuasion of an American woman to give up her independence, her mission work in India, for marriage—is decidedly relevant to Marita's voluntary status as an adjunct wife in *The Garden of Eden*. The Kipling work that Hemingway misremembers here is "The White Seal" in *The Second Jungle Book*, about the search by a white seal for a safe haven for his much-hunted species—hence Marita's remark in this chapter: "When he kissed me he looked like a white-headed seal" (13).

19. Doctorow, "Braver Than We Thought," 1, 44–45.

20. Ibid., 45.

21. Ibid. See also Kenneth Lynn's more complimentary suggestion, that "the Africa story bears a striking resemblance to Beryl Markham's account in *West with the Night* of her hunting experiences as a girl in Kenya," in *Hemingway*, 541n. Hemingway was an admirer of Markham's book (Lynn, 412) and would probably have been influenced by the chapters in book 2 on hunting with her dog Buller and her African friend Kibii (a name close to that of David's dog Kibo) and by the later paean to the intelligence and nobility of elephants in book 4, chapter 17.

22. John Updike, "The Sinister Sex," *The New Yorker*, 30 June 1986, 85–88. See especially p.88, where Updike finds the elephant's death "horrendous and moving" and the tale's "splicing and counterpoint" with the main narrative "quite brilliantly" managed. For Faulkner's criticism of Hemingway for staying within known limits, see Meyers, *Hemingway*, 432.

23. Doctorow, "Braver Than We Thought," 44–45.

24. Meyers, *Hemingway*, 70; Mizener, *The Far Side of Paradise*, 230.

25. See Gilbert and Gubar, *The Madwoman in the Attic*, 248–308; and *No Man's Land*, vol.2, *Sexchanges*, 341–43.

26. See, for example, Hemingway's *Selected Letters*, 759: "I remember how I could not let my father's death make any impression on me until I had finished re-write on A Farewell to Arms."

27. See Meyers, *Hemingway*, 480–81.

28. Baker, *Ernest Hemingway*, 713.

APPENDIX A: A SOURCE FOR THE MACOMBER "ACCIDENT"

1. See, in order of reference, *Selected Letters*, 179, 182; Beach, *Shakespeare and Company*, 77; Reynolds, *Hemingway's Reading*, 155; Brasch and Sigman, *Hemingway's Library*, 221, 240; Ernest Hemingway, "Monologue to a Maestro: A High Seas Letter," *Esquire* 4 (October 1935): 21, 174A, 174B; and Plimpton, "An Interview with Ernest Hemingway," 60–89.

2. Baker, *Ernest Hemingway*, 263.

3. The fourteen volumes contain the following novels and tales: *The Children of the New Forest; Frank Mildmay, or, The Naval Officer; Jacob Faithful; Japhet in Search of a Father; Joseph Rushbrooke, or, The Poacher; The King's Own; The Little Savage; Masterman Ready; The Mission, or, Scenes in Africa; Mr. Midshipman Easy; Newton Forster, or, The Merchant Service; Olla Podrida; The Pacha of Many Tales; Percival Keene; Peter Simple; The Pirate; The Phantom Ship; Poor Jack; The Privateer's Man; Rattlin the Reefer* (attributed to but only edited by Marryat); *Snarleyyow, or, The Dog Fiend; The Three Cutters; The Travels and Adventures of Monsieur Violet in California, Sonora, and Western Texas;* and *Valerie*.

4. In a private letter dated 5 February 1983.

5. Captain Frederick Marryat, *Percival Keene* and *The Poacher*, Illustrated Sterling Edition, 149, 328, 347. See also *Japhet in Search of a Father*, 1:151, where Major Carbonell says of the risk of another duel, "After all, what is it? . . . we all owe Heaven a death; and if I am floored, why then I shall no longer be anxious about title or fortune." For Hemingway's personal response to the original lines from Shakespeare, see his introduction to *Men at War* (1942), his anthology of "best" war stories, where he speaks of his own "sudden happiness and the feeling of having a permanent talisman" when a young British officer first wrote out the lines for him during his convalescence from shell and machine gun wounds in a Milan hospital in World War I (xiv). He also singles out for special praise a story about trench warfare in World War I, "Her Privates We," for which the Shakespeare lines serve as an epigraph (xvi, 775).

Attempts to minimize the importance of these lines for the Macomber story by critics like Warren Beck, cited below, should be measured against these registrations of the author's views.

6. Marryat, *Percival Keene*, 317.

7. For this sequence, see ibid., 312–14.

8. Marryat, *The King's Own / The Pirate / The Three Cutters*, Illustrated Sterling Edition, 267–69.

9. See especially Warren Beck, "The Shorter Happy Life of Mrs. Macomber," *Modern Fiction Studies* 1 (November 1955): 28–37; my critique of it as a New Critical misreading in "The Necessary Stylist: A New Critical Revision," *MFS* 6 (Winter 1960–61): 289–96; his long-delayed response to my critique in *MFS* 21 (Autumn 1975): 377–85; and our final exchange in *MFS* 22 (Summer 1976): 245–69. For an extension of the controversy, one curiously oblivious to all such precedents, see Kenneth G. Johnson, "In Defense of the Unhappy Margot Macomber," *Hemingway Review* 2 (Spring 1983): 44–47.

10. Hemingway, *Short Stories*, 34.

11. Beck, "The Shorter Happy Life of Mrs. Macomber," 37; Johnson, "In Defense of the Unhappy Margot Macomber," 46.

12. Marryat, *Percival Keene*, 149.

APPENDIX B: A RETROSPECTIVE EPILOGUE

1. James R. Mellow, "Reading Hemingway with One Eye Closed," *New York Times*, April 24, 1988, H33.

2. Ibid.

3. Ibid., H38.

4. D. H. Lawrence, *Selected Literary Criticism*, 427.

5. Edmund Wilson, "Hemingway: Gauge of Morale," 92–114.

6. Hemingway, *Selected Letters*, 245.

7. Baker, *Ernest Hemingway*, 236.

8. Showalter, *A Literature of Their Own*, 136–37.

9. For the Fauntleroy-Finn conjunction, see Thwaite, *Waiting for the Party*, 95. For the Teddy Roosevelt impress, see Reynolds, *The Young Hemingway*, 16, 23–35, 27–30 ff.

10. For Ernest's father's embarrassing tears, see especially Baker, *Ernest Hemingway*, 45–46, and *For Whom the Bell Tolls*, 401–6.

11. See Baker, *Ernest Hemingway*, 585, for Faulkner's famous judgment in 1947 that Hemingway "lacked the courage to get out on a limb of experimentation," which Hemingway characteristically misread as an attack on his physical courage.

12. *The Garden of Eden* Manuscript, 3/23/9, Hemingway Collection, Kennedy Library, Boston.

Works Cited

Arlen, Michael. *The Green Hat*. London: Cassell, 1968.

———. *The Romantic Lady*. New York: Dodd, Mead, and Co., 1921.

Baker, Carlos. *Ernest Hemingway: A Life Story*. New York: Bantam, 1970.

———, ed. *Selected Letters, 1917–1961*. By Ernest Hemingway. New York: Scribner's, 1981.

Beach, Sylvia. *Shakespeare and Company*. New York: Harcourt, Brace, and World, 1959.

Beck, Warren. "The Shorter Happy Life of Mrs. Macomber." *Modern Fiction Studies* 1 (November 1955): 28–37.

———. "The Shorter Happy Life of Mrs. Macomber—1955, 1975." *Modern Fiction Studies* 21 (Autumn 1975): 363–85.

———. "Mr. Spilka's Problem: A Reply." *Modern Fiction Studies* 22 (Summer 1976): 256–69.

Bell, Millicent. "*A Farewell to Arms*: Pseudoautobiography and Personal Metaphor." In *Ernest Hemingway: The Writer in Context*. Ed. James Nagel. Madison: University of Wisconsin Press, 1984.

Bellow, Saul. "Hemingway and the Image of Man." *Partisan Review* 20 (May–June 1953): 338–42.

Benson, Jackson. *Hemingway: The Writer's Art of Self-Defense*. Minneapolis: University of Minnesota Press, 1969.

Blackmore, R. D. *Lorna Doone*. New York and Boston: Thomas Y. Crowell, 1893.

Brasch, James D., and Sigman, Joseph. *Hemingway's Library: A Composite Record*. New York: Garland, 1981.

Brontë, Emily. *Wuthering Heights: An Authoritative Text with Essays in Criticism*. 2nd ed. Ed. William W. Sale, Jr. New York: Norton, 1972.

Buckley, Peter. *Ernest*. New York: Dial Press, 1978.

Burnett, Frances Hodgson. *A Lady of Quality*. New York: Scribner's, 1898.

———. *Little Lord Fauntleroy*. London: Collins, 1974.

Calder, Jenni. *Women and Marriage in Victorian Fiction*. New York: Oxford University Press, 1976.

"Captain Marryat at Langham." *Cornhill Magazine* 16 (August 1867): 149–61.

Colby, Vineta. *Yesterday's Woman: Domestic Realism in the English Novel*. Princeton: Princeton University Press, 1974.

Collins, Angus P. "Homosexuality and the Genesis of *Tender Is the Night*." *Journal of Modern Literature* 13 (March 1986): 167–71.

Collins, Philip. *From Manly Tears to Stiff Upper Lip: The Victorians and Pathos*. Wellington, New Zealand: Victoria University Press, 1975.

Craik, Dinah Mulock. *John Halifax, Gentleman*. London: A. & C. Black, 1922; London: Dent, 1961.

———. *Sermons Out of Church*. New York: Harper and Brothers Publishers, n.d.

Defoe, Daniel. *The Life, Adventures, and Pyracies of the Famous Captain Singleton*. Ed. Shiv K. Kumar. London: Oxford University Press, 1969.

Doctorow, E. L. "Braver Than We Thought." *New York Times Book Review*, 18 May 1986: 1, 44–45.

Donaldson, Scott. *By Force of Will: The Life and Art of Ernest Hemingway*. Harmondsworth, Middlesex: Penguin, 1978.

Fenton, Charles A. *The Apprenticeship of Ernest Hemingway*. New York: Viking Press, 1958.

 Fetterley, Judith. "Hemingway's Resentful Cryptogram." *The Resisting Reader: A Feminist Approach to American Fiction*. Bloomington: Indiana University Press, 1981.

Fiedler, Leslie. "Duplicitous Mark Twain." In *Mark Twain: A Profile*. Ed. Justin Kaplan. New York: Hill and Wang, 1967.

Fitch, Noel. "Ernest Hemingway—c/o Shakespeare and Company." *Fitzgerald/Hemingway Annual 1977*. Detroit: Gale Research, 1977.

Fitzgerald, F. Scott. *Tender Is the Night*. In *The Portable F. Scott Fitzgerald*. Ed. John O'Hara. New York: Viking Press, 1945.

Gay, Peter. *The Bourgeois Experience: Victoria to Freud*. Vol.1, *The Education of the Senses*. Vol.2, *The Tender Passion*. New York: Oxford University Press, 1984, 1986.

Gilbert, Elliot L. *The Good Kipling: Studies in the Short Story*. Athens: Ohio University Press, 1970.

Gilbert, Sandra, and Gubar, Susan. *The Madwoman in the Attic: The Woman Writer and the Nineteenth-Century Imagination*. New Haven: Yale University Press, 1979.

———. *No Man's Land: The Place of the Woman Writer in the Twentieth Century*. Vol.2, *Sexchanges*. New Haven: Yale University Press, 1989.

Gilligan, Carol. *In a Different Voice: Psychological Theory and Women's Development*. Cambridge: Harvard University Press, 1982.

Green, Martin. *The Great American Adventure*. Boston: Beacon Press, 1984.

Green, Roger Lancelyn. *Kipling and the Children*. London: Elek Books, 1965.

Griffin, Peter. *Along with Youth: Hemingway, The Early Years*. New York: Oxford University Press, 1985.

———. "Ernest Hemingway: In My Beginning Is My End." Ph.D. dissertation, Brown University, 1979.

Hannay, David. *Life of Frederick Marryat*. London: Walter Scott; New York, Boston, and Toronto: W. J. Gage, 1889.

Hemingway, Ernest. *Across the River and Into the Trees*. New York: Scribner's, 1971.

———. *The Complete Short Stories of Ernest Hemingway*. Finca Vigia Edition. New York: Scribner's, 1987.

———. *Death in the Afternoon*. New York: Scribner's, 1932; 1960.

———. *A Farewell to Arms*. New York: Charles Scribner's Sons, 1929.

———. *A Farewell to Arms* Manuscript. Hemingway Collection, Kennedy Library, Boston, Mass.

———. *The First Forty-Nine Stories and the Play "The Fifth Column."* New York: Modern Library, 1938.

———. *For Whom the Bell Tolls*. New York: Scribner's, 1940.

———. *The Garden of Eden*. New York: Scribner's, 1986.

———. *The Garden of Eden* Manuscripts. Hemingway Collection, Kennedy Library, Boston, Mass.

———. *Green Hills of Africa*. New York: Scribner's, 1935; 1963.

———. *Hemingway's Nonfiction: The Public Voice*. Ed. Robert O. Stephens. Chapel Hill: University of North Carolina Press, 1968.

———. *Islands in the Stream*. New York: Scribner's, 1970.

———. "The Last Good Country" Manuscripts. Hemingway Collection, Kennedy Library, Boston, Mass.

———. "Monologue to a Maestro: A High Seas Letter." *Esquire* 4 (October 1935): 21, 174A, 174B.

———. *A Moveable Feast*. New York: Bantam, 1965.

———. *The Nick Adams Stories*. Ed. Philip Young. New York: Bantam, 1973.

———. *The Old Man and the Sea*. New York: Scribner's, 1952.

———. *Selected Letters, 1917–1961*. Ed. Carlos Baker. New York: Scribner's, 1981.

———. *The Short Stories of Ernest Hemingway*. New York: Scribner's, 1966.

———. *The Sun Also Rises*. New York: Scribner's, 1954.

———. *To Have and Have Not*. New York: Scribner's, 1937.

———. *The Torrents of Spring*. New York: Scribner's, 1972.

———, ed. *Men at War: The Best War Stories of All Time*. New York: Crown, 1942.

Hemingway, Grace Hall. "A Record of Ernest Miller Hemingway's Baby Days." Books I–V. Hemingway Collection, Kennedy Library, Boston, Mass.

Hemingway, Leicester. *My Brother, Ernest Hemingway*. Cleveland: World, 1962.

Hemingway, Mary Welsh. *How It Was*. New York: Ballantine Books, 1977.

Home, Gordon. Introduction, *John Halifax, Gentleman*. By Dinah Mulock Craik. London: A. & C. Black, 1922.

Hovey, Richard B. *Hemingway: The Inward Terrain.* Seattle: University of Washington Press, 1968.

Hughes, Thomas. *Tom Brown's School Days at Rugby.* Boston: James R. Osgood and Co., 1875.

Jardine, Alice. "Death Sentences: Writing Couples and Ideology." In *The Female Body in Western Culture: Contemporary Perspectives.* Ed. Susan Rubin Suleiman. Cambridge: Harvard University Press, 1986.

Johnson, Kenneth G. "In Defense of the Unhappy Margot Macomber." *Hemingway Review* 2 (Spring 1983): 44–47.

Jones, James. *From Here to Eternity.* New York: Dell, 1980.

Jong, Erica. *Fanny: Being the True History of the Adventures of Fanny Hackabout-Jones.* New York: New American Library, 1980.

———. *Fear of Flying.* New York: Holt, Rinehart, and Winston, 1973.

Kert, Bernice. *The Hemingway Women.* New York and London: Norton, 1983.

Kipling, Rudyard. *The Jungle Book.* Vol.7 of *The Writings in Prose and Verse of Rudyard Kipling.* New York: Charles Scribner's Sons, 1898.

———. *Life's Handicap: Being Stories of Mine Own People.* Vol.4 of *The Collected Works of Rudyard Kipling.* New York: Doubleday, Doran and Co., 1941.

———. *The Light That Failed.* Vol.9 of *Writings.* New York: Charles Scribner's Sons, 1898.

———. *Many Inventions.* New York: D. Appleton and Co., 1896.

———. *Rudyard Kipling's Verse, Inclusive Edition, 1885–1918.* Garden City, N.Y.: Doubleday, Page and Co., 1922.

———. *Soldiers Three and Other Stories.* Vol.2 of *Collected Works.* New York: Doubleday, Doran and Co., 1941.

———. *Stalky & Co.* Vol.18 of *Writings.* New York: Charles Scribner's Sons, 1900.

———. *Under the Deodars.* New York: Doubleday, Page and Co., 1911.

Lapham, Aaron. "A Farewell to Machismo." *New York Times Magazine,* 16 October 1977, 51–55 and following.

Lawrence, D. H. *Selected Literary Criticism.* Ed. Anthony Beal. New York: Viking Press, 1956.

Lean, Florence Marryat Church. *Life and Letters of Captain Marryat.* 2 vols. London: Richard Bentley and Son, 1872.

Legman, Gershon. *Love and Death.* New York: Hacker Art Books, 1949.

Lewis, Robert W., Jr. *Hemingway on Love.* Austin: University of Texas Press, 1965.

Lloyd, Christopher. *Captain Marryat and the Old Navy.* London: Longmans, Green, 1939.

Loeb, Harold. *The Way It Was.* New York: Criterion Books, 1959.

Lynn, Kenneth S. *Hemingway.* New York: Simon and Schuster, 1987.

Markham, Beryl. *West with the Night.* Boston: Houghton Mifflin, 1942.

Marryat, Captain Frederick. *Frank Mildmay; or, The Naval Officer.* Ed. R. Brimley Johnson. London: J. M. Dent and Co.; Boston: Little Brown and Co., 1896.

———. *Jacob Faithful.* London and New York: George Routledge and Sons, n.d.

———. *Japhet in Search of a Father*. 2 vols. Philadelphia: E. C. Carey and A. Hart, 1835.

———. *The King's Own / The Pirate / The Three Cutters*. Illustrated Sterling Edition. Boston and New York: Dana Estes, 1896.

———. *Masterman Ready*. Ed. R. Brimley Johnson. Everyman's Library. London: J. M. Dent and Sons; New York: E. P. Dutton and Co., 1910.

———. *Mr. Midshipman Easy*. Ed. R. Brimley Johnson. Everyman's Library. London: J. M. Dent and Sons; New York: E. P. Dutton and Co., 1910.

———. *Percival Keene* and *The Poacher*. Illustrated Sterling Edition. Boston: Dana Estes, 1898.

———. *Peter Simple*. Ed. R. Brimley Johnson. Everyman's Library. London: J. M. Dent and Co.; New York: E. P. Dutton and Co., 1907.

———. *Peter Simple* and *The Little Savage*. Illustrated Sterling Edition. Ed. W. L. Courtney. Boston: Dana Estes, 1896.

———. *Snarleyyow; or, The Dog Fiend*. 2 vols. Philadelphia: E. L. Carey and A. Hart, 1837.

Masefield, John. *Salt-Water Ballads*. New York: Macmillan, 1913.

———. *The Story of a Round House and Other Poems*. New York: Macmillan, 1913.

———. *Victorious Troy; or, The Hurrying Angel*. New York: Macmillan, 1935.

Mellow, James R. "Reading Hemingway with One Eye Closed." *New York Times*, April 24, 1988, H33, H38.

Meyers, Jeffrey. *Hemingway: A Biography*. New York: Harper and Row, 1985.

Miller, Alice. *Prisoners of Childhood: The Drama of the Gifted Child and the Search for the True Self*. Trans. Ruth Ward. New York: Basic Books, 1981.

Miller, Madelaine Hemingway. *Ernie: Hemingway's Sister "Sunny" Remembers*. New York: Crown Publishers, 1975.

Mizener, Arthur. *The Far Side of Paradise*. Boston: Houghton Mifflin, 1951.

Montgomery, Constance Cappel. *Hemingway in Michigan*. New York: Fleet Publishing Co., 1966.

Moss, Robert. *Rudyard Kipling and the Fiction of Adolescence*. New York: St. Martin's Press, 1982.

Oldsey, Bernard. "The Original Beginning." In *Hemingway's Hidden Craft: The Writing of "A Farewell to Arms."* University Park: Pennsylvania State University Press, 1979.

Plimpton, George. "An Interview with Ernest Hemingway." *Paris Review* 18 (Spring 1958): 60–89. Reprinted in *Writers at Work: The "Paris Review" Interviews*. 2nd ser. New York: Viking Press, 1963.

Pullin, Faith. "Hemingway and the Secret Language of Hate." In *Ernest Hemingway: New Critical Essays*. Ed. Robert A. Lee. London and Toronto: Vision Press and Barnes and Noble, 1983.

Reynolds, Michael S. *Hemingway's First War: The Making of "A Farewell to Arms."* Princeton: Princeton University Press, 1975.

―――. *Hemingway's Reading, 1910–1940: An Inventory*. Princeton: Princeton University Press, 1981.

―――. *The Young Hemingway*. London: Blackwell, 1986.

Richards, I. A. "Sentimentality and Inhibition." In *Practical Criticism*. New York: Harvest, 1929.

Rodin, Auguste. "The Metamorphoses of Ovid." *Rodin Skulpturen*. London: Phaidon Press, 1934; 1953. New York: Allen and Unwin, Oxford University Press, 1934.

―――. *Rodin Sculptures*. Ed. Jennifer Hawkins. London: Her Majesty's Stationery Office, 1975.

―――. *The Sculptures of Rodin*. Ed. John Tancock. Philadelphia: Philadelphia Museum of Art, 1976.

Rosenfeld, Isaac. "A Farewell to Hemingway." *Kenyon Review* 13 (1951): 147–55.

Sanford, Marcelline Hemingway. *At the Hemingways: A Family Portrait*. Boston: Little Brown, 1962.

Scholes, Robert. "Decoding Papa: 'A Very Short Story' as Work and Text." In *Semiotics and Interpretation*. New York: Yale University Press, 1982.

Showalter, Elaine. *A Literature of Their Own: British Women Novelists from Brontë to Lessing*. Princeton: Princeton University Press, 1977.

Smith, Constance Babington. *John Masefield: A Life*. New York: Macmillan, 1978.

Smith, Paul. "The Tenth Indian and the Thing Left Out." In *Ernest Hemingway: The Writer in Context*. Ed. James Nagel. Madison: University of Wisconsin Press, 1984.

Sokoloff, Alice Hunt. *Hadley, The First Mrs. Hemingway*. New York: Dodd, Mead, 1971.

Spacks, Patricia Meyer. "The Adolescent as Heroine." In *The Female Imagination*. New York: Avon, 1976.

Spilka, Mark. "The Death of Love in *The Sun Also Rises*." In *Hemingway: A Collection of Critical Essays*. Ed. Robert P. Weeks. Englewood Cliffs: Prentice Hall, 1962.

―――. "Hemingway and Fauntleroy: An Androgynous Pursuit." In *American Novelists Revisited: Essays in Feminist Criticism*. Ed. Fritz Fleischmann. Boston: G. K. Hall, 1982.

―――. "The Necessary Stylist: A New Critical Revision." *Modern Fiction Studies* 6 (Winter 1960–61): 289–96.

―――. "A Source for the Macomber 'Accident': Marryat's *Percival Keene*." *Hemingway Review* 3 (Spring 1984): 29–37.

―――. "Victorian Keys to the Early Hemingway: Captain Marryat." *Novel: A Forum on Fiction* 17 (Winter 1984): 116–40.

―――. "Victorian Keys to the Early Hemingway: *Fauntleroy* and *Finn*." *Journal of Modern Literature* 10 (June 1983): 289–310.

―――. "Victorian Keys to the Early Hemingway: *John Halifax, Gentleman*." *Journal of Modern Literature* 10 (March 1983): 125–50.

————. "Warren Beck Revisited." *Modern Fiction Studies* 22 (Summer 1976): 245–55.

Stephens, Robert O. *Hemingway's Nonfiction: The Public Voice*. Chapel Hill: University of North Carolina Press, 1968.

————, ed. *Ernest Hemingway: The Critical Reception*. New York: Burt Franklin, 1977.

Svoboda, Frederick Joseph. *Hemingway and "The Sun Also Rises": The Crafting of a Style*. Lawrence: University Press of Kansas, 1981.

Tancock, John, ed. *The Sculptures of Rodin*. Philadelphia: Philadelphia Museum of Art, 1976.

Tate, Allen. "Good Prose." *The Nation* 122 (10 February 1926): 160–62.

————. "Hard-Boiled." *The Nation* 123 (15 December 1926): 642–44.

————. "Random Thoughts on the 1920s." *Minnesota Review* 1 (Fall 1970): 46–56.

————. "The Spirituality of Roughnecks." *The Nation* 123 (28 July 1926): 89–90.

Thomson, James. *Poems and Some Letters of James Thomson*. Ed. Anne Ridler. London: Centaur Press, 1963.

Thwaite, Ann. *Waiting for the Party: The Life of Frances Hodgson Burnett*. New York: Scribner's, 1974.

Updike, John. "The Sinister Sex." *The New Yorker*, 30 June 1986, 85–88.

Villard, Henry. "A Prize Specimen of Wounded Hero." *Yankee Magazine*. July 1979: 134–35.

Warner, Oliver. *Captain Marryat: A Rediscovery*. London: Constable, 1953.

Wasserstrom, William. *Heiress of All the Ages: Sex and Sentiment in the Genteel Tradition*. Minneapolis: University of Minnesota Press, 1959.

Westbrook, Max. "Grace under Pressure: Hemingway and the Summer of 1920." In *Ernest Hemingway: The Writer in Context*. Ed. James Nagel. Madison: University of Wisconsin Press, 1984.

Wilson, Edmund. "Hemingway: Gauge of Morale." In *Eight Essays*. Garden City, N.Y.: Doubleday-Anchor Books, 1954.

Woolf, Virginia. "The Captain's Death Bed." In *Collected Essays*. Vol. 1. Ed. Leonard Woolf. London: Chatto and Windus, 1966.

————. "An Essay in Criticism." In *Ernest Hemingway: The Critical Reception*. Ed. Robert O. Stephens. New York: Burt Franklin, 1977.

Young, Philip. "'Big World Out There': *The Nick Adams Stories*." *Novel: A Forum on Fiction* 6 (Fall 1972): 5–19.

————. *Ernest Hemingway: A Reconsideration*. University Park: Pennsylvania State University Press, 1966.

Index